JEAN ALLMAN, SUSAN GEIGER,
AND NAKANYIKE MUSISI, EDITORS

Women in African
Colonial Histories

INDIANA
University Press

Bloomington & Indianapolis

This book is a publication of

Indiana University Press
601 North Morton Street
Bloomington, IN 47404-3797 USA

http://iupress.indiana.edu

Telephone orders   800-842-6796
Fax orders   812-855-7931
Orders by e-mail   iuporder@indiana.edu

© 2002 by Indiana University Press

The paper used in this publication meets the minimum requirements of American National Standard for Infor-mation Sciences—Permanence of Paper for Printed Library Materials, ANSI Z39.48-1984.

Manufactured in the United States of America

Library of Congress Cataloging-in-Publication Data

Women in African colonial histories / edited by Jean Allman, Susan Geiger, and Nakanyike Musisi.
    p. cm.
   ISBN 0-253-34047-0 (hard) — ISBN 0-253-21507-2 (pbk.)
   1. Women—Africa—History. 2. Africa—Colonial influence.   I. Geiger, Susan. II. Musisi, Nakanyike.
III. Allman, Jean Marie.
   HQ1787 .W655 2002
   305.4′096—dc21

                                          2001003447

1 2 3 4 5   07 06 05 04 03 02

Nenda salama, Susan . . .

Contents

Acknowledgments

This project has accumulated many debts since its inception in 1996—far too many to list individually here. We would, however, like to take the opportunity to express our sincere gratitude to those whose essays make up this volume. As the project moved from a collection of short abstracts to a final copyedited manuscript, our contributors were endlessly patient and extraordinarily generous with their time and understanding. Over the past several years, the project encountered more than its fair share of obstacles, and it was their enthusiasm and support that always kept us on track.

We would also like to acknowledge the crucial support of Joan Catapano, former senior editor at Indiana University Press, and that of her successor, Dee Mortensen, who provided so much encouragement in the final stages. Marissa Moorman took care of many of the mechanical and editorial obstacles inherent in transforming thirteen essays into a uniformly formatted manuscript text. We are very grateful to Marissa and to the University of Minnesota for funding Marissa's work. The maps for the anthology were drawn by the expert hand of Jane Domier, director of cartographic services at the University of Illinois. Finally, we wish to thank the two anonymous readers whose careful comments and constructive criticisms helped us chart our way through one last round of revisions, and our very patient and expert copyeditor, Shoshanna Green, whose enormous skills have made this a much better book.

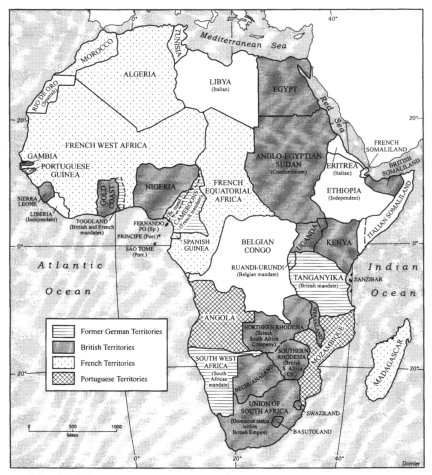

Colonial Africa, ca. 1941

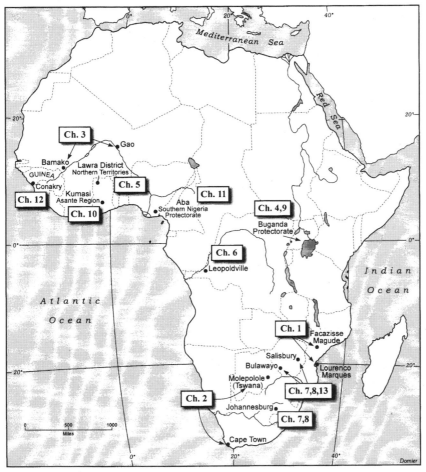

Mapping the Chapters

Women in African Colonial Histories

Women in African Colonial Histories: An Introduction

Jean Allman, Susan Geiger, and Nakanyike Musisi

The essays assembled here explore African women's encounters with European colonialisms. They focus on the ways in which women negotiated that range of political, economic, and social forces embraced by the term "colonial"—from European rule, missions, taxation, and cash cropping to biomedicine, labor migration, white settlement, and racialized discourses of power. While ever cognizant of the inherent violence of these encounters, be it the brutality of racist discourse or the coercive force which comes through the barrel of a gun, all of the chapters undermine any image of African women as hapless victims. Through their daily lives, through their families and their communities, in ritual and belief, in their travels, their struggles, and their travails, African women, as historical subjects, were active agents in the making of the colonial world. By considering the lives of farmers, queen mothers, urban dwellers, migrants, and political leaders in the context of particular colonial conditions at specific periods of time, the contributions to this volume challenge the notion of a homogeneous "African women's experience." They do so by drawing on a wide variety of methodologies and sources, including life histories, oral narratives, court cases, newspapers, colonial archives, and material objects.

The approaches to women's lives taken in these essays complicate the binaries and disrupt the chronologies that have tended to frame African colonial history more broadly. In these prevailing binaries—rural/urban, private/public, peasant/proletarian, production/reproduction, formal/informal, resistance/collaboration, citizen/subject—either women occupy half of the "dichotomy" or their experiences are erased altogether. They are pictured in rural areas, for example, reproducing the labor force, while men are shown migrating to productive, wage-paying jobs in urban areas. They are relegated to a fixed domestic sphere, while only men are shown to have access to the public. Their economic activity is deemed informal—marginal to the colonial economy. But women's diverse historical experiences defy such static representations. Boundaries between, for example, the male urban worker and the female rural reproducer shift and blur.

Women's colonial histories, moreover, challenge the chronological boundaries that have framed African colonial history generally, boundaries based largely on formal political markers, such as a decisive military defeat, a treaty of "protection," or the hoisting of the flag of independence. For the most part, such markers are not gender-neutral, but rather signify definitive moments in the colonial histories of male political elites. The essays collected here are grounded in gendered chronologies of colonialism which, depending on the place and time, begin well before or well after the formal onset of European political rule, and of which many extend into the present.

Historiographies of Women and Colonialism

This anthology benefits enormously from being situated in and engaged with a burgeoning historiography which, for well over two decades, has persistently fought to write women into the history of the African continent. We are particularly indebted to trail-blazing collections like *Women in Africa* (1976), *Women and Work in Africa* (1982), *African Women and the Law* (1982), *Women and Slavery in Africa* (1983), *Women and Class in Africa* (1986), and *Women and the State in Africa* (1989).[1] Since the 1970 publication of Ester Boserup's important work *Woman's Role in Economic Development,*[2] much of this collected historiography on African women, though certainly not all of it, has been centered on the impact of European contact on African women,[3] and these anthologies provide few exceptions. However, none of the collections to date has taken colonialism and women's modes of adjustment, negotiation, and resistance as its central problematic.

Yet since the publication of the foundational historical anthologies on African women over a decade ago our knowledge of women's colonial pasts has exploded, and we are now at a point where we can begin to explore trans-national or trans-colonial processes and to draw meaningful comparative insights into the ways women shaped and were shaped by the colonial world as they struggled to secure and defend their autonomy. In 1988, Jean Hay bemoaned the paucity of historical monographs on African women and the fact that only a handful of articles on women or gender had appeared in the leading journals of the profession.[4] The latest research in women's history increasingly appears in mainstream journals, and the number of monographs has multiplied dramatically since Hay listed the lone five which had appeared between 1971 and 1986.[5] This rich and dynamic historical literature has begun to bring elusive pasts into sharper focus, particularly around certain sets of questions.

As Ifi Amadiume has recently written in her important theoretical contribution to women's studies, *Re-inventing Africa: Matriarchy, Religion, and Culture,* "African women have . . . been concerned with the fundamental social issues of self-organization and the economy."[6] In many ways, that concern has been reflected in the sets of questions posed by much of the historical literature of the past decades. There is now an extensive scholarship on women and rural (re)production that places women at the center of agricultural and social transformations in the countryside,[7] as well as a rich and varied body of scholarship on women's organizations and strategies of protest and resistance.[8] That scholarship effectively challenges the collaboration/resistance paradigms of the broader colonial historiography, as it explores the ways in which women struggled against a reconfigured patriarchy rooted in both indigenous and colonial ideologies.

More recently, women's experiences in cities—in politics, churches, and schools, and in a range of cash-generating activities like petty trading, prostitution, and beer brewing—have been the focus of studies which have remapped our understanding of the urban colonial landscape, a landscape gendered male in much of the earlier historiography.[9] Other scholars have devoted considerable attention to the ways in which Victorian notions of domesticity were transplanted to the African continent in order to mold "better" mothers and wives, and how African women encountered and remade those strategies on their own terms. Others, like Carol Summers, have explored "intimate colonialisms" in an effort to grapple with the often violent sexual politics of colonial rule.[10] While much of this research has appeared in the form of articles or chapters in edited collections,[11] we are beginning to see more book-length monographs, which afford the author the space to engage simultaneously with multiple themes in complex and shifting settings.[12] That the first comprehensive textbook on African women's history, Hay and Stichter's *African Women South of the Sahara*, was recently updated and republished (1995; orig. 1984) and has been joined by two other systematic overviews of the field—Berger and White's edited volume *Women in Sub-Saharan Africa: Restoring Women to History* and Coquery-Vidrovitch's *African Women: A Modern History*—is a testament both to the strides made in the field of African women's history and to its expanding audiences.[13]

While engaged with this flourishing historiography on African women, the collection also speaks to some of the more pressing questions raised in broader, interdisciplinary scholarship, especially recent work on gender and colonial representation.[14] In important ways, it departs from the thrust of much of this literature, which has argued for a move away from women's history to gender history or to gender analyses, whereby men, as well as women, become "subjects and authors of gendered histories."[15] While the essays in this volume share as a primary objective the engendering of mainstream African history, they also reflect Ayesha Imam's concern that the term "gender analysis" can be—indeed often is—deployed to "neutralise and soften the challenge posed by the direct accusation of bias against women and the demand for the recognition and rights of women posed by feminist theory."[16] *Women in African Colonial Histories* is aimed at foregrounding women's colonial histories and women as historical subjects in gendered colonial worlds.[17]

A quick glance at recent publications in the broader field of African colonial history underscores the ongoing necessity of foregrounding women as historical actors. Despite the fact that feminist scholars have been writing women into African colonial histories for three decades, it is still very much the case that unless "women" or "gender" appears in the title, women do not have to be present in the text at all.[18] While women's history is now recognized by the profession as a legitimate field of inquiry and several books in women's history and gender history have won the coveted Herskovits Prize in North America for the best monograph in African studies,[19] the impact of women's history and gender studies on mainstream colonial historiography remains alarmingly minimal.[20] It is thus clear that feminist historians must continue to "work on both fronts simultaneously," as Zeleza has recently asserted. "Gender history cannot go far without the continuous retrieval of women's history, while women's history cannot transform the fundamentally flawed paradigmatic bases of 'mainstream' history without gender history."[21]

The Architecture

The anthology includes thirteen chapters grouped in three thematic parts: "Encounters and Engagements," "Perceptions and Representations," and "Power Reconfigured/Power Contested." In terms of regional coverage, five of the contributions are from western Africa, five from southern Africa, two from eastern Africa and one from central Africa. A range of colonizers appear on the stage—Portuguese, Belgian, French, and British—although British colonial rule forms the backdrop in nine of the chapters. Yet from the very beginning, we, as editors, were more concerned with thematic coverage than with equity in the representation of regions or colonizing powers. Far more important for African women's lives than their regional location or the particular form of colonial rule imposed by a specific European power were the trans-metropole colonial methods of extraction, taxation, and exploitation of the continent's human and material resources. Indeed, one colonial power, like Great Britain, could develop very different methods depending upon the specific configuration of resources in a particular setting. A quick comparison of British colonial rule in Southern Rhodesia and the Gold Coast (see the chapters here by Jackson and by Tashjian and Allman) underscores the difficulty of conceptualizing coverage in terms of region or of European colonizing power. Useful bases for synthesis and comparison, we would argue, are not necessarily regional or derived from differing colonial metropoles. They concern such critical factors as the presence or absence of European settlers, access to land, cash-cropping and subsistence agriculture, mineral wealth, gendered labor migrancy, urban and rural differentiation, and the social organization of power in the precolonial past.

Our twofold intent as editors, then, was to attain this kind of coverage and to do so by including contributions that could move from the specific—the life story of a midwife, the Women's War in southeastern Nigeria, or women travelers in southern Africa—to the more broadly synthetic and thematic. We wanted readers to be able to grapple with the lives of real women in a range of colonial histories and with the complexities and ambiguities of evidence for those histories. Toward that end, each contributor has located her or his chapter in the broader literature in African women's history, so that the specific topic of a chapter becomes the door through which the reader encounters an overarching theme in the literature, such as women's mobility in colonial Africa. In addition, each author has included a short primary source in her or his chapter, in order to provide readers with a concrete example of the kind of evidence upon which she or he relied. In most cases this text is set at the end of the chapter, though in three instances (the chapters by Gengenbach, Mianda, and Lyons) the source is fully integrated into the text. The range of primary sources foregrounded in this collection—personal narratives, court testimony, photographs, autobiographies, colonial reports—attests to the innovative methodologies women's historians have developed in order not only to render women visible, but to capture their diverse roles as active agents in the making of colonial histories.

On the basis of initial abstracts, we first envisioned a four-part anthology. Of our original thematic part titles, only "Perceptions and Representations" remains. Yet the story of how we got from our first conceptualization to the volume's present architecture offers insight into the ways in which this volume both complicates and disrupts standard assumptions about African history. The first part, "Encounters and Engagements," was originally called "African Women on the Eve of Formal Colonial Rule." This title "worked" for the chapters we tentatively placed there, and it had the advantage of a suitably momentous (and, of course, chronologically specific) ring. To present an anthology about women during the colonial period, we reasoned, we needed to begin with chapters that depicted African women "before" and "after" "colonial contact." As draft chapters came in, however, it became clear that the title, but more importantly this chronological conceptualization, was not satisfactory and obscured more than it revealed.

First, the idea that there was a "moment of colonial contact" for the peoples of the African continent is extremely problematic, as is the notion that such a moment is best equated with the establishment of "formal" colonialism (i.e., political overrule). The infamous Berlin Conference of 1885, at which European powers divided up the continent amongst themselves, marks the beginning of "formal" colonial rule through the European political metropoles, on paper and by treaty. But it goes without saying that no Africans—male or female—attended the conference, and most Africans had no knowledge of it. In fact, from the perspective of Africans rather than colonial rulers, there were as many moments of contact or encounter on the African continent as there were and are African societies. Moreover, colonial "contact" was seldom one defining experience. Rather, it was a series of experiences and interactions over time, sometimes cumulative, sometimes changing.

Although African men usually encountered and engaged the agents of colonial rule—soldiers, travelers, missionaries, explorers, officials—in relations of one kind or another before African women met them, the diversity and reflexivity of early contacts was apparent for both genders. It is this diversity, and the conscious way in which African women sought to achieve their own objectives through engagements with colonial agents and institutions, that the chapters in the reconstituted part reveal. This is not to argue that African women, any more than African men, necessarily controlled the context in which encounters and engagements with Europeans occurred, or that they necessarily controlled the terms and consequences of relations established. African women were, however, motivated by their own agendas—agendas that were frequently at odds with those of the Europeans, and sometimes completely incomprehensible to them.

Our second part, "Perceptions and Representations," is the only one that survived the metamorphosis from prospectus to book, and that is perhaps because it was the only part we initially conceived without reference to chronological parameters. Like many Africanist historians, we understand that, from the very beginning, colonial perceptions and representations of African women profoundly affected the ways in which women lived their lives and negotiated social relationships. Such perceptions and representations—born of Western ideological assumptions and arrogance, fears, ignorance, and, always, the need to exercise control—often circumscribed or negated women's economic activities, mobility, political power and institutions, and status in their respective societies.

For example, it is well documented that in many parts of the continent, colonial administrators perceived African women as alarmingly diseased and, in particular, worried about whether they would give birth to a sufficient number of healthy children to reproduce the colonial workforce. The introduction of Western biomedicine was frequently a product of such perceptions, as was the colonial obsession with African women's bodies, which were both clinically represented and frequently invaded in the name of colonial "science" and control.[22]

Similarly, colonial court systems imposed throughout the continent reflected perceptions and representations of African girls and women as willful and properly subordinate to men—to chiefs, fathers, brothers, and husbands. African relational concepts such as "daughter," "wife," and "mother" were redefined, often through court cases and disputes, to better conform to Western ideological notions of these female social positions. Such redefinitions were undertaken with the full support of African (male) authorities, fathers and husbands, who often welcomed the opportunity to exercise greater control over the females in their households and societies.[23]

Colonial perceptions and representations of status and class difference were also affixed to African women through Western educational systems that fostered concepts of marital and household relations mirroring the nuclear family and the functions of the "civilized" wife and mother. A "civilized" African wife knew about tables and chairs, doilies and crockery, curtains and bedspreads, books and polite conversation. In order to be successful in the "modern" sector of any colonial urban area, an African man needed a wife to keep his home and children up to the "civilized" (i.e., Western) standard of housekeeping and childrearing. Perceptions and representations of many kinds were thus adopted and manipulated by African women and men who aspired to elite status within diverse colonial settings.[24]

To point out that this second part of the anthology survived the collection's many recastings is not to say that it is, therefore, the least disruptive of conventional paradigms. During the decades of colonial overrule, African women in many parts of the continent were increasingly characterized as limited in their economic activities, mobility, political interests and associations, and, indeed, character and mental capacity. As colonial regulations circumscribed their movements and opportunities, the African woman as "rural subsistence farmer" became a stereotype that historians themselves adopted as "the norm." In this part, however, the normative female subsistence farmer emerges as nuanced, multifaceted, and complicated. She is not defined solely by, or understood only in terms of, her labor as an agricultural producer.

We originally conceived of the final part, "Power Reconfigured/Power Contested," as two parts: "Differentiation and Change, Adjustments and Resistance" and "Struggling for Freedom." But as arguments and themes began to develop, we became increasingly dissatisfied with the first of the two part titles because the concepts seemed vague and overgeneralized—common buzzwords that did not do justice to the content of the essays placed in that part. Moreover, the divvying up of chapters between the two parts seemed increasingly random, as we tried unsuccessfully to read substantive differences into concepts like "resistance" and "struggling for freedom."

During the colonial period, African women "struggled" in many ways that have expanded our understanding of the term "political" far beyond direct organized action against the colonial state and its functionaries. Nor has their quest for greater "freedom" or autonomy been limited to what has traditionally been considered the political (i.e., public, formal) sphere. The title "Power Reconfigured/Power Contested" allows us to include essays that not only address examples of women's loss of political power as a result of colonial overrule, and their action and participation in a range of organizations, but also consider shifts in other forms of power, from the economic to the familial.

Chapter by Chapter

Part One. Encounters and Engagements

The three chapters in the first part focus on the complex, changing, and frequently ill-understood ways in which African women encountered and engaged colonialism in diverse regions of the continent. They also foreground critical discussion of sources in reconstructing African women's historical subjectivity. In "'What My Heart Wanted': Gendered Stories of Early Colonial Encounters in Southern Mozambique," Heidi Gengenbach explores women's actions vis-à-vis "the colonizer," as recounted not only in available European written sources but in women's own accounts as well. She demonstrates how African women's explanations of historical change and their narrative constructions of their own lives reveal both the ambiguities of colonial encounters and the nature and range of women's strategic engagements with the colonial order. Wendy Urban-Mead's "Dynastic Daughters: Three Royal Kwena Women and E. L. Price of the London Missionary Society, 1853–1881" uses the journals of a European woman missionary to analyze the ways in which individual subjectivity and larger-scale political, cultural, and economic forces combined to shape the options of three royal African women in the decade before the formal onset of colonial rule in southern Africa. The chapter considers the problems and opportunities for historical writing when reconstructions of European and African women's nineteenth-century encounters are largely limited to sources produced by European women. In "Colonial Midwives and Modernizing Child-birth in French West Africa," Jane Turrittin draws on a relatively rare historical source for African women's history, the autobiography. Focusing on the fascinating life of Aoua Kéita, as recounted in Kéita's own words, Turrittin examines how a colonially-trained midwife's resistance to her Eurocentric training contributed to a reevaluation of her cultural tradition and to her social and political radicalization.

Part Two. Perceptions and Representations

The chapters in this part subject colonial and postcolonial perceptions and representations of African women to thorough critical analysis. Nakanyike Musisi's "The Politics of Perception or Perception as Politics? Colonial and Missionary Representations of Baganda Women, 1900–1945" takes on a colonial archive filled with European representations of Baganda women—an archive, she argues, that is part and parcel of a larger story of domination and control. By exploring both women's rejection of colonial biomedical practices and their selective use of them, Musisi demystifies that documentary archive and demonstrates how Baganda women struggled to maintain control over their lives and bodies. In "'The Woman in Question': Marriage and Identity in the Colonial Courts of Northern Ghana, 1907–1954," Sean Hawkins uses a different genre of colonial archive, court records, to explore how colonial courts sought to define women's social identities. He argues that although courts largely marginalized LoDagaa women, their records nonetheless reveal that the greatest challenge to British control was the relative autonomy women enjoyed outside the courts. Gertrude Mianda's chapter, "Colonialism, Education, and Gender Relations in the Belgian Congo: The *Évolué* Case," extends the discussion of colonial perceptions by exploring how they were internalized by African elites. Mianda uncovers the attitudes of évolués (self-styled African advocates of modernity) toward women's issues, such as marriage, family, work, mobility, and sexuality, and concludes that colonial representations and perceptions served the strategic purposes of African male elites by consolidating their position and subordinating women.

The last two chapters of this part, "Virgin Territory? Travel and Migration by African Women in Twentieth-Century Southern Africa," by Teresa Barnes, and Lynette Jackson's "'When in the White Man's Town': Zimbabwean Women Remember *Chibeura*," challenge the androcentric framing of migration and travel in colonial Africa and reveal how collective memories of suffering among women urban migrants are articulated and remembered. Barnes demonstrates the ways in which contemporary literature has perpetuated the myth that mobility, travel, and migration are a male preserve, thus consigning women to mass immobility. She argues that such misconceptions drive women off of the center stage, freezing them in a perpetual economic powerlessness as "passive rural widows." Jackson explores how colonial fears of "unattached" and mobile women led to the development of chibeura—the coercive practice which compelled women to open their legs to be "inspected" by agents of colonial authority when they sought access to towns—and how women remember these painful experiences of violation.

Part Three. Power Reconfigured/Power Contested

The anthology's final part explores two closely intertwined themes: the multiple ways in which gendered systems of power and authority were recast during the colonial period, and the ways in which African women contested, individually and collectively, reconfigurations of patriarchal power. Holly Hanson's "Queen Mothers and Good Government in Buganda: The Loss of Women's Political Power in Nineteenth-Century East Africa" analyzes the system of gendered political power in Buganda in which the queen mother had autonomous authority, grounded in land ownership, which she used to check the excesses of the king and safeguard the interests of the nation. Hanson demonstrates how, even before formal colonization, the position of the queen mother was gradually undermined by long-distance trade, including an escalation in the trade in slaves, which enriched and empowered provincial chiefs while weakening centralized authority. Victoria Tashjian and Jean Allman's "Marrying and Marriage on a Shifting Terrain: Reconfigurations of Power and Authority in Early Colonial Asante" demonstrates that it was not only women of high rank and status whose positions were undermined by colonial rule and the dramatic economic changes which often preceded it. Shifting the focus from queen mothers to commoner women, from the arena of formal politics to the realm of domestic economies, the authors explore how the introduction of cash cropping in Asante and the increasing monetization of the economy recast conjugal relations, afforded husbands greater rights to wives' labor, and ultimately increased the labor burdens of most women. Misty Bastian's "'Vultures of the Marketplace': Southeastern Nigerian Women and Discourses of the *Ogu Umunwaanyi* (Women's War) of 1929" moves our focus from the ways in which women's economic and political positions were undermined during the colonial period to women's collective action against the forces and symbols of colonial rule, as Bastian revisits one of the better-known events in African women's history. She is concerned here with highlighting the continuities between women's prewar forms of collective action, especially song and dance, and their verbal rhetoric and nonverbal displays during the war. Elizabeth Schmidt's "'Emancipate Your Husbands!' Women and Nationalism in Guinea, 1953–1958" is similarly concerned with the ways in which women made use of preexisting "cultural systems" in mobilizing support for the nationalist struggle in Guinea. Schmidt explores how some of those efforts violated entrenched gender norms, yet did not result in women's emancipation in the post-independence period. The questions of nationalist struggle and the prospects for women's emancipation posed by Schmidt are revisited in the anthology's final chapter. In "Guerrilla Girls and Women in the Zimbabwean National Liberation Struggle," Tanya Lyons looks at the experiences of women combatants. She argues that women's roles in the armed struggle for independence were extensively glorified during the war in order to garner international support, and that a close examination of women's lived experiences as combatants reveals how patriarchal power was reconfigured both during the war of liberation and after independence.

• • •

The end of colonial rule—even when brought about through protracted liberation struggles that violated gender norms—did not, in the final analysis, result in women's emancipation in Zimbabwe, Guinea, or elsewhere. The essays collected here provide ample historical evidence of, and reasons for, the resilience of colonial patriarchies. But at the same time we hope that these chapters, by foregrounding African women as active agents in the making of colonial histories, have implications for how we think about women's emancipation, and for how we weigh the prospects for autonomy and security in a postcolonial world.

NOTES

1.   Indeed, in the case of Misty Bastian's chapter here on the Ibo Women's War, we are revisiting some of the same historical events and themes first explored in one of those early collections. See Judith Van Allen, "'Aba Riots' or Igbo 'Women's War'? Ideology, Stratification, and the Invisibility of Women," in *Women in Africa: Studies in Social and Economic Change,* ed. Nancy J. Hafkin and Edna G. Bay (Stanford, Calif.: Stanford University Press, 1976), pp. 59–85. See also Edna G. Bay, ed., *Women and Work in Africa* (Boulder, Colo.: Westview, 1982); Margaret Jean Hay and Marcia Wright, eds., *African Women and the Law: Historical Perspectives* (Boston, Mass.: Boston University, African Studies Center, 1982); Claire C. Robertson and Martin A. Klein, eds., *Women and Slavery in Africa* (Madison: University of Wisconsin Press, 1983); Claire Robertson and Iris Berger, eds., *Women and Class in Africa* (New York: Holmes and Meier, 1986); Jane L. Parpart and Kathleen A. Staudt, eds., *Women and the State in Africa* (Boulder, Colo.: Lynne Rienner, 1989). Both Margaret Jean Hay and Luise White have discussed the negative consequences of so much women's history appearing in edited anthologies rather than in mainstream journals. Hay wrote, "[T]he vast majority [of articles] appear only in edited collections or special issues of journals—collections that may simply be disregarded by other historians and thus seem to reinforce the ghettoization of women's history." See Margaret Jean Hay, "Queens, Prostitutes, and Peasants: Historical Perspectives on African Women, 1971–1986," *Canadian Journal of African Studies* 23, no. 3 (1988): 432, and Luise White, "Anthologies about Women in Africa," *Canadian Journal of African Studies* 28, no. 1 (1994): 127–33.

2.   Ester Boserup, *Woman's Role in Economic Development* (New York: St. Martin's, 1970).

3.   Women's history's initial focus on the colonial past was not mirrored in the broader discipline. As Margaret Strobel wrote in 1982, that focus was, in fact, "ironic, given the struggle in the early years of African history to insist that Africa had a past prior to European contact." See Margaret Strobel, "African Women: A Review," *Signs: Journal of Women in Culture and Society* 8, no. 1 (1982): 131. See also Nancy Rose Hunt, "Placing African Women's History and Locating Gender," *Social History* 14, no. 3 (1989): 360–61.

4.   Hay, "Queens, Prostitutes, and Peasants," pp. 432–33.

5.   Ibid., pp. 432. The book-length works she lists are Margaret Strobel, *Muslim Women in Mombasa, 1890–1975* (New Haven, Conn.: Yale University Press, 1979); Claire C. Robertson, *Sharing the Same Bowl? A Socioeconomic History of Women and Class in Accra, Ghana* (Bloomington: Indiana University Press, 1984); Nina Emma Mba, *Nigerian Women Mobilized: Women's Political Activity in Southern Nigeria, 1900–1965* (Berkeley: University of California, Institute of International Studies, 1982); Cherryl Walker, *Women and Resistance in South Africa* (London: Onyx, 1982); and Kristin Mann, *Marrying Well: Marriage, Status, and Social Change among the Educated Elite in Colonial Lagos* (Cambridge: Cambridge University Press, 1982). Since Hay compiled this list, the number of book-length monographs in African women's history has increased enormously—to the point that it is not possible to provide a comprehensive list without risking omissions. White echoes Hay's concerns about the paucity of women's history in mainstream journals in "Anthologies" (p. 133). Some improvement in recent years is evident, for example, in the *Journal of African History, Africa,* the *International Journal of African Historical Studies,* the *Canadian Journal of African Studies,* and *African Studies Review.* Some articles in African women's history have also appeared in non-Africanist mainstream historical journals such as *Comparative Studies in Society and History, Past and Present, Social History,* and the *American Historical Review,* though their impact remains minimal.

6.   Ifi Amadiume, *Re-inventing Africa: Matriarchy, Religion, and Culture* (London: Zed, 1997), p. 196.

7.   See, for example, Jean Allman and Victoria Tashjian, *"I Will Not Eat Stone": A Women's History of Colonial Asante* (Portsmouth, N.H.: Heinemann, 2000); Belinda Bozzoli with Mmantho Nkotsoe, *Women of Phokeng: Consciousness, Life Strategy, and Migrancy in South Africa, 1900–1983* (Portsmouth, N.H.: Heinemann, 1991); Helen Bradford, "Women, Gender, and Colonialism: Rethinking the History of the British Cape Colony and Its Frontier Zones, c. 1806–70," *Journal of African History* 37, no. 3 (1996): 351–70; Judith Carney and Michael Watts, "Disciplining Women? Rice, Mechanization, and the Evolution of Mandinka Gender Relations in Senegambia," *Signs: Journal of Women in Culture and Society* 16, no. 4 (1991): 651–81; Barbara M. Cooper, *Marriage in Maradi: Gender and Culture in a Hausa Society in Niger, 1900–1989* (Portsmouth, N.H.: Heinemann, 1997); Jean Davison with the women of Mutira, *Voices from Mutira: Lives of Rural Gikuyu Women* (Boulder, Colo.: Lynne Rienner, 1989); Elizabeth Eldredge, "Women in Production: The Economic Role of Women in Nineteenth-Century Lesotho," *Signs: Journal of Women in Culture and Society* 16, no. 4 (1991): 707–31; Beverly Grier, "Pawns,

Porters, and Petty Traders: Women in the Transition to Cash Crop Agriculture in Colonial Ghana," *Signs: Journal of Women in Culture and Society* 17, no. 2 (1992): 304–28; Jane Guyer, "Female Farming in Anthropology and African History," in *Gender at the Crossroads of Knowledge: Feminist Anthropology in the Postmodern Era*, ed. Micaela di Leonardo (Berkeley: University of California Press, 1991), pp. 257–77; Margaret Jean Hay, "Luo Women and Economic Change during the Colonial Period," in *Women in Africa*, ed. Hafkin and Bay, pp. 87–109; Allen Isaacman, *Cotton Is the Mother of Poverty: Peasants, Work, and Rural Struggle in Colonial Mozambique, 1938–1961* (Portsmouth, N.H.: Heinemann, 1996); Jean Koopman, "Women in the Rural Economy: Past, Present, and Future," in *African Women South of the Sahara*, ed. Margaret Jean Hay and Sharon Stichter, 2nd ed. (New York: Longman, 1995), pp. 3–22; Margot Lovett, "Gender Relations, Class Formation, and the Colonial State in Africa," in *Women and the State*, ed. Parpart and Staudt, pp. 23–46; Elias Mandala, *Work and Control in a Peasant Economy: A History of the Lower Tschiri Valley in Malawi, 1895–1960* (Madison: University of Wisconsin Press, 1990); Henrietta Moore and Megan Vaughan, *Cutting Down Trees: Gender, Nutrition, and Agricultural Change in the Northern Province of Zambia, 1890–1990* (Portsmouth, N.H.: Heinemann, 1994); Elizabeth Schmidt, *Peasants, Traders, and Wives: Shona Women in the History of Zimbabwe, 1870–1939* (Portsmouth, N.H.: Heinemann, 1992); Marcia Wright, "Technology, Marriage, and Women's Work in the History of Maize-Growers in Mazabuka, Zambia: A Reconnaissance," *Journal of Southern African Studies* 10, no. 1 (1983): 71–85.

8. Again, a comprehensive list is not possible here, but see, by way of example, Iris Berger, *Threads of Solidarity: Women in South African Industry* (Bloomington: Indiana University Press, 1992); Hilda Bernstein, *For Their Triumphs and Their Tears* (London: International Defense and Aid Fund, 1985); LaRay Denzer, "Constance A. Cummings-John of Sierra Leone: Her Early Political Career," *Tarikh* 7 (1981): 20–32; Susan Geiger, "Women in Nationalist Struggle: TANU Activists in Dar es Salaam," *International Journal of African Historical Studies* 20, no. 1 (1987): 1–26, and *TANU Women: Gender and Culture in the Making of Tanganyikan Nationalism, 1955–1965* (Portsmouth, N.H.: Heinemann, 1997); Cheryl Johnson-Odim and Nina Mba, *For Women and the Nation: Funmilayo Ransome-Kuti of Nigeria* (Urbana: University of Illinois Press, 1997); Tabitha Kanogo, "Kikuyu Women and the Politics of Protest: Mau Mau," in *Images of Women in Peace and War: Cross-cultural and Historical Perspectives*, ed. Sharon MacDonald, Pat Holden, and Shirley Ardener (Madison: University of Wisconsin Press, 1987), pp. 78–99; Ellen Kuzwayo, *Call Me Woman* (London: Women's Press, 1985); Rina Okonkwo, ed., *West African Nationalists* (Enugu: Delta, 1986); Cora Ann Presley, "The Mau Mau Rebellion, Kikuyu Women, and Social Change," *Canadian Journal of African Studies* 12, no. 3 (1988): 502–27; Timothy Scarnecchia, "Poor Women and Nationalist Politics: Alliances and Fissures in the Formation of a Nationalist Political Movement in Salisbury, Rhodesia, 1950–6," *Journal of African History* 37, no. 2 (1996): 283–310; Van Allen, "'Aba Riots'"; Walker, *Women and Resistance*.

9. See, by way of example, Teresa Barnes, *"We Women Worked So Hard": Gender, Urbanization, and Social Reproduction in Colonial Harare, Zimbabwe, 1930–*

1956 (Portsmouth, N.H.: Heinemann, 1999); Judith Byfield, "Innovation and Conflict: Cloth Dyers and the Interwar Depression in Abeokuta, Nigeria," *Journal of African History* 38, no. 1 (1998): 77–100; Gracia Clark, *Onions Are My Husband: Survival and Accumulation by West African Market Women* (Chicago: University of Chicago Press, 1994); Mann, *Marrying Well;* Jane Parpart, "'Where Is Your Mother?': Gender, Urban Marriage, and Colonial Discourse on the Zambian Copperbelt," *International Journal of African Historical Studies* 27, no. 2 (1994): 241–71; Mamphela Ramphele, "The Dynamics of Gender Politics in the Hostels of Cape Town," *Journal of Southern African Studies* 15, no. 3 (1989): 393–414; Robertson, *Sharing the Same Bowl,* "Traders and Urban Struggle," *Journal of Women's History* 4, no. 3 (1993): 9–42, and *Trouble Showed the Way: Women, Men, and Trade in the Nairobi Area, 1890–1990* (Bloomington: Indiana University Press, 1997); Kathleen Sheldon, *Courtyards, Markets, City Streets: Urban Women in Africa* (Boulder, Colo.: Westview, 1996); and Luise White, *The Comforts of Home: Prostitution in Colonial Nairobi* (Chicago: University of Chicago Press, 1990).

10. By way of example, see Jean Allman, "Making Mothers: Missionaries, Medical Officers, and Women's Work in Colonial Asante, 1924–1945," *History Workshop Journal* 38 (1994): 23–47; Deborah Gaitskell, "Devout Domesticity? A Century of African Women's Christianity in South Africa," in *Women and Gender in Southern Africa to 1945,* ed. Cherryl Walker (Cape Town: David Philip, 1990), pp. 251–72; Karen Tranberg Hansen, ed., *African Encounters with Domesticity* (New Brunswick, N.J.: Rutgers University Press, 1992); Nancy Rose Hunt, "'Le Bébé en Brousse': European Women, African Birth Spacing, and Colonial Intervention in Breast Feeding in the Belgian Congo," *International Journal of African Historical Studies* 21, no. 3 (1988): 401–32, and "Domesticity and Colonialism in Belgian Africa: Usumbura's *Foyer Social,* 1946–1960," in *Ties That Bind: Essays on Mothering and Patriarchy,* ed. Jean F. O'Barr, Deborah Pope, and Mary Wyer (Chicago: University of Chicago Press, 1990), pp. 149–77; Diana Jeater, *Marriage, Perversion, and Power: The Construction of Moral Discourse in Southern Rhodesia, 1894–1930* (Oxford: Oxford University Press, 1993); Meredith McKittrick, "Faithful Daughter, Murdering Mother: Transgression and Social Control in Colonial Namibia," *Journal of African History* 40, no. 2 (1999): 265–84; Susan Pederson, "National Bodies, Unspeakable Acts: The Sexual Politics of Colonial Policy-Making," *Journal of Modern History* 63, no. 4 (1991): 647–80; Carol Summers, "Intimate Colonialism: The Imperial Production of Reproduction in Uganda, 1907–1925," *Signs: Journal of Women in Culture and Society* 16, no. 4 (1991): 787–807; Lynn Thomas, "Imperial Concerns and 'Women's Affairs': State Efforts to Regulate Clitoridectomy and Eradicate Abortion in Meru, Kenya, c. 1910–1950," *Journal of African History* 39, no. 1 (1998): 121–46; Megan Vaughan, *Curing Their Ills: Colonial Power and African Illness* (Stanford, Calif.: Stanford University Press, 1991).

11. It is important to note that much women's history research continues to appear in edited collections organized around particular themes. One of the most recent examples is Dorothy Hodgson and Sheryl McCurdy, eds., *Wicked Women and the Reconfiguration of Gender in Africa* (Portsmouth, N.H.: Heinemann, 2001).

12. Most recently, see, for example, Allman and Tashjian, *"I Will Not Eat Stone";*

Edna G. Bay, *Wives of the Leopard: Gender, Politics, and Culture in the King-dom of Dahomey* (Charlottesville: University of Virginia Press, 1998); Berger, *Threads of Solidarity;* Bozzoli, *Women of Phokeng;* Cooper, *Marriage in Maradi;* Geiger, *TANU Women;* Sandra Greene, *Gender, Ethnicity, and Social Change on the Upper Slave Coast: A History of the Anlo Ewe* (Portsmouth, N.H.: Heinemann, 1996); Nancy Rose Hunt, *A Colonial Lexicon of Birth Ritual, Medicalization, and Mobility in the Congo* (Durham, N.C.: Duke University Press, 1999); Anne Mager, *Gender and the Making of a South African Bantustan* (Portsmouth, N.H.: Heinemann, 1999); Moore and Vaughan, *Cutting Down Trees;* Robertson, *Trouble Showed the Way;* Schmidt, *Peasants, Traders, and Wives;* Pamela Scully, *Liberating the Family? Gender and British Slave Emancipation in the Rural Western Cape, South Africa, 1823–1853* (Portsmouth, N.H.: Heinemann, 1997); Marcia Wright, *Strategies of Slaves and Women: Life Stories from East/Central Africa* (New York: Lillian Barber, 1993).

13.   Hay and Stichter, *African Women South of the Sahara;* Iris Berger and E. Frances White, *Women in Sub-Saharan Africa: Restoring Women to History* (Bloomington: Indiana University Press, 1999); Catherine Coquery-Vidrovitch, *African Women: A Modern History* (Boulder, Colo.: Westview, 1997).

14.   See, for example, the introduction and accompanying essays in Nancy Rose Hunt, Tessie Liu, and Jean Quataert, *Gendered Colonialisms in African History* (Malden, Mass.: Blackwell, 1997).

15.   Nancy Rose Hunt, introduction to *Gendered Colonialisms,* ed. Hunt, Liu, and Quataert, p. 323.

16.   Ayesha Imam, "Engendering African Social Sciences: An Introductory Essay," in *Engendering African Social Sciences,* ed. Ayesha Imam, Amina Mama, and Fatou Sow (Dakar: CODESRIA, 1997), p. 6.

17.   In this way it departs from the intellectual genealogy set out in Hunt's intro-duction to *Gendered Colonialisms,* which argues that the field has moved from women's history to gender history. "Histories of gender in Africa," she writes, "have moved far from the first generation of women's history in their con-tents and analytic frames, in their use of social theory and evidence, and in authorship" (p. 325).

18.   This is not the place to list books or take on the entire profession, but any quick perusal of the book review sections of the *Journal of African History,* the *International Journal of African Historical Studies,* or *Africa* will evidence this point.

19.   For example, Strobel's *Muslim Women in Mombasa;* Robertson's *Sharing the Same Bowl;* White's *The Comforts of Home;* Moore and Vaughan's *Cutting Down Trees;* and, most recently, Hunt's *Colonial Lexicon.*

20.   This case is most powerfully made by Tiyambe Zeleza, "Gender Biases in Afri-can Historiography," in *Engendering African Social Sciences,* ed. Imam, Mama, and Sow, pp. 81–116.

21.   Zeleza, "Gender Biases," pp. 110–11.

22.   See, for example, Jeater, *Marriage, Perversion, and Power;* Pederson, "National Bodies"; Summers, "Intimate Colonialism"; Vaughan, *Curing Their Ills.*

23.   See, for example, Jean Allman, "Adultery and the State in Asante: Reflections on Gender, Class, and Power from 1800 to 1950," in *The Cloth of Many Col-*

ored Silks: Papers on History and Society, Ghanaian and Islamic, in Honor of Ivor Wilks, ed. John Hunwick and Nancy Lawler (Evanston, Ill.: Northwestern University Press, 1996), pp. 27–65; Martin Chanock, *Law, Custom, and Social Order: The Colonial Experience in Malawi and Zambia* (Cambridge: Cambridge University Press, 1985), and "Making Customary Law: Men, Women, and Courts in Colonial Northern Rhodesia," in *African Women and the Law,* ed. Hay and Wright, pp. 53–67; Sally Falk Moore, *Social Facts and Fabrications: "Customary" Law in Kilimanjaro, 1880–1980* (New York: Cambridge University Press, 1986); Penelope Roberts, "The State and the Regulation of Marriage: Sefwi Wiawso (Ghana), 1900–40," in *Women, State, and Ideology: Studies from Africa and Asia,* ed. Haleh Afshar (Albany: State University of New York Press, 1987), pp. 48–69; Kristin Mann and Richard Roberts, eds., *Law in Colonial Africa* (Portsmouth, N.H.: Heinemann, 1991).

24. For example, see Mann, *Marrying Well.*

Part One.   *Encounters and Engagements*

*The chapters in this first part challenge the salience and gener-
alizability of the images of African women frequently invoked by
historians of the "colonial encounter": helpless victims, passive
objects, collaborators, resisters, or mindless vessels of "tradition."
They remind us that there was no single moment, much less
form of contact, that marks a common starting point for the colonial epoch throughout the continent. Rather, historical chronologies, the actors involved, and the consequences of women's
engagement with the colonizers and those associated with European rule depended upon numerous factors, not the least of
which were the needs, wishes, and understandings of the women
in question. In approaching the women who are the subjects of
their essays, the authors share an interest in the use of women's
personal narratives—life stories, a journal, an autobiography—
in the historical reconstruction of women's relationships to the
agents and institutions associated with the European colonial
presence. Yet each scholar understands that the documents they
bring to the fore—whether oral or written—constitute representations of women's colonial experience that must be contextualized and interpreted.*

1 "What My Heart Wanted": Gendered Stories of Early Colonial Encounters in Southern Mozambique

Heidi Gengenbach

When in mid-1995 I first moved onto the grounds of the former Swiss mission station at Antioka, in the locality of Facazisse (Magude District) in southern Mozambique, I was received by the community as a harbinger of the return of *valungu* (whites) to the area for the first time since the end of the war between Renamo and the Mozambican government, which laid waste to the country between 1976 and 1992.[1] Many people believed I was a missionary, some thought a doctor, and one woman suspected I was an arms trader from "America" come to reignite the conflict. Yet whoever they thought I was, everyone expected me to behave in a particular way toward local authorities, beginning with visiting them and explaining the reasons for my presence. I dutifully made the rounds and what I thought were the necessary introductions, meeting with representatives of the governing party, Frelimo;[2] with locality officials; and with male leaders in the "traditional" chiefly system.[3] It was only after several months had passed that I learned I had made some critical omissions. What finally alerted me was the regular occurrence of incidents that, on their own, seemed unremarkable: troops of giggling young women knocking on my door at all hours of the day and night; elderly women repeatedly stopping by my hut to discuss their health problems; murmurs from my translators that certain powerful women—spirit mediums—were wondering when "the little white person" was planning to visit *them*. There were, I belatedly realized, female as well as male authorities, with their own views of the meaning of my presence in their midst, and their own constituencies watching to see how I positioned myself within a field of social relations crisscrossed by multiple networks of status and power.

Trying to understand these gendered responses has helped me to think about some intriguing fragments of written evidence from the Magude area between the mid–nineteenth and early twentieth centuries, all composed by Europeans and all narrating their initial or early encounters with African women. These written sources only began to make sense to me as I conducted life history interviews with women in Magude and explored other forms of women's history-telling, such as pottery, tattooing, spirit possession, and land-use practices.[4] These bodies of feminine evidence also "speak," in their own ways, about early colonial interactions; most importantly, they tell us that African women's behavior in this context defies analysis through the categories—such as "resistance" and "collaboration"—that dominated the historiography of early colonial Africa from the 1960s to the late 1980s. Simply put, this scholarship focuses on the period of European military and political conquest of Africa (c. 1880–1900) and argues that Africans responded to colonial aggression either by struggling actively against it or by cooperating with European colonizers.[5] While many historians in the past decade have recognized that such analytic binaries fail to capture the multivalent, negotiated, and kaleidoscopic character of African relationships with Europeans,[6] work on gender and women's history in particular has forced scholars to reconsider the theoretical constructs through which colonial encounters in Africa have been narrated and explained.[7] The gendered trajectory of African historiography on this subject is obviously linked to the gendered narratives embedded in colonial written sources. The Magude area, for instance, was one of the first places in southern Mozambique to experience the conversion efforts of the Swiss Mission, and one of the last to be subdued politically by the Portuguese. According to documentary evidence, Magude's history for the first several decades after Europeans' arrival contains numerous personalities that do seem to fit one pole or the other of the "resistance" paradigm: political rebels, clandestine labor migrants, and tax evaders on the side of resistance; colonial chiefs, soldiers and police, and African evangelists on that of collaboration. Yet even if we provisionally grant the adequacy of these categories, it is significant that most of the individuals inscribed within them are men. Colonizers themselves often perceived African women's actions during this period as too ambivalent, too changeable, and too contradictory to be classified so neatly along these lines.

Yet women's conduct did not lack reason or coherence, and patterns in their behavior in—and their representations of—early interactions with Europeans suggest an alternative to the "resistance" framework. I propose that in early colonial Magude, and perhaps in rural southern Mozambique more broadly, we might conceptualize women's actions in relation to colonizers as *strategic engagement,* the terms, objectives, and meanings of which not only were gendered and negotiated, but also changed over time. Most studies of the gendered terrain of colonial encounters in Africa have concerned themselves primarily with the extent to which European agents sought to establish "control" over African women. Yet "control" is itself a colonial construct, and tells us very little about women's understanding of the meaning or stakes of these encounters. This chapter, then, reexamines African women's experiences of early colonial contact in southern Mozambique by reading European written sources in light of women's accounts of this historical moment—in particular, women's memories of their early relationships with Europeans. Even the scant references to African women in the reports of European travelers and officials in the Magude area indicate that these interactions were far more complex than historians have portrayed them. Early mission records from the Antioka station furnish an especially provocative glimpse of gendered struggles over the spiritual and material meaning of the Swiss presence. In these struggles, African women were clearly motivated by their own agendas, engaging things European with the aim of buttressing feminine forms of knowledge, power, and authority in local communities.

The alternative vision of "colonial encounter" that these sources suggest, which I discuss in the first part of this chapter, stands out even more vividly when we turn to the narrative portraits in women's life stories, perhaps most dramatically of all in the case of one woman, Rosalina Malungana, who tells the history of her involvement with the Portuguese colonial order principally through recollections of interracial sexual relationships. Like the other women I interviewed who were born before 1930, Rosalina remembers the early years of colonialism as not a period of European "control" so much as a time when a new cast of characters—with novel ideas, behaviors, and material trappings—began to appear on the rural landscape and to acquire meaning for African women through subjective, narrated experience. While they did not always determine the conditions under which colonial encounters took place, Rosalina and her peers interpreted these encounters largely in terms of cultural mappings that were shaped by the life stories of their mothers and grandmothers, whose own memories predated the beginning of European rule. As the excerpt from Rosalina's life story at the end of this chapter illustrates, even in as power-laden a field of "contact" as interracial marriage African women constructed their actions according to a worldview that did not ascribe supreme authority to Europeans—and within which women were able to exercise considerable autonomy and influence by claiming to follow the uncontrollable impulses of their "hearts."

• • •

In the centuries prior to formal colonization, the area now known as Magude District was a place of population movement, cultural flux, and sociopolitical change. Traversed by the Nkomati River, it lay along one of the major trade and travel routes between the Indian Ocean coast and the lands west of the Lebombo hills, which straddle the present-day border between southern Mozambique and South Africa. Oral traditions and clan genealogies narrate a complex history of migrations, invasions, and political conquests and the emergence of new ethnic identities in this area through the end of the nineteenth century, with local small-scale societies regularly confronting, accommodating, or otherwise reconciling themselves to newcomers.[8] Although the imposition of rule by immigrants of the Khosa clan (from present-day Natal) in the early eighteenth century and the region's incorporation into the Gaza Nguni kingdom in the nineteenth century[9] enlarged the territorial scope of local political authority, nominally subject chiefdoms in the Magude area seem to have retained a measure of cultural and political independence in their dealings with outsiders—a category that by mid-century included European traders, hunters, and explorers.[10] Thus in 1860, when the Portuguese hunter-trader Diocleciano Fernandes das Neves reached what he believed was "the town of the great chief Magudzu [Khosa],"[11] he was shown great hospitality by the local subchief and the community despite Magudzu's absence.[12] Das Neves' narrative of this journey includes the first published description of contact between Europeans and African women in this area, and in his account of his first night at "Magud's" he draws a vivid portrait of women's manners and motives in what was evidently their first encounter with a *mulungu* stranger:

> As soon as it grew dark, and I lit a candle, a perfect legion of native women appeared at the door of my hut. This troop of African beauties was headed by four lovely matrons, who entered first, and then all the rest followed, until my hut was full. . . . They commenced to question me very minutely, examining my hair, which they thought very smooth, and at last they asked me for [beads]. I gave each of the wives of the chief a bunch of beads, and four rows to every girl. They thanked me in a graceful manner, and went away clapping their hands and laughing, in what I thought derisive uproar.[13]

The following day, according to das Neves, after he had disposed of a giant hippo that had been menacing farmers along the riverbanks, an old woman went out of her way to thank him, on behalf of the community, for finally ridding them of the "sorcerer" that had been devouring their crops.[14] Frederick Elton, a British explorer who passed through a nearby village about a decade later, recorded a similar impression of female assertiveness: "At Magud's," he wrote, "we were besieged and annoyed by women, who came down to our camp after the men had retired for the night."[15]

These depictions of African women actively courting contact with Europeans, and interpreting the visitors' presence to their advantage, merely hint at the gendered quality of early colonial encounters in this area. We might be tempted to dismiss them, except that the same pattern is echoed and amplified in the writings of the first Christian missionaries to the area in the 1880s and 1890s. The foundations of the Swiss Presbyterian Mission in the land the missionaries called "Khocene" were formally laid by Yosefa Mhalamhala, who had fled with his parents from their home north of the Nkomati as refugees from the Gaza succession war (1858–61) and resettled in the Transvaal, where Yosefa attended the Swiss Mission school at Valdezia and converted to Christianity. In 1882, Yosefa returned to the land of his birth and, with Magudzu's permission, began a successful evangelizing campaign in the chief's territory.[16] Like the other African missionaries who succeeded him, Yosefa depended heavily on the female members of his household to woo audiences and win converts, principally through the women's daily conversations with neighbors and visitors.[17] More importantly, the new Christian community that Yosefa and his family fostered was initially composed almost entirely of women. While local men, especially chiefs and other male authorities, were wary of the political implications of cooperating with this European agent (and Magudzu himself abruptly ended his relationship with Yosefa in 1884), women of all ages and political ranks—including the wives and daughters not only of Chief Magudzu but of the Gaza kings Muzila and Ngungunyana as well—came from near and far to "listen to the Word," often risking social "persecution" and defying explicit orders from their husbands.[18] Some of these women, according to Yosefa's letters, sought consolation in the wake of personal tragedy; others claimed that curiosity, spiritual "thirst," or a "voice" calling them to "pray" brought them to Yosefa's door. The vast majority of Yosefa's first converts, though, were *young* women, about whom a visiting Swiss missionary wrote in 1886 that

> for [them], faith is not an affair of the intelligence, for their ignorance is great even on a number of [essential] doctrines. It is truly their *heart* that has been captured. All of them . . . have recognized first of all their state of sin, their fear of condemnation, their often poignant agonies, and finally the peace that they have found in thinking of . . . Jesus.[19]

The fervor of these young women proved instrumental to Yosefa's evangelizing campaign, for they channeled it directly into pressuring men in their communities—including their chiefs—to renounce such customs as beer drinking, polygyny, and, above all, anything related to what the missionaries called "sorcery."[20]

This trend continued after the Antioka mission station was built in 1889–90. However, the Swiss personnel who replaced Yosefa viewed women's behavior in relation to Christianity as rife with contradiction. Throughout the 1890s, women consistently outnumbered men at Antioka's prayer and worship services, a pattern the Swiss attributed in part to male labor migrancy and in part to the fact that men were often preoccupied with "political matters." Girls and women also continued to form the majority in catechism classes and on the lists of African converts and baptized church members.[21] Yet, according to the Swiss, women were also generally less "interested and attentive" in worship than men, "seizing any pretext for making noise" and "amusing themselves, laughing and doing one another's hair" during the sermon.[22] And while a handful of women were the missionaries' most ardent converts, most women in the area confronted the Swiss with open "mockery," "hardened" resistance to schooling, and stubborn opposition to efforts to eliminate drinking, belief in witchcraft, and so-called "pagan" rituals concerned with ancestor spirits and death.[23] Indeed, the lack of fear of or respect for the white missionaries among some women had been plain from the moment of their arrival in Khocene, for although the Swiss negotiated with local chiefs to obtain a site for the station, they were prevented from occupying it until they had paid one pound sterling and several bolts of cloth in "compensation" to the women who were cultivating the land the missionaries wanted.[24] Perhaps most telling of all, although women were at first skeptical of Swiss claims to knowledge in the realms of rainmaking and biomedicine, it was also women who displayed the most interest in these branches of the missionaries' "power" and who more often decided to convert after being cured of illness (or helped through a dangerous childbirth) in Swiss hands.[25]

Patterns in the incidence and character of early female conversions, which can be traced through mission records from the mid-1890s on, suggest that it was precisely in matters of doctoring that Christianity's appeal to women was most powerful, ambivalent, and contentious. Like Yosefa, the first Swiss missionaries at Antioka quickly attracted a community of followers composed predominantly of young women.[26] However, the Swiss reported drawing two additional categories of women whose zealous embrace of the new religion was just as striking: elderly women, and women suffering from physical or mental health problems. In 1893 and 1894, missionaries' writings included brief references to a "women's asylum" at Antioka—a building they had given over to the individuals who, at the time, constituted nearly their entire congregation. Residents of the "asylum" included a woman with leprosy, a young blind woman, an adolescent girl "fleeing the temptations of town," and an older woman who had come to Antioka afflicted by what the Swiss called "madness" and then undergone a "miraculous transformation," received baptism, and stayed on at Antioka to further her Christian education.[27] In 1895, and again in 1897, the outbreak of war between the Portuguese and Gaza armies drove many elderly and invalid women to seek refuge on the mission grounds; a number of them quickly announced their desire to embrace the Christian faith, on the grounds that their "heart was suffering" and they had heard "voices" telling them to "follow Jesus"—by whom they often meant the missionaries themselves.[28] By 1904, Antioka had a special catechism class for elderly women; around the same time, the Swiss began to intensify their requests to the Mission Council that funds be provided to build a hospital at Antioka, for they had realized that their "medical mission" did "far more for the progress of their work" than proselytizing on its own.[29] As one missionary doctor wrote, "hospitalization presents especially great advantages for evangelization among the sick. . . . Trust [in our medical work] already exists, in many places to an astonishing degree. Our influence can be extended still more, the path is open . . . [if] we permit the sick to benefit from the spiritual resources of the station."[30]

Clearly, one reason the missionaries were able to tout the compelling power of their medicine may have been the well-documented ravaging of the Magude area by waves of famine, cattle epidemics, and human illness around the turn of the century. At this moment of ecological crisis, as malnourished rural communities battled familiar scourges such as malaria and diarrhea along with the new, migrancy-linked afflictions of tuberculosis and venereal disease, the Swiss offered treatments whose novelty alone may have convinced desperate families to try them.[31] However, increased recourse to missionary doctoring did not necessarily mean that more people in Khocene were opening themselves to Christianity. In fact, burgeoning demand for European medical intervention coincided with another trend at Antioka: from about 1900 on, even as their annual reports noted an increasing number of conversions, improved attendance at worship services, and a more "receptive" attitude to the "Gospel," the Swiss became more and more concerned about the "lack of fervor" and apparent shallowness of faith among their converts—above all, their enduring susceptibility to "pagan superstitions" and their reluctance to abandon local herbal and spirit healers.[32] These worries were deeply gendered, for missionaries blamed spiritual backsliding among converts mainly on the influence of non-Christian women, whose "terrible" outspokenness and "immorality" were most shockingly manifest in all-night "orgies" of drinking and dancing—activities in which many female converts were also taking part.[33] Although they avoided writing explicitly about such matters, the missionaries' frequent references to "sorcery" in this context imply that these "orgies" often involved spirit possession and spirit-medium divination ceremonies, the most powerful (and, to the Swiss, "satanic") form of local healing. In other words, if the mission doctors at Antioka were experiencing heightened demand for their medical services at this time, so were Khocene's local doctors; and the constant fussing in mission reports over the "spiritual torpor" and furtive, nocturnal sinning of Antioka Christians suggests that the Swiss were concerned not only about African souls, but about a mounting contest to determine who had superior powers of healing.

The missionaries recognized soon after their arrival in Khocene that medical doctoring was not only a strategy but also a major battleground in their campaign for spiritual and social hegemony. As one wrote confidently in 1890, "people look like they've had enough of their doctors, and they have great faith in ours."[34] It took over a decade, though, for the Swiss to realize that local doctors were just as keen to augment their own powers as the Swiss were to establish their authority as healers; yet, in fact, the signs were there from the beginning, in the identities of the women who were the missionaries' first and most eager customers. Old women, known as *masungukati*,[35] possess special healing abilities in Tsonga-Shangaan[36] society: besides having an extensive knowledge of herbal remedies for physical ailments ranging from flu to infertility, they are reputed to be the masters of a certain kind of supernatural power, which enables them to combat the malignant work of witches and to bewitch people themselves. They are also responsible for ritual leadership and practical guidance in matters related to birth, sexuality, marriage, and death, and for ceremonies to protect the land from crop pests and drought.[37] Young women (roughly between the ages of fourteen and twenty-five), on the other hand, along with women suffering from chronic physical or nervous disorders, have been the people most susceptible to spirit possession since at least the late nineteenth century, when Swiss doctors began documenting this phenomenon in Magude and elsewhere in southern Mozambique.[38] There is no space in this chapter to explore the complex character or causes of spirit possession in this region; what is important here is that the most common treatment for possession was training and initiation into a community of spirit mediums (*vanyamusoro*), after which initiates would pursue potentially lifelong careers as healers—not only of possession, but of a wide range of illnesses, psychological problems, and witchcraft. Between these two groups of female doctors, masungukati and vanyamusoro, women dominated the everyday practice of medicine in late-nineteenth-century Khocene, using their considerable powers to mend bodies, spirits, crops, and the land; to counsel the suffering and the outcast; and to guide relationships between men and women, old and young, rich and poor, the living and the dead.

Female healers did not stand by passively as the Swiss intruded with their own notions of how doctoring should be done. Mission sources document increasingly public tensions between them and the Swiss between 1890 and 1910, with missionaries on more than one occasion waging "oratory combat" to persuade ailing Christians that European healing methods were superior to African ones.[39] One particularly dramatic incident in 1899 illustrates that women doctors took advantage of the Swiss medical presence to claim greater supernatural and social power for themselves, vis-à-vis both European healers and local political authorities. The following passage was written by a missionary's wife at the height of an epidemic of bubonic plague in Magude, when the Swiss and Portuguese officials were finding their efforts to control the disease thwarted by very different local methods of explaining and handling it:

> The Khosa seemed grateful that the [missionary] had discovered the illness that was killing their people and had denounced this thing to the government, but now they forget, and what are they doing? They are listening to an old sorceress who utters lies and nonsense; she says she is their *savior,* she recounts that she met one night with the *baloi* (evil spirits), fought with them, conquered them and made them promise to keep their hands off the Khosa. "Kill," she supposedly said to them, "all that you want in Ntimane, but watch out for the Khosa, I have taken them under my protection!" And now she says to whoever wants to listen that it was she who saved people, and everyone applauds her speeches . . . adoring every word. One day, she asked the young chief to get her feathers of the *nkulukulu* bird [Purplecrested Lourie] . . . in order to make herself a royal head-dress; immediately the young people threw themselves into a campaign to satisfy her desire. The poor people do not see that she is simply stealing their money, . . . getting herself invited to their orgies around pots of beer and called by the pompous title of "queen of the desert" (*nkosi ya mananga*)! . . . These Khosa . . . do not believe any less in their superstitions, even while they say yes and amen to everything. Alas! We are powerless. Only God can change their hearts.[40]

Of course, in her last comment, the writer hits the most critical issue on the head: neither the missionaries then, nor we now, can know with certainty what motivated certain women at this time to seek a relationship with the Swiss; what exactly these women did with this relationship in their private lives or in spheres of local public life to which the missionaries had no access; or why, and with what consequences, other women shunned such interaction and openly positioned themselves as the missionaries' rivals and antagonists. What, for instance, do we make of the repeated claims that young women's adoption of Christianity was not "intelligent" but a matter of the "heart," sometimes so intense (according to European reports) as to border on hysteria—especially when Swiss doctors characterized female victims of spirit possession (i.e., future spirit mediums) in exactly the same manner? How do we explain some women's zealous use of their new faith to modify the behavior of husbands and chiefs, or to escape from, supplement, or even challenge the doctoring powers of older generations of women? How, on the other hand, are we to understand those women who courted contact with the Swiss through more casual interaction on their own terms, by participating in prayers and worship without formally converting, by consulting both African and missionary doctors, or by staying for a time in the "women's asylum" and then returning home? Women were clearly selective and pragmatic in their approach to the Swiss in other respects, flocking to prayers during periods of drought, filling the sewing classes offered by missionaries' wives, and sending their children to work or live at Antioka when times were lean.[41] In a symbolic sense, these feminine forms of strategic engagement are not unlike the visit das Neves received back in 1860: women arrive at the Europeans' door, study their hair, ask for beads (for reasons unknown to the white men), and then go away laughing when their request has been fulfilled.

Swiss stories of the gendered ambivalence in African conduct offer a number of tantalizing hints that women not only chose what they wanted of Christian teachings and medical techniques and ignored the rest, but turned around and used what they acquired from Europeans to enhance the very kinds of authority that Europeans were trying to appropriate, eliminate, or transform. Early European traders in the area, like das Neves, often found that the only goods Africans would accept from them were particular colors of imported cloth and beads— almost exclusively identical to the ones that spirit mediums, then and now, require for their costumes and ceremonies. In like manner, Swiss missionaries introduced novel material objects (such as crocheted hats and medicine bottles), theological constructs (such as "savior"), and forms of religious expression (such as hymns) that female healers did not hesitate to borrow; and other members of the community seem to have interpreted the meaning of these borrowings as they interpreted the practices of the missionaries themselves, in terms of their power to "doctor" along local rather than European lines. Moreover, missionary writings make it clear that what African women most often sought from the Swiss tended to be precisely what indigenous female doctors also offered: rituals to call rain, "medicines" to ward off supernatural dangers, assistance in childbirth, cures for bodily illness, family and marriage counseling, and—perhaps most importantly—an affective community defined by its concern with social health, broadly defined as physical, spiritual, and moral well-being. Thus what the missionaries read as signs of their deepening influence we might also interpret as women's selective appropriation of resources that colonizers made available, with the aim of reinforcing gendered constructions of local authority according to which a woman's capacity to "heal" conferred enormous social power, potentially rivaling even the power of chiefs.

If Swiss records often provide no more than fleeting glimpses of early encounters between Europeans and African women in the Magude area, interactions between women and Portuguese actors are considerably more difficult to "see" in archival sources. Portuguese material on early colonial Magude is limited in quantity, and such documents as do exist rarely acknowledge the presence of African women. Moreover, conceptualizing these encounters presents a different kind of challenge: "strategic engagement" seems less suitable for describing African women's behavior in relation to colonizers who were (notoriously) willing to use a good deal more coercion than the Swiss in their dealings with Africans, and who made fewer pretensions to be exercising power in African interests. In fact, official sources suggest that the first representatives of Portuguese colonialism in Magude were generally too concerned with their *lack* of authority to pay much attention to the ordinary activities of local women. Although a Portuguese envoy tried to persuade Chief Magudzu to pay tribute as early as 1883,[42] no Portuguese personnel were stationed in the area until 1891. For the next twenty years, the fledgling colonial government in what was then Magude Circumscription was preoccupied with a series of overt political challenges. Portuguese documents from this period reflect officials' overriding concern with the uncertainty of their administrative presence, in terms of both the instability of their "rule" and how little they knew about the "natives" that they were supposed to be governing.[43] Women occasionally appear in these sources in, again, curiously ambivalent ways, as when the mother of Magudzu's successor (a young boy named Xongela) is said to have pleaded with Portuguese officials in 1892 for protection against Ngungunyana; and as in 1896 when female prisoners in the makeshift jail allegedly informed on two male prisoners who had escaped, for no apparent reason except to help the Portuguese track the men down.[44] Other than these fragments, written sources tell us virtually nothing about women's actions in this period, creating the impression that while men evaded and "resisted" Portuguese power in whatever ways they could, women simply sat by and allowed (or even encouraged) colonization to happen.

Women's oral accounts and life stories, however, represent this process in a rather different way. The first challenge they pose to the implied narrative of Portuguese documents is one of chronology, for the colonizers' claims to rule—carefully recorded in the 1890s in so-called "treaties of vassalage" with local chiefs—are belied by women's memories of colonization as a much later, much more incremental, and much less dramatic and disruptive event than official sources contend. And while I recognize that my identity and the circumstances of interviewing may have had some effect on the content of women's recollections, certain patterns were so pronounced that it is difficult to dismiss them as fictions of my ethnographic imagination.[45] Women as a group acknowledged that the Portuguese monopolized a certain kind of power from the moment of their arrival: they were the new "chiefs," after all, and backed their authority and demands with the threat of violence, imprisonment, or punishments such as forced labor; and they were always making unreasonable laws, such as the one compelling all African schoolchildren to learn Portuguese. They also, women asserted, often treated African *men* abominably, throwing them into jail or beating them at the slightest hint of disobedience. Yet when women recalled their own and their foremothers' early interactions with valungu—a category that, for them, embraced all non-African actors, including South Asian ("Banyan") merchants and shopkeepers[46]—they highlighted, not abuse and exploitation, but two other, contrasting patterns. First, women emphasized the ways in which early colonizers "helped" them, through such diverse measures as introducing new fashions of dress, building hospitals and maternity clinics, freely dispensing a kind of "tea" (a soupy mix of bread, sugar, and water) to customers at their shops, extending seeds or food on credit in times of drought, and providing transport so that women could go visiting and trading over longer distances. Second, women all over Magude narrated similar stories about early encounters between African women and valungu that occurred within feminine spaces in the most ordinary fields of everyday life. According to these accounts, which refer roughly to the period between 1890 and the 1930s, African women of all ages drank, danced, visited, and negotiated sexual unions and fictive kinship with valungu men from every conceivable sector of colonial society: merchants, farmers, settlers, bureaucrats—even, in some cases, local administrators.

Perhaps the most neglected face of the colonial encounter in African historiography, interracial relationships—typically involving European or Asian men and African women—are an especially delicate topic for scholars of former Portuguese colonies, where the myth of *lusotropicalismo* has indelibly stamped "miscegenation" as a branch of Portuguese imperial policy.[47] Yet studies of colonial intermarriage in the Americas and Asia have demonstrated that such unions were a crucial site for the construction of new race, class, and gender identities; for the negotiation of ties of economic and political cooperation between colonizers and indigenous communities; and for everyday struggles over the boundaries and meaning of colonial rule.[48] In a context such as Magude, intimate relationships between valungu men and African women could play a pivotal role in constituting the "frontier" of colonial contact, as the new arrivals (either bachelors or men whose wives were still overseas) found that political and commercial influence could be fostered through the creation of kinship with local families, and as local populations sought to demystify—in a sense, domesticate—the lighter-skinned strangers by integrating them into their own cultural and social universe. The balance of power in these relationships depended to a great extent on the circumstances in which sexual encounters took place, and obviously could vary a great deal between genuinely consensual unions and "arranged" coupling negotiated by a woman's father or male guardian for purposes of his own. However, women's perceptions of how and why they entered such relationships, embedded in their understanding of the range of marital options available to them and the consequences of their actions whichever path they decided to follow, were an equally important ingredient in the power dynamics of interracial unions. Where women had little experiential evidence of European political or social hegemony, yet saw certain advantages in marriage to a mulungu, there was no reason for them to view this alternative as innately more oppressive or exploitative (or less desirable) than marriage to an African man. Indeed, under these conditions, a temporary interracial relationship or informal marriage could serve as a woman's first "strategic engagement" with the world of the colonizers, even when it occurred many years after the formal imposition of European rule. As many older women's oral accounts suggest, it was often the moment of this "encounter" more than anything else that established, for them, the subjective foundation of colonial society.

By way of illustration, I would like to share a passage from the life stories[49] of one woman, Rosalina Malungana, whose memories offer a particularly dramatic and challenging example of women's "strategic engagement" with colonialism in southern Mozambique. When I first met Rosalina in 1995, she was an eighty-one-year-old woman living alone in one of the abandoned infirmary huts on the Antioka church grounds, less than twenty feet from the hut I would occupy for the duration of my time in Magude. She woke every morning before dawn to kindle a fire for what she called, in Portuguese, her "breakfast"—a routine that on its own marked her as a person with an educated, urban past. Yet soon after sipping the last of her tea, Rosalina would set off barefoot down the path toward her fields, teetering slightly under the weight of the hoe slung over one shoulder. She never returned until almost dusk, long after most younger women had left off farming and gone home; and she rarely returned without an additional burden of some kind—firewood, fresh corn, manioc dug from the ground of her late mother's homestead, an interesting insect to show her new mulungu neighbor. As Rosalina and I were first getting to know each other, she was fond of repeating three observations about me: first, that I reminded her of "Miss Randin," her favorite teacher at the Swiss Mission girls' school in the colonial capital, Lourenço Marques, which Rosalina attended from 1928 to 1932; second, that my mother must have beaten me a lot when I was young, since I was "not afraid of hard work"; and third, that my husband's quiet manner reminded her of her own late husband, a Portuguese truck driver named Agosto Capela.

Rosalina's comments were overtures to me, but they also reveal the principal motifs of a life whose complexities and contradictions force us to confront the ambiguities of colonialism as it is enacted through one woman's subjective portrayal of her negotiations with European society.[50] She was born in 1914 into a prominent family in rural Guijá connected to the Swiss Mission, and her earliest recollections include traveling on foot with her mother to visit her maternal uncle's homestead in Mazimhlopes (near present-day Chokwe). Here she had her first encounter with the Portuguese colonial order, in the form of settlers who used to come to buy leopard and kudu skins from her uncle, Patapata Tivane. One of Rosalina's most vivid memories from this period is of a mulungu man who used to wink lecherously at her when she accompanied her aunt to the local shop—the incident with which she opens the narrative below. As a teenager, Rosalina defied the strict Christian discipline of the paternal uncle, Dane Malungana (an evangelist for the Swiss), in whose Caniçado homestead she lived after her father's death in 1918; but she did so in what might appear to be contrary ways: by, on the one hand, sneaking out with her girlfriends to "pull" (i.e., elongate) her labia (kukoka mitsingi), a rite of adolescence her non-Christian mother and grandmother insisted she undergo; and, on the other hand, by tacitly accepting the romantic overtures of young Portuguese and mestiço men during her years as a student at the Swiss Mission girls' school in Lourenço Marques. It was during this time that Rosalina met Agosto Capela, the man with whom she had her first and most serious sexual relationship. Neither colonial law nor Rosalina's uncle would permit the couple to marry formally; yet Rosalina remembers Agosto as her only "husband" (*nuna*), describing him as an ideal mate for reasons that draw on both Christian norms and those that men and women of Rosalina's generation identify as "traditional": he was an "Adam" to her "Eve," because he was kind and never beat her; and he was a model son-in-law (*mukon'wana*) because he regularly visited and "helped" Rosalina's maternal kin.

Rosalina's fond memories of Agosto have not erased the reality of what for her was clearly an agonizing and life-marking experience of interracial courtship, when the young woman's determination to steer her own course through the many different worlds of colonial southern Mozambique—countryside and town, *xilandin* ("black"/Shangaan) and *xilungu* (European) ways, indigenous spiritualism and mission Christianity—ran up against a wall of often contradictory social expectations about the shape her life should take. The following passage, which recounts this story, was prompted by my asking Rosalina to tell me more about the "husband" she was always mentioning in our conversations. This question in turn arose in the context of a prolonged discussion about the practice of labia elongation, and Rosalina's mother's determined effort to make sure that her daughter did not neglect this "duty" despite the risk of a severe beating from her uncle if he found out. I have selected this particular narrative out of the many hours of Rosalina's recorded testimony because it represents, through one woman's eyes, a colonial encounter of the most intimate and "ordinary" kind; yet it is an extraordinary story, and it illustrates just how multifaceted, contested, and profoundly gendered the meanings and outcomes of such encounters could be.

> I've *never* sat down with you to tell you my whole life, to tell you everything. Never. And if sometimes you meet up with other people who—who else can tell you my life? Because am I not the only one who knows my life? My life, to tell it—I haven't yet told everything. I—I don't know what I had, my star. I can say that, it's been my luck[51] that only white men wanted me, since I was a child. Mmm. I don't know, if God when I was born had already—well, I don't know! He'd already given me this luck, that my whole life would be the life of the whites. It happened this way. When I was about ten or eleven years old, sometimes I went to Mazimhlopes, to the house of my uncle, Patapata. And there, sometimes I stayed with my mother's oldest sister, Xintomanyana. Mmm. Sometimes we would go to the shop, with . . . Carolina, Sofia, Domeyana—we were all in the same family. We used to go to the shop to sell *piri piri* [hot peppers], so we could buy salt. And there, a Portuguese man named Cartaxana used to come to that shop. Albino Cartaxana, that was his name. . . . And then, there was one day, when I went to the shop with those sisters of my mother. Tenda, the one who had spirits. And Mapfuxana. . . . Later, when I went into the shop [raises her voice], there was that white man, always going around and spying on me, because he wanted to buy me! So that when

I grew up, I could be his wife. Because there were some [whites] who bought girls, so that when they grew up they could be their wives. [HG: When you say "buy," what do you mean?] Buy, I mean give bridewealth for them [*kulovola*]. Later, another day when I went there, with my aunts, my mother's sisters, that one, Tenda, and Mapfuxana, there he was, sitting there and writing his business, and when I went in with my aunts, he began to look at me! And he did this, with his eye [winks]! He did that! And I didn't understand! I said, "Heh! So that mulungu, he's doing that, he's insulting me!" Because since I was a small child, sometimes when you were annoyed with another child, you would do that, "*eee*" [winks]. That thing, that's an *insult* [*kurhuketela*⁵²]. Eee!! . . . Ah! He's insulting me! And me, I'll say "*eee*" to him! [she winks back]. . . . That mulungu, when he did that, closed his eye, it was to tell me that he liked me! And I said, "Hmm! Mm! Mm-mm! Eh! Hah, he's insulting me! Mama, mama," I said to Tenda. "Do you see him? Do you see that mulungu, how he's insulting me? He says '*eee*' [winks], so I'm saying '*eee*' right back to him!" [winks both eyes, squeezes them tight]. . . . Because I wanted to show him, "I'm insulting you too!" [laughs] Ah! And then, my aunts, they began to laugh, saying "Heh! You, Cartaxana! You're insulting our daughter, what are you insulting her for?" "I'm not insulting her at all!" But then, "Mmm!" [he winks at her] So I said, "Mmm!!" [furiously winks both eyes back] Tenda said, "Eh, Buxeni!⁵³ Truly, that mulungu, he wants you, that's why he's doing that." "He wants me, what does he want? He's insulting me! So I'm doing it back to him!" And she began to laugh, because she knew that I, poor thing, I didn't know that he was courting me!

Well! I went home, because I had to go to school. I started going to school when I was only eleven! . . . Later, I was about twelve years old. And sometimes I went to my mother's home, to visit my mother's brother. . . . Later, I went back to the shop with Xintomanyana. And when he saw me, he said, "Heh! That girl has already grown big! Isn't that Patapata's grand-daughter [*ntukulu*]?⁵⁴ It was him, that Cartaxana. . . . So he said, "Mmm. I'm going to talk to Patapata, to see if he'll let me marry [*kulovola*] her." Another day, Patapata went to the shop, to drink wine, because he always used to go there, to sell animal skins. Mmm. . . . So he said, "Heh, Pata-pata! I saw your niece—she's already big, and so pretty! Eh! Won't you let me buy her? I really want that girl, she's beautiful!" And Patapata said, "Eh! I don't have a daughter for you to buy, to give bridewealth for. Because that girl is my sister's child. Only if you speak to her uncle, her father's brother, the one who is the pastor. Me, no. If you want her, you can speak to her uncle." . . .

Well, that passed. When I was already fourteen or fifteen—I was four-teen when I started at the Internato [Girls' School, Lourenço Marques]. I was at the Internato in 1928, '29, '30. That's when it started with Eduardo Capela. . . . That Eduardo, he was Agosto's boss. He had a shop, up there in

Chibuto. And later he called his cousins to come work with him, in the shop—he was the first one [in his family] to come here from Portugal. And his truck, Eduardo's truck, it was that truck that always picked us up from home [Guijá], to drop us off at Xinavane, so we could catch the train to Lourenço Marques. This was in '28, '29, '30. That's when he began to talk with my uncle, to tell him he wanted me. Listen well, Heidi! This is what he said to Dane [her uncle]. "Eh, *mufundhisi* [pastor]. I want your niece, the one who is at the Internato." . . . [HG: He spoke Shangaan?] Mmm! He spoke Shangaan. That whole family spoke Shangaan, perfectly! If he was speaking outside [and you couldn't see him], you'd think it was an African speaking! And then the pastor, that Dane, said, "Eh, Capela! You're *married*. Yet you still want my niece!" . . . [55] He was the first one to ask my uncle, to tell my uncle he loved me. Agosto already wanted me, but he was still afraid, because I was the daughter of the mufundhisi. . . . Meanwhile Eduardo had already spoken to my uncle. But my uncle said, "Eh, Capela. You have Sofia at the shop. In Lourenço Marques, you have Lucia, and Maluissia. And now you want my niece? Why? Eh! No. I don't want to have a white man in my house, taking my daughters. I want them to marry men of their own race. That's what I want." . . .

Later, we were coming home for the vacation. That Agosto, he was very quiet, very shy. It was hard for him even to tell me, "Look Rosalina, I want you." [drops her voice] All he did, he sent me a little letter. He gave it to his assistant. . . . "Go to the home of the Malunganas, but in secret, you know? I don't want the pastor to see you. He'll want to know what you want there at his house. . . . You must hide, do you understand?" And he came, in the dark, with his bicycle. . . . He came from Chibuto, in Capela's truck. Because, when Eduardo married Sofia, then her brother Agosto came [to Mozambique], to be his driver. . . . So that Agosto and Capela could always go to Xinavane, to pick up *magayisa* [migrant workers] coming home from South Africa. . . . And at that time, Agosto, he wasn't well, because of Eduardo. He went around wondering, "How will I ever get that girl? I love that girl, I don't know what I'm going to do!" And on the holidays, when we got off [the train] at Xinavane, we met Agosto, who was there with his truck, waiting for magayisa, because we always went home on Saturdays. And on the thirty-first of July, we took the train home, it was the school holidays. If it was in November, the thirty-first [*sic*] of November, we had to go home, because they closed the schools, for the holidays. Eeh. . . . We always met him there, in his car, it was the car that we always rode in! Well. Capela [Eduardo] was already going around to my father.[56] And later, Agosto also began to come after me. Sending letters. [HG: What did he say in his letters?] In his letters he said that he wanted to take me to be with him, because he loved me. . . . And me, when I found those letters, I had to send them back, saying, "Look. I don't want to go around with a white man. Because I want to get married, I want to put the veil over my head, to see many people behind me singing. No, I won't marry you, you're a mulungu, and I'm black, I'll find a black man to marry."

Well. It was '30, when he started to insist, and began to write me letters. Thirty, '31, he kept it up. '32, that's when I left the Internato. And he was already, you know, with my uncle, because he had already said, "I want Rosalina." And my uncle said, "Eh! What will I do?! Capela also is beginning to threaten me about Rosalina! Now you too!" Look, there at home, I had that Patrício, . . . the brother of João Leão, who has a shop in Caniçado. . . . And he too was coming after me, so I'd be with him! And Raul Emílio, who was coming after me, he was a *misto* [i.e., of mixed race]. And there was Ishmael Panishandi. He was a misto, his father was Indian, from India. He had a black wife, who had six children with him! . . . And my uncle was going around like this, eh! I don't know, he was so upset. But what am I going to do? Sometimes he called me, "Call Rosalina, to come to me!" And I went into the house. "Sit down. Rosalina." Or, sometimes he called me Buxeni, or Racelina.[57] "Uncle?" "What am I going to do with you? So many valungu are coming to threaten me—one of these days I'll get shot! What am I going to do with you? I mean, here at home there are many girls, but you—I'm not very pleased with you! Because there are all these white men and mistos who want you!" And I said, "Eh! Uncle. I don't know, uncle. There was that man, Jaime Massingue, who wanted to marry me. You didn't accept him. He was black. You said you didn't like him because he belonged to that race of people from Beira. Then came Jeremia. He wanted to marry me. You said, 'I don't want him, he's a heathen, he just joined the church a short time ago, and certainly he came into the church because he wanted you! Because as soon as he started coming to church, he sent me a letter asking to marry you!' And then came Silva Mohambe. He wanted to marry me. And you said that he was no good because his mother is a heathen, his father is a heathen. He was black. That's already four! Because there was another, called João Mabunda. From over near Caniçado. But it's always the same thing! Now I too, I don't know what my uncle wants! Because those men, for sure, among those four, I could have married one of them, I could have loved one of them! But you, you didn't let me. Now, if these white men are coming, threatening you that they want to *lovola* me, whatever they want—I'm not to blame for that!" And he said, "Yes. I see, for sure, I see that one of these days I'll be shot to death. I'm afraid of these Portuguese men! . . . They'll kill me. I don't know, but one day you're going to disappear from here, from my home, so that I can live in peace! Just because you're the prettiest one in the house!" And I said, "Look, I don't know, that is my luck." He said, "Ah! [disgusted] One day soon, I'll decide what I'm going to do with you."

Later, I went to tell my mother. "Mama. Uncle called me, to tell me that one of these days, I'm going to disappear from this house, because he's unhappy with me, because all the time—first it was Capela. And now it's Agosto. Now it's Patrício, and Raul, and Ishmael Panishandi. All of them, they're all white, or misto. But it wasn't me who invited them! They're the ones who want me. . . . Now he's saying that I'm going to disappear one of these days!" And then my mother, she said thus. "All right. This is what I see. One of these days, for sure, I know that you'll go to get firewood, and he'll go and kill you himself, so that he can be at peace, and he won't have to see those valungu in his home. It's better for you to go to Mazimhlopes, to my brother's house. There's a church there, you can go to church, and for sure you will find some boys who will want to marry you. . . . " I said, "All right. I see that I must do as you say." But there was a girl, the niece of my uncle's wife, called Virgínia. She heard everything, and then she went to complain to my uncle. She said, "Rosalina said this and this and this. . . . " And later, Dane came to make trouble with my mother. "If you want to disappear, disappear—I don't care. Because my brother, when he died, I took you in to live with me, to look after you and your children. And now, I see that you want to take your daughter away." Mama said to him, "No, that's not what I said. She is suffering! And those four boys, why don't you let her choose one of them, to marry him? What fault does she have? She's a girl here in your home! And with her luck, she's pretty—it wasn't she who invited those men!" . . .

And later, there was one day, I got up in the morning and I packed my things. So that I could get the boat, António's boat, that crossed [the river] to go to the shop, so I could catch the train to Mazimhlopes. And later, I don't know who told him . . . he got on his bicycle and came after me. Dane. He found me in the street. I was just about to reach the boat, to cross the river. He took what I was carrying on my head. Mmm. And he said, "Look. I know that you're going to those Capelas, or somewhere. In my house, you will never again enter my house." And he took the clothing that I had on my head. . . . And I was already near the house of Ishmael Rigonanti, who was with my cousin, Joana. He had two wives, Rosana and Joana, who was my cousin. . . . When my uncle took my clothing, he went home. I was left with just the clothing that I was wearing. . . . I went to Joana's house, crying. . . . Joana and Rosana, they told me, "It would be better, since you weren't able to get away, and he took all your clothing, we have to go and tell Agosto." *Luck,* Heidi! That day, Agosto was leaving from Chibuto, from the Capelas' place. With his truck full of sacks of corn, to distribute to the shops at Xibabela, and Javanyani, and Ngomane. And when he heard what had happened, eee! That "the mufundhisi went by, carrying all of Rosalina's things, saying that Rosalina was going to your house. That [Dane] ran after her because of you." And he said, "Ah, I see. But I just came from there, I didn't see her." Later, there was another boy, who was in the shop, buying things. He said, "Eh, it's true. I know that she's at Ishmael's house now. Without her clothing! She has only the clothing she is wearing, he even took the scarf from her head!" Eh! This story!

But God exists in this world—God exists in this world, in the heavens! God saw *everything* that my uncle had done.

Well. . . . Later, Agosto said, "All right. She's at her cousin's house. He [Dane] ran after her because of me. All right. That's fine, that he did so. I wanted that girl, so much, and now he's done this! Well. The clothing that he took, I don't care about that." And I was [at Joana's house], crying. But my cousin Joana said, "Look. If Agosto knew that [Dane] had done this, taken your clothing, because of him, and said that you were Agosto's wife. . . . If this were Patrício, no. But Agosto, that's a different matter! Because . . . Agosto Capela, '30, '31, even '32 he's still coming after you!" And later, when [Agosto] returned from Ngomane, he came to Ishmael Rigonanti's house. On that same day, when he had finished distributing the corn. . . . We saw the truck, pulling in. Everyone said, "Sheee! Here comes Capela's truck! Did someone already tell Capela, or what's going on?" . . . Agosto came in, he met the owner of the house, Ishmael Rigonanti. They greeted each other [in Shangaan], "Hey, ho, mulungu!" "Heh, welcome, Capela! Welcome, Capela!" Well! . . . "When I passed through Javanyani, I heard about this. In Ngomane too, I heard it. That that Dane ran after Rosalina, because of me. There was a boy, he said, 'Yes, I saw that girl, she was even crying, she went into Ishmael Rigonanti's house, crying. He took all the clothing that she had.'" . . . Well. [Agosto said,] "What I'm going to do—it's already been many years that I've wanted that girl, now she can't be with any other man. Not white, not black. Because everyone knows now that she's my wife. Her uncle abandoned her—he ran after her because of me. Not because of the others. I have been pleading since '30 until now, '32, going after that girl, because she's the one I want." And later, I said, "No. I'm going to my uncle's house [i.e., Patapata]." He said, "No. I know that if you go to Patapata's house, I'll never be able to be with you, and I love you. Don't you love me?" I said, "Mmm! Even though I love you, I'm preparing to marry, to find someone of my race to marry. It's not because I don't want you! What I'm worried about, the thing that bothers me, is that you could leave me!" And he said, "Look. I promised you that I wouldn't leave you. I want you to be my wife! It's already been four years that I've come after you, Rosalina! So many years! And do I have a wife at home? No! There you are. It's because long ago I promised that you would be my wife. Many Portuguese men here have black girls living with them, but not me. But you think that you, Rosalina, you can run to your uncle's house, and I'll see you with another man?! No, better I kill myself! Because he [Dane], he insulted me too! Saying that you're already my wife, when you're not my wife, not yet. No, it can't be. You are here, you're coming to my house." And Rigonanti, Ishmael, he said "Yes, for sure. Rosalina, there's no alternative, except for you to go with Agosto." . . . And so he took me there, to his house. And I was crying, Heidi. Because what I wanted was to marry in the *church*. Like I'd seen other girls marry, that way. I wanted that. But I had to go with him. And I was afraid, ah! . . . Because I knew he would want [to have sexual inter-course with me], and I had never been with a man before. And they say that it hurts, the first time! [HG: But how did you feel about him then? Did you love him?] Mmm, eee. I loved him. But I was afraid, I was afraid that he would leave me. But I loved him, I loved him. Much more than any of the others. . . . And so, I went to live with Agosto. Ah! Heidi. This story!

• • •

Rosalina and Agosto lived together for less than five years, until Agosto died suddenly of an asthma attack in 1937. After his death, Rosalina says, she vowed never to "marry" again and risk harnessing herself to a man who might not love her or treat her as well as Agosto. Here she was consciously following her mother's advice; yet like her mother, who was widowed early after a formal lovola marriage to a man who (according to Rosalina) "really, really loved her," Rosalina did periodically enter relationships with other men—although, in her case, all of these men were Portuguese, and she distinguishes them from Agosto in her memory by referring to them, always in Portuguese, as "lovers" (*amantes*, sing. *amante*). And while Rosalina recalls them in affectionate terms, she narrates the history of these relationships with little of the romantic nostalgia that suffuses her tale of Agosto's courtship. She "accepted" the others, she says, because they offered her housing, nice clothing, an urban network of "family" and friends, and the means to pursue economic activities of her choice: marketing, beer brewing, needlework, hospital midwifery, and farming on land Rosalina acquired through carefully wrought webs of real and fictive (often interracial) kinship.

Significantly, these interracial relationships also offered Rosalina a wider array of spiritual resources than she grew up with in her uncle Dane's household in Caniçado. Over the years she developed an eclectic repertoire of beliefs and divination methods combining Christianity, spirit mediumship, dream inter-pretation, and a Portuguese dice-throwing game called "Napoleon Bonaparte." This spiritual patchwork not only helped Rosalina to weave herself more tightly into a diverse range of affective communities, but multiplied the frameworks of explanation—and kinds of "luck"—she increasingly needed to make sense of her life choices, which have not been without personal cost. Rosalina's lack of socially recognized in-laws, for instance, and most especially her childless-ness,[58] means that she has had to struggle harder than most other women her age to maintain kinship-based support networks into the present, networks which today encompass Facazisse—where she moved in the early 1970s to look after her dying mother—as well as urban and peri-urban neighborhoods in Chokwe, Chibuto, and the capital city. Moreover, Rosalina's status as never for-mally "married," and her reputation as a woman who "wanted only white men," encourages some of her neighbors in Facazisse to refer to her as a "prostitute" or (worse) a "witch," most predictably when Rosalina's well-known diligence with her hoe pays off in abundant harvests. Yet Rosalina does not view herself in these terms, nor appear to regret any of the turns she took in the course of navigating her way through Mozambique's colonial society. On the contrary, she insists that she always did "what [her] heart wanted"—a formulation many women used in interviews when they wanted simultaneously to assert, deny, and justify their agency in shaping the content of their life, even under what historians have portrayed as the most brutal colonial circumstances. Even today, living alone and almost entirely dependent on farming for her survival, Rosalina declares that she has "never suffered"—that, indeed, she has been able to look after not only herself but her late mother and her late brother's family—because she has been blessed with a kind of "luck" that, in fact, she earned on her own. "I never liked to just sit," Rosalina explains, "without working to take care of myself, like my mother taught me. Ah, I know how to work. And because I work, my daughter, I have luck in my life."

More telling still, Rosalina's evocation of "heart" echoes the discursive construct the Swiss recorded the women of Khocene using to explain their interest in Christianity back in the 1890s. Its formulaic repetition in Rosalina's and other women's life stories, in southern Mozambique and elsewhere in Africa,[59] suggests a way for us to think about gendered agency and "strategic engagement" in the context of early encounters between African women and European colonizers. What Rosalina's heart wanted changed in the course of her lifetime, as she weighed what her mother, aunts, and grandmothers told her of family history and the "ways of long ago" (ntumbuluko ya khale), what she learned in mission schools and towns, and what she discovered through personal experience in colonial society against her own creative and dynamic understanding of what she herself needed to be happy. Yet there is also continuity in the history of Rosalina's heart's longings, whether we privilege her self-conscious narrative portrayal of that history or the patterns in narrated events of which she might not be consciously aware. "Heart," in other words, is as much an individual as a social construction, as much a deliberate assertion of self as an admission that there are influences, external to the self, that dictate how a person should live. In the same way that elderly women courted contact with the first missionaries and spirit mediums appropriated Christian trappings to enhance their doctoring powers, Rosalina's self-narrated patterns of engagement with the colonial order—illustrated in the turbulent romantic history presented above—reveal her preoccupation with, and deference to, gendered fields of moral authority that defined themselves neither in opposition to nor in collaboration with European "control." Albino Cartaxana's lewd advances, in Rosalina's memory, are not intimidating but "insulting," in the same way that elderly women's kurhuketela ceremonies "insult" threats to the harvest: because they flout conventions of sexual propriety and customary rules of courtship. Rosalina's acquiescence to Agosto is similarly told as a decision precipitated by the actions of her legal guardian, the paternal uncle responsible for negotiating her marriage in any case; but Dane, according to the story, is driven to his furious rejection of Rosalina by the traitorous revelations of his niece and the subversive intervention of Rosalina's mother—who risks her position in Dane's household in order to save her daughter from further emotional suffering and physical danger. Agosto, too, emerges through the narrative as worthy of Rosalina's love because he meets a set of recognizably local and feminine standards: he respects his own kinship obligations (e.g., following his sister and cousin to Mozambique); he performs services considered vital to the welfare of agrarian communities (e.g., returning migrant workers to their homes, delivering food to rural shops); he too follows his "heart" despite years of rejection and the wrath of Rosalina's uncle; and his final proposal is inspired in part by Dane's "insult" to his own masculine honor and code of romantic conduct.

Indeed, Rosalina's narrative demonstrates how women's memories enact what may be the most potent form of "strategic engagement" of all—the act of historical interpretation. Listening to the life stories of Rosalina and other women of her generation, whose inherited and experiential knowledge of the past straddles those ambiguous decades of early European presence, it is not difficult to imagine the Antioka missionaries' first "converts" returning home from worship or medical treatment with similar tales of "accepting" xilungu prescriptions for reasons that had little to do with Christianity or "civilized" notions of healing, and that construed acceptance not in terms of submission to European colonizers but as a positive, "heart"-led ethic of individual and collective survival under continuing forms of feminine authority and control.[60] Preserving and passing on such tales of "colonial encounters" enabled these women to add valungu to the already crowded field of social actors among and against whom they had to maneuver in order to go on living as, in their eyes, they had always done: tilling the land, tending families, and safeguarding the health of agrarian society.

NOTES

Earlier versions of this essay were presented at the 1997 annual meeting of the African Studies Association (Columbus, Ohio, 14 November 1997) and to the "Social History of African Women" seminar at the University of Minnesota in May 1998. My thanks to the participants at both sessions, and particularly to Jean Allman, Bill Bravman, John M. Collins, Susan Geiger, and Alda Saúte for their helpful comments and suggestions.

1. "Renamo" is the acronymic name of the Mozambique National Resistance, originally a South African–backed guerrilla army created to destabilize the Mozambican government after independence and today the largest opposition party in Mozambique's multiparty democracy. Recent studies of the Mozambican war include William Finnegan, *A Complicated War: The Harrowing of Mozambique* (Berkeley: University of California Press, 1992); and Alex Vines, *Renamo: Terrorism in Mozambique* (London: University of York, Centre for Southern African Studies, in association with James Currey, 1991). On Renamo's transformation from guerrilla army to political party, see Carrie Manning, "Constructing Opposition in Mozambique: Renamo as Political Party," *Journal of Southern African Studies* 24, no. 1 (1998): 161–90.

2. Frelimo (Front for the Liberation of Mozambique) was formed in 1962, initi-

ated an armed struggle against Portuguese colonialism in 1964, and took over the government of independent Mozambique in 1975. See Thomas Henrikson, *Revolution and Counter-revolution: Mozambique's War of Independence, 1964–1974* (Westport, Conn.: Greenwood, 1983); Allen Isaacman and Barbara Isaacman, *Mozambique: From Colonialism to Revolution, 1900–1982* (Boulder, Colo.: Westview, 1983); Eduardo Mondlane, *The Struggle for Mozambique* (London: Zed, 1983); and Barry Munslow, *Mozambique: The Revolution and Its Origins* (London: Longman, 1983).

3.　The present-day locality and former *regulado* (chieftaincy) of Facazisse was created by the Portuguese colonial administration in 1900, as part of an effort to strengthen their hold on this area—the site, in 1897, of the last anticolonial uprising in southern Mozambique. The Portuguese carved up the powerful chiefdom of Magudzu Khosa into nineteen small regulados (including Facazisse) and appointed one of Magudzu's male descendants to rule over each one. Because chiefly political power remained within the royal Khosa lineage, and because the Portuguese interfered relatively little in the internal workings of chiefly government in Facazisse, most local residents view (and explicitly refer to) this system and its authorities as part of the "traditional" order.

4.　Heidi Gengenbach, "Where Women Make History: Pots, Stories, Tattoos, and Other Gendered Accounts of Community and Change in Magude District, Mozambique, c. 1800 to the Present" (Ph.D. diss., University of Minnesota, 1998). I lived and conducted field research in Magude District for a total of thirteen months between May 1995 and December 1996. This research was made possible by funding from the Social Science Research Council, the Graduate School of the University of Minnesota, and the Norwegian Refugee Council.

5.　Key examples include Michael Crowder, ed., *West African Resistance: The Military Response to Colonial Occupation* (New York: Africana, 1971); Allen Isaacman and Barbara Isaacman, "Resistance and Collaboration in Southern and Central Africa," *International Journal of African Historical Studies* 10, no. 1 (1977): 33–65; T. O. Ranger, "The People in African Resistance," *Journal of Southern African Studies* 4, no. 1 (1977): 125–46, and *Revolt in Southern Rhodesia, 1896–1897* (London: Heinemann, 1976); A. Adu Boahen, ed., *Africa under Colonial Domination, 1880–1935*, volume 7 of the UNESCO *General History of Africa* (London: Heinemann, 1990), chapters 3–9.

6.　Frederick Cooper and Ann Stoler were among the first to argue that the resistance paradigm treats power reductively, neglects evidence of interaction among colonial actors, and falsely homogenizes "Europeans" and "Africans." See Frederick Cooper and Ann Stoler, "Tensions of Empire: Colonial Control and Visions of Rule," *American Ethnologist* 16, no. 4 (1989): 609–21. For a review of research trends and debates on this topic, see Frederick Cooper, "Conflict and Connection: Rethinking African Colonial History," *American Historical Review* 99, no. 5 (1994): 1516–45; and Sherry Ortner, "Resistance and the Problem of Ethnographic Refusal," *Comparative Studies in Society and History* 37, no. 1 (1995): 173–93.

7.　See, for example, Caroline Ifeka-Moller, "Female Militancy and Colonial Revolt: The Women's War of 1929, Eastern Nigeria," in *Perceiving Women*, ed. Shirley Ardener (London: Malaby, 1975), pp. 127–57; Cora Ann Presley,

Kikuyu Women, the Mau Mau Rebellion, and Social Change in Kenya (Boulder, Colo.: Westview, 1992); Susan Rogers, "Anti-colonial Protest in Africa: A Female Strategy," *Heresies* 9, no. 3 (1980): 222–25. For a broader gendered critique of the historiography of colonial Africa, see Nancy Rose Hunt, "Placing African Women's History and Locating Gender," *Social History* 14, no. 3 (1989): 359–79. Hunt's fascinating study of the medicalization of childbirth in the Congo similarly demonstrates (among many other things) how a gendered analysis disrupts the foundational paradigms of the field and renders even the more recent "colonial encounter" framework problematic. See Nancy Rose Hunt, *A Colonial Lexicon of Birth Ritual, Medicalization, and Mobility in the Congo* (Durham, N.C.: Duke University Press, 1999).

8. See Gerhard Liesegang, "Lourenço Marques antes de 1895: Aspectos da História dos Estados Vizinhos, da Interacção entre a Povoação e Aqueles Estados e do Comércio na Baia e na Povoação," *Arquivo* 2 (1987): 19–75; Pedro de Mesquita Pimental, "4a Circumscripção: Magude," in F. X. Ferrão de Castelo Branco, *Circumscripções de Lourenço Marques: Respostas aos Quesitos* (Lourenço Marques: Imprensa Nacional, 1909); António Rita-Ferreira, *Presença Luso-Asiática e Mutações Culturais no Sul de Moçambique (até c. 1900)* (Lisbon: Instituto de Investigacao Científica Tropical do Ultramar, 1982); Alan K. Smith, "The Peoples of Southern Mozambique: An Historical Survey," *Journal of African History* 14, no. 4 (1973): 565–80; Francisco Toscano, "Raças, Tribos, e Famílias Indígenas na Província do Sul do Save," *Boletim da Sociedade de Estudos da Colónia de Moçambique* 37 (1938): 201–13.

9. In the early 1820s, during the turbulent period of state-building, war, and migration in southeastern Africa that is known as the *mfecane,* the Ndwandwe (one of the northern Nguni chieftaincies at the eye of the political storm) dispersed into a number of breakaway war bands. One Ndwandwe group, under Nxaba Maseko, moved northward into Mozambique, recruiting soldiers from the local population and conquering smaller chieftaincies en route to Sofala. In the 1830s, another Ndwandwe leader, known as Soshangane, broke away to establish his own authority in southern Mozambique. The Gaza kingdom, as Soshangane's state came to be known, endured until the capture of its last ruler, Ngungunyana, by the Portuguese in 1895; at the height of its power, it included much of the land south of the Zambezi River. The Magude area occupies the southwestern fringe of the territory subjected to Gaza raids and tribute-taking in the nineteenth century. See Gerhard Liesegang, "Nguni Migrations between Delagoa Bay and the Zambezi, 1821–1839," *African Historical Studies* 3, no. 2 (1970): 317–37; Malyn Newitt, *A History of Mozambique* (Johannesburg: Witwatersrand University Press, 1994), chapter 11. On the mfecane itself, see Carolyn Hamilton, ed., *The Mfecane Aftermath: Reconstructive Debates in Southern African History* (Bloomington: Indiana University Press, 1996).

10. The first European known to have crossed this area was Louis Trigardt, who led a party of *trekboers* on an extension of the Afrikaner "Great Trek" from the Transvaal to the Portuguese coastal settlement at Lourenço Marques in 1837–38. Trigardt's travel diary is published in Claude Fuller, *Louis Trigardt's Trek across the Drakensberg, 1837–1838* (Cape Town: Van Riebeeck Society, 1932).

11. According to most oral and written sources from this period, Magudzu was

more "friend" and "ally" than "vassal" of the Gaza king Muzila. See A. Grandjean, "L'Invasion des Zoulou dans le Sud-Est Africain: Une Page d'Histoire
Inédite," *Bulletin de la Société Neuchateloise de Géographie* [hereafter *BSNG*]
11 (1899): 63–92; *Bulletin Missionaire* [hereafter *BM*] 4, no. 45 (1882): 42.
The *BM* published the correspondence of Swiss Presbyterian missionaries
stationed in Africa.

12. Later Europeans also commented on the warm hospitality offered to strangers
in Magudzu's domain. See, for example, A. Grandjean, "Voyage à Antioka,"
BM 7, no. 87 (1889): 338.

13. D. Fernandes das Neves, *A Hunting Expedition to the Transvaal*, trans. B. Mon-
teiro (Pretoria: State Library, 1987), pp. 33–34.

14. Ibid., pp. 41–42.

15. Frederick Elton, "Journal of an Exploration of the Limpopo River," *Journal of
the Royal Geographical Society* 42 (1872): 36.

16. For the early history of the Swiss Mission in Mozambique, see Jan van Butselaar, *Africains, Missionnaires, et Colonialistes: Les Origines de l'Eglise Presbyte-
rienne du Mozambique (Mission Suisse), 1880–1896* (Leiden: E. J. Brill, 1984).

17. *BM* 6, no. 64 (1886): 9–10.

18. *BM* 4, no. 47 (1882): 94; *BM* 4, no. 50 (1883): 217; *BM* 5, no. 58 (1885): 170;
BM 6, no. 64 (1886): 11; *BM* 6, no. 71 (1887): 213; *BM* 8, no. 88 (1890): 16;
BM 12, no. 146 (1898): 104. See also van Butselaar, *Africains, Missionnaires, et
Colonialistes*, pp. 37–40.

19. *BM* 6, no. 64 (1886): 11 (my emphasis). On Yosefa's young female converts,
see also *BM* 6, no. 64 (1886): 9; *BM* 8, no. 94 (1891): 205; *BM* 8, no. 100
(1891): 356; *BM* 7, no. 87 (1889): 87.

20. *BM* 4, no. 45 (1882): 41; *BM* 7, no. 81 (1888): 171; *BM* 7, no. 87 (1889): 343.

21. *BM* 7, no. 87 (1889): 342; *BM* 8, no. 92 (1890): 155, 157; Swiss Mission
Archive (hereafter SMA) 872F, A. Grandjean, "Rapport sur la Marche de la
Station d'Antioka pendant l'Année 1891," p. 3; SMA 472I, A. Eberhardt, "Rapport sur la Marche de la Station d'Antioka pendant l'Année 1897 (Statistique
de la Station)."

22. *BM* 7, no. 87 (1889): 342; *BM* 8, no. 92 (1890): 157.

23. *BM* 7, no. 87 (1889): 339; *BM* 7, no. 92 (1890): 152, 153, 156; *BM* 10, no. 122
(1895): 362; *BM* 11, no. 130 (1896): 130; SMA 82I, A. Grandjean, "Rapport
sur la Station d'Antioka pendant l'Année 1893," p. 5; SMA 82J, A. Grandjean,
"Rapport sur la Marche de la Station d'Antioka pendant l'Année 1894," pp. 5–
6; P. Jeanneret, "Les Ma-Khoça," *BSNG* 8 (1894–95): 138.

24. *BM* 7, no. 87 (1889): 342–44; *BM* 8, no. 88 (1890): 15–19; *BM* 8, no. 92
(1890): 154–56. See also Paul Berthoud, *Les Negres Gouamba ou Les Vingt
Premières Années de la Mission Romande* (Lausanne: Georges Bridel, 1896),
pp. 157–58.

25. On rainmaking, see *BM* 11, no. 121 (1895): 333. On women's ambivalence
toward Swiss medical interventions, see *BM* 8, no. 92 (1890): 159; *BM* 11,
no. 104 (1891): 361; Grandjean, "Rapport . . . 1891"; SMA 82F, Dr. G.
Liengme, "Rapport d'Antioka, 1892"; SMA 472N, A. Eberhardt, "Rapport
sur la Station d'Antioka pour 1898."

26. Grandjean, "Rapport . . . 1891."

27. *BM* 11, no. 130 (1896): 189–90; Grandjean, "Rapport . . . 1893"; Grandjean,
"Rapport . . . 1894." See also A. Grandjean's letters to P. Leresche, Secrétaire de

la mission Romande à Lausanne, 21 August and 23 October 1893. In the 1895 report, a missionary lamented that Antioka was a "church of eight members, of whom two are crippled and three are invalids" (SMA 1254D, N. Jaques, "Rapport de la Station d'Antioka pendant l'Année 1895").

28. *BM* 11, no. 126 (1895): 57–58; Jaques, "Rapport . . . 1895."

29. *BM* 8, no. 92 (1890): 159; SMA 1148A(2), Dr. A. Sechehaye, "Rapport sur l'Oeuvre Missionnaire à Antioka en 1904."

30. SMA 1148A(3), Dr. A. Sechehaye, "Rapport sur l'Oeuvre Missionnaire à Antioka en 1905." For a discussion of similar evangelizing strategies elsewhere in colonial Africa, see Megan Vaughan, *Curing Their Ills: Colonial Power and African Illness* (Stanford, Calif.: Stanford University Press, 1991).

31. Patrick Harries, *Work, Culture, and Identity: Migrant Laborers in Mozambique and South Africa, c. 1860–1910* (Portsmouth, N.H.: Heinemann, 1994), pp. 145ff.

32. SMA 479F, A. Eberhardt, "Rapport sur la Station d'Antioka pour 1900"; SMA 480B, A. Eberhardt, "Rapport sur la Station d'Antioka pour 1901"; SMA 480K, A. Eberhardt, "Rapport au Conseil de la Mission Romande sur la Station d'Antioka pour l'Année 1902"; SMA 1212A, Dr. A. Sechehaye, "Rapport sur l'Oeuvre Missionnaire á Antioka pendant l'Année 1903"; Sechehaye, "Rapport . . . 1904"; Sechehaye, "Rapport . . . 1905"; SMA 1212A, H. Guye, "Rapport sur la Marche de la Station d'Antioka pendant l'Année 1906"; SMA 106A, H. Guye, "Rapport sur la Marche de la Station d'Antioka du 1 Janvier au 31 Octobre 1907,"; SMA 1208B(4), H. Guye, "Rapport sur la Marche de la Station d'Antioka pendant l'Année 1907–1908"; SMA 106B, H. Guye, "Rapport sur la Marche de la Station d'Antioka, 1908–1909"; SMA 106C, F. Paillard, "Rapport sur la Station d'Antioka durant l'Année 1910."

33. *BM* 8, no. 92 (1890): 156; Guye, "Rapport . . . 1906"; Guye, "Rapport . . . 1907–1908."

34. *BM* 8, no. 92 (1890): 159. As early as 1886, Henri Berthoud wrote of Khocene that "the priests and prophets . . . are our natural enemies, and their number is legion." *BM* 6, no. 64 (1886): 7.

35. In Shangaan, a postmenopausal woman may be referred to as "grandmother" (*kokwana*), "old woman" (*xikoxana*), or *nsungukati*. However, the latter term is reserved for the very eldest women in a community, whose age and accumulated experience give them "wisdom" (*vutlhari*) and unsurpassed knowledge of the "laws" (*milawu*) and customs of "long ago."

36. The origins of "Tsonga" ethnicity in southern Mozambique and South Africa are the subject of much academic debate (see, for example, Patrick Harries, "The Roots of Ethnicity: Discourse and the Politics of Language Construction in South-East Africa," *African Affairs* 346 [1988]: 25–52). In Mozambique, "Tsonga" is considered an umbrella category for three ethnolinguistic subgroups—Shangaan, Ronga, and Tswa. Shangaan is the largest (numerically and geographically) of the three, and the term is often interchanged with Tsonga to refer to the indigenous peoples who occupy most of Maputo and Gaza provinces in southern Mozambique. The label "Shangaan" itself derives from the name of the Gaza Nguni king Soshangane.

37. See Heidi Gengenbach, "'I'll Bury You in the Border!': Women's Land Struggles in Postwar Facazisse (Magude District), Mozambique," *Journal of Southern African Studies* 24, no. 1 (1998): 9–36; H. A. Junod, *The Life of a South*

African Tribe, 2nd ed. (London: University Books, 1962), vol. 1, pp. 36ff, 199ff; J. Stevenson-Hamilton, *The Low-Veld: Its Wild Life and Its People*, 2nd ed. (London: Cassell, 1934), pp. 220ff.

38.   H. A. Junod, "Deux Cas de Possession chez les Ba-Ronga," *BSNG* 20 (1909–10): 387–402; G. Liengme, "Quelques Observations sur les Maladies des Indigènes des Provinces de Lourenço Marques," *BSNG* 7 (1894–95): 180–91; Stevenson-Hamilton, *The Low-Veld*, p. 229; Júlio Afonso da Silva Tavares, "A Arte de Curar entre os Indígenas das Terras de Magude: Relátorio do Facultativo do 2a Classe—28 de Agosto de 1909," *Moçambique—Documentário Trimestral* 14, no. 53 (1948): 111–32.

39.   *BM* 11, no. 132 (1897): 242. The first recorded occasion of a struggle of this kind is noted in Liengme, "Rapport . . . 1892."

40.   *BM* 12, no. 164 (1899): 539–40 (my emphasis on "saviour").

41.   Grandjean recognized early on that, to be persuasive, the missionaries had to "seek to enter into the material preoccupations of these poor ignorant people, in order to win their attention" (*BM* 8, no. 94 [1891]: 205). On the relationship between church attendance or conversion and drought (along with other crises, such as illness, war, and, in at least one case, donkeys devouring a woman's crops), see *BM* 11, no. 126 (1895): 57–58; SMA 472G, N. Jaques, "Rapport de la Station d'Antioka pendant l'Année 1896"; Eberhardt, "Rapport . . . 1897"; Eberhardt, "Rapport . . . 1898"; SMA 479B, A. Eberhardt, "Rapport sur la Station d'Antioka pour 1899"; Sechehaye, "Rapport . . . 1904"; Sechehaye, "Rapport . . . 1905"; SMA 106E, F. Paillard, "Rapport sur la Station d'Antioka en 1911–1912"; SMA 106F, F. Paillard, "Rapport sur la Station d'Antioka, 1913."

42.   *BM* 4, no. 50 (1883): 218.

43.   See, for example, the correspondence between officials in Cossine/Magude Circumscription and the governor of Lourenço Marques districts, from 1891 to 1900, in Fundo do Século 19, Governo do Distrito de Lourenço Marques (GDLM), Arquivo Histórico de Moçambique, (AHM), Caixas 105 and 106; and between officials at the Uanetzi Military Post and the governor of Gaza Military District, from 1898 to 1900, in Fundo do Século 19, Governo do Distrito Militar de Gaza, AHM, Cota 8-4, M1. See also Manuel José da Costa Couto, "Governo de Lourenço Marques: Secção Militar," *Boletim Oficial do Governo Geral da Província de Moçambique* 43 (1895): 409–10; Secção Especial, AHM, Direcção dos Serviços de Administração Civil, Processo No. 342, "Tentativa de Rebelião dos Indígenas no Distrito Militar de Gaza," 1904; Alfredo Freire d'Andrade, *Relatórios sobre Moçambique*, vol. 1 (Lourenço Marques, 1907), pp. 258 ff; de Mesquita Pimental, "4a Circumscripção."

44.   On Xongela's mother, see GDLM, Caixa 105, doc. 2, 25 May 1892; on the jailbreak, see GDLM, Caixa 105, doc. 116, 23 September 1896.

45.   I tape-recorded over two hundred interviews with eighty-one women from various parts of Magude District. Although my fluency in Shangaan improved during the course of field research, I continued to conduct interviews with the assistance of interpreters—two local women, Ruti Nkuna and Aida Dzamba—whom I hired to translate between Shangaan and Portuguese. Interview tapes are in my possession; copies of key interviews will be deposited at the Arquivo Histórico de Moçambique in Maputo.

46. The earliest written reference to "Banyans" in the Magude area is in *BM* 6, no. 64 (1886): 6.

47. First articulated in the 1950s by the Brazilian sociologist Gilberto Freyre, and developed in a series of studies published by the Portuguese government, the theory of *lusotropicalismo* ("lusotropicology") asserts that Portuguese colonial expansion in the tropics from the fifteenth century onward resulted in the creation of a new, racially integrated civilization, in which European and non-European peoples were harmoniously fused in large part through the biological "interpenetration of cultures"—that is, through intermarriage, miscegenation, and the emergence of a mixed-race population in colonized territories. See, for example, Freyre's *Portuguese Integration in the Tropics* (Lisbon: Realização Gráfica da Tipografia Silvas, 1961). Freyre's thesis sparked much debate among Portuguese, Brazilian, and African scholars in the 1950s and 1960s, and was denounced as a myth particularly because of its characterization of Portuguese "assimilation" policies in Africa as benevolent rather than racially segregationist and exclusionary in intent.

48. On native women in the North American fur trade, see Sylvia van Kirk, *Many Tender Ties: Women in Fur-Trade Society, 1670–1870* (Norman: University of Oklahoma Press, 1980). For a Latin American example, see Verena Martinez-Alier, *Marriage, Class, and Colour in Nineteenth-Century Cuba* (Ann Arbor: University of Michigan Press, 1987). Ann L. Stoler's work on this topic has been especially provocative; see, for instance, her "Sexual Affronts and Racial Frontiers: European Identities and the Cultural Politics of Exclusion in Southeast Asia," *Comparative Studies in Society and History* 34, no. 3 (1992): 514–51. For a rare example from Africa, see George E. Brooks, Jr., "The *Signares* of Saint-Louis and Gorée: Women Entrepreneurs in Eighteenth-Century Senegal," in *Women in Africa: Studies in Social and Economic Change*, ed. Nancy J. Hafkin and Edna G. Bay (Stanford, Calif.: Stanford University Press, 1976), pp. 19–44.

49. I began my fieldwork expecting that I would interview a small group of elderly women and from those interviews produce a "life history" for each. However, I quickly ran into a number of problems. It is not possible to translate the term "life history" into Shangaan; moreover, my ideas about what a "life history" should consist of were quite different from the ways women talked about their pasts. For instance, rather than producing seamless, linear accounts of the unfolding of their lives, women told anecdotal, episodic stories about their experiences. These stories ranged widely across time and space; relied on common themes, language, images, and plots which often echoed features of women's "fictional" narratives (*minkaringana*, sing. *nkaringana*); and rarely isolated the speaker as the central actor in remembered events. Moreover, through telling life stories women expressed subjectivities and identities that were not only insistently multiple (a quality reflected in each woman's possession of several personal names) but inextricably intertwined with those of other women. By labeling women's recollections "life stories" rather than "life history" I am deliberately emphasizing this ontological plurality, rather than trying to write it away.

50. I lived for a total of thirteen months as Rosalina's neighbor, student, and ultimately "daughter." I tape-recorded twelve formal interviews with her (total-

ing over forty hours), and spent innumerable hours in informal conversation and listening to Rosalina tell impromptu stories about her life. The following discussion draws on both taped interviews and my field notes. The interview tapes and transcripts are in my possession; copies will be deposited at the Arquivo Histórico de Moçambique in Maputo.

51. Here Rosalina was speaking Portuguese and used the word *sorte*, which can mean good luck, fate, destiny, fortune, chance (but not bad luck). At other times she used *dyombo*, a Shangaan word that seems principally to mean good fortune, rather than fate or destiny (which imply that the speaker is a passive victim of something she would rather not have happen to her). "Fate" in Shangaan is expressed either as *makumu* (end, conclusion) or *khombo*, although the latter is more commonly used to refer to misfortune (e.g., a death in the family).

52. Although Rosalina told the bulk of this story in Portuguese, at critical points such as this one she reverted to Shangaan. The kind of "insult" she is referring to has a very rich (and gendered) cultural meaning. Elderly women, for instance, perform an elaborate ceremony known as *kurhuketela* whenever crops are suffering from drought or a pest of some kind. This "insulting" involves dancing naked through the fields, hurling obscenities at any men whose paths the women cross, and mockingly pantomiming sexual intercourse. It is a demonstration of the powerful relationship between women's sexuality and fertility and the "health" of the land—and to be the target of such "insults" is considered very dangerous to one's health.

53. Like all older women in the area, Rosalina had several personal names, some given to her by various female relatives when she was born and others given to or chosen by her later in life. "Buxeni" is one of Rosalina's birth names, given to her by one of her father's sisters. See Heidi Gengenbach, "Naming the Past in a 'Scattered' Land: Memory and the Powers of Women's Naming Practices in Southern Mozambique," *International Journal of African Historical Studies*, forthcoming.

54. In Shangaan, a man's sister's child is his *ntukulu*, a term normally translated into English as "grandchild."

55. As often happened in interviews with women, Rosalina interrupted this narrative of her own life to tell a "life story" about one of the characters in her account. This story explained how Eduardo, who had two African "wives" in Chibuto, had to marry his Portuguese cousin—Agosto's sister Sofia—because she was pregnant with his child. Sofia then accompanied Eduardo back to Mozambique.

56. *Bava*, referring to Rosalina's uncle Dane.

57. Racelina is the name Rosalina received when she was baptized, in 1927. Agosto renamed her Rosalina.

58. Rosalina became pregnant three times during her years with Agosto, but she lost all three babies through either miscarriage or stillbirth.

59. Although the discursive power of "heart" to direct and justify women's life choices is evident in women's personal narratives from other parts of Africa, there has been no attempt to theorize the meaning of "heart" as trope in feminine historical memory or experience. See, for example, Marjorie Shostak, *Nisa: The Story of a !Kung Woman* (New York: Vintage, 1981); and

Jean Davison with the women of Mutira, *Voices from Mutira: Lives of Rural Gikuyu Women* (Boulder, Colo.: Lynne Rienner, 1989).

60. Recent scholarship on African women and European missionary endeavors paints a similar picture of women's selective, constructive engagement with colonial Christianity and its medical and educational offerings. See, for example, Jean M. Allman, "Making Mothers: Missionaries, Medical Officers, and Women's Work in Colonial Asante, 1924–1945," *History Workshop* 38 (1994): 23–47; and Hunt, *Colonial Lexicon.*

2 Dynastic Daughters: Three Royal Kwena Women and E. L. Price of the London Missionary Society, 1853–1881

Wendy Urban-Mead

In August of 1866, at Molepolole, the capital of an African kingdom in what today is known as Botswana, a Tswana woman named Bantsang asked the wife of the local missionary, Elizabeth "Bessie" Price, to teach her English. When Bessie declined, saying that her domestic duties were too overwhelming to permit time for English instruction, Bantsang persisted:

> why cannot you find time to teach & to apply yourself to me?—what have you to do?—you have a cook—a sewer—a washer—a nurse for [your infant son]—you don't pick (cultivate) your ground nor sew [your] corn—nor harvest it—nor build your house nor smear it as we do—What do you do? . . . Well, even tho' you thus refuse to teach me, I shall never cease worrying you to do so![1]

In this passage we hear Bantsang's voice as mediated by Bessie Price, whose written words constitute evidence of a personal relationship between them.

This chapter explores how individual African women responded to the teachings of Christian missionaries. The African women in question are three daughters of the Tswana chief Sechele: Ope, Kuanteng, and Bantsang. Since our knowledge of Sechele's daughters is mediated by the writings of Bessie Price, the daughter and wife of missionaries, she figures centrally as well. The chapter considers how the Christian identity of all four women shaped their life choices and informed their interactions with others in their families, particularly their fathers and husbands.

All four had as a common link and determining condition their status as daughters of regionally prominent Christian men. Bessie Price's father was Robert Moffat, an agent of the London Missionary Society (LMS) and head of Kuruman Mission from 1825 to 1870. Under Moffat's leadership, Kuruman Mission became an important center of Christianizing efforts throughout the area. For his part, Sechele was the Christian king of an independent African kingdom. As chief of the Kwena branch of the Tswana people from 1831 to

1892, Sechele enjoyed wide-ranging contacts with the other Tswana chiefdoms, the Cape Colony, the Boer Republics,[2] and other independent African polities.

Bantsang's interest in learning the English language, and her forthright manner in challenging Bessie Price's refusal to teach her, represent one of a variety of attitudes that women in nineteenth-century southern Africa could bring to the process of Christian conversion. Bantsang's sisters, Ope and Kuanteng, made very different choices in their approach to the multilayered package of faith, literacy, and cultural practices offered by agents of the LMS. The choices they made included a vigorous pursuit of book-learning, all-out rejection of the entire package, and a struggle to maintain Christian piety while living with a non-Christian spouse.

Bessie Price's responses were also complex, combining a continued commitment to her parents' vision of Christianizing the Tswana people with a deeper understanding of, and appreciation for, Tswana culture than her parents had. Thus Bessie Price cannot fairly be essentialized as representing the British-imperial, female, Christian point of view[3] any more than Bantsang, Ope, or Kuanteng can be said to represent the "essential" African woman.

In examining the stories of these four women, we must consider important questions of historiography and methodology. Africanist scholars have shown increasing interest in reassessing the encounter between Africans and European missionaries in the years before and during colonial rule.[4] Historians have long since given up writing heroic mission histories about European men such as David Livingstone, who entered the "Dark Continent" for the sake of sharing with its natives the "benefits" of commerce and Christianity. In recent decades, scholars have frequently depicted the missionary project as a largely one-sided affair, with European missionaries as cultural imperialists imposing an alien and even destructive system of thought and practice as part of a collective effort to "subdue Africans to European domination."[5] In such a depiction, those Africans who took on mission Christian teachings must be seen as little more than unwitting victims of colonialism.[6]

Among the significant contributors to this ongoing discussion are Jean and John Comaroff and Paul Landau.[7] Their studies focus on the history of Christianity among the Batswana[8] and directly engage the question of African agency in the making of Christian mission history in Africa. As cultural anthropologists with a strong interest in history, the Comaroffs use an approach to the past which emphasizes continuities over time.[9] While the Comaroffs have viewed "agency" as always compromised by forces such as colonialism and modernity, Landau, who is a historian, insists that the Batswana "have to be recognized as generating their own conflicts, and so their own history."[10] Landau's *Realm of the Word* highlights how the Ngwato leader, Khama, successfully appropriated LMS Christianity to enhance his own authority.

Among the many aspects of Tswana Christianity not yet addressed by historians, however, are women's responses to conversion in the earliest years of Tswana-missionary contact.[11] Bessie Price's letters to her sister and children—letters Price referred to as her "journals"[12]—offer an unparalleled opportunity to explore African women's engagements with Christianity in this early period.[13] Since Price wrote to her family members almost daily, the letters indeed have a journal-like, up-to-the-minute quality and allow us to explore how the mission's Christian message resonated both in her own life and in the lives of Sechele's daughters.

Of course, relying on Bessie Price's journals raises the contested issue of representation. There is an inherent problem when the only words in the documentary record are those of Bessie Price, or Bessie Price's versions of the words spoken by Bantsang or Ope.[14] However, legitimate concerns about representation should not lead us to assume that Bessie Price's position during her years at Sechele's capital was unambiguously powerful. Granted, she had more power than those she wrote about, in the sense that it was her pen that recorded her interactions with Sechele's daughters, and in the sense that she was British, belonging to the group that was the colonial authority at the Cape Colony. But it is also true that Sechele ruled an independent African kingdom, where the African elites (i.e., members of the Kwena royal family) were free to take or reject aspects of the Christian message. We shall see, however, that friendship with the Prices could be advantageous, given their influence with Sechele. Sources such as Bessie Price's letters are invaluable for what they can reveal about the lives of African women from a time beyond the reach of the present. By paying attention to the context of the journals, and situating the writings in time and place,[15] I hope to demonstrate that limitations on the claims that can be made regarding the lives of Sechele's daughters need not prevent us from making fruitful use of the material.

The Kwena kingdom under Sechele has been largely ignored in recent scholarship.[16] Yet during the years focused on in this chapter, 1854–83, the Kwena were the dominant Tswana group. During the height of his power, Sechele was a major player in regional politics, having a close relationship with Robert Moffat and the LMS, diplomatic and military interactions with both the Cape Colony to the south and the Boer Republics to the east, and wide-ranging influence and contacts with the Tswana chiefdoms, as well as other African polities from Mzilikazi's Ndebele kingdom on the Zimbabwe plateau to Moshoeshoe's Sotho kingdom in the southeast.[17]

Bessie Price's father, Robert Moffat, was well positioned in the Tswana-speaking region at roughly the same time as Sechele. Respected by African leaders and Boers alike, Moffat was sought after as an intermediary and adviser by many, including Sechele. The LMS mission station he presided over, Kuruman, was an oasis of foliage, fruit trees, and irrigated crop cultivation in an otherwise quite arid region.[18] The last outpost of European "civilization" for traders heading north as well as an important center for the education and evangelization of Tswana-speaking people, Kuruman became the parent station of a series of smaller LMS establishments to the north and east. Moffat was also the founder of something of a "missionary dynasty": three of his daughters married missionaries and one of his sons became a missionary, all based in southern Africa.[19]

As the daughter of Robert and Mary Moffat, Bessie was raised to embrace certain views of the Africans among whom her parents worked and of herself as the future wife of a missionary, for this was the role envisioned for her by her parents. Mary and Robert's opinions as to how to conduct themselves in their work among Africans were negatively influenced by the (in their view) reprehensible example set by an earlier LMS missionary in the Cape Colony, Johannes van der Kemp. Van der Kemp had married an indigenous woman and adopted local dress and eating patterns.[20] The Moffats felt it was crucial that a European missionary have a European wife, and that their home serve as an example of how to live according to "civilized" (European) Christian domestic values.

Bessie was raised on the mission station, spent six years being educated in England, and returned home to teach in the Kuruman mission school in 1854, when she was fifteen. Her sister Jane (Jeanie) similarly was schooled in England and began to teach four years after Bessie. The girls backed each other up in their conflicts with their mother, chafing against the isolation of life at the mission station and the sometimes unruly students—Sechele's children among them—in their charge.[21] Bessie married Roger Price, an LMS agent, in 1861, and since he was the missionary to Sechele from the 1860s to the 1880s, her contact with Sechele and his children continued over the next several decades.

Bessie's ideas of how to conduct herself as the wife of a missionary were largely informed by her mother's example. Mary Moffat had originally imagined missionary life as a partnership, in which she would accompany her husband on his visits to scattered African villages. Indeed, she saw herself as not only providing domestic comforts but also sharing in the preaching and teaching. She also dreamt of running a school for African girls.[22] As much as Robert, then, Mary felt called to Africa for the sake of the gospel. However, before the 1880s, "missionary" denoted a *male* evangelist,[23] and technically only Robert was the LMS agent. And in any case, within a year of her 1819 arrival in southern Africa, Mary found that maintaining "a civilized standard of living" on the frontier while bearing and rearing children demanded a reassessment of her dreams.[24] Her role, she determined, was to be Robert's "help-meet"; her ministry, to provide a "civilized" home where Robert could be restored and renewed, both spiritually and physically. In this capacity, Mary would share his trials and pray with him, and raise their children with the aim and the hope that they might follow in their parents' work.

Like her mother, Bessie regarded her husband's teaching and preaching as the "real" work of the mission, and her own work as supportive of his. Nonetheless, she never quite reconciled herself to remaining perpetually in the domestic sphere. After bearing twelve children (of a total of fourteen) and serving for twenty years solely as Roger's "help-meet," she acquired the help of a governess. With the governess there to look after her youngest children, Bessie resumed some of the teaching work which she had come to enjoy despite her earlier restlessness as a young woman at Kuruman.[25]

Bessie's assessment of Tswana people changed over time, as she came to see them in a more favorable light than her parents ever did. Not long after her mother's death in 1871, Bessie and Roger and their children took a four-year furlough to England. They returned to Sechele's capital at Molepolole in 1879, where Bessie immediately found that the people there were more to her liking, less materialistic and rushed than those she had met in England. From this time on she referred to herself as an African, and she came to disdain what she regarded as excessive attention to the niceties and superfluities of civilization. For example, she reveled in the freedom not to style her hair, boasting in a letter to her older children at school in England that she and the younger children had cut their hair short and were free to dunk their heads in a barrel of water to cool off during the hot season.[26] Such a practice would have met with severe disapproval from the more rigidly conventional Mary Moffat.

Ope, Kuanteng, and Bantsang

Embracing a Christian identity entailed acceptance not only of the specific beliefs which were professed prior to baptism—such as the divinity of Christ and the rejection of polygynous in favor of monogamous marriages—but also the adoption of certain elements of European civilization, such as wearing European-style clothing. Literacy was also a primary marker of those who were associated with the new religion.[27] For Africans in Sechele's kingdom, as well as for the European missionaries and their wives, the idea of becoming Christian without also, to some extent, "Europeanizing" was inconceivable. Sechele's home reflected this: it boasted a wide range of European furnishings, and meals offered to guests included tea and cakes served at a table spread with a linen cloth. The Christian members of Sechele's royal family were the first to wear European clothing.

In 1853, Sechele brought his wife, Ma-Sebele,[28] and several of his children to Kuruman for schooling, as Robert Moffat had agreed.[29] Among the children were Sechele's elder daughters, born of the wives whom he "put away" upon being baptized.[30] The eldest was Ope, a second daughter of Kereboletswe; the next was Kuanteng, the daughter of a lesser wife or concubine. The younger children included Sechele's son and heir Sebele (about age ten) and daughter Bantsang. Sebele and Bantsang returned to Kuruman for further education in 1857. All of the females, including Ma-Sebele, learned domestic skills such as dressmaking, sewing, and cooking. The primary texts used in the Kuruman mission school, and at LMS stations throughout the Setswana-speaking region during the mid- to late nineteenth century, were the Setswana grammars, Bible, hymn books, and catechism translated and written by Robert Moffat. English was not the language of instruction.

Ope makes herself known to us in Bessie's letters as the dignified royal daughter who as a girl kept herself aloof from Mary Moffat's instruction, but as an adult sought Bessie's support in her attempt to practice Christian piety in the home she shared with a non-Christian husband. Ope was born no later than 1835, probably earlier;[31] her mother, Kebalepile, was Sechele's cousin. By marrying her cousin (son of her father's brother), Kebalepile became Sechele's wife of honor, since cousin marriage was a preferred Tswana custom.[32] "Marry me, cousin, and retain the *bogadi* [bridewealth] cattle in the family fold."[33] As the oldest child of the chief's (former) wife of honor, Ope was considered the leader of her siblings. This perhaps explains why the Moffats characterized her behavior at Kuruman as haughty. In Bessie's view, Ope was "a very handsome girl, quite queenly in appearance and manners . . . clever & courteous . . . , but always with a certain degree of hauteur, rather resenting rebuke or correction of any kind."[34]

An incident that occurred after Ope's return from Kuruman in 1854 indicates that she was not afraid to defy her father. This episode was not recorded by Bessie, since at that time she was still in England; rather, it appears in her father's journals, which provide a crucial supplement to our knowledge of Ope's character at this time.[35] Robert Moffat visited the Kwena capital in both June and November of 1854.[36] During his June visit, he sought to influence Sechele's decisions about Ope's participation in Kwena initiation rites and her marriage.

At this time, Ope and her sisters were rebelling against Sechele, who had ordered them not to participate in the *bojale*, or girls' initiation rites. Bojale entailed a month-long period of seclusion and instruction for an age-set of girls who had reached puberty. Older women taught the girls the importance of wifely submission and gave explicit information about how to be sexually pleasing to their husbands. Both boys' and girls' initiations included a requirement to bear excruciating pain stoically.[37] For both sexes, completion of initiation brought adult status; in Tswana society only initiated adults were permitted to marry.

Ope led her sisters in their insistence that they join the bojale despite Sechele's explicit command that they not participate.[38] Their defiance suggests that they did not want to isolate themselves from the rest of Kwena womanhood by failing to participate in ceremonies which would bind their generation into a common age-grade association which, as royal daughters, they could expect to lead.[39]

Ope had been betrothed to her father's brother, Khosilintsi, since before 1848. Moffat, however, strongly disapproved of this "unnatural and unscriptural" betrothal of Ope to her uncle.[40] In the end, Sechele acceded to Moffat's arguments, and Khosilintsi, out of loyalty to his brother, agreed to let Ope be married to someone else. We know that by the 1880s Sechele's zeal for many of the missionary-imposed prohibitions of customs such as polygyny, rainmaking, and initiation rites had waned. However, in the 1840s and 1850s Sechele had divorced all of his wives but one, was attempting to do without rainmaking, and tried to keep his own children out of initiation ceremonies.[41]

While Ope's "queenly" demeanor as a girl at Kuruman and insistence on participating in bojale indicate a resistance to the Christianizing project, three decades later she sought Bessie Price's support in her struggles against her "heathen" husband, who objected to her desire to pray aloud at home and attend church services. What had happened in the intervening years to bring about such a change? Although the record is incomplete and we cannot know for certain, we have enough details about her life to make conjecture possible.

After Moffat succeeded in blocking Ope's betrothal to Khosilintsi in 1854, she was married to Sefunelo, the Christian son of the chief of the Rolong,[42] a Tswana polity to the east in the Boer Transvaal republic. She was married to him with the promise that she would be his only wife. When Sefunelo died not long afterward, Ope returned with her small son to Sechele,[43] whereupon Khosilintsi renewed his request to marry her. This time Sechele agreed to their union, and because of her high status Ope became Khosilintsi's chief wife, though she was not his first. According to Bessie, Ope was as "beloved of [Khosilintsi] as Rachel of old by Jacob."[44] Ope never bore another child, and her son by the Rolong prince died after he had reached maturity and returned to his father's people. This would have been a significant source of grief for Ope, since a woman's honor grew with her capacity to bear children.[45]

In 1880, when she was at least forty-five years old and certainly five years older than Bessie, Ope sought out Bessie's company.[46] Bessie wrote,

> Well—Ope has just been to see me, poor thing, & has been telling me about this [the death of her son] & other troubles. . . . She undergoes a sort of persecution fr. her doating husband for her efforts after the truth. He watches her closely, and forbids her any freedom in religious matters beyond going to church and reading her Bible, w. he would fain also forbid if he did not feel it would be going too far—as the Bakwena go [to] church and read the Bible & hymn book printed in their language as a matter of course, whether they are Christians or no.[47]

Thus the proud girl who resisted correction by Mary Moffat and rebelled (we presume successfully) against her father's ruling that she not participate in bojale had become the devoutly Christian wife of Khosilintsi.

Khosilintsi himself had led a powerful faction within the Kwena polity that opposed Sechele's moves toward Christianity. Sechele had ceded the job of supervising initiation rites to Khosilintsi, which gave the king's brother a significant amount of power among the Bakwena.[48] Although he had learned to read along with Sechele when Livingstone was their missionary, he mistrusted all Europeans and particularly hated the Boers. Like Sechele, he had valued the link with Livingstone because of the access to firearms that it provided.[49] He claimed to respect the person and teachings of Jesus, but found Jesus' adherents among the Europeans a very sorry representation of Christian teaching, and therefore had no use for the religion.

In the 1860s, when Bessie and Roger Price first arrived at Sechele's capital of Molepolole, Khosilintsi and Ope brought their children to the Prices with an official request that they be schooled by Roger. Yet Khosilintsi and his followers also reminded Sechele of his duties as rainmaker and pressured him to fulfill them. By the 1880s, Khosilintsi's opposition to Christianity and all things European had hardened into hostility,[50] even while he remained loyal to Sechele throughout their lives.

Ope's distress over Khosilintsi's attempts to limit her Christian practice should not necessarily be interpreted along the lines Bessie presented. Bessie described Ope as undergoing some "sort of persecution," calling her "poor thing." However, Ope's position as Sechele's daughter enabled her to differ, to a certain degree, from Khosilintsi on matters of religion.

In the early 1880s, Ope also used her status as one of the most "civilized" women of the ruling family—and friend of the missionaries—to undermine her father's marriage to a young woman, Kholoma, from Mzilikazi's Ndebele kingdom (in what is today Zimbabwe), after the death of Ma-Sebele. Kholoma arrived wearing skins rather than European-style clothes, did not know the table manners practiced in Kwena Christian homes, and was not a Christian. According to Bessie Price, Ope led the Kwena women in ridiculing and harassing Kholoma:

> Today we had a visit from Khosilintsi and his wife. . . . She came quite with the object of seeing if your Father [Roger Price] could not use his influence to make Sechele put away this raw Matebele woman with whom they are all more or less disgusted.[51]

Also according to Bessie Price, Kholoma suffered from scorn at the hands of the Kwena royal women, and when she finally died shortly after her arrival amongst the Kwena, these same women were relieved.[52]

We can never know what Ope's motivations were for these actions. What we can see, however, is that Ope used Christian teachings very differently at various points of her life. In each case she was clearly unafraid to pursue actions which led her into conflict with powerful male relatives. As a very young woman, Ope set herself in opposition to LMS Christian teachings regarding initiation rites. Early in her life the male authority Ope resisted was her father's, while thirty years later she defied, not Christian and "civilizing" practices, but her husband's refusal to allow her to pray and attend church. She also used her good standing with Bessie Price and her husband in invoking Christian teaching against marrying "heathens" to justify opposing her father's marriage to Kholoma.

In a path nearly the opposite of Ope's, Kuanteng proved herself Mary Moffat's most receptive pupil while she was at Kuruman; yet, as an adult, Kuanteng resoundingly rejected the LMS message. Kuanteng, the lower-status daughter of one of Sechele's concubines, had been Ope's "maid of honor."[53] While at Kuruman, Kuanteng's "gentle manners" and receptivity to teaching had won her special affection from Mary Moffat. Bessie wrote that her mother remembered Kuanteng as "comely & of a perfectly sweet & humble disposition, wh. made her a great favorite of my Mother's especially as she was, thro' her humility, a delightful pupil who progressed well."[54] Yet as a mature woman Kuanteng rejected all contact with Europeans, and with the Moffat family in particular. She refused to attend Christian worship services and put away her European-style dresses, preferring to wear skins. Kuanteng's story contrasts sharply with that of her half-sisters Bantsang and Ope, whose Christian identities and links with Bessie only strengthened with time.

After their return from Kuruman to Sechele's capital of Dithubaruba in 1854, Sechele had hoped that Kuanteng, Ope, and their sister Kereboletswe would teach others to read and write. Instead, he found that his daughters were disinclined to teach and his people were disinclined to learn. Although his children and Ma-Sebele gathered regularly to read among themselves, they did little to share their new knowledge with others.

Kuanteng supported Ope when she insisted on undergoing the bojale and said that if Ope did so, she and Kereboletswe would go also.[55] By the time Moffat returned to Dithubaruba in November 1854, he found that Kuanteng was now "Madame Wilson," having married British trader and explorer J. H. Wilson, with Sechele as matchmaker.[56] After four years together, Wilson returned to England without Kuanteng. Available sources are unclear as to whether Wilson invited Kuanteng to go with him and she refused, or whether she asked her father for permission to accompany Wilson and Sechele refused. Bessie herself wrote two somewhat conflicting accounts of what happened: one in 1863, the other much later, possibly around 1900. In the latter, Bessie suggests that Kuanteng had wanted to go to England, but had been refused permission by Sechele. Yet the 1863 version states that "she shrunk from the offer" to go to England and returned to Sechele on her own.[57]

> Mr. Wilson . . . travelled with her as far as [Lake Ngami], and intended to take her on to England with him by Walwich Bay, but she shrunk fr. the offer, & remained at Lake Ngami with her little half-caste boy, until an opportunity occurring back to her father's (an express conveyance, I think) she returned to him. Thence again she was taken & married by a respectable man of this place,[58] but a thorough & naked heathen. Gradually she gave up her European style of dress—her books & her church going habits (Mr. Schulenbourg's church[59])—and became in fact a pure heathen in manners dress & tastes. Khame [Khama] & Khamane [Khama's brother Kgamane] were just then commencing their civilized & Christian life under Mr. Schulenbourg and they sought her up & requested of her to teach them & help them on in reading &c. &c.—but she refused, and kept aloof in every way fr. them & their instructors. I have never *seen* her even. She evidently avoids me, for I have made repeated enquiries & can never see her.[60]

Other contemporary accounts support this version.[61]

We do not know how Kuanteng felt about her Ngwato husband, nor do we know what became of her child by Wilson. Like Ope's, perhaps Kuanteng's new husband refused to allow her any connection with her former life as a "civilized" Christian. On the other hand, it is possible that Kuanteng herself felt betrayed in her contact with Europeans and wanted nothing more to do with the Moffat family. If this is the case, we could read Kuanteng's lifestyle choices and silence toward Bessie as a strategy of resistance against the Europeanizing changes implied by Christian identity.[62] Kuanteng's Christian identity was, in Bessie's view—as well as in Kuanteng's own, I suspect—synonymous with her "civilized" identity as a wearer of dresses and reader of books. Church attendance, dresses, and literacy were all of a package. Refusing to wear European dress went together naturally with her refusal to speak with Bessie, attend church, or teach at the school in Shoshong after her remarriage to the Ngwato man.

Of all of Sechele's daughters, Bessie Price clearly felt the warmest rapport with Bantsang, whom she appreciated for her willingness to be blunt and penetrating in their discussions of family, faith, and politics. Both women were intellectually curious; in their forties they even collaborated in teaching a class to elite Kwena women. Unlike Ope and Kuanteng, Bantsang separated from her non-Christian husband. The youngest of Sechele's daughters educated at Kuruman, Bantsang was at least ten years Ope's junior, born about 1849.[63] Her mother was Mokgokong, known as Ma-Bantsang, daughter of the Ngwato chief Kgari. Ma-Bantsang was a "clever sensible" woman to whom the Ngwato elite, Sechele, and other male leaders looked for advice on important political matters.[64]

Bantsang lived at Kuruman along with Ope, Kereboletswe, Kuanteng, Sebele, and Ma-Sebele in 1853–54, and later returned with Sebele for an additional year in 1857. During the latter stay, Bessie and Bantsang became acquainted. Bessie, now eighteen years old, was teaching in the Kuruman school. Bantsang was probably between ten and twelve. By all accounts, Bantsang was an intelligent and lively girl. Moffat referred to her "fine, mild, intelligent countenance."[65] Of Bantsang and her brother Sebele, Bessie wrote in 1857, "They are very clever & possess really beautiful disposition[s]. The girl goes on pretty well—& her only fault is an almost uncontrollable merriment which makes her sometimes keep up a constant shaking & tittering till I send her away."[66]

Robert and Mary Moffat took a more negative view of Bantsang's character. In Mary's opinion, Bantsang became an increasingly burdensome charge, with her mischief spilling over into disobedience. For their part, Bantsang and Sebele accused Mary of starving them because she sent them to bed without their suppers on a few occasions.[67]

During the bojale episode of 1854, Bantsang, despite her mischievous streak and conflicts with Mary Moffat while at Kuruman, did not follow her elder half-sisters in revolt against Sechele's authority. After her half-brother Sebele stated that he would not be initiated, Bantsang came out boldly with "'Nor do I wish to go to the circumcision.'"[68] Sebele eventually changed his mind and agreed to be initiated, and Ope was as well. However, it is not clear from the available written sources whether Bantsang held to her refusal.[69]

If Bantsang was not initiated, this does not seem to have posed a barrier to her marriage to one of the first sons of the "heathen" faction amongst the Kwena. Sometime between 1857 and 1866, she was married to Khosilintsi's son, Bakwena. Perhaps Bantsang's high status, as a daughter of Sechele and a descendent of both the Kwena and the Ngwato royal lines, compensated for any lack of womanhood by the usual Tswana standards. By 1866, Bantsang had borne two children, but was dissatisfied with the marriage, ostensibly because Bakwena wanted to take a second wife. She came to Roger Price in 1866 to ask for his support in appealing to Sechele for permission to leave her husband and live at home again as Sechele's child.[70] Her appeal was apparently successful, for in early 1867, she separated from her husband.[71]

Around this time, when Roger and Bessie were newly established at Sechele's new capital of Logagen,[72] Bantsang visited Bessie frequently, and they had a series of spirited conversations which Bessie put in writing. From these we learn that Bantsang was very eager to learn English. The conversations continued, although Bessie tried to explain that she was busy from morning till night and that Bantsang herself had small children who would prevent her from concentrating on a properly rigorous course of English instruction. Bessie's reasoning prompted a burst of laughter from Bantsang:

> My children! Besi! do I know them?—do you suppose I nurse & follow them about as you do yours? Not I!—I never see them—this one & that one nurses them.

Bessie also insisted that teaching Setswana and Bible stories was more pertinent to the missionary's job than teaching English. Even if she had time to devote to teaching, these would take precedence. As it was, Bessie explained that she didn't have time anyway:

> my work as the Muruti's [missionary's] wife is not so much to teach with him as to keep him comfortable & his home civilized and Christian-like—& to train my children and servants likewise. I must teach you by setting an example in my home life.[73]

But Bantsang did not give up when Bessie refused to teach her English. The following month, she became the only female worshiper at the English-language service offered by Roger.[74]

Fourteen years later, when Bessie and Bantsang were in their forties, Bantsang was still as inquisitive, unbowed, and devoted to book-learning as ever. By this time Bessie had acquired the help of a governess, and was free to teach as she had not been in 1866. She chose to establish a class for the "ladies," high-status churchgoing women attached to the Kwena royal family. They would study the Setswana translation of *The Pilgrim's Progress*. Bantsang was a regular participant and helped Bessie as leader and expositor whenever Bessie's faulty Setswana failed.[75] Bantsang also complained to Bessie that her children's father and grandfather (Bakwena and Khosilintsi) would not permit her to have them attend church or school.[76]

Bantsang's commitment to literacy, church attendance, and friendship with the missionaries did not cloud her prescient insights into the political realities facing the Kwena kingdom. Increased pressure from the neighboring colonial state and economy, evident by 1880, had created a more hostile environment for the missionaries than had existed in the 1860s. Men who had worked as migrant laborers in the diamond mines had returned changed by their experiences.[77] The Anglo-Zulu war of 1879 was proof of Britain's capacity for military aggression against African kingdoms. Bantsang responded strongly to pictures of the Anglo-Zulu war that Bessie showed to her and Ope one day:

Yes! and you white people are coming upon us directly to conquer and kill us—and you know we have nothing but a handful of powder to defend ourselves with.

To Bessie's credit, she sought and appreciated Bantsang's pressing questions and forthright commentary: "I always like to get [Bantsang] in my talks with the women, because she is not shy of me at all and asks all sorts of questions and makes remarks wh. enable the other women to join too." In response to Bantsang's accusation against "you white people," Bessie admitted that she knew "full well we [missionaries] must always *appear* to be the ones who open the door of your country to the conquering English."[78]

Conclusion

Robert Moffat held that Christian conversion of the Tswana people had to entail radical rejection of much of Tswana culture and religion and adoption of European-style dress and customs, as well as of the LMS's particular brand of Protestant Christianity. His wife, Mary Smith Moffat, shared his views. When she found herself required to come to terms with domesticity, she resigned herself to letting her daughters become her surrogates in the schoolroom that she had once dreamed would be her sphere of mission work. Instead, she devoted herself to keeping a home in the European manner, offering hospitality to all visitors, and training her daughters and servants in the domestic arts.

Bessie Price blended loyalty to her father's vision of Christianizing and "civilizing" the "poor Bechuanas" and acceptance of her mother's vision of the domestic role with a more appreciative view of Tswana culture. She took advantage of her isolation on the frontier to eschew the dictates of European fashion and, in time, came to recognize missionaries' apparent complicity in the colonizing process, which accelerated in her later years. Bessie also permitted herself more intellectual freedom than her mother ever had. Her readings of Tolstoy and Martineau led her to develop unorthodox religious views.[79] As an old woman, inspired by Tolstoy, she even became a vegetarian, arguing that hunting and killing animals was as "uncivilised" as any African custom the missionaries had tried to stamp out.[80]

It was Bessie Price's own reading of Christian scripture that goaded her to be more tolerant than her parents even while she remained essentially condescending in her attitude toward Africans. She felt responsible for their well-being, comparing her work to that of the Good Samaritan who succored the injured traveler.[81] Advocating greater tolerance, patience, and gentleness of approach, she still sought to "raise up" the Tswana into a Europeanized Christianity.

Ope, Kuanteng, and Bantsang were all deeply affected by their father Sechele's checkered path toward Christianization. Ope and Bantsang were daughters of Sechele's discarded wives. All three of them were sent to Kuruman to learn reading and writing, European domestic skills, and Christian beliefs from the Moffats. Each of them had her own responses to this experience.

Ope began by resisting: remaining distant and unresponsive at Kuruman, insisting on her right to be initiated as a Tswana woman in the traditional bojale ceremony. Yet later in life she emerged as the wife of a "heathen" husband—Khosilintsi—determined to practice the Christian faith and use European-derived manners and dress. When, in his old age, Sechele married a fully "heathen" Matabele woman, Kholoma, it was Ope who led the cadre of royal Kwena women in harassing her literally to death for her lack of "civilization." These efforts suggest that African women had different kinds of influence and spheres for action depending on whether they moved in their capacity as sister, daughter, or wife. Clearly Ope as well as Bantsang found it most advantageous to act as Sechele's daughter, not as a wife.[82]

Kuanteng, initially the most receptive and pliant of Mary Moffat's Kwena daughter-pupils, in the end made the most thorough rejection of all things European, Christian, or "civilized." Perhaps Kuanteng's position as the daughter of a concubine, not a proper wife of Sechele, influenced the direction she took. Had she been able to stay near her father's home like Ope and Bantsang, perhaps she might also have balanced marriage to a "nonbeliever" with the Christian and "civilized" ways she had learned at Kuruman.

In the end, Bantsang proved the most consistently loyal to her father's priorities. As a child, at least initially, she sided with her father against Ope's defiance of his prohibition of bojale. She parlayed her position as Sechele's daughter and friend of the missionaries into an opportunity to reject her husband once he became a polygynist. Finally, she assertively pursued book-learning and the English language.

In this chapter, I have sought to consider the worldviews of both European and African protagonists in a "single analytical field"[83] by directing attention to the personal experiences and interactions of four women, all daughters of formidable men. Three were daughters of Sechele, the Kwena ruler from 1831 to 1892, and the fourth, a daughter of Robert Moffat, the preeminent missionary to the Batswana from 1822 to 1875. Bessie, Ope, Kuanteng, and Bantsang shared a formative period as girls at the LMS station at Kuruman, and their varied responses to the teachings they received in that time are brought to light by Bessie's letters to her sister and children.

The idea that women act—are agents—if not always under circumstances of their own choosing, is central to the stories we have explored here. Bessie Price's writings vividly illustrate the interplay between the power of societal and cultural trends and the agency exercised within these constraints in individual lives, both her own and those she observed. She makes judgments that reinforce prevailing missionary views of African women, even while she offers descriptions of individual women that undermine them.

These four "notable women" were daughters of regional "big men." Although we cannot know Sechele's daughters through their own words, Bessie's words provide important insight into their lives, and therefore into the processes of Christian conversion in the years immediately preceding colonial rule in southern Africa. Our lens permits us to move beyond casting Bessie as a white imperialist missionary and Sechele's daughters as African victims of hegemonic forces. All four women developed their own responses to the Christianizing projects of their parents. In each case, Christian teaching took a different place in individual strategies for negotiating a way through domestic, marital, and familial situations.

Primary Document

Elizabeth Lees Price, *The Journals of Elizabeth Lees Price: Written in Bechuanaland, Southern Africa, 1854–1883, with an Epilogue, 1889 and 1900,* ed. Una Long (London: Edward Arnold, 1956), p. 426.

[The following is excerpted from a letter written by Bessie Price to her children, who were in Britain for schooling, on 18 October 1880, at Molepolole. The original letters are in the Cory Library for Historical Research at Rhodes University, Grahamstown, South Africa. The excerpt is from document number 5919A.]

> Well—Ope has just been to see me, poor thing, & has been telling me about this & other troubles, not that those of wh. I have told have just happened. No! her son died while we were in England. I have always thought Ope so shy & reserved & was glad to see her the other day coming of her own accord to see me, & still more glad when I found she was thirsting & longing after the one thing needful. She undergoes a sort of persecution fr. her doating husband for her efforts after the truth. He watches her closely, and forbids her any freedom in religious matters beyond going to church and reading her bible, wh. he would fain also forbid her if he did not feel it would be going too far—as the Bakwena go [to] church and read the Bible & hymn book printed in their language as a matter of course, whether they are Christians or not. "Yet" she remarked "when I come fr. church I sit down in my home, and just tremble when I hear my husband coming—altho' I know I have done nothing wrong & nothing new—but just because I know he feels so angry at my going." Then she told me what at first I could not understand—that he would not allow her to pray—that for a long while he held out sternly and refused— but wearied I suppose by her supplications he at last yielded—& now she prayed. Now we would think it much easier for any tyrant to prevent our reading or church going than our praying but it is not so with them. Shall I tell you why?—because they are like little children, and cannot pray easily without doing it audibly—that is, so that they can hear themselves speak & then believe that God hears them too. Poor things! My heart just yearned compassionately over Ope, as I caught the idea—after looking awhile wonderingly at her, not understanding what she meant by not being allowed to pray. *You* may wonder too that Mama, after living all these long & many years in Bechwana land, never discovered or under-

stood this before. I, too, feel rebuked & sad to think it should be so—but one excuse for me is this, that I have so many little folks to look after & care for all alone; & I had not always our dear good Miss Wallace to take half, or more than half my work, off me as she does now—leaving me free to help & cheer & care for my poor Bechwana friends.

NOTES

1. This passage appears in a letter written by Bessie Price to her sister Jeanie Moffat, dated 22 August 1866, in which she paraphrases Bantsang's words. Elizabeth Lees Price, *The Journals of Elizabeth Lees Price: Written in Bechuanaland, Southern Africa, 1854–1883, with an Epilogue, 1889 and 1900,* ed. Una Long (London: Edward Arnold, 1956), pp. 215–16.

2. "Boer" means "farmer" in Dutch. The term was used in southern Africa in the eighteenth and nineteenth centuries by both English settlers and the "Boers" themselves to refer to rural settlers of European ancestry who spoke a language derived from Dutch and were affiliated with the Dutch Reformed Church. In the 1830s several thousand Boers left the Cape Colony to establish their own polities, independent of British control, beyond the Orange and Vaal Rivers. These two republics became known as the Orange Free State and the Transvaal (or South African Republic), respectively.

3. See Margaret Strobel, *European Women and the Second British Empire* (Bloomington: Indiana University Press, 1991); and Nupur Chaudhuri and Margaret Strobel, eds., *Western Women and Imperialism: Complicity and Resistance* (Bloomington: Indiana University Press, 1992).

4. Some works in this vein are Richard Elphick, "Writing Religion into History," in *Missions and Christianity in South African History,* ed. Henry Bredekamp and Robert Ross (Johannesburg: University of Witwatersrand Press, 1995); Richard Gray, *Black Christians and White Missionaries* (New Haven, Conn.: Yale University Press, 1990); Robert Hefner, ed., *Conversion to Christianity* (Berkeley: University of California Press, 1993); Lamin Sanneh, *Translating the Message: The Missionary Impact on Culture* (Maryknoll, N.Y.: Orbis, 1989); and numerous works by Terence Ranger, most recently *Are We Not Also Men? The Samkange Family and African Politics in Zimbabwe, 1920–64* (Portsmouth, N.H.: Heinemann, 1995). See also Jean Comaroff and John Comaroff, *Of Revelation and Revolution,* vol. 1, *Christianity, Colonialism, and Consciousness in South Africa,* and vol. 2, *The Dialectics of Modernity on a South African Frontier* (Chicago: University of Chicago Press, 1991–97); and Paul Landau, *The Realm of the Word: Language, Gender, and Christianity in a Southern African Kingdom* (Portsmouth, N.H.: Heinemann, 1995).

5. Quoted from "Toward the History of African Christianity," a talk given by Thomas Spear at the University of Minnesota, 2 May 1997. Examples of such works might include T. O. Beidelman, *Colonial Evangelism: A Socio-historical Study of an East African Mission at the Grassroots* (Bloomington: Indiana University Press, 1982); Elizabeth Schmidt, *Peasants, Traders, and Wives: Shona Women in the History of Zimbabwe, 1870–1939* (Portsmouth, N.H.: Heine-

mann, 1992); Charles van Onselen, *Chibaro: African Mine Labour in Southern Rhodesia, 1900–1933* (London: Pluto, 1976), pp. 182–86.

6.   Both the heroic mission history and that of cultural imperialism have been criticized for their Eurocentrism, for ignoring the possibility that Africans were not merely passive recipients of dynamic forces, whether beneficial or oppressive, emanating from Europe. The wish to acknowledge African "agency," to explore how Africans were active makers of their own history, has changed the way scholars write about the history of Christian missions in Africa. For an approach which recognizes both African and missionary input into the Christianizing process and is also concerned with the LMS as a missionizing agent, see Pier M. Larson, "'Capacities and Modes of Thinking': Intellectual Engagements and Subaltern Hegemony in the Early History of Malagasy Christianity," *American Historical Review* 102, no. 4 (1997): 969–1002.

7.   See Comaroff and Comaroff, *Of Revelation and Revolution,* and Landau, *Realm of the Word.*

8.   A word about terminology. "Batswana" is a plural noun referring to the Tswana people. "Botswana" is the name of an independent African nation where the majority of the people speak the Setswana language. Before gaining independence in 1966, what is now Botswana was known as the Protectorate of Bechuanaland. Not all Batswana live in Botswana. Many Setswana speakers live in the Republic of South Africa in what was successively called British Bechuanaland, the Cape Province, and (under apartheid) the "homeland" of Bophuthatswana.

9.   Comaroff and Comaroff, *Of Revelation and Revolution,* vol. 2, p. 52.

10. Landau, *Realm of the Word,* p. xxii. The Comaroffs' introduction to the second volume of *Of Revelation and Revolution* addresses Landau's concerns. They also respond to similar criticism from Terence Ranger and other historians. See vol. 2, pp. 44ff.

11. Janet Hodgson's *Princess Emma* (Craighall, South Africa: A.D. Donker, 1987) is one of the few offerings which explores in depth a southern African woman's responses to Christian conversion and mission education in the mid–nineteenth century. Emma, the daughter of the Xhosa king Sandile, was educated in an Anglican school—Zonnebloem College—in Cape Town in the 1850s.

12. Price, *Journals.* The original letters of Elizabeth Price are held at the Cory Library for Historical Research at Rhodes University in Grahamstown, South Africa. Una Long, who edited them for publication, was a white South African academic; she is strongly identified with the Cory Library. Her father was a journalist and a politician, her grandfather a Church of England clergyman in Norwich, U. K. Long was a Field-Worker in History at Rhodes University, where she was charged with the task of locating, and securing for the Cory Library, privately owned unofficial manuscripts relating to the history of South Africa. Included among these are the letters of Elizabeth Lees Price. Sandy Rowoldt, librarian at the Cory Library, personal communication, 9 July 1998.

   After extensive research in Botswana (then known as the Bechuanaland Protectorate) and the United Kingdom, Long edited, annotated, and introduced the Price letters. Elizabeth Price's daughter, Christian Wallace Price, had produced typescript copies of her mother's letters. Both the originals and the typescript copies were at Long's disposal. For several of the key passages used in this chapter I was able to check Long's published version of the text against photocopies of the original hand-written letters. These copies were kindly provided by the staff of the Cory Library.

13. Although the Comaroffs, Landau, and others have made use of the Price journals, they are not interested in Price as an individual. The Comaroffs mine Price's letters for references to evidence of domesticity-as-imperialism. Landau and others have used her detailed accounts of the contemporary scene to reconstruct the political history of the region. This is particularly true of Frederick Jeffress Ramsay, Jr., "The Rise and Fall of the Bakwena Dynasty of South-Central Botswana, 1820–1940" (Ph.D. diss., Boston University, 1991). Edwin Smith drew heavily on Price's journals in his *Great Lion of Bechuanaland: The Life and Times of Roger Price, Missionary* (London: Independent Press for the London Missionary Society, 1957).

14. Kuanteng's words do not appear in these stories, only her actions. But these also can "speak."

15. Personal Narratives Group, *Interpreting Women's Lives: Feminist Theory and Personal Narratives* (Bloomington: Indiana University Press, 1989), p. 13. Women scholars from the formerly colonized world, as well as others, have pointed out the ways that Western feminist scholars gloss over painfully real differences in power, values, and life circumstance when they claim to represent women from other parts of the world on the strength of a shared female identity. For example, see Trinh T. Minh-Ha, *Woman, Native, Other: Writing Postcoloniality and Feminism* (Bloomington: Indiana University Press, 1989). One of the more scathing indictments of the efforts of Western female scholars' work in African women's history is Kirk Hoppe, " 'Whose Life Is It, Anyway?': Issues of Representation in Life Narrative Texts of African Women," *International Journal of African Historical Studies* 26, no. 3 (1993): 623–36. See also Heidi Gengenbach's rebuttal to Hoppe, "Truth-Telling and the Politics of Women's Life History Research in Africa: A Reply to Kirk Hoppe," *International Journal of African Historical Studies* 27, no. 3 (1994): 619–27.

16. An exception to this is Ramsay, "Rise and Fall of the Bakwena Dynasty." The last major published work on Sechele in English was Anthony Sillery's *Sechele: The Story of an African Chief* (Oxford: George Ronald, 1954). Wolfgang Proske's recent study, in German, of the Hermannsburg missionaries in Tswana country devotes considerable attention to Sechele without substantively changing the perspectives offered by Sillery. See Wolfgang Proske, *Botswana und die Anfaenge der Hermannsburger Mission* (Frankfurt-am-Main: Peter Lang, 1989). William Duggan, *An Economic Analysis of Southern African Agriculture* (New York: Sage, 1986), and Gary Okihiro, "Hunters, Herders, Cultivators, and Traders: Interaction and Change in the Kgalagadi, Nineteenth Century" (Ph.D. diss., University of California, Los Angeles, 1976) treat Molepolole and its environs, but they do not put principal focus on Sechele's kingdom.

17. Sechele's leadership of the Kwena is a compelling example of an attempt at Christian African kingship, earlier, though less famous, than that of Khama III's rule of the Ngwato kingdom, highlighted by Landau in *Realm of the Word*. The Ngwato kingdom did not gain ascendancy until late in the nine-

teenth century. In addition, Landau's period of study begins in earnest with the declaration of the British Protectorate over Bechuanaland (1895), while the Comaroffs' lack of emphasis on "event history" means that they pay little attention to the period 1850–80.

18. For more on the symbolic importance of irrigation to missionaries in general and those located at the springs of Kuruman in particular, see Nancy Jacobs, "The Flowing Eye: Water Management in the Upper Kuruman Valley, South Africa, c. 1800–1962," *Journal of African History* 37, no. 2 (1996): 237–60, especially pp. 239–44.

19. Bessie married LMS missionary Roger Price and her eldest sister, Mary, married David Livingstone. Their sister Ann married Paris Evangelical Mission Society agent Jean Fredoux, and Jane "Jeanie" Moffat remained unmarried, serving at Kuruman as a teacher until her father's retirement. The Moffats' youngest son, John Smith Moffat, served as an independent missionary and later joined the LMS, serving at the LMS station at Inyati in Matabeleland (now in Zimbabwe) from 1859 to 1865. He then took over at Kuruman when his father retired, and in the end left mission work altogether to work for the British colonial service in South Africa and Rhodesia (Zimbabwe).

20. See Elizabeth Elbourne, "Concerning Missionaries: The Case of Van der Kemp," *Journal of Southern African Studies* 17, no. 1 (1991): 153–64; and Janet Hodgson, "Do We Hear You, Nyengana? Dr. J. T. Vanderkemp and the First Mission to the Xhosa," *Religion in Southern Africa* 5, no. 1 (1984): 3–47.

21. By 1860 Mary despaired of her daughters' staying at the station, and was preparing to send them to live "in the Colony" at Capetown. Mora Dickson, *Beloved Partner: Mary Moffat of Kuruman: A Biography Based on Her Letters* (1974; reprint, Kuruman and Gaborone: Kuruman Moffat Mission Trust/ Botswana Book Centre, 1989), p. 158.

22. See Dickson, *Beloved Partner*.

23. Valentine Cunningham, " 'God and Nature Intended You for a Missionary's Wife': Mary Hill, Jane Eyre, and Other Missionary Women in the 1840s," in *Women and Missions: Past and Present: Anthropological and Historical Perceptions,* ed. Fiona Bowie, Deborah Kirkwood, and Shirley Ardener (Providence, R.I.: Berg, 1993), p. 89. See also Cecillie Swaisland, "Wanted—Earnest, Self-Sacrificing Women for Service in South Africa: Nineteenth-Century Recruitment of Single Women to Protestant Missions," ibid., pp. 70–83. LMS policy on admitting single or married women to the mission field as missionaries in their own right was reflected in the policies of other Protestant mission societies as well: women did not, in general, officially act as missionaries until the last two decades of the nineteenth century. See also Jane Hunter, *The Gospel of Gentility: American Women Missionaries in Turn-of-the-Century China* (New Haven, Conn.: Yale University Press, 1984).

24. Dickson, *Beloved Partner*, p. 62.

25. For more on how Bessie and her sister Jeanie changed from resisting to embracing their teaching job at Kuruman, see Dickson, *Beloved Partner*, p. 198.

26. Price, *Journals*, p. 433.

27. The extent to which literacy, the rejection of certain "traditional" African customs, and the adoption of certain European cultural practices became bound up with the process of Christian conversion has been addressed in scores of articles and books. The lines drawn on these issues varied from one

mission society to another and changed in broadly uniform ways over the course of the nineteenth and twentieth centuries. Relevant scholarship includes Landau, *Realm of the Word*, especially p. 17; and Hodgson, "Do We Hear You, Nyengana?". An extensive literature treats the question of female circumcision among the Kikuyu in the 1920s; see, for example, Susan Pederson, "National Bodies, Unspeakable Acts: The Sexual Politics of Colonial Policy-Making," *Journal of Modern History* 63, no. 4 (1991): 647–80. For a useful anthology, see Torben Christensen and William R. Hutchison, eds., *Missionary Ideologies in the Imperialist Era: 1880–1920* (Cambridge, Mass.: Harvard Theological Review, and Aarhus, Denmark: Aros, 1982).

28. Sechele's wife's name was Selemeng. She was referred to, however, as "Ma-Sebele," or "mother of Sebele." Mary Moffat was similarly called "Ma-Mary" by the Batswana, since her first-born child was also named Mary.

29. While Sechele was traveling from his capital, at that time located at Dithubaruba, to Cape Town, he left the members of his family at Kuruman. He went to Cape Town to protest against the terms of the 1850 Sand River Convention, which ruled that Europeans in the Cape would no longer sell arms to Africans, while continuing to sell arms to the Boers living beyond the Cape's borders. The Boers had recently attacked Dithubaruba. Sechele spoke with Governor George Cathcart, who dismissed his concerns as beyond the responsibility of the colonial government. Robert Moffat pointed out, in a letter of 1852, that Sechele brought his family to Kuruman in part for reasons of security: "[I have been given] the charge of Sechele's children whom he sent to my care for their education. . . . after the attack of the Boers, [he sent] his wife and little ones, with a considerable retinue for safety." Robert Moffat, *The Matabele Journals of Robert Moffat, 1829–1860*, ed. J. P. R. Wallis (Salisbury: National Archives of Rhodesia, 1976), vol. 1, p. 278.

30. In response to Sechele's persistent requests that the LMS assign a missionary to live at the Kwena capital, Moffat sent his son-in-law, David Livingstone (married to his eldest child, Mary), to be Sechele's missionary in the 1840s. From Livingstone Sechele learned to read and write, and was baptized in 1848.

31. Bessie Price wrote that Ope, at about age twelve, had been betrothed to Khosilintsi before Sechele's baptism by David Livingstone in 1848. Price, *Journals*, p. 424.

32. Bessie termed Ope's mother Sechele's "Chief Wife" (Price, *Journals*, p. 67). In spite of Kebalepile's status, Sechele retained Selemeng (Ma-Sebele) as his sole wife when he converted to Christianity, since Selemeng was the mother of his male heir, Sebele.

33. Solomon T. Plaatje, *Sechuana Proverbs with Literal Translations and the European Equivalents* (London: Kegan Paul, Trench, and Trubner, 1916), p. 74.

34. Price, *Journals*, pp. 67–68.

35. Moffat, *Matabele Journals*, vol. 1, pp. 164–78.

36. Moffat was on his way from Kuruman on one of his many journeys to Matabeleland, the Ndebele kingdom led by Mzilikazi in what is now Zimbabwe. He stopped at Sechele's capital on his way both to and from Matabeleland.

37. Boys were circumcised, while girls had a hot rod pressed against the inside of the thighs. For both sexes, the ability to bear pain was an ingredient of adult

status. See Margaret Kinsman, "'Beasts of Burden': The Subordination of Southern Tswana Women, ca. 1800–1840," *Journal of Southern African Studies* 10, no. 1 (1983): 39–54; and Jean Comaroff, *Body of Power, Spirit of Resistance* (Chicago: University of Chicago Press, 1985), pp. 114–15.

38. Smith, *Great Lion of Bechuanaland,* p. 162.

39. See Thomas Tlou, "The Batawana of Northwestern Botswana and Christian Missionaries: 1877–1906," *Transafrican Journal of History* 3, nos. 1–2 (1973): 112–28, for more on age-grade associations among the Tswana. This was not the first recorded instance in which a Tswana woman defied Sechele and the missionaries to participate in her age-grade's bojale. David Livingstone, the first missionary to Sechele, wrote in 1846 of a woman who feared her daughter, a Christian, would not be accepted by the people at Chonwane since she had not been "boyalified" (David Livingstone, *Family Letters, 1841–1856,* ed. with an introduction by Isaac Schapera [London: Chatto and Windus, 1959], vol. 1, p. 173).

40. Finding that "neither Ope nor Khosilintse were believers [i.e., Christians]," Moffat told Sechele to forbid the match, impressing upon him that it was his duty "to leave Ope to be the spouse of a young man whom she could love." Moffat, *Matabele Journals,* pp. 161–62.

41. His political situation, in light of the strength of Khosilintsi's anti-Christian faction, would not permit Sechele to impose a kingdom-wide ban on initiation ceremonies. This is one of the striking differences between Sechele's situation and that of Khama III as depicted by Landau in *The Realm of the Word.* In the Ngwato kingdom during that later period, facing a more aggressive British colonial presence and wielding a very different type of authority, Khama III was able to impose wide-reaching bans on "heathen" practices such as the brewing of beer. Sechele's attempts to maintain Christian teachings as rigidly as his political situation permitted were partly motivated by his need for Moffat's support in matters of strategic security.

42. Sefunelo was the son of Moroka, chief of the Rolong. Price, *Journals,* p. 425 n. 1.

43. There is a rumor that Ope's son, Motlhware, was in fact not the son of Sefunelo, but of Tshipinare, a relative of his who took Ope as a levirate wife. See Colin Murray, *Black Mountain: Land, Class, and Power in the Eastern Orange Free State, 1880s to 1980s* (Washington, D.C.: Smithsonian Institution Press, 1992), pp. 22–24. This would suggest that Ope had a total of three husbands, not two.

44. Price, *Journals,* p. 425.

45. Ibid.

46. At this time Bessie's husband Roger had recently resumed his place as missionary to Sechele after a four-year furlough.

47. Ibid., pp. 426–27.

48. Stephen Volz, "Chief of a Heathen Town: Kgosi Sechele and the Arrival of Christianity among the Tswana" (M.A. thesis, University of Wisconsin, Madison, 1999), p. 84.

49. Similarly, he tolerated Sechele's bid to bring in the German Lutherans, though in the end Khosilintsi reviled them as mere Boers and was influential in getting Sechele to end his support for the Hermannsburg missionaries.

50. Khosilintsi delivered a searing speech for Moffat's benefit in 1854 about the hypocrisies of British "native" policy in the region. The Sand River Convention had made the purchase of firearms illegal only for Africans. Khosilintsi resented that his continued use of guns only earned him a self-righteous reminder from missionaries that it was against God's law to promote war. He said, "Are we only to obey the word of God because we are black? Are white people not to obey the word of God, because they are white?" (Moffat, *Matabele Journals*, p. 378). In contrast, Sechele's hopes for British protection against the Boers never wavered. By the 1880s, after the 1879 Anglo-Zulu war and other regional conflicts between African polities and British colonial interests, there was marked tension in Sechele's capital between Europeans and the Africans of the "pagan" camp.

51. Price, *Journals*, p. 476.

52. Ibid., p. 484.

53. Price, *Journals*, p. 150.

54. Ibid., p. 68.

55. Moffat, *Matabele Journals*, p. 174.

56. Moffat goes on to say, "So there is one of Sechele's school-mistresses disposed of. . . . I said nothing. It was too late. My heart, however, felt grieved at the conduct of Sechele giving a young woman to a man whose shameless character is a joke in the country." Moffat, *Matabele Journals*, p. 345. Later Moffat refers to Wilson as a "whoremonger" (p. 351).

57. Price, *Journals*, pp. 68, 150. In the earlier account Bessie writes that Kuanteng and Wilson were "married, somehow," but in the later she calls Kuanteng his "mistress." How many children they had is unclear as well; the earlier account mentions only one, but the later refers to "children." W. C. Baldwin, *African Hunting from Natal to the Zambezi: From 1852 to 1860*, 2nd ed. (London, 1863), pp. 286–90, also mentions only one, and this seems more likely to be correct than Bessie's reminiscences very late in life.

58. "This place" refers to Shoshong, the capital of the Ngwato branch of Tswana, ruled in 1863 by Segkhoma. The Ngwato polity was later famous among Europeans as the realm ruled by Segkhoma's son, Khama. Khama was already an important player in Ngwato politics by this time. Bessie and Roger Price began their married life at Shoshong in 1863 before settling at the Kwena capital, Molepolole, under Sechele in 1866.

59. Schulenburg was the Hermannsburg Society's Lutheran missionary stationed at Shoshong. He returned to Germany not long after the Prices' arrival. For more on the Hermannsburg mission to the Tswana, see Proske, *Botswana*.

60. Price, *Journals*, pp. 150–51.

61. W. C. Baldwin, a British hunter, wrote of his 1858 encounter with Kuanteng shortly after Wilson had left for England. Some days after leaving Lake Ngami, he said, "I came across the Bechuanas—Wilson's wife, Sechele's daughter. Wearied and footsore, unused to walking, she was dead-beat and unable to proceed. I acted the part of the Good Samaritan and gave her and her brat a seat in the wagon all the way to Sechele's." Baldwin, *African Hunting*, p. 286.

62. As Kirk Hoppe says, "silence is a strategy." Hoppe, "Whose Life Is It, Anyway?" p. 631.

63.   She was most likely born in 1848 or 1849, since Livingstone felt compelled to bar Sechele from church membership not long after his baptism because he had resumed sexual relations with Mokgokong. See Neil Parsons, *King Khama, Emperor Joe, and the Great White Queen: Victorian Britain through African Eyes* (Chicago: University of Chicago Press, 1998), p. 39, and Price, *Journals*, p. 178 n. 1.

64.   Price, *Journals*, p. 177. After Sechele divorced her, Mokgokong returned to the Ngwato capital at Shoshong and remarried.

65.   Moffat, *Matabele Journals*, p. 165.

66.   Price, *Journals*, p. 71.

67.   See Dickson, *Beloved Partner*, p. 163. For a detailed account of how Robert Moffat viewed Bantsang and Sebele's behavior while at Kuruman in 1853–54, see his letter to his wife in *Matabele Journals*, p. 351. Among other things, the passage richly illustrates Moffat's arrogant assurance that for all Sechele's pretensions to Christian, "civilized" status, he was still "too great a heathen" to know how to properly raise his own children.

68.   Moffat, *Matabele Journals*, p. 174. Let it be clear, however, that female initiation among the Tswana did not include circumcision, though boys were circumcised as part of their initiation ritual.

69.   Ramsay, "Rise and Fall of the Bakwena Dynasty," vol. 1, pp. 127–28. See also Volz, "Chief of a Heathen Town," pp. 84–85, for a discussion of the initiation episode, highlighting the fact that Khosilintsi and Sechele disagreed vigorously with one another over whether Sechele's children ought to be initiated. The fact that most, if not all, of the children decided to defy their father and be initiated indicates one way that Sechele's Christianity undermined his authority as *kgosi* or king.

70.   Price, *Journals*, p. 245.

71.   Ibid., p. 255.

72.   Logagen was later known as Molepolole.

73.   Price, *Journals*, pp. 215–16. The liveliness of this account is fueled by the fact that Bessie was describing it in a letter to her sister Jeanie, who would have remembered Bantsang from their days at Kuruman. Jeanie was at this time still living with their parents at Kuruman, and perhaps Bessie expected Jeanie to share news of Bantsang with Robert and Mary as well.

74.   Ibid., p. 230.

75.   Ibid., p. 436.

76.   Ibid., pp. 416–17.

77.   Ibid., pp. 487–88. Here Bessie describes how the cook she had had before her four-year furlough in England had come back to his job a changed man, more reserved, more unfriendly. He had been to the diamond mines in the intervening years.

78.   Ibid., p. 458, emphasis in original.

79.   According to a valediction written about Bessie Price by her daughter, Christian Wallace Price. See ibid., p. 537.

80.   Ibid., p. 10.

81.   Ibid., p. 410.

82.   See Iris Berger, "'Beasts of Burden' Revisited: Interpretations of Women and Gender in Southern African Societies," in *Paths toward the Past: African His-*

torical *Essays in Honor of Jan Vansina,* ed. Robert W. Harms, Joseph C. Miller, David S. Newbury, and Michele D. Wagner (Atlanta: African Studies Association Press, 1994), pp. 123–41.

83. Frederick Cooper and Ann Laura Stoler, "Between Metropole and Colony: Rethinking a Research Agenda," in *Tensions of Empire: Colonial Cultures in a Bourgeois World,* ed. Frederick Cooper and Ann Laura Stoler (Berkeley: University of California Press, 1997), p. 4.

3 Colonial Midwives and Modernizing Childbirth in French West Africa

Jane Turrittin

When the colonial administration opted to promote Western medicine in French West Africa (*Afrique Orientale Française*—AOF) as an aspect of their *mission civilisatrice,* they found it necessary to create a new social strata of educated Africans—the *évolués*—that ultimately played a very different role from that originally intended. Because the French viewed Western medicine as "an indication of all the benefits which our occupation can give them [the Africans],"[1] and recognized that training African women could further their project of social domination by facilitating access to African families,[2] they included a school of midwifery in the medical center they established in Dakar in 1918. *L'École des sages-femmes* was the first school of midwifery in Africa. Several évolués who trained as medical auxiliaries at the Dakar medical center, including a handful of colonial midwives, became militants in the anti-French independence movement.

The other colonial powers also trained African medical auxiliaries[3] to promote public health but, whereas in the AOF the colonial state took responsibility for health promotion from the beginning, medical auxiliaries in the British colonies and in the Belgian Congo were trained in missionary institutions. Only later was their training subsidized by the colonial state.[4] Midwifery education in Uganda, for example, was introduced in 1919 by the wife of a Church Mission Society missionary.[5] In both the French and English colonies, medicine was one of the first fields in which women had an opportunity for post-primary education.[6] This chapter examines the modernizing role of the colonial elite of Franco-African évolués by focusing on the work of colonial midwives who, from the end of World War I to independence, disseminated the French model of childbirth and other aspects of Western medicine to subject peoples throughout the AOF.

Creating an indigenous medical corps was congruent with the French colonial administration's political interests after World War I. However, the catalyst for the establishment of the Dakar medical center was a demand made by Blaise Diagne, the first African elected to represent the *quatre communes* (Four Communes) in the French Chamber of Deputies, for France to expand its colonial health services in recompense for the contributions Africans had made to the war.[7] The medical center, made up of three faculties—*L'École africaine de médecine* (the African Medical School), popularly known as *L'École le Dantec* for its first director, Dr. Aristide Le Dantec; *L'École Jules Carde,* a pharmaceutical school; and *L'École des sages-femmes*—was a crucial component of the state-sponsored health service the French put in place to promote preventive and social health in the postwar period.[8] Colonial midwives were the most highly educated women in the AOF until 1938, when teachers' training schools for women were opened in Rufisque, Senegal, and Katibougou in the Ivory Coast.[9] Each of the more than five hundred midwives who graduated from the School of Midwifery between 1920 and 1957, when it was annexed to the reorganized Medical School in Dakar,[10] was obligated to serve in the *Service de santé* (Health Service) for a period of at least ten years. As members of pioneering teams of medical auxiliaries sent to introduce Western medicine into the French African colonies of Senegal, Guinea, Soudan, Ivory Coast, Upper Volta, Niger, Dahomey, the Cameroun, and Togo, colonial midwives were a significant occupational group.[11]

The main source for this chapter is the autobiography of an African midwife, Aoua Kéita—*Femme d'Afrique* (Woman of Africa).[12] Few African women have written autobiographies, and autobiographies by women active during the colonial period are even rarer. *Femme d'Afrique* is a valuable social document because it provides us with the voice of an African woman who was "a militant civil servant during the colonial epoque, and because it shows the difficulties of a woman in Malian society."[13] Kéita's active career as a pioneering midwife and political militant from 1931 to 1968 coincided with the transition from colonial domination in the former French Soudan to national independence in Mali. Born in Bamako in 1912, Kéita attended the *École des filles* and the *Orphelinat des métisses* and then the School of Midwifery in Dakar, from which she graduated in 1931. She worked for the Colonial Health Service throughout what was then the French Soudan, delivering more than nine thousand babies before retiring from midwifery.[14] She received her political apprenticeship in the health workers' union (Symedvétopharsa, the *Syndicat des médecins, vétérinaires, pharmaciens, et sages-femmes* [Union of Doctors, Veterinarians, Pharmacists, and Midwives],[15] an umbrella organization of all health care workers) and, as a union member, participated in major strikes in the period leading up to independence. In conjunction with her union activity, she became a well-known militant in the Soudanese branch of the *Rassemblement democratique africain* (USRDA), a radical party opposed to French colonialism. She achieved national leadership in the USRDA when she was the first woman ever to be appointed to the party's central committee. She and Aissata Sow, president of the Teachers' Union, co-founded the Union of Salaried Women of Bamako. As a deputy elected to the independent Republic of Mali's national assembly in 1960 and as head of the women's branch of the party, the National Union of Malian Women (*Union nationale des femmes du Mali*—UNFM), Kéita made a significant contribution to Mali's 1962 constitution by promoting marriage legislation which enhanced women's rights. Kéita went into exile in 1968 when Modibo Kéita was deposed in a military coup. She died in Bamako in 1979.

Kéita expresses évolué "liberationist self-representations" and values in *Femme d'Afrique*, which she wrote to ensure that her views on the events in which she had participated would become part of the public record.[16] In addition, she recorded a great deal of information about her experiences as a colonial midwife on the French model. Kéita's access to alternative knowledge led her to question aspects of African traditions, as well as to work to change the "traditional" place of women in African societies by promoting women's rights and opposing both French colonialism and patriarchy. Her life story illustrates the dilemmas experienced by évolué women who struggled to reconcile the habits imparted to them by the colonial education system with the African values to which they were socialized as children.[17] Yet one must be cautious in generalizing from Kéita's experiences to those of colonial midwives as a group, because few were as willing as Kéita to be publicly active in the anti-colonial movement.[18] The excerpts selected from *Femme d'Afrique* for this chapter illustrate experiences colonial midwives tended to share, rather than those which were unique to Aoua Kéita.

In analyzing colonial midwives' experiences, it is important to remember that the production of knowledge, including scientific understandings of reproduction and birthing[19] in the industrialized and nonindustrialized worlds, is shaped by different material, social, and political conditions. The case of midwifery in Africa is especially interesting because it exemplifies a local knowledge system that is controlled by women.[20] While men controlled obstetrics in France in the 1930s, in Africa the profession was controlled by postmenopausal women, who derived considerable prestige and material rewards from their activities. Thus both the colonial midwives who promoted the Western model of birthing and the local representatives of African systems of birthing and reproduction with whom they were in competition were women.

Historians and anthropologists have used a number of approaches to make sense of African medical systems and the history of Western medicine in Africa.[21] I draw upon the work of feminist historians who have examined the dynamics of race, gender, and class in relation to state and missionary promotion of medicine during the colonial period. For example, in *Divided Sisterhood*, a study of the nursing profession in South Africa, Shula Marks documents how "medical services are profoundly gendered":

> Relations of domination and subordination are not simply a result of class and racially defined divisions, but also result from inequalities of power between men and women, and between white, brown and black women.[22]

Megan Vaughan has examined how medical discourse has been used to delineate the "politics of difference" and shows how Africans have responded with contestation, resistance, redefinition, and rejection to the differences "bestowed" upon them by the British.[23] Vaughan has worked with a group of historians of colonialism in the former British East Africa who use the concept of hegemony to analyze colonial medical history. They argue that, since medical professionals "largely accepted the values the colonizers attached to medical intervention and carried them beyond the confines of the colonial enclaves," they "provide a window on the operation of hegemony."[24] As this chapter demonstrates, such professionals often "contested" the colonial administration's hegemony.[25]

The School of Midwifery in Dakar

Students were selected for training at the School of Midwifery on the basis of competitive examinations given annually throughout the territories of the AOF.[26] The costs of their education were covered by tax revenue generated within the AOF. Most, including Kéita, were from privileged backgrounds; more were Christian than Muslim. Kéita's father was an *ancien combattant* who, after serving France in Europe in World War I, became a civil servant employed at Bamako's central laboratory.

In 1935, the School of Midwifery, whose premises had been in temporary buildings, moved into an "elegant" pavilion which contained an obstetrical clinic and was attached to the 250-bed Le Dantec Hospital, where midwifery students did their practical training. The pavilion's design was inspired by Sudanese architecture, but its spatial organization reflected French, rather than African, conventions.[27] The colonial administrators and educators modeled the school's curriculum after midwifery curriculums current in France.[28] Convinced of the superiority of French medical knowledge and techniques, they made little effort to promote African, experientially based, "prescientific" knowledge of birthing and reproduction.[29] The educators' racialized, ethnocentric understandings are reflected in a statement in a 1935 brochure describing the school, which notes that the training emphasized "practical competency rather than . . . theoretical knowledge."[30]

> [E]very effort is being made to make the course simple and concrete, and to bring it as far as possible into line with modern practice and in touch with the pathological problems of French West Africa.[31]

> [T]he most notable feature of the students' training was the half-day clinics and hospital sessions in which they participated daily with their professors from the first year onward.[32]

In their first year, the young women studied:

	Periods per week
Obstetrics, tutorials, exercises on lay figures	5
Infant welfare	1
Elementary anatomy and physiology	1
Hygiene	1
Public health visiting (first year)	1
Course of general education (orthography, French, and arithmetic)	5[33]

Discussion and teamwork were encouraged. Instead of lecturing, teachers dictated clear notes to which students could refer throughout their careers. According to the brochure, this method not only had better results but also offered "the additional advantage of developing in our students a facility in expressing themselves orally in the French language."[34]

The school's paternalistic operating philosophy encoded the colonialists' belief that medicine and morality were linked.[35] The effort to shape students' morals was so thorough that in the dormitory students were under the constant supervision of two European women able to "advise them in all the details of their everyday life . . . [give] moral guidance and . . . inculcate habits of order and regularity and proper behavior":

> This supervision . . . is neither over-strict nor interfering. Every effort is made to leave the students a certain degree of liberty and some scope for initiative, so that later on, when they are left to their own devices, they may already have learned self-control.

> On every possible occasion . . . [students are reminded] of what they owe personally to France. . . . By unobtrusive but unremitting efforts on these lines we endeavor to ensure that later on they may become thoroughly loyal servants of the Government.[36]

Students were evaluated on their behavior (*conduite*) as well as their academic work (*travail*). Kéita portrays herself as a rebel in a brief comment about the three years of serious study (*de bonnes études*) she spent at the School of Midwifery:

> [W]ith respect to behavior, my turbulence was not appreciated by the supervisors whom I teased to amuse myself. In these conditions, bad grades for behavior rained down on me. Happily, my work did not suffer because of it.[37]

Midwifery training was aimed at rendering students fully committed to French birthing practices and French culture.[38] Kéita declared that when she graduated, at the age of nineteen, she had gained "confidence in myself and in the future" (27). Moreover, she had acquired a set of expectations about social, familial, and personal life qualitatively different from the values imparted to her in childhood by her traditional Soudanese education (15–26). She was happy and proud to learn that she would be working in distant Gao, where she could use her "modest knowledge in the service of a population who had never known what a midwife was" (28). Kéita, like other colonial midwives, was motivated to relieve human misery, spread évolué values, and help her sisters to *sortir de tradition* (leave tradition behind), activities which gave them the moral satisfaction of serving the social good.[39]

The Colonial Health Service (*Service de la santé*) and the Colonial Midwives Corps

In 1918, health services in French West Africa were transferred from military to civilian control.[40] Yet their military origins were carried over to the Colonial Health Service's philosophy of health care and are visible in its authoritarian, bureaucratic organizational structure, which continued to be character-ized by "medical apartheid."[41] Its *cadre supérieur* was made up of ex-army and foreign doctors and its *cadre inférieur* of African medical auxiliaries.

To fulfill its mandate to enlarge "the cadre of medical assistants . . . [and ori-ent them] toward hygiene and preventive and social medicine,"[42] to reduce in-fant mortality, and to increase the productivity of the labor force,[43] the French colonial administration embarked on a campaign to build an infrastructure of medical posts. By 1946, they had established 152 such posts throughout the AOF.[44] Each post was headed by a doctor (*médecin-chef de lieu*), who was aided by male or female nurses and a midwife. The ideal was that each post would have a car with a chauffeur, in order that personnel could make inspection tours, carry out vaccination campaigns, and evacuate those needing emergency medi-cal care. The cadre supérieur did undertake regular inspection tours to super-vise the work of the medical auxiliaries in the posts under their jurisdiction, but the reality was that only a few posts had cars. Medical personnel made their rounds by bicycle.[45] Because of logistical difficulties, African auxiliary person-nel often acted independently. Although the cadre supérieur had more educa-tion and status and earned more, the auxiliary personnel's work was very similar to that of the cadre inférieur.[46] Materials were frequently in short supply[47] and there was a constant turnover of French and foreign doctors, who were over-worked and often spoke no local languages. The administration had such diffi-culty staffing the more remote centers that, as early as 1927–29, one-fifth of all the doctors in the AOF were in Dakar.[48]

As a member of the Health Service's medical team, a colonial midwife was responsible for a wide range of tasks.[49] She supervised obstetric and infant care, promoted health education, and managed maternity wards on medical posts. Her duties were strictly regulated by a series of administrative decrees (*arrêtes*). She was authorized to give vaccinations, but legally obligated to call upon an auxiliary doctor in cases of difficult or pathological births.[50] Only certain kinds of medical instruments could be included in her *trousseau de sage-femme*. The medications she could use and prescribe were confined to "a list . . . fixed by the code made by medical specialists."[51] At baby-weighing clinics and during con-sultations she instructed mothers about personal hygiene during pregnancy, vaccinations, reproductive matters, nutrition, and general hygiene and sanita-tion (clean drinking water, the danger of dirty hands). She encouraged women's use of maternity centers as educational resource centers for matters pertaining to maternal and child health and other issues of interest to women.[52] In addi-tion, she trained traditional birth attendants (TBAs) and maternity assistants.[53] Management of a post's maternity center necessitated organizing the work en-vironment; hiring, training and supervising personnel; and ordering and main-taining supplies. A midwife had to secure the collaboration of clients and sub-ordinates, to whom Western hygienic practices made little cultural sense, in order to enforce and maintain the hygienic standards which she learned at the School of Midwifery. The continuous supervision of maternity personnel, who were responsible for cleaning, laundry, and cooking, necessitated considerable social skill. Kéita was criticized for three months by staff who did not like her *toubab*[54] rules about keeping the maternity clean, but she "remained insensible, if not indifferent and uncompromising," until "people understood and the situation reverted to normal" (95; see also 68).

A novice midwife generally began her career at an isolated post, moving to less isolated, better-equipped posts as she gained experience and seniority.[55] It was Colonial Health Service policy to send auxiliary medical staff to posts in areas other than their place of origin. For this reason, a midwife sometimes had to learn a new language before she could do her work effectively.[56] Indeed, Aoua Kéita's career reflects the mobility midwives could experience. Between 1931 and 1956 she worked at eleven posts, her stay at each varying from less than six months to six years.[57] A midwife could augment her salary by working overtime, but there was a limit on overtime earnings. She could also supplement her wages by delivering the children of Europeans and Lebanese.[58]

As in the military, employees of the Health Service could move upward through a number of grades. Once a colonial midwife reached a certain rank, she was obligated to take a six-month refresher course, followed by an examination, to qualify for promotion. Midwives usually took this course after six to eight years.[59]

> [T]he refresher course . . . best serves to demonstrate the extent to which the students who have qualified at the school have made good in their profession. Of the twenty-five midwives who underwent the refresher course by 1934, ten were classed as "excellent," while eleven have exhibited a satisfactory measure of devotion to their work and an adequate capacity for resisting that temptation to stagnation which besets the path of every practitioner who has to bury himself away in the bush.[60]

There were eight grades, or ranks, in the Health Service. Thirty percent of midwives reached the four highest. The salary paid at the lowest rank (*3è classe stagiare*) was approximately half that paid at the highest (*principale 1ère classe*).[61] Kéita made her way through the ranks, although it took her seven years to be promoted from the second highest to the highest.

The Long Arm of the Job[62] (1): Encountering Resistance

Bearing children is a fundamental aspect of African women's social identity, in no small part because economic production in Africa is largely dependent on human labor power. For this reason, children are viewed as sacred,[63] motherhood as a benediction, and childbearing as a sign of women's strength and power.[64] Because childbirth can lead to the death of both mother and infant, several cultures conceptualize it metaphorically as women's "field of battle." Kéita writes,

> Sonrai, Bambara, Wolof, Malinke, Kassonke, Sere, Samo, Peul, Diola, Sarakole, and Bobo women that I had occasion to assist in the course of my long career as a midwife, all had the same behavior when faced with the pain of childbirth, with rare

exceptions. . . . Because of the value given to personal honor, [they] . . . make it a point of honor to give birth without expressing their suffering [so as not to bring shame on their families or themselves]. (260–61, 262)

The eternal refrain is the following: women do not participate in battle, nor in hunting parties, nor do they fish. . . . The field of battle is childbirth, whose pain they must support with courage and dignity. . . . For them, it is an ordeal which must be supported in honor. They have only the right to invoke the name of God. (261)

Indeed, as several authors have shown, African women could enhance their social status through ritual elaboration of their childbearing roles.[65]

Cognizant of the significance Africans accorded to childbearing, the French administration believed that African women would welcome the "superior" birthing techniques introduced by colonial midwives,[66] yet the opposite proved to be true. African women welcomed colonial midwives' ability to save mother and infant in times of crisis, but otherwise strongly resisted the birthing practices the French promoted.

There were many reasons for this resistance. African women of childbearing age did not find the French model of childbirth easy to assimilate to their own knowledge systems and beliefs. Moreover, postmenopausal women who were TBAs saw no need to cede their power and status to colonial midwives. More importantly, perhaps, colonial midwives' class identity as évolués, their toubab habits, and their ethnocentrism interfered with their efforts to promote the French model of childbirth.[67]

In her autobiography, Kéita conscientiously reports African women's resistance to the type of care dispensed at government maternity centers:

Next, the new mothers and their women friends began to dance and all of them formed an impenetrable block against me. Then the rumor began to sweep through the town: "Aoua has begun to tire the women with her toubab ways, she forbids spitting on the ground, this is unforgivable. Sick mothers don't even have the right to keep a little plate of rice under their bed. She separates mothers and babies, the former in their beds, the latter in their cribs. We've never seen that before." They all condemned me.[68] (95)

In addition to contesting maternity rules concerning infant care, eating, and cleanliness, African women, who delivered their babies in an upright or stooping position on mats at home, were unfamiliar with delivering in a supine position on beds.[69] Moreover, women who gave birth in maternity centers missed the constant emotional and social support of friends and family members.[70] Women remained in the maternity centers for seven to eleven days, and visitors were not allowed during siesta hours. It was customary for women who gave birth at home to be visited by women friends during those hours.

As the first colonial midwife posted to Gao, Kéita was thrust into a situation in which local women who "had never known what a midwife was" strongly distrusted anything European and hid from her to avoid pelvic examinations (28, 31).[71] Her work was "limited [at first] . . . to caring for mothers and infants after the birth, cutting the umbilical cord, disinfecting the eyes, [and] examining the placenta" (32). As a result of her more spectacular procedures, however —"digital *curetage* in the case of hemorrhage after an abortion, . . . artificial deliveries, animation of infants who appear to be stillborn . . . " (32)—Kéita won the local population's respect and earned a "sensational" reputation. Babies were born at home until 1936 when, due largely to Kéita's efforts, the first maternity center opened (45).

Colonial midwives' ethnocentrism sometimes prevented them from responding appropriately when confronted with culturally distinctive behavior. The Moors, according to Kéita, valued the husband's presence at birth. When she assisted a Moor woman at childbirth, she did not know how to manage the woman's husband's presence:

> I was amused for a short while [by the husband's comings and goings]. Then, I simply freed the poor man, ordering him not to come back to the maternity until after the baby had been born. (260)

Yet working among various peoples gave colonial midwives a comparative perspective on birthing and reproductive beliefs. Though a "Bambara," Kéita was critical of a belief held by Bambara speakers that a child whose first bath was not done properly would have a disagreeable odor all its life. On the other hand, she considered some indigenous practices as efficacious as, and even superior to, French practices. She describes approvingly how the "infants of the Kingdom of the Askias" (in Gao) are "washed" with a fine, clean sand especially prepared for that purpose, and then confesses that

> we, midwives at that epoch, washed the little Africans with a lot of water to keep our clientele. However, at the principal hospital in Dakar, the first bath of newborn Europeans was made with paraffin oil and was not given to the child until the umbilical cord had fallen off and the wound caused by cutting the cord had healed completely. (268–70)

Kéita's confession reveals an irony—the way colonial midwives bathed newborns gave African women ideas about what was "modern" which devalued even those local practices which colonial midwives approved. When Kéita asks her readers how "we can act to eliminate certain customs . . . without losing the support of the masses" (288), she expresses the frustrations of many évolués who sought to promote the French model of birthing and particular aspects of French culture.

The Long Arm of the Job (2): Contesting Discrimination

If Kéita dedicated herself to promoting a French model of birthing, she also continually and publicly opposed French colonialism and the inequities associated with it. As members of the health workers' union (Symedvétopharsa), she and other members of the midwifery corps participated in strikes held throughout the AOF in 1945 and 1952 to protest French colonial policies (253–57). Moreover, she did not subscribe to the belief, widespread in the French Soudan, that women were inferior to men. Her contestation of gender discrimination began at an early age. As "emancipated" women, colonial midwives were somewhat exempt from traditional expectations of female subordination, but this did not protect them from gender discrimination. Kéita was on friendly terms with a number of French expatriates and other Europeans whom she considered *large d'esprit* (progressive; 44). But as an African woman working with male European and African medical colleagues, she had to negotiate carefully to promote her interests in a context in which social and cultural rules governing gendered behavior supported white and male interests. For example, Kéita describes how shocked she was by racial discrimination on the Niger River steamer she took to travel to remote Gao shortly after graduating from the School of Midwifery. All African passengers except Kéita herself, including her twelve-year-old sister, were confined to third- and fourth-class steerage (29).

In another example, Kéita describes how, during her exile in the Casamance for her anti-French activism (discussed below), she met the inspector general of the Colonial Health Service. He confided to her that she had been sent to a relatively pleasant place, rather than the distant AEF, because she had prepared a meal for him many years before when, as a *médecin commandant* on tour, his car had broken down. It was "an act he would never forget in life" (190). Their conversation over, the inspector general got up, shook Kéita's hand cordially, and ordered his chauffeur to drive away:

> From his car, which took off violently, he made a little gesture of goodbye with his left hand as a sign of friendship to me, but it also conveyed a shocking and undisguised paternalism. (191)

As "emancipated" women, colonial midwives were highly critical of the male mentality (African or French) which supported male privilege. Most also had deep respect for women's social and political aspirations for equality and were critical of African women who believed that women should be subordinate to men.[72] Kéita frequently found it necessary to assert her right to speak for herself (and the right of other women to speak for themselves) when men—African and French—tried to keep her silent (13, 66, 91, 144). She addressed the problem of male colleagues' chauvinism in her first public speech, made at the Symedvétopharsa Congress in 1954, in which she delivered a "pressing call to unmarried doctors and midwives, inviting them to work with greater solidarity and understanding in order to establish, if not peaceful coexistence, at least a climate of cooperation and reciprocal confidence" (292). Kéita reports that her struggles against hypocritical male colleagues, whose publicly avowed belief in gender equality did not prevent them from dominating female colleagues when it was in their interest to do so, were "especially appreciated" by other midwives (292).

The Long Arm of the Job (3): Bridging Difference

Colonial midwives searched for ways to bridge the class and cultural gap that separated them from the peoples among whom they worked. Kéita found that class-based bureaucratic procedures were not effective. In the Casamance, she issued certificates to thirty pregnant women "forbidding them to work in the rice beds" in the last months of pregnancy. Four women thanked her, but the others laughed and asked her, "how and with what are my husband and children going to live if I don't produce rice?" (211). She had greater success bridging African and European worldviews when she operated on the basis of friendship. Her use of friendship with local women to promote French birthing techniques and her own political values is a model of how politics across difference can work.[73] Africans defined maternity centers as "female" space, out of men's hearing, where women were free to express themselves.[74] Kéita, who was an accomplished seamstress, encouraged local women to join her to sew on the verandah of the maternity, and in some cases in her living quarters, during siesta hours. Once the women gathered, conversation inevitably moved beyond fashion to more serious topics, such as family and political life. As a result of the solidarity that developed between the women, they organized *mutuelles des femmes* (women's mutual aid groups) in some of these regional centers to help with family ritual celebrations, such as baptisms, marriages, and funerals (299). In three centers, the women redefined the functions of the *mutuelle des femmes* to include political action. Colonial midwives especially favored developing working relationships with TBAs, whom they believed "could play an important role in our campaigns . . . [if they were] well trained and conscientious" (279). But the desired collaboration between the two types of professionals rarely materialized.[75] As members of specialized kin groups in which knowledge about reproduction and birthing was passed down from mothers to daughters, TBAs were often reluctant to share their knowledge with outsiders.[76]

Among many Soudanese groups, responsibility for young women's sexual education was given to older women who were prenuptial ritual specialists, called *magnamagans* in Bambara. Kéita felt that there was a "great" need to educate young people about sexual behavior and venereal disease, but that "the customs and manners of our country did not permit a young midwife . . . to deal with" these topics (271).[77] She regarded some of the instruction she received from a magnamagan at the time of her own marriage as useful, but most as "stupid" (272, 274). The prenuptial education magnamagans gave was one of the matters colonial midwives wished to "clean up" (*nettoyer*). But Kéita's ability to make friends with local women sometimes gave her an opportunity to learn more about TBAs and prenuptial rituals. She describes a conversation between herself and Sokona Dioune, a Sarakole magnamagan and TBA, whom she met when she was posted to Nara near the Mauritanian border, and who, like Kéita, opposed polygamy (281–87). Viewing loss of blood before birth, breech presentations, and other problems as "signs of mourning," Dioune asked Kéita to give her, "in the name of . . . friendship" and despite their "difference in ethnicity, age, and condition . . . the secrets that the whites had given her in this domain" (275, 278). Yet Dioune declined Kéita's invitation to participate in the training workshop Kéita organized for traditional birth attendants, citing her belief that knowledge and practices surrounding birth should be passed on from mother to daughter, and shrugging off Kéita's suggestion that her "secrets" could only be obtained through long exposure to the French educational system. Dioune saw no need to go to French schools. Kéita avowed that she did not intend to condemn magnamagans (273), but wanted only "to demonstrate how young women can go to extremes in their effort to practice all the recommendations that magnamagans give them in good faith" (288). Thus, Kéita informed Dioune's initiates about ways to avoid getting pneumonia from the cold baths that were part of the training (278). Writing two decades later, Kéita noted with "satisfaction" that not for twenty years had magnamagans assisted in a "newly married couple's first contact," and that social attitudes toward the sexual education of girls may also "adapt . . . harmoniously with the country's evolution" (274).

The relationship between Aoua Kéita and Sokona Dioune shows that TBAs "were drawn unwittingly into the dominion of European 'civilization' while at the same time often contesting its presence and the explicit content of its worldview."[78] Kéita's efforts to protect Dioune's initiates from the dangers she saw in Dioune's training reveal aspects of the social dynamic through which colonial midwives were implicated in the hegemonic processes which undermined local medical practitioners' knowledge and practices. Having adopted the French medical establishment's attitudes toward magnamagans, Kéita misunderstood the significance of and did not acknowledge the importance of their knowledge and ritual activity.

Kéita may not have valued Dioune's expertise as a ritual specialist, but she did value her as an ally in the emerging women's movement against polygyny. She discovered that developing friendships with local women was an effective strategy for political mobilization. In her efforts to mobilize support for the independence movement, Kéita sought out local women leaders as allies and encouraged them to work with her to promote their common interests (96).[79] In political matters, Kéita valued local women's points of view; reciprocally, local women appreciated Kéita's efforts to promote their empowerment (69, 144).

The effectiveness of Kéita's mobilization of local women to promote common goals is demonstrated by the testimonials of women in Gao with whom she worked to raise support for the USRDA. Kéita was warmly welcomed by the people of Gao as a "leader" and "the mother of our children" when she returned in 1951 after an absence of thirteen years (94). Within a year, the French administration sent her into exile because her political activities were seen as a threat. On the eve of her departure, Bollo Yattara, who was the wife of a prominent merchant and who had worked with Kéita to get out electoral support for the USRDA, praised her, saying, "You are the only literate person among us.

Since you arrived, the women have become conscious of their power and the role that they must play. This is an important fact that all the world must recognize" (146). The exchange between Kéita and Dioune and the testimony of the women of Gao bring into stark relief the complex and contradictory processes in which colonial midwives were implicated as they disseminated the French model of childbirth, while at the same time actively resisting French colonial power.

Conclusion

It is a paradox that, in disseminating Western science in the form of the French model of childbirth, colonial midwives contributed to processes which both eroded aspects of local women specialists' knowledge and authority about childbirth and the sexual education of marriageable girls, and mobilized women to promote their collective interests as women and to oust the colonial "masters." Colonial midwives appreciated the fact that local African women operated in a material and scientific context which was socially and psychologically very different from their own, but, as the beneficiaries of French colonial education, they were uncritical of male-biased Western technology and science, which they viewed as the key to the modernization of their own societies. For this reason, colonial midwives participated in the French medical establishment's attack on magnamagans, whose practices they viewed as both inferior to and incompatible with modern science.

Only a few of the newly independent states, such as Guinea and Mali, opted to put their resources into public health promotion following the pattern introduced by the French colonial administration.[80] Yet an increasing number of health activists are working to ensure greater collaboration between cosmopolitan and traditional health workers in their efforts to improve maternal and infant health, eradicate female genital mutilation, and lower maternal fertility rates in order to slow down population growth.[81] Charles Good, a development theorist who believes that Africans' health needs would be better served by strengthening the interface between modern and traditional medical practices, regrets the closing of the Dakar medical center, which he regards as an "outstanding colonial program."[82] Like Aoua Kéita, some health activists are effectively collaborating with TBAs.

The contradiction between the debt colonial midwives felt to the colonizers, who introduced a whole "arsenal of modern discoveries"[83] to French West Africa, and their contestation of the French administration's power, exemplified in their participation as Health Union members in the general strikes of 1945 and 1952, is fundamental to understanding midwives' and other évolués' professional identity. As "emancipated women," colonial midwives were influential in disseminating the évolué lifestyle to the mass of the people. Their advocation of young people's right to choose their own spouses, women's right to participate in political life, and women's economic autonomy grew out of their reevaluation of African social, familial, and conjugal traditions, as well as their defense of women's interests in the face of opposition from their évolué brothers and the more conservative older generation. Upholding an image of African women as hard-working and economically independent, colonial midwives opposed the lifestyle adopted by some urban bourgeois women who expected their wage-earning husbands to support them in leisurely dependence (240). Aoua Kéita played a leading role in the populist movement to reform marriage laws and to eradicate polygyny. As a colonial midwife, she was a pioneer in the continuing struggle of African women to gain greater freedom of expression and greater control over their lives and bodies.

Primary Document

Aoua Kéita, *Femme d'Afrique* (Paris: Présence africaine, 1975), pp. 276–79. Translated by Jane Turrittin.

One day when we were alone . . . Sokona said to me, "Aoua Gaffoure, you know that my mother is a midwife like you?"

"No, Sokona, I didn't know that."

"Ah, well, she is the one who assists all the women at Goumbou. . . . Like her grandmother and her mother, she began as a magnamagan and became a midwife later. In my maternal family, all the women exercise that profession, if God gives them a long life and strength. After the age of forty, they teach the profession of magnamagan to their daughters and they exercise the profession of midwife starting about the age of forty-five or fifty, after the menopause."

"What is the relationship between menopause and the profession of midwife?"

"It is when a woman no longer menstruates and is normally no longer obliged to be occupied during the night, so that she has plenty of time to conscientiously occupy herself with childbirth, women giving birth, and babies. In a few years, I will have to go live in Goumbou so that I will be able to accompany my mother to the villages where she always goes to help women in labor. Thus I will undergo my apprenticeship and be able to effectively replace her on the day of her disappearance, which I hope will be as far in the future as possible."

"But why don't you do your apprenticeship with me, here?" I said to her. "I have trained and equipped numerous midwives in Kita, Tougan, and Gao."

"No, Gaffoure, among us Soninkes this profession is only taught by mothers to daughters. And that's not all. In order to do this work, there are magic, beneficent words to be used while massaging women's stomachs that you others, toubabs, are able neither to understand nor to teach. . . . I prefer to be initiated by my mother, who will at the same time convey all the secrets and necessary talismans to me, as she did when she initiated me to my present profession, which I now exercise to my clients' satisfaction. However, my dear Aoua, I have something to confide to you, and I caution you to discretion, because I would be very upset if the midwives of Ouagadou got word of it."

"I am listening, Sokona; you can be sure that I will keep your secret."

"*Voila!* As soon as the midwives of my region are confronted with a breech presentation, a shoulder or a face, they make a somber prognosis. . . . Unfortunately, it is often the death of the two [mother and infant]. . . . Loss of blood before childbirth and the prolapse of the umbilical cord are both considered signs of mourning. For us, all infants who come by the posterior, the arm, or the mouth, all those who show their cords early, are not called to life. Often they drag their mothers toward death. It is said in town that you manage to keep mother and child in good health when faced with these sorts of presentations. The praise-singer from Boumba, Faragaba, whom you saved and whose daughter is named after you, speaks about it wherever she goes. . . . In the name of our close friendship, I would like you to give me the secrets the whites have given you about these things."

After having furnished Sokona with some explanations about abnormal presentations which worry any midwife, I added, "What I have just told you can only be acquired after certain instruction. It is necessary to go to school in Nara to earn the primary certificate, then to secondary school in Bamako. Finally, for a proper technical education, it is necessary to pass an examination and to go to Dakar or to France. . . . "

Sokona, who listened to me with a particular attention, sneezed at the end of my exposé. She declared, "God approves the truth of that which you have just said. You have not put tobacco in my nostrils. One only sneezes spontaneously at the truth."

NOTES

1.   Ringenbach and Guyomarch, "Notes de géographie médicale de la section française de la mission de délimitation Afrique équatoriale française–Cameroun en 1912–1913: variole, paludisme, maladies vénériennes," *Bulletin de la Société de pathologie exotique* 8 (1915), p. 202, quoted in Rita Headrick and Daniel R. Headrick, *Colonialism, Health, and Illness in French Equatorial Africa, 1885–1935* (Atlanta: African Studies Association Press, 1994), p. 46.

2.   Pascale Barthélemy, "La formation des institutrices africaines en A.O.F.: Pour une lecture historique du roman de Mariama Ba, *Un si longue lettre,*" *CLIO* 6 (1997), p. 158.

3.   The Dakar training center served as a model for the Yaba Medical Training College, established in Nigeria in 1930. Adell Patton, Jr., *Physicians, Colonial Racism, and Diaspora in West Africa* (Gainesville: University Press of Florida, 1996), p. 33. See also David Arnold, *Imperial Medicine and Indigenous Societies* (Manchester: Manchester University Press, 1988); and Roy MacLeod and

Milton Lewis, eds., *Disease, Medicine, and Empire: Perspectives on Western Medicine and the Experience of European Expansion* (New York: Routledge, 1988).

4. See Megan Vaughan, "Health and Hegemony: Representation of Disease and the Creation of the Colonial Subject in Nyasaland," in *Contesting Colonial Hegemony: State and Society in Africa and India,* ed. Dagmar Engels and Shula Marks (London: British Academic Press, 1994), p. 184.

5. Mary Elizabeth Carnegie, *The Path We Tread: Blacks in Nursing Worldwide, 1854–1994* (New York: National League for Nursing, 1995), p. 275.

6. LaRay Denzer, "Women in Government Service in Colonial Nigeria, 1862–1945" (Boston, Mass.: Boston University, African Studies Center, Working Papers in African Studies no. 136, 1989), p. 6.

7. G. Wesley Johnson, "The Impact of the Senegalese Elite upon the French, 1900–1940," in *Double Impact: France and Africa in the Age of Imperialism,* ed. G. Wesley Johnson (Westport, Conn.: Greenwood, 1985), p. 163.

8. Jules Carde later became governor general of the AOF. A veterinary school was established in Bamako in 1924; a training school for visiting or district nurses was created in Dakar in 1930. See W. Bryant Mumford and Major G. St. J. Orde-Brown, *Africans Learn to Be French* (1935; reprint, New York: Negro Universities Press, 1970); and A. N'Daw, "L'École des sages-femmes de Dakar," *Afrique médicale* 120 (1974): 493–96. Substantive research is needed on colonial midwives in the AOF. No scholarly study has been made of the Dakar medical training center. See K. David Patterson, "Disease and Medicine in African History: A Bibliographical Essay," *History in Africa* 1, no. 1 (1974): 141–48; and Judith N. Lasker, "The Role of Health Services in Colonial Rule: The Case of the Ivory Coast," *Culture, Medicine, and Psychiatry* 1 (1977): 277–97. Dr. M. Sankalé's overview of the development of the French colonial medical service, *Médecins et action sanitaire en Afrique noire* (Paris: Présence africaine, 1969), lacks theoretical and critical sophistication. For an excellent analysis of the influence of metropolitan women's beliefs about infant welfare on practices in the Belgian Congo, see Nancy Hunt, " 'Le Bébé en Brousse': European Women, African Birth Spacing, and Colonial Intervention in Breast Feeding in the Belgian Congo," *International Journal of African Historical Studies* 21, no. 3 (1988): 401–32. A study of the history of Western medicine in the AOF from the perspective of political economy, such as that made by the Headricks in *Colonialism, Health, and Illness* for French Equatorial Africa (*Afrique Equatoriale Française*—AEF), is needed. The Headricks document the disastrous consequences of French contact in the AEF, where epidemics of previously little-known diseases took a severe toll, and appalling conditions in work camps resulted in high death rates among migrant railroad workers. See also Jean Mark Ela, *African Cry,* trans. Robert T. Barr (Maryknoll, N.Y.: Orbis, 1985).

9. Prior to 1938, women teachers were recruited from among those who completed higher primary school. See Barthélémy, "La formation des institutrices africaines," p. 1.

10. Ten to fifteen midwives graduated annually. Between 1920 and 1953, 582 doctors graduated from the School of Medicine and 87 pharmacists from the School of Pharmacy. Between 1920 and 1934, 191 midwives, compared to 148 doctors, received diplomas. Sankalé, *Médecins et action sanitaire,* p. 39.

11. For studies of nurses in Africa, see Denzer, "Women in Government Service"; Hilda Kuper, "Nurses," in *An African Bourgeoisie: Race, Class, and Politics in South Africa*, ed. Leo Kuper (New Haven, Conn.: Yale University Press, 1965), pp. 216–33; and Shula Marks, *Divided Sisterhood* (New York: St. Martin's, 1994). For studies of professional Francophone African women in the independence period, see Diane L. Barthel, "The Rise of a Female Professional Elite: The Case of Senegal," *African Studies Review* 18, no. 3 (1975): 1–19; Danielle Bazin-Tardieu, *Femmes du Mali* (Ottawa: Lemeac, 1975); Carmel Dinan, "Pragmatists or Feminists: The Professional 'Single' Women of Accra, Ghana," *Cahiers d'études africains* 17, no. 1 (1977): 155–76; Judith Van Allen, "Memsahib, Militante, Femme Libre: Political and Apolitical Styles of Modern African Women," in *Women in Politics*, ed. Jane Jacquette (New York, 1974), pp. 304–21.

12. Aoua Kéita, *Femme d'Afrique: La vie d'Aoua Kéita racontée par elle-meme* (Paris: Présence africaine, 1975). See Jane Turritin, "Aoua Kéita and the Nascent Women's Movement in the French Soudan," *African Studies Review* 36, no. 1 (1993): 58–89, and *"Femme d'Afrique:* la vie d'Aoua Kéita racontée par elle-meme," in *Dictionnaire des oeuvres littéraires négro-africaines de langue française (1979–1989)*, ed. Ambroise Kom, 2 vols. (San Francisco: International Scholars Publications, 1996).

13. Robert Pageard, *Littérature négro-africaine d'expression française* (Paris: L'école, 1979), p. 70. This and all other translations from French sources are my own. For an overview of autobiographical and biographical literature by and about African women, see Marcia Wright, "Autobiographies, histoires de vie, et biographies de femmes africaines en tant que textes militants," *Cahiers d'études africaines* 109, issue 28, no. 1 (1988): 45–58.

14. Kéita, *Femme d'Afrique*, p. 236.

15. Sankalé, *Médecins et action sanitaire*, p. 368; Kéita, *Femme d'Afrique*, p. 252.

16. Megan Vaughan, "Introduction: Discourse, Subjectivity, and Differences," in *Curing Their Ills: Colonial Power and African Illness* (Cambridge: Polity, 1984), p. 16.

17. Barthélémy, "La formation des institutrices africaines," p. 161.

18. Ruth Schachter Morganthau, *Political Parties in French-Speaking West Africa* (Oxford: Clarendon, 1964), p. 287.

19. See Sandra Harding, "Gendered Ways of Knowing and the 'Epistemological Crisis' of the West," in *Knowledge, Difference, and Power: Essays Inspired by Women's Ways of Knowing*, ed. Nancy Rule Goldberger et al. (New York: Basic, 1996), p. 433.

20. Ibid.

21. More research is needed before the colonial midwives' corps can be examined from the point of view of the sociology of the professions. See Terence J. Johnson, *Professions and Power* (London: Macmillan, 1972); Patton, *Physicians;* Marks, *Divided Sisterhood;* Murray Last and G. L. Chavunduka, eds., *The Professionalization of African Medicine* (Manchester: Manchester University Press, 1988).

22. Marks, *Divided Sisterhood*, p. 3.

23. Vaughan, *Curing Their Ills.*

24. Maryinez Lyons, "The Power to Heal: African Medical Auxiliaries in Colonial Belgian Congo and Uganda," in Engels and Marks, *Contesting Colonial Hege-*

mony, p. 202. See also Vaughan, *Curing Their Ills,* p. 191, and David Arnold, "Public Health and Public Power: Medicine and Hegemony in Colonial India," in *Contesting Colonial Hegemony,* ed. Engels and Marks, pp. 131–51.

25.   Lyons, "Power to Heal," p. 202.

26.   Students had to attain a standard approaching that required for the Primary Certificate. A study of the entrance tests reprinted in *L'éducation africaine* (a bulletin published by the French colonial administration) over a twenty-year period shows that this standard was relatively low.

27.   Sankalé, *Médecins et action sanitaire,* p. 155.

28.   François Hacquin, *Histoire de l'art des accouchements en Lorraine des temps anciens au XXè siècle* (Saint-Nicholas-de-Port: Imprimerie STAR, 1979), pp. 254–57. See also Philip Altbach and Gail Kelly, *Education and Colonialism* (New York: Longman, 1978), p. 19; and Barthélémy, "La formation des institutrices africaines."

29.   The French had little understanding of African beliefs and practices surrounding reproduction and birth at the time the Dakar School of Midwifery was established. "[S]ome physicians were interested in the possibilities of medicinal plants [but] traditional medicine as a whole was treated as a regressive force." Albert Saurraut, *La mise en valeur des colonies françaises* (Paris: Pagot, 1923), p. 285. More positive attitudes toward traditional African medicine were expressed after independence. Dominique Traoré, author of *Pharmacopie traditionnelle du Soudan* (Paris: Présence african, 1965), wrote "to aid the Europeans . . . who arrive on this land of the Soudan with the very noble mission to *civiliser,* to become knowledgeable about the milieu in whose center they are called to live" (n.p., introduction).

30.   Peggy Sabatier, "Elite Education in French West Africa: The Era of Limits, 1903–1945," *International Journal of African Historical Studies* 11, no. 2 (1978): 252.

31.   Mumford and Orde-Brown, *Africans Learn,* p. 152.

32.   Sabatier, "Elite Education," p. 252.

33.   Mumford and Orde-Brown, *Africans Learn,* p. 152. Given our interest in examining the French medical establishment's construction of African women's sexuality, gender identity, and family roles, it would be useful to learn about the content of "infant welfare" and "public health visiting." See Vaughan, *Curing Their Ills.*

34.   Mumford and Orde-Brown, *Africans Learn,* p. 152.

35.   Lyons, "Power to Heal," p. 204.

36.   Mumford and Orde-Brown, *Africans Learn,* p. 154.

37.   Kéita, *Femme d'Afrique,* p. 26. Further quotations from this work are cited in the text. Midwives' training was three years long, compared to four years for auxiliary doctors. Mumford and Orde-Brown, *Africans Learn,* p. 154.

38.   Barthélémy, "La formation des institutrices africaines," p. 158.

39.   Nafissatou Diallo, *De Tilene au Plateau: Une enfance dakaroise* (Dakar: Nouvelles éditions africaines, 1973), p. 118. Diallo, who graduated from the School of Midwifery in the 1950s, describes her experiences as a student in her autobiography. Diallo's father criticized her for her "'*occidentalism*' but credited her with respecting the ways of her people." See also Barthélémy, "La formation des institutrices africaines," p. 158.

40.   The colonial administration had a virtual monopoly on health care delivery in

the AOF; few missionaries were involved. A separate health service, the Military Health Corps (*Corps de santé militaire*), later came under the jurisdiction of medical officers of the French Navy. See Sankalé, *Médecins et action sanitaire*, p. 32; J. H. Ricosse, "Comparative Aspects: French West and Equatorial Africa," in *Health in Tropical Africa during the Colonial Period*, ed. E. E. Sabben-Clare, D. J. Bradley, and K. Kirkwood (Oxford: Clarendon, 1980), p. 230; and Patton, *Physicians*, p. 23.

41. Its head office was in Dakar, but its general direction came from Paris. See William B. Cohen, *Rulers of Empire: The French Colonial Service in Africa* (Stanford, Calif.: Hoover Institution, 1971), p. 238 n. 124, and Headrick and Headrick, *Colonialism*, p. 412.

42. Circular from Governor General Merlin, quoted in Guy Belloncle and Georges Fournier, *Santé et développement en milieu rural africain: réflexions sur l'expérience nigérienne* (Paris: Editions économie et humanisme, 1975), p. 28.

43. See Lasker, "Role of Health Services," p. 285, and Ela, *African Cry*, p. 96. Policies to improve maternal and infant health were introduced earlier in the AOF than in the AEF. Maternal and child health were not priorities during the first phase of the colonial period (from the 1890s to the 1930s), when the French emphasized control of epidemic diseases. They became increasingly important in the 1930s, however, when population issues were "fiercely debated" as the administration grew alarmed about high infant mortality rates (Headrick and Headrick, *Colonialism*, pp. 412, 105).

44. J. Suret-Canal, *French Colonialism in Tropical Africa* (London: C. Hurst, 1971), p. 414.

45. Kéita, *Femme d'Afrique*, p. 56, 68.

46. Suret-Canal, *French Colonialism*, p. 414.

47. Ibid., p. 292; Headrick and Headrick, *Colonialism*, p. 194.

48. "Another fifth were in the rest of Senegal [though] that city and territory together had [only] one-tenth of the population of the federation." Headrick and Headrick, *Colonialism*, p. 408.

49. Diane Barthel retains the French term *sage-femme* to refer to the female professional elite in Senegal, rather than the English translation "midwife," to indicate the wide-ranging duties of these highly trained professionals. Barthel, "Female Professional Elite," p. 17.

50. Since only women were generally present at childbirth, the stipulation that an auxiliary (male) doctor be called in case of a difficult birth was culturally inappropriate. One wonders if the Colonial Health Service would have had more success promoting aseptic techniques and other aspects of reproductive health care if it had conformed to African gender expectations.

51. "Grades et diplomes d'état," *L'éducation africaine: Bulletin de l'enseignement de l'Afrique occidentale française*, nos. 8 and 9 (1951): 46.

52. Sankalé, *Médecins et action sanitaire*, p. 156; Kéita, *Femme d'Afrique*, pp. 65, 69.

53. Sankalé, *Médecins et action sanitaire*, p. 157; Kéita, *Femme d'Afrique*, p. 279.

54. The word *toubab* is widely used as a pejorative in French West Africa to refer to the "Western" lifestyle and higher standard of living characteristic of whites as well as educated black Africans.

55. As a disciplinary action, the administration sometimes sent a midwife to a post which did not correspond to her rank. Kéita, *Femme d'Afrique*, p. 203.

56. Ibid., p. 31.
57. Kéita was posted to Gao in 1931. In 1936, a year after her marriage, she and her husband, an auxiliary doctor, were posted to Kita. They moved to Tougon, in what is now Burkina Faso, in 1943; to Kayes in 1946; and, in 1947, to Niono in the Office du Niger. Kéita continued to work at the Office du Niger after her divorce, but at different posts: Kokry in 1949 and Marakala in 1950. In 1951 she returned to Goa where, as a result of her political activism, she was "disciplined" by the French administration and sent out of the Soudan to Bignona, in Senegal's Casamance region. When she returned to the Soudan in 1953, she was given a posting at Nara du Sahel, on the Mauretanian border, which did not correspond to her seniority. In 1956, she was sent to a relatively luxurious post in Kati, and finally to Bamako in 1957, where she headed the new center for the Protection of Maternal and Infant Health. Kéita regarded the post at Niono in the Office du Niger, which had a spacious, well-provisioned hospital and maternity ward made of cement, as best, and that at Nara du Sahel, which was made of wattle and dab and had very small rooms, as worst.
58. Kéita charged Europeans and Lebanese 10,000 CFA for delivering their babies. Kéita, *Femme d'Afrique*, p. 72.
59. Mumford and Orde-Brown, *Africans Learn*, p. 155.
60. Ibid., p. 156.
61. "L'arrête du 5 septembre 1953, no. 6613—règle le fonctionnement de l'École de médecin," *L'éducation africaine: Bulletin de l'enseignement de l'Afrique occidentale française*, no. 22 (1954): 15.
62. See Martin Meissner, "The Long Arm of the Job: A Study of Work and Leisure," *Industrial Relations* 10 (1971): 239–60.
63. Cyrille Aguessy, "Rôle des médecins et sages-femmes auxiliaries de l'A.O.F. dans l'assistance médicale indigène," *L'éducation africaine* 8 (1932): 198.
64. V. Y. Mudimbé, *Les corps glorieux des mots et des êtres* (Montréal: Humanitas, 1994), p. 113.
65. See, for example, Carol P. MacCormack, ed., *Ethnography of Fertility and Birth* (London and New York: Academic Press, 1982).
66. Aguessy, "Rôle des médecins," p. 198.
67. Ibid., pp. 40, 73.
68. Kéita wrote that being called toubab "pained" her because it connoted "being a stranger to the city and to the Soudan" (p. 289).
69. Kéita describes witnessing her mother give birth alone on two occasions, something which was not common among Bambara-speaking women (pp. 265–66).
70. See George Way Harley, *Native African Medicine, with Special Reference to Its Practice in the Mano Tribe of Liberia* (1941; reprint, London: Frank Cass, 1970); and Lucille F. Neuman, "Midwives and Modernization," *Medical Anthropology* 5, no. 1 (1981), special issue: 1–11.
71. See Carolyn Sargent, *Maternity, Medicine, and Power: Reproductive Decision in Urban Benin* (Berkeley: University of California Press, 1989), and Headrick and Headrick, *Colonialism*, p. 206.
72. Kéita, *Femme d'Afrique*, p. 397. Kéita's mother tried to sabotage her father's efforts to send her to school. In addition, she encountered opposition from her mother-in-law, who did not look favorably upon Kéita's role as an "eman-

cipated" woman. When it became apparent that Kéita could not bear a child, her mother-in-law insisted that her son divorce Kéita.

73.   Lorraine Code, *What Can She Know? Feminist Theory and the Construction of Knowledge* (Ithaca, N.Y.: Cornell University Press, 1994), pp. 306–12.

74.   Sankalé, *Médecins et action sanitaire*, p. 156; Kéita, *Femme d'Afrique*, pp. 65, 69.

75.   Kéita does not report that traditional birth attendants perceived her as an agent of French colonialism. See Frantz Fanon, "Medicine and Colonialism," in *The Cultural Crisis of Modern Medicine*, ed. John Ehrenreich (New York: Monthly Review, 1978), pp. 229–51, and Hazel H. Weidman, "The Transcultural View: Prerequisite to Interethnic (Intercultural) Communication in Medicine," *Social Science and Medicine* 13B (1979): 85–87. For insightful discussion of the complexities associated with interactions of midwives trained in Western medical practices and traditional birth attendants, see Carolyn Sargent, "Prospects for the Professionalization of Indigenous Midwifery in Benin," and Carol MacCormack, "The Articulation of Western and Traditional Systems of Health Care," both in Last and Chavunduka, *Professionalization of African Medicine*, pp. 137–49, 151–62; and Sargent, *Maternity, Medicine, and Power*.

76.   Arthur Kleinman, *Patients and Healers in the Context of Culture: An Exploration of the Borderland between Anthropology, Medicine, and Psychiatry* (Berkeley: University of California Press, 1980), p. 209.

77.   Female circumcision or genital mutilation was widely practiced in the former French Soudan, but Kéita does not refer to it in her autobiography. Her silence on this issue was shared by other medical observers of the time (Sankalé, *Médecins et action sanitaire*; Anne Retel-Laurentin, *Infécondité en Afrique noire: Maladies et consequences sociales* [Paris: Masson, 1974]), despite the fact that novelists Yambo Ouologuem (*Le devoir de violence* [Paris: Éditions du Seuil, 1968]) and Ahmadou Kourouma (*Les soleils des indépendances* [Paris: Édition du Seuil, 1970]) had exposed the issue to public scrutiny. Awa Thiam published interviews with African women who denounced these practices in *La parole aux negresses* (Paris: Denoel, 1978).

78.   Jean Comaroff and John Comaroff, *Of Revelation and Revolution*, vol. 1, *Christianity, Colonialism, and Consciousness in South Africa* (Chicago: University of Chicago Press, 1991), p. 26.

79.   Code, *What Can She Know?* pp. 284 ff.

80.   Fred G. Burke, *Public Administration in Africa: The Legacy of Inherited Colonial Institutions* (Syracuse, N.Y.: Maxwell Graduate School of Citizenship and Public Affairs, Syracuse University, 1967), p. 349.

81.   Charles M. Good et al., "The Interface of Dual Systems of Health Care in the Developing World: Toward Health Policy Initiatives in Africa," *Social Science and Medicine* 130 (1979): 141–54.

82.   Ibid. See also Rene Dumont, *L'Afrique noire est mal partie* (Paris: Éditions du Seuil, 1962); Ela, *African Cry*, p. 104; Thomas Kargbo, "Traditional Midwifery in Sierra Leone," in *African Medicine in the Modern World* (University of Edinburgh, Centre of African Studies, 1986), pp. 87–113.

83.   Fanon, "Medicine and Colonialism," p. 237.

Part Two.   *Perceptions and Representations*

Through critical readings of archival documents (court records, census statistics, police files, and missionary records) and oral materials that recall the colonial period and its aftermath, this section explores perceptions and representations of African women. The contributors treat "perception" as a process of cultural interpretation and consider "representation" a political act whereby particular ideologies (patriarchy, modernity, racism) shape perceptions of reality. Although concerned with a range of times and places, the chapters grapple with the common and salient perception, often shared by colonial officials, missionaries, and indigenous elite men, that wayward, recalcitrant, or rebellious women were disrupting the "traditional" family ideal. The perceived problem of unruly women necessitated the disciplining of female bodies, behavior, thought, and mobility.

4 The Politics of Perception or Perception as Politics? Colonial and Missionary Representations of Baganda Women, 1900–1945

Nakanyike Musisi

In 1897, under the auspices of the Church Missionary Society (CMS), Dr. Albert Cook and Catherine Thompson (later to become Mrs. Cook) arrived in Buganda to embark on a project that saw the establishment of Uganda's modern medical structure. Until their deaths, the two worked tirelessly on Baganda social and medical issues. They founded hospitals, maternity training schools, and maternity and child welfare centers; led a campaign for moral purity; headed commissions of inquiry; and presented papers at both national and international conferences. They published widely on their perceptions of illness and health among the Baganda, particularly among women and children. Their medical writings expressed concern over certain social and biological aberrations (Baganda women's supposedly deformed pelvises) and over what they considered to be a pathological diminishing of a "virile race,"—the Baganda. Indeed, the entire Ugandan medical structure that developed around their pioneering work began from this one great concern: that the Baganda, as a "race," would be extinct within a few years.[1]

Hardly any aspect of the "natives'" lives escaped the observing eyes of early colonialists and missionaries such as the Cooks, or was left undiscussed in their papers, letters, and memoirs. Over the years, this colonial writing enterprise has attained the status of an archive that academic researchers are required to consult. Attracted by the long debate between Dr. Cook and other colonial doctors about the nature of Baganda women's pelvises, I offer in this chapter a critique of missionary and colonial representations of Baganda women that embodied a series of assumptions about them, and of the politics those representations engendered. I locate Cook's representation of Baganda women's gynecological anatomy within the larger context of the politics of "seeing" and "writing" in a colonial setting. Representation, whether by colonial administrators or by missionaries, is an interpretative process, and it took place in a historically and socioculturally charged period of unequal power relations between Europeans and the Baganda.

The essay is composed of five sections. Section one presents "eyes and pens" as indispensable constructors of colonialism. Section two explores colonial processes of hierarchization and marginalization. "Under Dr. Cook's Microscopic Observation," the third section, exposes the danger of accepting scientific knowledge at face value. The fourth section locates Cook's perception and representation of Baganda women's gynecological problems in the ambit of power. It argues that the representations created by depictions in colonial and missionary reports, learned and refereed journals, private correspondence, and artifact collections, as well as in photographs, were not simply secondary to the practices and realities of a colonial encounter in Buganda. These depictions constituted political actualities in themselves. The final section considers the value and limitations of focusing on an archive.

I begin from the premise that colonial and missionary records in London, Entebbe, and elsewhere constitute a series of evidentiary fragments which record colonial administrators' and missionaries' activities.[2] These sources' conception of the "true" nature of the Baganda rested on two basic fallacies. First was the idea that the Baganda were a distinct and separate culture and a people that needed to be saved from extinction. Second was the quasi-scientific thinking espoused mostly in medical writings. I argue that the knowledge contained in missionary and colonial documents, such as Cook's, is not only inherently partial but also ideologically committed and culturally biased. More broadly, I try to show why colonial and missionary documents should draw our attention to the historical conditions of knowledge production and power within which perception and representation take shape. We must read missionaries' and colonial administrators' documents as expressions of how they perceived the "natives" and consider their context: why they were written, by whom, and for whom. Most of these documents were not intended for the colonized population. They were aimed at readers in the colonial metropolis and were intended to incite debate and provoke sympathy and curiosity. Within this broader context, this chapter explores both the perception that the Baganda were in danger of extinction and the representations of Baganda women that that perception produced.

On Sources: Eyes and Pens in the Construction of Images

I ought to say that, while many of the missionaries do realize how much we value and depend upon Annual Letters, it is not universally realized that they are not a luxury for us but an absolute necessity. . . . I am tempted to utter a reminder that the writing of Annual Letters is one of the Regulations to which all missionaries have agreed![3]

It is now virtually a truism that knowledge is power. In a colonial setting, what was observed and committed to writing became knowledge. For this reason, keen observation and writing came to be considered central to what travelers, colonial administrators, and missionaries did in Africa. The above quotation is just one example of an admonition from CMS headquarters in Salisbury Square, London, to missionaries in the field. Europeans who labored in Africa gained fame for their skill in recording their observations.[4] The images they created were widely circulated in books, learned journals, magazines, memoirs, and pamphlets. The colonial home office, as well as religious and lay sponsors, required Europeans to write detailed daily, monthly, and annual descriptions.

Though not all were published, these documents offered missionaries and colonialists a privileged venue through which they were able to confirm their identity as members of a "higher civilization." Equally important, "they could also account for themselves, [and] reflect on and transmit that construction of self and the work they were engaged in back to those at home."[5] And, for the most part, the authors represented themselves in a rather positive light. The reason is transparent. They had constituencies; they needed to advertise their work, satisfy their donors, and solicit recruits and funds. In 1923, G. F. Saywell, the CMS editorial secretary, wrote,

> One of our greatest problems here at home is how to keep the supporters of the society well informed as to the progress of the work in the field. For there is no doubt that interest in missionary work, if it is to be vital and permanent, and if it is to result in adequate gifts and personal service, must be based upon knowledge. . . . it is an additional help when the letter gives us some local colour, some description of the background and the changing conditions under which work is done . . . last but not least, something of its disappointments and anxieties. . . . [Letters from missionaries are necessary] to give our best assistance to the supporters of the society at home, to enter into a sympathetic understanding of your work and its many problems.[6]

Five years later, the general secretary of the CMS, Wilson Cash, was more explicit: "We at home are responsible for keeping the home fire burning, and it is upon the continual supply of information and news that the prayers' backing depends."[7] In this effort, African societies were observed, imagined, and projected in ways that were not always entirely consistent with, nor reflective of, reality.

Culture, Ethnicity and Race, and Gender: Strategies of Hierarchization and Marginalization

The fact that the Baganda received the first travelers and missionaries with pomp and ceremony earned them the notorious label of "collaborators" in earlier histories of African responses to colonialism.[8] The welcome the travelers and missionaries received influenced their perceptions of the Baganda. Early travel, missionary, and colonial accounts often called the Baganda the "most advanced and intelligent" of all central African societies.[9] Colonel Lambkin, quoting Sir Harry Johnston, described them as "the Japanese of the dark continent, the most naturally civilized, charming, kind, tactful, and courteous of black people."[10] Travelers, colonialists, and missionaries did not reflect on their bias toward the Baganda, precisely because the Baganda were welcoming or fought on their side.[11] The fact that they did so was taken as indicative of their innate, essential nature. Perceiving the Baganda as exceptional allowed Europeans to essentialize them in the colonial discourse of governance of the Uganda Protectorate.

Europeans imagined that the Baganda belonged to a distinct political and social order and were thus privileged over other ethnic and cultural groups in the area. According to Sir Harry Johnston, Buganda was

> perhaps one of the best organised and most civilised of African kingdoms at the present day. In fact, putting aside the empires of Abyssinia and Morocco (as entirely independent states ranking with other world powers), Uganda would take a high place among those purely Negro kingdoms which retain any degree of national rule.[12]

Buganda's cultural and political institutions were thus perceived as worth exporting to adjacent conquered territories, and its distinctive order worth preserving, even if certain faults would need to be addressed through planning, education, medical science, and Christianity. Buganda was an "ideal" model through which indirect rule could be effected. As such, it required not only "protection" and codification of its "native customs and laws," but also a precise anthropological diagnosis. John Roscoe, first a missionary and later the first amateur anthropologist in Buganda, championed this conviction.[13] Yet some missionaries perceived Buganda differently. They disagreed with Roscoe and saw only barbarism and an absence of order in Buganda's institutions and culture. For example, Archdeacon Walker showed open disgust at Roscoe's decision to return to Uganda as an anthropologist rather than as a missionary. He reviled Roscoe's work as "hunting about in the rubbish heaps of Uganda for foolish and unclean customs."[14]

Although Europeans disagreed about what in Buganda needed to be preserved and institutionalized, they all agreed that certain customs and aspects of culture needed to be refined by colonial administration and the missionary projects. At the heart of this refining was the colonial policy of indirect rule through collaboration with elite male Baganda chiefs: a "modern" form of government founded on the consent of the governed.[15] Indirect rule was formalized in 1900, when the colonial government and the Baganda male elite, with the help of missionaries, signed the Buganda Agreement. The agreement secured for the Baganda a special status in the colony and an endorsement of their cultural and political institutions. But it was premised on and stressed cultural, racial, and gender differences. Indirect rule provided for the ideological procedures by which the cultural space and practices of the Baganda were observed, imagined, and disrupted. The images which resulted were then reinscribed according to the needs of the British colonial project: eugenics (reproduction), administration (governance), extraction of resources, and ideology (spiritual and religious, educational, and moral).

Baganda chiefs fully cooperated with the colonial and missionary projects and were always delighted to see the colonial government and missionaries perceiving "realities" in the Kiganda way, and refining those aspects of culture or politics which did not fit Buganda's imagined status as a "great nation."[16] They were particularly concerned with gender and class issues. For example, although the founding of Gayaza Girls School in 1906 caused some anxiety among chiefs, four years later chiefs had become staunch supporters and patrons of the school. In the presence of about fifty important chiefs, Prime Minister Apolo Kagwa, Buganda's prime policy maker, congratulated the missionaries on their success and contrasted aristocratic girls' current activities with their "former idle existence . . . concerned with mainly dressing their finger nails and letting them grow long." He stressed that "such girls now did the ordinary work of women, [and are] not being spoilt," as those who opposed female education assumed them to be.[17] In their efforts to preserve customs and traditions, the British reshaped gender and class configurations through biased laws and regulations.[18]

Indeed, gender became a crucial dimension in the politics of preservation, protection, modification, and Christianization of the "great nation." In the end, the treatment of women became the key measure of Buganda's greatness and its ability to advance as a modern nation. Missionary and colonial images of Kiganda practices that debased women were held up as reasons for Buganda's regretful state and failure to progress.[19] At least prior to 1900, the missionaries were for the most part restricted to the capital, and what they saw of women's condition and treatment was not necessarily representative of the rest of Buganda. But these were the images they sent back home.[20] According to the missionaries' ideological, essentialist, and culturally biased worldview, the Baganda needed to be saved from dying out as a race, and this depended on the roles of women.

One fact is clear: missionaries, the Buganda Lukiiko (parliament), the colonial state, and anthropologists all agreed that women had to play a central role in the regeneration of Buganda and its progress toward modernity. The new representations envisioned women as the embodiment not only of civilization but equally of moral Christian order. "Civilization" thus required their emancipation, in every realm from hygiene and home management to the bearing and rearing of children. Within this framework, womanhood was equated with motherhood and motherhood equated with wifehood. The perception that Buganda was in a state of moral, nutritional, and medical crisis lent additional force to social engineering efforts that specifically focused on the significant role women were expected to play in societal rejuvenation. Perceived as free, yet as a "beast of burden," ignorant and diseased, the woman/wife/mother thus became the target not only of colonial and missionary education policies but also of medical examinations, practices, and policies.[21] Baganda women became objects of scientific inquiry and thus gave missionaries, colonial administrators, and the Bugandan state entry into the most private aspects of Baganda lives. Cook's argument that Baganda women's gynecological problems were a result of their status as "beasts of burden" is perhaps the best illustration of the power of "scientific knowledge" in the politics of perception and the construction of the "other."

Under Dr. Cook's Microscopic Observation: Baganda Women's Pelvises, Scientific Knowledge, and the Construction of the "Other"

Concerned about the imminent demise of the Baganda, Cook set out to do two things. First, he sought to observe and classify the causes of depopulation and the factors influencing health and mortality rates. Second, he proposed solutions to the problem. His inquiries were all based, however, on one central assumption (paranoid fantasy?), which was endlessly repeated: that the "uncontrollable sexual drive of the Baganda, which was combined with disease and ignorance, damaged their fertility."[22] According to his research, the causes for this regretful situation fell into three categories: harmful native customs and behavior, sexually transmitted diseases, and ignorance of Western medicine.[23] Cook wrote,

> we have three principle foes to attack. For long ages, entrenched behind the triple ramparts of ignorance, superstition and dirt, i.e. unsanitary conditions, they have defied attack, but now their trusted defenses are being rapidly breached and their ancient thrones are tottering. The three foes are harmful native customs . . . the widespread occurrence of syphilis, and the absence of skilled help in abnormal cases.[24]

Having taken meticulous measurements of Baganda women's pelvises, Cook became convinced that some of those "harmful native customs" caused deformity. He concluded that Baganda girls were victims of a cultural burden; because they carried heavy loads, a culturally determined female function, they were likely to suffer from "degenerate," "flattened," "deformed," and "contracted" pelvises and reproductive organs.[25] As he crystallized his perceptions into a theory, Cook became the first person in the medical history of Uganda to champion a direct link between the size and shape of women's pelvises and reproductive organs and the level of civilization. Cook's scientific discourse regarding Baganda women's bodies reversed the long-held conviction that anatomy was destiny. For Cook, culture became destiny.[26] Within this argument, maternal problems were encapsulated in culture and heathen customs.

As might be expected, Cook's view provoked an intense and potentially explosive response from doctors in the colonial administration's service. At first, the debate was conducted in private, but by 1938–39, hot disagreements were publicized in medical journals and at regional conferences. Dr. J. P. Mitchell, superintendent of Mulago Hospital and principal of its medical school, called

Dr. Cook's theory "mere guess work." Dr. R. Y. Stones considered such insistence on blaming native customs and medicine for Baganda women's antenatal difficulties "not only unfortunate" but also "dangerous." In his opinion, while the administration of native drugs was most unscientific, obstinacy like Cook's could prevent further investigation.[27] Writing in the *East African Medical Journal*, Mitchell revealed,

> I know that much can be said in favor of clinical observations against laboratory tests. Nevertheless, in our own early records I find many examples of credibility and loose thinking in relation to this subject (native medicine, culture re: obstructed labor). Fixed convictions of any kind have undoubtedly a perverting effect upon one's clinical honesty and acumen. . . . I have refrained for some years from discussing this subject publicly in the hope that by private endeavor the teaching of what I believe to be a myth would cease. I do so now because I find that it continues.[28]

But Cook hated to be challenged. He quoted scientific work published in Europe to back up his arguments and to defend himself from Mitchell's characterization of his theory as "mere guess work." He authoritatively declared, "I learnt my theoretical midwifery in the early nineties from Galabin and Guy." Quoting these well-respected authorities of his time, Cook called upon his readers to empathize with what he had observed: "Who with this in mind does not look with anxious eyes upon the little girls of five or six staggering along carrying heavy 'ensuwa' of water from the well or a massive bunch of 'matoke.'" Defiant and insistent on blaming indigenous customs and medical knowledge, Cook concluded,

> No one can have seen, as my colleagues and I have done, scores of these unnecessary deaths without endeavoring to impress on those being trained the folly of trusting to native medicine. . . . I can assure Dr. Mitchell that . . . the two great Maternity Native Training Schools in the Protectorate . . . have seen the evil effects of reliance on "native medicine.[29]

The colonial government doctors, such as Mitchell, argued for further scientific investigation into what was being propagated as a medical truth. Mitchell wrote,

> I believe that to this cause [culture] are attributed many obstetric tragedies which could be avoided by more careful investigation of the pelvic passage and its relation to the passing foetal head.[30]

Stones agreed, adding,

> If the Baganda women are peculiar in having a contracted pelvis the girls are certainly not peculiar among Africans in alone carrying heavy head loads. . . . There is undoubtedly room for further investigation in these matters. . . . Already there are signs that the Baganda, who are well known to be an intelligent people, realize the value of ante-natal examinations and are availing themselves of the opportunities of safe delivery these examinations afford their women. It is to be hoped that, thus,

early causes of obstruction . . . will be revealed and the reason for the many still-births among this people be brought to light.[31]

Colonial government doctors, such as Mitchell and Stones, disagreed not with Cook's observations but rather with his representation of the facts and his analysis of them. In reality, Cook's story of "deformed, flattened, contracted pelvises" was not just "mere guess work," as Mitchell charged. Cook was very careful in his empirical observations, noting the varying sizes of most of his Baganda women patients.[32] However, the significance of Mitchell's and Stones's critiques lies in their demand that Cook come to terms with difference. The two colonial doctors were willing to accept birth as a product of the interaction of cultural and medical preferences. Certainly, beliefs about proper roles for men and women have always shaped birth rituals, as has physiology. Indeed, as Stones pointed out,

> the custom of giving these drugs can hardly have been so long accepted if their effect were only detrimental. Native customs, even when known to be wrong, are notoriously hard to kill, but it is very reasonable to suppose that some parturient women are helped by these drugs.[33]

By refuting and correcting what they saw as medical misconception and misrepresentation, Mitchell and Stones were drawn into a public disagreement with Cook over the hypothetical links between culture, "deformed pelvises," and obstructed labor. Mitchell attempted to correct Cook's notion of "deformed pelvises." He explained that Baganda women's pelvises were unfortunately small, rather than "deformed," and that it was this inherent small size that was the cause of women's antenatal difficulties. His rebuttal was encased in racialist, evolutionist language. He wondered,

> Who has not been struck by the extraordinary narrowness of the Negroid hip? Viewed behind in the erect position at the level of hips the female Negroid body is narrow and round as compared with the "broad beam" of the average European woman, and when the dried pelvises of each are placed alongside each other the explanation is obvious, the Muganda's bone looks like that of a child in size and in the fineness of its structure. . . . The negroid races have a shape of pelvis which is intermediate between the protomorphean races and those of the higher civilised types. . . . The brim, as in the apes, is long-oval in shape.

Regrettably, such a conceptualization was not absurd to many accustomed to Darwinist racialized stereotypes in an era of colonial imperialism. Arguing linearly, Mitchell continued, "With the development of races the long-oval brim changes to the round or cordate type and the pelvis as a whole becomes more upright and compact."[34]

Mitchell compared a collection of local female pelvises with those held by the museum of the Royal College of Surgeons. His conclusion foregrounded the racialized, evolutionist underpinnings of his approach: "It will be seen that the inlets of the pelvises of the blacks are not only smaller but they are also round and not reniform as in the whites."[35] Mitchell was convinced that "[s]ome of the black races . . . appear to be living still in the transitional period." He was even more precise in his racialized, evolutionist argument when it came to the Baganda: "From the evidence provided by the bones of these unfortunate young mothers, and from the story of the high incidence of obstructed labour in Uganda, one cannot but suggest that the Baganda are afflicted with the hereditary stigma."[36] In many ways, Cook's science supported a discourse of racial superiority premised on human anatomy, behavior, and culture. To Cook and Mitchell, the differences between "normal" and "abnormal" deliveries called for greater scrutiny of the subtleties of Baganda women's anatomy. Mitchell's unfortunate likening of Baganda women's pelvises to those of apes closely echoed earlier anatomical categories of African women developed in Europe and the United States. Through their use of evaluative language such as "deformed," "flattened," "contracted," "childlike," and "between protomorphean races and those of the higher civilised types," the doctors reinforced their power to judge and classify. In characterizing Buganda prenatal practices as dangerous and backward, and Baganda women's pelvises as less- or underdeveloped, they maintained Western white women's bodies as the norm. Within this binary approach to cultural and anatomical progress, Baganda women's pelvises were classified as anomalous.[37]

Indeed, as Stephen Jay Gould states, "Science is no inexorable march to truth; it is mediated by the collection of objective information and the destruction of ancient superstition. . . . Scientists as ordinary human beings unconsciously reflect in their theories the social and political constraints [i.e., biases] of their time."[38] Certainly Cook's theory and the responses it provoked support this argument. There was a good deal of cultural and ideological colonialism in Cook's medical theories and practice in Buganda. From his ideological position, he endlessly preached, lectured, and published in learned journals, as he sought to transform what was simply different from and unpalatable to "modern" medicine. W. D. Foster poignantly sums up Cook's medicine: "Cook's epidemiological notions were led astray by his missionary keen nose for sin."[39] He looked at Baganda women's illnesses solely in terms of what Christianity and civilization could effect and perfect. Backwardness, sin, and racial difference thus appear as the actual causes of "deformed," "flattened," "contracted," and "childlike" pelvises, as well as of high maternal and child mortality rates. No doubt, missionary and colonial doctors' anxiety about population decline shaped their enterprise in Buganda, but their preoccupation with women's anatomy cannot be understood outside of the larger context of scientific assumptions during this period, namely the triumph of Darwinism in colonial medical thought.

Cook's discourse was meant to address those aspects of Bugandan culture that prevented the kingdom from realizing its destiny as a great and populous nation. Yet by 1908, he had come to focus on modernity and civilization as the primary dangers. Cook and the CMS had begun their missionary medical enterprise by attacking indigenous culture and advocating for Christianity, commerce, and civilization. By 1908, they were arguing that civilization was the culprit responsible for the near extinction of the "race" they so much wished to preserve. Meanwhile, Colonel Lambkin alerted Cook and the CMS to another and related danger—Christianity. In 1908, he discussed

> the suppression by Christianity of the tribal laws and customs which formerly prevailed, under which the liberties of women were greatly restricted and the unchastely were severely punished. Christian teachers have brought about the abandonment of polygamy and of a control over female liberty which was formerly exerted, and under which immorality and promiscuous intercourse did not exist. . . . [T]he chiefs of the Baganda tribe, the majority of whom had become Christians, decided to remove all such restrictions as being contrary to Christian teaching, and to set the women free. This was done, and the women were left at liberty to roam about to do as they liked, with the result of establishing a system of promiscuous sexual intercourse and immorality.[40]

The CMS's leadership in Buganda was quick to react to Colonel Lambkin's diatribe. Bishop Tucker responded,

> The state of the case in my opinion is simply this. For ages the social restraints in the national life of the Baganda have been due entirely to the existence of a very complete system of feudal ties. The land was held on a service tenure terminable at the will of the king or chief. There was no fixity of tenure. Without such fixity of tenure it had come to be realised by those in authority that there could be no proper development of the country. Consequently, the tendency of all legislation in Uganda in recent years has been towards the creation of a class of landed proprietors. . . . The result has been the abolition of the service tenure, . . . and the complete break up of that feudal system which with all its restraints, wholesome and unwholesome, has yet, I believe, done good service in the making of Uganda.

According to Bishop Tucker, the result was "not merely liberty" but license to sin. He denied that Christianity had anything to do with the breakdown of the feudal system. He continued,

> It is a fundamental principle of our work to interfere as little as possible with tribal laws and customs. The breakdown of the feudal system has been due not to Christian teaching—for Christian teaching had no controversy with it—but to government legislation.

Cautiously, he added, "In saying this I do not wish in the very least to reflect upon the policy of the administration, which I am sure has been actuated by the highest and best motives."[41]

Likewise, Cook refused to accept Lambkin's submissions. His response was short yet very firm: "I must give emphatic denial to the assumption that Christianity has been the chief cause of this epidemic. It has been all the other way. Read 'civilization' for 'Christianity' and there may be some amount of truth in it." He added, "Christianity from the very beginning acted as a deterring and restraining force and when intelligently accepted it would be the only true prophylaxis to this terrible scourge."[42] Nonetheless, Cook and the CMS leadership in Buganda had at least acknowledged a painful truth: the supposed imminent extinction of the Baganda was rooted in the very civilization their projects advocated. The missionaries came face to face with the proposition that modernity extracted the "natives" from their roots and placed them in a hybrid state[43] that was neither "civilized" nor "traditional." But like cultural backwardness, sin, and ignorance, the forces of hybridity had to be systematically countered with a body of scientific knowledge, practices, and institutions.

Perception and Representation: An Apparatus of Power

Efforts to deal with moral crisis and population decline would inevitably focus on women's behavior and the customs pertaining to their freedom of movement and education. Almost everything having to do with the organization of custom or urban life was to be executed in the name of the noble and rational cause of preserving and protecting the "fine and virile race."[44] Intervention was thus manifest in a series of regulations that arose not only from Cook's work, but from a colonial commission of inquiry headed by Colonel Lambkin in 1907 and by Colonel Sparke, Captain Keane, and Lieutenant Traves in 1908.[45] Inevitably, concern over the quality of the Baganda "race" spurred colonizers not only to monitor and reform birthing practices but also to initiate Western medical training. Out of these commissions and numerous related efforts, the first colonial hospital, Mulago, was founded. Makerere Medical School developed from Mulago, and Makerere College (later University) evolved from it. Subsequently, several other treatment and training centers were opened in up-country areas.

The entries in the colonial archive demonstrate that medical intervention was highly specific, ideologically informed, and very intrusive.[46] The positive value of some of this intervention, especially the establishment of maternal and child welfare centers, maternity training schools, Mulago Hospital, and Makerere Medical School, cannot be denied. Yet these institutions significantly reordered life for political purposes, demonstrating clearly that the welfare of women and infants had become a matter of national concern, rather than a private issue for clans and families. And government and colonial intervention in this aspect of family life was primarily justified on these grounds.

For the most obvious reasons, the missionaries' bid to attack sexual immorality (which they considered the primary cause of venereal diseases) and high maternal mortality rates was connected to the semantics of sin.[47] Through their pedagogy and medicine, missionaries like Cook managed to make sexuality, particularly women's, not only a religious concern but a secular one as well, one that needed to be regulated by the colonial state. To be more explicit, sex became an area that required legislation that would put individuals under colonial surveillance. The medical and sociopolitical project of managing births, children, and mothers' lives required that sexual morality itself be controlled by the state rather than by clan and kinship groups.

In an effort to rescue the Baganda through a scientifically learned apparatus of control, the most rigorous interventions were first applied with intensity among the chiefs, the economically privileged and politically dominant stratum of Bugandan society. The missionary and colonial establishments believed that educational and medical interventions would be more acceptable to the Baganda and more widely disseminated if they began with this stratum. Through interventions by the Anglican Synod, Colonel Lambkin's commission, and the strong arm of the Lukiiko, this social stratum was first alerted to the pathology of sexual immorality, the urgent need to keep it under close watch, and the need to devise a rational body of laws to control it.[48] Indeed, it was members of this chiefly social stratum, as recipients of missionary and colonial education and of medical instruction and practices, whose birthing practices and sexual morality first became Westernized. And through vigilant political surveillance of prominent chiefs, this chiefly social stratum was the first to commit itself to rigorous sexual censorship.

Yet the lower classes did not manage to escape the colonial and missionary apparatus of power. With the help of the chiefs, they were subjected in specific ways to missionary and colonial surveillance. Colonel Lambkin was a strong believer in the power of the chiefs to bring about desired changes more easily than had been possible for the colonial state in India. He subsequently prided himself on having left behind in Buganda a network to handle the situation. Through this network, persons afflicted with sexually transmitted diseases were reported to the medical authorities and forced, with the help of chiefs, to receive treatment. Treatment rooms were opened up in various localities throughout Buganda.[49]

At another level, Lukiiko decrees obliged chiefs to provide housing and food for midwives in their areas.[50] Maternity and child welfare centers became individual community projects with direct missionary and government participation in their staffing and surveillance.[51] Nonetheless, the Westernization of birth and childrearing practices penetrated the lower classes slowly, in what appear to have been four successive stages, though at times these stages overlapped. The first stage involved the Lambkin Commission's problematization of the negative consequences of the weakening of cultural values and the privileging of Christian monogamous ethics. The second stage regarded the organization of "conventional family care" as a crucial mechanism for the surveillance of the quality of the "race." In this phase, the massive Moral Purity Campaign (sponsored by the colonial government, headed by the Cooks, and blessed by the Buganda Lukiiko) tried to improve the morals of the lower classes. The third stage came in the early 1920s, with the development of maternity training schools to preserve what was perceived as a dwindling population.[52] This was the moment when moralization through Christian ethics and a general acceptance of Western medical practices spread more broadly through the entire social body of Buganda, with the active participation of the Buganda Lukiiko. Cook could even afford to boast about men's securing Western medicines for their pregnant wives: "Husbands often make a journey many miles to obtain the valued drug for their wives who are unable to walk the distance—they would not do that if they did not see the result in healthy families."[53] Finally the lower strata were brought under surveillance through Western education, urban spacing and regulation, and public hygiene and sanitation laws.[54]

The Value of Focusing on the Archive

Focusing on the archive allows the historian to understand the ethnography of a colonial encounter. However, the perceptions and rhetoric preserved in missionary and colonial archives also serve to underscore three important characteristics of those archives. These are, first, the constructed and artificial nature of many of the missionary and colonial accounts; second, the fragmented nature of those accounts; and third, the asymmetrical production and consumption of images of the "natives." Colonial and missionary documents give us only partial cultural and historical truths about the colonial moment in Buganda. They should not be seen as anything but fragmentary perceptions.

Published colonial documents, apart from disguising and censoring failure, camouflage difficult truths that were often explicit in private letters to or from missionaries. For example, thanks to the work of Carol Summers and Megan Vaughan,[55] much is already known about Cook's work on sexually transmitted diseases in Buganda. However, the extent to which these diseases were not only a "native" problem, or a problem for the "immoral Arabs," but a European colonial problem is concealed in Cook's public lectures and writings. Yet his correspondence files are full of letters from Europeans asking for treatment of and advice about their venereal diseases.[56] Cook never mentions this fact in his numerous writings on the subject, nor does he use these letters to calculate the percentage of Europeans in the colony infected with such diseases, as he did with his "native" patients, or the numbers of those likely to further infect the "natives." Cook's suppression of this knowledge created an overall racialized perception that immorality was a "native" problem.

The perception that Buganda was in a state of moral crisis lent force to the new ideology of social engineering. Both the colonial administration and missionaries depicted the Baganda as ignorant, childlike, immoral, and diseased, and strongly believed that they could be uplifted only through education, the reorganization of societal values, and social regulation based on medical and scientific knowledge. Women's central role in this process of uplift was registered from the beginning. Thus the missionary and colonial imaginings of "womanhood," "motherhood," and "wifehood" were directly shaped by broader concerns over population decline, excess maternal and child mortality rates, women's education, and national food shortages. The image of the "Muganda woman" as potentially embodying the virtues of chastity, fecundity, and life was internalized in an essentialist manner in colonial and missionary circles; women became the symbol of agricultural productivity in the nation, and hence its lifeline. Missionary and colonial administrators assumed that this image captured the "natural" role society assigned to women.[57] Imagined and essentialized in this manner, Baganda women were to be the objects of a more intrusive, patronizing, and controlling discourse. The "ignorant" and "diseased" women, mothers, and wives were to be transformed not only through education but equally through medical practices and policies. Their centrality as an index of progress and morality meant that their productive and reproductive capabilities were put under continued, intrusive, microscopic scrutiny.

Although missionaries' and administrators' perceptions of Baganda women were unfavorable, they nonetheless implicitly underscore the importance of women to Buganda. Baganda women's centrality in society was never denied. Missionaries and colonial administrators believed that improvement in women's education and the return to precontact mechanisms of social control were needed if colonial and missionary projects were to succeed. Ironically, the colonial project now rested on the belief that precontact social relations, however oppressive they might have been, were especially vital in order to control women and thereby maintain a stable social order, guaranteeing the nation adequate food production and good health. As Frantz Fanon wrote more generally, "There is a quest for a Negro, the Negro is in demand, one cannot get along without him, he is needed but only if he is palatable in a certain way. Unfortunately the Negro knocks down the system and breaks the treaties."[58]

There is no doubt that Baganda women were in demand, and that they were destabilizing the designs of missionary and colonial agendas at every opportunity. There is also no doubt that any form of resistance on their part led to desperate appeals from missionary and colonial agents.[59] Indeed, Colonel Lambkin bluntly asserted that it was premature for missionaries to consider freeing Baganda women from centuries of control. Comparing Baganda women to Western "liberated women," he blamed Christian missionary teaching and practice for facilitating the establishment of "a system of promiscuous sexual intercourse and immorality." In 1908 Lambkin justified restricting Baganda women:

> The freedom enjoyed by women in civilized countries has gradually been won by them as one of the results of centuries of civilization, during which they have been educated; and women whose female ancestors had for countless generations been kept under surveillance were not fit to be treated in a similar manner. . . . They were, in effect, merely female animals with strong passions, to whom unrestricted opportunities for gratifying these passions were suddenly afforded.[60]

Perceptions and representations that produced texts such as this were integral to the colonial moment in Buganda. The work of Cook, Lambkin, and Mitchell suggests more specifically how information and regulation in a particular policy field—health—were simultaneously a colonizing project and a vehicle for more general surveillance and further intervention. Equally important, medical literature such as they produced became the privileged, though not the only, site of explicit engagement with racial difference during this period in Buganda. I do not wish to label Dr. Cook, who worked tirelessly in Buganda, nor any other colonial doctors racist; rather, I want to expose how cultural and ideological assumptions and systems of representation of Baganda women were backed by a "science" through which individual colonial and missionary doctors understood their connection and existence within colonial Buganda.

Conclusion

There is no doubt that the "quality" and "quantity" of the Buganda population were central concerns of the missionary and colonial administration from the very beginning of contact.[61] The British officials in Buganda, from Sir Harry Johnston in 1900 to Sir Charles Dundas in 1945, seem to have been committed to protecting them. Mortality and fertility rates took a primary place in all colonial statistics, especially the Annual Reports.[62] Vital statistics were issued in each Medical and Sanitary Annual Report and, according to Cook, "careful statistics were kept at Mengo Hospital."[63] Missionary doctors and colonialists felt that it was their responsibility to foster population growth. Because of this, they scrupulously observed Baganda women. They represented Baganda women's culture, bodies, and health in writing and images. Out of their perceptions, measures were implemented, some of which were no doubt to the benefit of Baganda women: for example, the founding of maternity training schools. These not only increased women's restricted employment opportunities but also prompted girls' schools to include some basic science subjects in their curricula. At the same time, the surveillance of immorality, especially of a sexual nature, was seen as a way to improve the health, and increase the population, of the Baganda. How to do this was, to the Cooks, the missionaries, and the colonial administrators, the central question behind the intensification of the Moral Purity Campaign and the problematization of health. Equally important, irrespective of whatever other things Cook wrote and said, he saw himself as having a positive impact on Buganda, and some Baganda agreed. Empowered by their (Christian) ideological convictions and their endless energy, Cook and his wife perceived themselves as uplifting and saving a "race" that was in danger of becoming extinct.

To understand the power relations within which perceptions and representations of Baganda women were articulated and developed, we must situate these relations in the crucial area of colonial power over and knowledge about the "natives." Knowledge about the colonized inscribed and justified different forms of control. European perceptions of Baganda women were indeed part of this larger history of domination, control, and accommodation. Granted, Baganda women, as a colonized people, were medically dominated. Yet even in Cook's own work there is evidence that they were never completely assimilated to Western medicine. The persistent use of local medicines from the colonial period to the present time, to the annoyance of the medical establishment, is evidence that Baganda women were not fully dominated and that they maintained some form of control over their medical conditions and knowledge. This is a subject that needs further careful investigation. Women's persistent rejection or selective use of modern medical practice (which became the ground of

Cook's continuing fight) is another indication of the extent to which colonial projects were met with indigenous resistance and accommodation. While the Cooks and the colonial state imposed Western medicine on Baganda women, the women strategically appropriated its benefits—services and knowledge. Indeed, the frequent insistence that Western colonizing control and Christian values needed to be affirmed demonstrates Baganda women's noncompliance and resistance. Is it not significant that Dr. Albert Cook repeated the same message (regarding dangerous customs and ignorance) from the day he began his career in medical practice in Buganda to the day he retired?

Primary Documents

1. Secretary, MTS Committee, Mengo Hospital, to the provincial commissioner, 1920. Albert Cook Medical Library Archives, Mulago Hospital, Makerere University, box "Mengo Hospital Incoming Correspondence (Including MTS), 1919–1921, 1925–1930."

> May I ask your sympathetic help in pressing upon the representatives of the Native Government in various Districts to which qualified Midwives are being sent, their responsibility in carrying out instructions laid down in the accompanying letter. . . .
>
> The aim is to bring home to the Native Lukiiko in each District the paramount duty of the Native Government to promote by every means in its power the object for which the Midwives have been trained VIZ to diminish in every way the excessive mortality among Baganda mothers and their infants and the enormous annual loss to the Protectorate of what might be useful lives owing to the prevalence of venereal diseases and dangerous Native treatment by poisonous drugs. [The drugs referred to here are the indigenous prenatal medicines that Dr. Cook had serious reservations about, and that he tried to weed out of Buganda.]

2. Alfred R. Tucker, Bishop of Uganda, "Syphilis in Uganda," letter to the editor, *The Lancet*, 24 October 1908, 1246.

> Sir, My attention has been drawn to an article in your issue of Oct. 3rd on "Syphilis in Uganda" and to certain statements therein contained as to the bearing of Christian teaching upon the tribal laws and customs of the Baganda and the disastrous consequences which, it is alleged, have resulted therefrom. May I be permitted to say that I disagree altogether with the assumption from which the conclusion is drawn?
>
> The state of the case in my opinion is simply this. For ages the social restraints in the national life of the Baganda have been due entirely to the existence of a very complete system of feudal ties. The land was held on a service tenure terminable at the will of the king or chief. There was no fixity of tenure. Without such fixity of tenure it had come to be realised by those in authority that there could be no proper development of the

country. Consequently the tendency of all legislation in Uganda in recent years has been towards the creation of a class of landed proprietors with the freehold of their lands. The result has been the abolition of the service tenure, the imposition of rent, and the complete break up of that feudal system which with all its restraints, wholesome and unwholesome, has yet, I believe, done good service in the making of Uganda. With this sweeping away of the feudal system has come in not liberty merely but licence, and the result we have stated for us in Colonel Lambkin's paper. Christianity, in my opinion, has had nothing whatever to do with these lamentable consequences. It is a fundamental principle of our work to interfere as little as possible with tribal laws and customs. The breakdown of the feudal system has been due not to Christian teaching—for Christian teaching had no controversy with it—but to Government legislation. In saying this I do not wish in the very least to reflect upon the policy of the administration, which I am sure has been actuated by the highest and best motives. But it is well, I think, that we should be clear in our minds in a case like this as to the causes to which such results as these set forth by Colonel Lambkin are traceable.

3. J. P. Mitchell, O.B.E., M.D., superintendent of Mulago Hospital, Kampala, and principal of the medical school, "On the Causes of Obstructed Labour in Uganda," Part 1, *The East African Medical Journal* 15 (1938–39): 176–210.

There is an impression that African women have little or no difficulty in parturition. In Buganda it requires only the shortest acquaintance with obstetrics to discover that abnormal distress in labour is frequent and that the incidence of foetal and maternal casualties from disproportion is high. It is disconcerting, too, to find that the explanations of these casualties are not always convincing. The causes are frequently obscure.

There is no poverty in Uganda. There is an abundance of good food and sunshine. The women cultivate; they are active and handsome; they have no mutilating customs. Rickets is unknown and yet that they have long been acquainted with labour difficulties is suggested by certain practices and customs which are not generally known and are of interest.

Sir Harry Johnston in his "Uganda Protectorate" refers to the Baganda women as poor breeders. He observed that it is customary for men to acquire wives from neighbouring territories either by raiding or through the agency of slave traders. . . .

Racial characteristics of negroid pelvises. The negroid races have a shape of pelvis which is intermediate between the protomorphean races and those of the higher civilised types. Of the protomorpheans the Bushmen of South Africa and the Veddas of Ceylon are examples. In these sex differences are not well marked. The brim, as in the apes, is long-oval in shape, the true conjugate being longer than the transverse diameter. . . .

With the development of races the long-oval brim changes to the round or cordate type and the pelvis as a whole becomes more upright and compact.

A number of local female pelvises were collected. When comparing them with different types in the museum of the Royal College of Surgeons I was struck by their similarity to a number of Andaman bones.

It will be seen that the inlets of the pelvises of the blacks are not only smaller but they are also round and not reniform as in the whites. General anatomists regard the latter feature as racially characteristic of the blacks. . . .

The custom of carrying heavy loads in childhood is immemorial and universal among the blacks. Yet I can find no reference to flattening resulting from this cause except in Sir Albert's reports. Surely the Baganda are not peculiar in this respect. Where adverse social conditions exist the blacks flatten equally with the whites but the causes are pathological and not mechanical.

NOTES

1. Sir Albert R. Cook, *Uganda Memories: 1897–1940* (Kampala: The Uganda Society, 1945), p. 329. *The Lancet,* a medical journal, reiterated this fear: "As things are at present, the entire population is in danger of being exterminated by syphilis in a very few years, or of being left a degenerate race fit for nothing." Colonel Lambkin, "Syphilis in Uganda," *The Lancet,* 3 October 1908, p. 1022.

2. These records are preserved in the *Church Missionary Intelligencia, Church Missionary Notes, Church Missionary Gleaner, Church Missionary Annual Reports,* and other sources.

3. G. F. Saywell, CMS editorial secretary, "Re: Annual Letters," 31 July 1923, Albert Cook Medical Library Archives, Mulago Hospital, Makerere University (hereafter ACMLA), box "Incoming Correspondence from CMS London, 1919–1932."

4. See, for example, John Hanning Speke, *Journal of the Discovery of the Source of the Nile* (Edinburgh: Blackwood and Sons, 1863); H. M. Stanley, *Through the Dark Continent,* vol. 1 (New York: Harper and Brothers, 1879); Alexander M. Mackay, *A. M. Mackay: Pioneer Missionary of the Church Missionary Society in Uganda* (London: Hodder and Stoughton, 1891); Sir Harry Hamilton Johnston, *The Uganda Protectorate,* vol. 1 (London: Hutchinson, 1902); John Roscoe, *The Baganda: An Account of Their Native Customs and Beliefs* (London: Macmillan, 1911); Cook, *Uganda Memories.*

5. Catherine Hall, "Missionary Stories: Gender and Ethnicity in England in the 1830s and 1840s," in *Cultural Studies,* ed. Lawrence Grossberg, Cary Nelson, and Paula A. Treichler (New York: Routledge, 1992), p. 241.

6. Saywell, "Re: Annual Letters."

7. Wilson Cash, CMS general secretary, letter no. 9, 9 February 1928, ACMLA, box "Incoming Correspondence from CMS London, 1919-1932."

8. Terence Ranger, "African Reactions to Imposition of Colonial Rule in East and Central Africa," in *Colonialism in Africa, 1870-1960,* ed. L. H. Gann and Peter Duignan (Cambridge: Cambridge University Press, 1969), vol. 1, pp. 293-324; T. O. Ranger, ed., *Emerging Themes in African History* (Nairobi: East African Publishing House, 1968); Andrew Roberts, "The Sub-imperialism of the Baganda," *Journal of African History* 3, no. 3 (1962): 435-50; H. B. Thomas, "*Capax Imperii:* The Story of Semi Kakungulu," *Uganda Journal* 6 (1939): 125-50.

9. Speke, *Journal;* Stanley, *Dark Continent;* Johnston, *Uganda Protectorate;* Roscoe, *The Baganda;* Cook, *Uganda Memories;* Sir Albert Cook, "Notes on the Disease Met With in Uganda, Central Africa," *Journal of Tropical Medicine* 4 (1901): 175.

10. Lambkin, "Syphilis in Uganda," p. 1022.

11. M. S. M. Semakula Kiwanuka, *A History of Buganda: From the Foundation of the Kingdom to 1900* (London: Longman, 1971); Sir Gerald Portal, *The British Mission to Uganda in 1893* (London: Edward Arnold, 1894).

12. Johnston, *Uganda Protectorate,* p. 636.

13. Roscoe, *The Baganda.*

14. Archdeacon Walker to Baylis, 13 March 1907, Church Missionary Archives, University of Birmingham.

15. Roscoe, *The Baganda.*

16. See, for example, C. W. Hattersley, *The Baganda at Home* (London: Frank Cass, 1964), and *Uganda Notes,* vol. 5 (November 1905). "Kiganda" refers to or describes the customs of the Baganda people.

17. Miss Allen, annual letter, 28 November 1910, G. 3. A7/05, Church Missionary Society Archives, Birmingham.

18. Nakanyike B. Musisi, "Transformation of Baganda Women: From the Earliest Times to the Demise of the Kingdom in 1966" (Ph.D. diss., University of Toronto, 1991).

19. Catholic Church in Buganda, *Eddini YaKatonda* (Marseilles: 1894), pp. 459-60; Robert Pickering Ashe, *Chronicles of Uganda* (London: Hodder and Stoughton, 1894).

20. J. M. Waliggo, "The Catholic Church in Buddu Province of Buganda" (D.Phil. diss., Cambridge University, 1976).

21. Catherine Thompson, "Mothers in Mengo," *Mercy and Truth* 4 (1900): 219.

22. Albert R. Cook, "The Medical History of Uganda, Part 2," *The East African Medical Journal* 13 (1936-37): 105.

23. The equation in operation was transitive and contained four terms: A (freedom from religious and cultural constraints: freedom of movement) = B (immorality: syphilis and other STDs) = C (high maternal and child mortality rates: degeneration of the "race" and depopulation) = D (race extinction).

24. Dr. Albert Cook, "The Influence of Obstetrical Conditions on Vital Statistics in Uganda," *The East African Medical Journal* 9 (1932-33): 327.

25. Ibid. See also Albert R. Cook, "Notes on Dr. Mitchell's Paper on the Causes of Obstructed Labour in Uganda," *The East African Medical Journal* 15 (1938-39): 190-92.

26. In fact, he called Baganda customs surrounding pregnancy and childbirth "useless and dangerous." See Cook, *Uganda Memories*, p. 328.

27. Dr. R. Y. Stones, "On the Causes of Obstructed Labour in Uganda," letter to the editor, *The East African Medical Journal* 15 (1938–39): 218.

28. Dr. J. P. Mitchell, "On the Causes of Obstructed Labour in Uganda, Part 1," *The East African Medical Journal* 15 (1938–39): 188–89.

29. Cook, "Notes on Dr. Mitchell's Paper," pp. 213–17.

30. Ibid.

31. Stones, "Obstructed Labour," 218.

32. See Clinical Notes and Files, ACMLA; Cook, "The Influence of Obstetrical Conditions," pp. 321–22.

33. Stones, "Obstructed Labour," p. 218.

34. Mitchell, "Obstructed Labour, Part 1," pp. 181–83.

35. Ibid., p. 183.

36. Dr. J. P. Mitchell, "On the Causes of Obstructed Labour in Uganda, Part 2," *The East African Medical Journal* 15 (1938–39): 210–11.

37. For a discussion of comparative anatomy, see Nancy Stephan, *The Idea of Race in Science: Great Britain, 1800–1960* (Hamden, Conn.: Archon, 1982).

38. Stephen Jay Gould, *Ever since Darwin: Reflections in Natural History* (New York: W. W. Norton, 1979), p. 15.

39. W. D. Foster, *The Early History of Scientific Medicine in Uganda* (Nairobi: East African Literature Bureau, 1970), p. 83.

40. Lambkin, "Syphilis in Uganda," p. 1023.

41. Bishop Alfred R. Tucker, "Syphilis in Uganda," letter to the editor, *The Lancet*, 2 October 1908, p. 1246.

42. Sir Albert Cook, "Syphilis in Uganda," *The Lancet*, 12 December 1908, p. 1771.

43. I borrow this term from Homi K. Bhabha, *The Location of Culture* (London and New York: Routledge, 1994).

44. Ibid., p. 328.

45. Cook, "The Medical History of Uganda, Part 2," p. 99.

46. Carol Summers, "Intimate Colonialism: The Imperial Production of Reproduction in Uganda, 1907–1925," *Signs: Journal of Women in Culture and Society* 16, no. 4 (1991): 787–807; Megan Vaughan, *Curing Their Ills: Colonial Power and African Illness* (Stanford, Calif.: Stanford University Press, 1991).

47. Foster, *Early History*, p. 81.

48. Lambkin, "Syphilis in Uganda," p. 1023; Cook, "The Medical History of Uganda, Part 2," p. 100. For a fuller discussion of the development of laws to curb immorality in Buganda, see Musisi, "Transformation of Baganda Women."

49. Lambkin, "Syphilis in Uganda," p. 1023. Also see Cook, *Uganda Memories*, p. 342.

50. Letter from the secretary of the MTS Committee, Mengo Hospital, to the provincial commissioner, 1920. Luganda version. ACMLA, box "Mengo Hospital Incoming Correspondence (Including MTS) 1919–1921, 1925–1930."

51. Cook, "The Influence of Obstetrical Conditions," p. 329, and "The Medical History of Uganda, Part 2," pp. 101–102.

52. Cook, "The Medical History of Uganda, Part 2," p. 102.

53. Dr. Albert R. Cook, "The Treatment of Ante-natal Syphilis," *Kenya and East African Medical Journal* 6 (1929–30): 15.

54. Cook, *Uganda Memories*, pp. 335–36.

55. Summers, "Intimate Colonialism"; Vaughan, *Curing Their Ills*.

56. See, for examples, letters marked "Cook Box 10" in box "Mengo Hospital Incoming Correspondence (from CMS London) (Including M.T.S.), 1919–1921, 1925–1930 (Including Some Apolo Kagwa Correspondence)" at ACMLA, especially letters from J. G. Nunes, Mr. S., and J. W. Braganza.

57. See Herbert G. Jones, *Uganda in Transformation, 1876–1926* (London: S.C.M. Press, 1926), p. 340.

58. Frantz Fanon, *The Wretched of the Earth*, trans. Constance Farrington (New York: Grove, 1968), p. 147.

59. Archdeacon Walker to family, 25 October 1896, A7/G.3 Letter 337, Church Missionary Society Archives, Birmingham University; John Roscoe, *Twenty-Five Years in East Africa* (Cambridge: Cambridge University Press, 1921), p. 170; John Roscoe, "Uganda and Some of Its Problems," *Journal of the African Society* 22 (1922): 96–108, 218–25.

60. Lambkin, "Syphilis in Uganda," p. 1023.

61. Johnston, *The Uganda Protectorate*.

62. Cook, "The Influence of Obstetrical Conditions," pp. 316–17. Also see R. R. Kuczynski, *Demographic Survey of the British Colonial Empire* (London: Oxford University Press, 1949), pp. 230–324.

63. Cook, *Uganda Memories*, pp. 329–30.

5 "The Woman in Question": Marriage and Identity in the Colonial Courts of Northern Ghana, 1907–1954

Sean Hawkins

In August 1944, a woman by the name of Angmin appeared before a British colonial officer in the northwest corner of what was then the Northern Territories of the Gold Coast (today Ghana). She was appealing against decisions made by two lower Native Authority courts. From the transcript of the hearing we learn that Angmin had been betrothed as a child to a man with whom she had had five children over fifteen years. Her husband had died the previous year, and since then his nephew, who was also his heir, had been putting pressure on her to take another husband so that the conjugal payments of his late uncle would be returned to him by her new husband. The nephew had also taken Vaare, a suitor of hers, to court to force him to present conjugal payments because of "an act constituting marriage." It was alleged that Vaare had taken Angmin to his house and slept with her. According to Angmin, her late husband's heir had stopped feeding both her and her children in an effort to force her into an unwanted union, and so she had accepted assistance from a suitor; however, she denied having married Vaare.

A Native Authority court ruled against Vaare, forcing him to present 1,450 cowry shells and three cows to Angmin's late husband's nephew. But Angmin then appealed to a higher Native Authority court and, finally, to the district commissioner of Lawra District as the local representative of the Supreme Court of the Gold Coast Colony. In her testimony to this last court, Angmin denied having slept with Vaare or having become his wife. But she did admit to using him to improve her conditions as a widow, explaining, "As Vaare is after me if I see that he does not treat me well I will not agree to follow Vaare, as his lover." At the end of the colonial period, former husbands asserted proprietorial interests as compensation for their loss of the control over women that administrators had granted to men at the beginning of the century. For Angmin, taking a lover was quite distinct from taking a husband. She made this very clear as she explained why she opposed the decision of the Native Authority courts that Vaare should take her as a wife.

> I resist this because I have five children and cannot marry another man thereby leaving my children. I also resist the claim in that I have not married Vaare & do not intend to do so, & that Vaare, not being a new husband, is not liable for the repayment of dowry [conjugal payments]. . . . Vaare has never asked me to marry him. . . . I would not like to marry Vaare even if I could take the children with me. I want to remain in my late husband's house to see his tomb.

Vaare admitted to wanting to take Angmin as a wife, but explained how unrealistic this was, as she was "unwilling to sacrifice her children, & not wishing in any case to marry again."

This case was very unusual for several reasons. First, appeals to the district commissioners of the Northern Territories of the Gold Coast were very rare. Second, it was even rarer for a woman to appear as a litigant before any court. Third, Angmin was successful in her case. The district commissioner ruled that she had been forced to marry against her will.[1] As we will see at the end of this chapter, Angmin's case, even though it was exceptional, tells us a great deal about the motivations and desires of other women in this part of the West African savanna whose voices have otherwise been lost in the colonial court records. In particular, it alerts us to women's often hidden ability in the colonial period to define their own identities in the world beyond the courts.

In the court record books of the area where Angmin lived, Lawra District, clerks began using the phrase "the woman in question" from the early 1950s—as the colonial period was coming to an end—to refer to women like her. The phrase eventually became almost as ubiquitous as "defendant," "plaintiff," and "witness" in the court records. Although it disguised women's identities and reduced them to a generic status, the phrase is apposite given that women only very rarely participated in the courts as litigants, even though most disputes were about matters that directly affected their lives.[2] When women appeared, they did so almost always as witnesses, interested bystanders without recognized rights. If the attitudes of male litigants were taken to indicate the freedom of women under colonial rule, women would appear to have been virtually passive beings, devoid of any social agency or personal autonomy. But even where most oppressed, social actors have agency. What makes agency meaningful is personal autonomy, i.e., the freedom to exercise that agency. We know that women in this area possessed both agency and autonomy simply because these were the fundamental causes of most litigation; without such agency and autonomy disputes between males would have been severely curtailed.

The phrase "the woman in question" is also apt because during the fifty-year period in which litigation came before colonial courts, the identity of women was constantly questioned. The most persistent question was whose wife a woman was.[3] The contextual manner in which such a question was answered by the social norms of the people who occupied most of Lawra District, the

LoDagaa,[4] meant that the issue was ambiguous and hotly contested at the beginning of the colonial period. Over the course of the next half century, this uncertainty was slowly reduced, and male disputes more readily resolved, as a proprietorial definition of the social status of "wife" was introduced.

This chapter is about how colonial courts attempted to shape the social identities of LoDagaa women between 1907 and 1957, and in so doing eroded aspects of their freedom. More specifically, it is about the ambivalence of colonial attitudes toward women's freedom, as well as the rigidity in assumptions concerning the proper behavior of wives and the ease with which marriage might be defined. It is also about the gap between the rhetoric of court proceedings and the actions of women. Finally, it is about how the courts began to allow current and former husbands to claim interests in their wives as a form of property, and so inflict material punishments on their rivals. Overall, this chapter argues that concepts such as "wife," "marriage," "lover," and "adultery" became increasingly problematic in the colonial courts during the first half of this century because indigenous practices were not commensurable with these categories of colonial control.

Even though women might have been conspicuous by their almost complete absence as litigants, women were by no means peripheral to the courts. Women spoke as witnesses to disputes about their own lives, and, because it was often the evidence most relevant to disputes, men told stories about women. Colonial courts almost always either denied or ignored women's aspirations and interests, but they also highlighted the importance of control over women to the colonial project. This part of the project was distinctly patriarchal, conceived of through the conjuncture of the attitudes of British officers and the interests of a colonial elite of chiefs, elders, and other prominent men. The greatest challenge to British colonial rule of the LoDagaa was the relative autonomy that women enjoyed outside of the courts. Denied an active voice in the courts, women did not fail to exercise agency outside them, speaking through actions rather than words. One way of finding out about these actions is through court records.

Because colonialism's assumptions, as well as its architects, were largely patriarchal, its effects on women and their reactions to it were once quite obscured. Thanks to the work of numerous historians in the last two decades, that gendered myopia has begun to be corrected. For example, the work of Elizabeth Schmidt and Diana Jeater, as well as the chapter by Lynette Jackson in this volume, highlights just how central control over African women in Southern Rhodesia (today Zimbabwe) was to the economic and social objectives of British colonialism.[5] Just as women were once thought to have been at the margins of the colonial project, colonial courts have been often treated as marginal to colonialism. However, court proceedings were not peripheral. In exploring litigation before colonial courts we find ourselves at the heart of the exercise of colonial power.[6] In a history of colonial courts in Nyasaland (today Malawi) and Northern Rhodesia (now Zambia), Martin Chanock noted that "in terms of the time which officials claim to have spent on it, [family law] was one of the colonial government's most important interventions into African life."[7] Most of this litigation centered on the idea of marriage, and yet colonial courts often found this cultural concept very difficult to elucidate from the give and take of conjugal practices in many African societies. Recent studies of marriage in a variety of African societies, from the Ewe of southern Ghana to the Tswana of Botswana, have consistently shown how difficult it is to define this concept in terms of indigenous criteria and in terms of how women understood their autonomy and exercised their agency.[8] This lack of convergence between colonial paradigms and the reality of women's lives is especially evident in the colonial history of the LoDagaa.

Freedom, Property, and Women

In 1907, the annual report for the Northern Territories noted that among the LoDagaa "the constancy with which a woman changes her husband would be humorous if it were not for the trouble it gives." This situation was diagnosed as the product of "the absence of any strict laws or even customs over matrimony."[9] A year later it was reported that "[t]he women do not make good wives and their chief fault is their unfaithfulness."[10] A generation later, in 1938, and despite an intensive period of colonial rule, the district commissioner of the area wrote that "the ever-recurring problem of the district is the marriage problem."[11] Administrators did not define marriage, attempt to ascertain whether it was an indigenous category of experience, investigate its nature, or place it within the context of other indigenous social practices. Instead, they merely identified it and conveniently ascribed to it all possible social conflicts, thereby ignoring the complex and separate issues that informed such disputes. The identification of marriage as a social problem was highly significant for the colonial and postcolonial history of the LoDagaa. Not only were indigenous means of resolving disputes suppressed and displaced by the imposition of foreign judicial structures, but litigants before these courts were forced to define disputes in terms of marriage, their ascribed cause.

Litigation before colonial courts addressed relationships between women and men, almost always to the advantage of the latter. Perhaps unsurprisingly, social historians have generally accepted that these were marriage cases, that is, disputes about an indigenous African institution in which women were disadvantaged. Yet this does not seem to have been the case in many African societies, where "ideological valuations" and "ritual elaborations" of the types found in many Eurasian societies were "conspicuously absent."[12] As Jane Guyer, a contemporary anthropologist, has observed, "conjugality is not a key institution in Africa either as an architecture within which people live their sexual and reproductive lives or a channel through which property is transmitted." Why then was marriage used as a paradigm for understanding gender relations in colonial Africa? The period from the 1920s through the 1940s witnessed what she calls the "conceptual normalization of marriage in comparative anthropology," whereby order and clarity were imposed on indigenous practices in order to eliminate ambiguity and diversity. Anthropologists and administrators shared this need for such order and clarity, as "many peoples lacked a criterion that could be unambiguously translated into colonial legal criteria for differentiating marriage from transactions involving slaves and debt pawns, both of which transferred rights in people against other items of value."[13] What kept LoDagaa women from being property, or slaves, was men's lack of physical control over them as well as their own capacity for autonomous action.[14] But the relationship between women and conjugal payments was problematic for colonial administrators and anthropologists because of their attitudes toward the autonomy of women, especially as wives. The meaning of this relationship became even more troubled in the courts.

It is difficult to reconcile the male-centered perspective of litigants and administrators with the reality of women's lives. This difficulty is compounded by the gender-specific perspective enshrined in the explanatory models of conjugal payments once offered by anthropologists. In the 1950s, anthropologists risked confusing African conjugal arrangements with purchase. Although they might disclaim economic connotations, anthropological analyses were often based on implicit notions of purchase because of their emphasis upon the twinned concepts of exchange and rights.[15] Their jural language obscured the consideration of women as property, but because rights were seen in terms of commercial exchange, women were necessarily, if unintentionally, interpreted as property. But analyses grounded in the language of rights and exchange do not "necessarily describe what happens to women," implying as they do "powerlessness and lack of initiative, will, or feelings on the part of women."[16] The adherence to a rigidly directional perspective, which required the payments presented to equal the rights received, ignored the ethnographic complexities of actual practices.[17] These commercial interpretations were echoed in the views of both administrators and male litigants throughout Africa.

At the beginning of this century, it was reported of the LoDagaa that "ideas of property existing among pagan races consist of cattle and livestock, wives, children, clothes and ornaments."[18] Although we do not know whether this was an accurate reflection of indigenous ideas, by the 1960s commercial language had entered into male interpretations of conjugal payments among the LoDagaa. In justifying his claim to the custody of his former wife's new child, a husband used the following metaphor to describe the effect of the conjugal payments that were still in the keeping of his former wife's household: "If I buy a female animal I need it to multiply."[19] Such statements must be understood for what they were: bold rhetorical claims with little relation to reality outside the courts. Despite the interests or rights a husband may have expected in a wife, there was no way men could actually compel women to comply with these expectations—except when they came to court. As colonial administrators frequently complained, women usually did not recognize such rights.[20] The notion of a set of jural norms establishing marriage among the LoDagaa was countered by a corresponding set of actions that women engaged in. In the 1980s an anthropologist working in a LoDagaa settlement far to the south of Lawra District noted that the actual behavior of women made apparent the "illusion" of patriarchal control, "leaving men to sort out the consequences."[21] However, such a subtle and sophisticated understanding of the autonomy of women was slow in coming.

From an early date administrators demonstrated a decided inclination to return women to their former husbands even though they had new ones. The case of *Rex vs. Bowo*, which was heard in 1908 according to the criminal laws of the Gold Coast relating to seduction, clearly illustrates the divergence between colonial assumptions and indigenous practices. Kabiri came to complain that his rival Bowo had "caught" his wife and "slept with her and otherwise ill-treated her." Questioned by the district commissioner, Bowo admitted to having done so even though he knew she had been a wife to Kabiri. When asked why he did it, he attempted to explain according to the logic of LoDagaa social practices, which did not protect conjugal relations by any explicit social sanction against such action on the part of a rival: "I wanted to marry her."[22] Evidently he was not understood, as he was sentenced to three months at hard labor and twenty-four lashes. Before the arrival of the British, the LoDagaa did not have chiefs, let alone courts for the resolution of potentially violent disputes that fell outside of the authority of households or localities. The logic of marrying the wife of another man had been unassailable.[23] There was no wider political structure through which a household could prosecute a rival household that had taken a wife from it; direct retaliation would have been the only recourse. Colonial rule quickly changed these dynamics by substituting summonses for retaliation. As soon as British officers began hearing disputes "the natives, the ice once broken, flocked in with complaints and summons." It was noted that "they evidently appreciate a judge who can enforce his decisions."[24] Through their close contact with the district commissioner and his court, the chiefs whom the British selected, appointed, and imposed upon the LoDagaa quickly learned the solutions made possible by judicial structures and procedures, particularly the use of coercive punishments based on judicial authority.[25]

One reason district commissioners were eager to provide coercive sanctions to protect conjugal unions against the interference of rivals was to protect the interests of migrant laborers. The protection of migrant workers' conjugal unions was central to the work of colonial officers throughout Africa. It was nowhere more obvious than in the areas that supplied labor to the Copper Belt of Northern Rhodesia.[26] Although somewhat less prominent in the Northern Territories, such protection was very important in areas, such as Lawra District, that supplied a disproportionately large number of workers to the south. These workers had been recruited by the administration through its "labour crusade" to supply the southern economies of the Gold Coast with the north's only readily exploitable resource.[27] Two cases from 1908 illustrate such protection. In the first, *Kompailah vs. Naiver*, the plaintiff left his wife and went south to work in the mines. When he returned he learned that the defendant had taken her. Kompailah did not try to secure the return of his wife by any indigenous strategy, such as retaliatory action, but came immediately to the court to issue a summons against Naiver. Before capitulating with no further record of dissent, the defendant explained his action: "I have got no wife so when I saw this woman I took her. I knew she was the Plaintiff's wife but she said her husband had gone away." The woman, Kompo, was returned to her husband, Kompailah, even though she said, "I don't want to go back to either man. I want to go home, my husband's brother flogged me for going after other men when my husband went away."[28]

The second case, *Depang vs. Quiniari,* is worth citing to reiterate the willingness of the district commissioner to protect the interests of husbands, particularly when they were migrant laborers, as well as the logic of social practices. Depang, also a miner, returned home to find that Anwosa, once a wife to him, had been driven away from his compound by his elder brother and had been taken as a wife by the defendant from her household compound and with her parents' consent. Furthermore, Quiniari had already presented the conjugal payments to the woman's parents to be returned to Depang. The following was Quiniari's explanation of his own actions: "I have no wife. . . . I knew the woman was Depang's wife. I knew he paid headmoney." Anwosa corroborated this evidence and said she did not want to return to Depang, explaining that she liked her husband, "but his elder brother drove me from my house so I went [and] lived with my people and my mother gave me to defendant. I won't go back to Depang." Nevertheless, the district commissioner restored her to the plaintiff.[29]

It was not only cases involving migrant laborers that were decided by the district commissioner in a manner that transformed male interests in control over women into practical rights before the court. In *Loab vs. Chiapuun,* heard in 1909, Loab explained that Battyelle, formerly a wife to him, had "asked leave" to go to her father's compound in a neighboring settlement a fortnight before, but had not returned because another man, Chiapuun, had "caught" her from her parents. The district commissioner then questioned Battyelle.

Q: Why did you go to Defendant when you were married to Plaintiff?
A: I told my husband that if I went to my father I would not come back.
Q: Did you tell Chiapuun that you had another husband?
A: Yes I told him.

Battyelle's actions were a common indigenous strategy for women wishing either to renegotiate their conjugal unions or to leave their husbands.[30] However, in the court's view they constituted a violation of the conjugal union. Chiapuun admitted knowing that the woman was already another man's wife, but this, he explained, mattered little to him as the woman had been willing to go with him. He was fined ten shillings and Battyelle was returned to Loab despite her evident desire to leave him.[31] Cases such as this might be said only to demonstrate the deficiencies of administrative understanding of LoDagaa society. Yet both types of action, the elopement of wives and ensuing retaliatory action, were being discouraged. The difference was that when litigation was substituted for retaliatory action, the woman was invariably returned to the original husband, most often without consideration of her wishes, and in contravention of indigenous social practices. Before colonial rule, retaliatory action could only have deterred further infringements of a household's interests: it could not have brought about the restitution of a wife.

On the one hand, administrators were applying their own gendered constructions of morality to LoDagaa society and, on the other, they were ensuring that women's freedom did not discourage men from "volunteering" for labor recruitment. Women's freedom, together with the need for labor, required administrators to apply their particular ideology of marriage. By protecting the unions of migrant laborers, they redefined such relationships for all men, denying women the ability to leave unions if their former husbands came to court. What was being lost was the highly contextual language of conjugal unions that had accommodated and reflected the unprecedented latitude that women had been able to exercise at the beginning of the colonial period. Among the LoDagaa, what was commonly translated as "marriage" were the gender-specific and locational terms *de pog*, "take a woman," and *kul sir*, "go to a man." There was no term to refer to the institution of marriage, only to the agreement of a man and woman to live together.[32]

The marital career of Pornu of Tugu, recorded in 1913, illustrates a typical pattern for women. Before the turn of the century, she had entered a union with a man named Chafo, with whom she had three children. This union dissolved and was replaced by her relationship with another man, named Nabile, with whom she stayed long enough to have two more children. She was repudiated by Nabile, an uncommon cause of conjugal dissolution, but shortly after entered a union with Muyah, by whom she had another child. Since all her children were at least three years apart in age, these events probably took place over at least eighteen years.[33] The term "marital career" is appropriate because even though women often changed husbands before finding or negotiating a stable union, they remained married—that is, resident with one man or another—for the duration of their lives.[34] Barbara Cooper, who has used the same term to talk about the lives of Hausa women in Niger, has noted that most women are "perennial migrants" in their own societies.[35] Women such as Pornu often had several short-term conjugal unions in addition to a few long-term ones, thereby making their careers even more varied.

By the mid-1930s, blatant action by district commissioners to protect conjugal relationships from the prevalent competition over women by giving some relationships the legal status of marriage became rarer. At the same time, however, fewer cases were coming before the district commissioner's court, while the number being heard by the chiefs' tribunals was increasing. There are unfortunately no records of the tribunals' decisions for this period, but even if the chiefs were not directly protecting conjugal relationships, both chiefs and litigants were using seduction charges to the same effect. Although the district commissioners became less involved in conjugal litigation during the 1930s, litigants sought elsewhere the help the commissioners had provided in controlling their wives. During the first generation of colonial rule, the civil and complaint record books of Lawra District show that various district commissioners imposed judgments that probably favored husbands over rivals. It is important to recognize that this colonial patriarchal alliance was not synonymous with gender relations, being mediated almost as much by considerations of age and power. However, colonial rule did change attitudes toward women by introducing male British notions of appropriate female behavior and fostering the adoption of similar ideas by LoDagaa men. Some of these ideas were not necessarily unprecedented—they may have been implicit in LoDagaa men's views of women before colonial rule—but explicit colonial attitudes validated them, while colonial courts applied them.

Wives, Morality, and Divorce

The milieu of political relations that resulted from colonial rule was decidedly male, and, in the beginning at least, unreflectively so. Officers showed little to no interest in the welfare or rights of women during the early years of colonial rule, and when attention was focused on the subject in later years, it was only in response to metropolitan concerns. In 1918, roughly a decade after the beginning of colonial rule, an officer referred to absconding and recalcitrant wives as "shrews" and was heard to lament, "It is a pity that the ducking stool and bridle . . . have gone out of fashion."[36] Whether or not there was any congruence between their decisions to return women to former husbands and indigenous practices did not matter to officers, as they were settling disputes between men, in which context the interests of women were perceived to be peripheral. Some officers did express concern over the welfare of young betrothed girls, but these concerns were unnecessary so long as women were still free to leave such unions by entering into a subsequent union of their own choosing.[37] Officers obviously did not expect such freedom and, when they became aware of it, they were ambivalent about whether it was a good thing for LoDagaa society.

When the chief commissioner of the Northern Territories issued warnings about child betrothal in 1911, the acting secretary for native affairs argued that officers should not be unduly concerned. It was possible for them not "to judge the institutions of primitive people by the standards of the twentieth century," he asserted, without any prejudice to the "moral or social welfare" of their colonial subjects.[38] In the first published account of the peoples of the Northern Territories, A. W. Cardinall, a colonial officer, wrote that although he referred to conjugal unions as marriage, the terms was "misleading."

> A woman is looked upon primarily as a begetter of children, and secondly as a preparer of food. . . . The essential thing is the children, and they, no matter who their father, belong to the owner of their mother. Every woman has, beside her husband, one or two favourite lovers to whom her husband has no objection.[39]

Despite these hesitations, the court record books persistently described conjugal unions as marriages. Such a categorization was extremely convenient for administrators because it subsumed a variety of social disputes, and, accordingly, minimized their importance. This meant they were more readily relegated to the jurisdiction of the chiefs. The volume of "matrimonial" litigation was a source of aggravation to district commissioners and a direct challenge to their amateur and inexperienced grasp of the indigenous issues behind such disputes. Writing of conditions before the 1920s, Cardinall added that women chose husbands on their own:

> This last is progress, but unfortunately it leads to a maze of entanglements. . . .
> Many of these women, having tasted emancipation, are not satisfied until they
> have tried as many as ten husbands. It is not the white man who has brought this
> about. Such has been the practice for long past. It led to murder and war and raids;
> today it leads to disputes and complaints beyond number, and incidentally at times
> to a half-crazy Commissioner.[40]

These comments highlight the dilemma that the related phenomena of conjugal instability and women's autonomy presented to officers throughout the colonial period. The rate of conjugal dissolution was often seen as a sign of moral deficiency, or at least as an inconvenient social fact, but the only immediate means of restricting such dissolution was to limit the freedom of women. Attitudes toward such limitation were ambiguous. Evidently mindful of the growing rights of women in Britain, Cardinall noted that although the freedom available to women in the Northern Territories had led to "prevalent immorality," their freedom nonetheless represented "progress."[41]

Even if indigenous practices did not fulfill the "ideological valuations" of marriage defined by observers, the administration could not countenance categorizing such disputes under any other heading—e.g., purchase. The characteristics that administrators felt were appropriate to marriage, especially stability of unions and constancy of wives, may not have existed, but this did not eliminate their belief that they should have existed. Nor did it do away with their obligation to adjudicate such disputes as matrimonial issues.

Administrative attitudes toward LoDagaa women exhibited a degree of cultural relativism when compared with acceptable male attitudes toward British women in the metropole. In 1930, the colonial secretary's request for information about female circumcision elicited an articulation of the implicit indifference characteristic of administrative attitudes. One officer noted, "[T]his raises a very large question as to what is detrimental to the health and well being of the people. I suggest many African customs would be detrimental to a European but are apparently not so to an African."[42] Similarly, the assistant medical officer for the protectorate concluded his report:

> [I]t will thus be seen that the only objections to the operation of clitoridectomy
> are its brutality and its uselessness. It must be remembered that the operation has
> been judged from the European point of view. The African would not consider this
> operation as brutal and its suppression by law would probably appear to him to be
> in the nature of religious persecution.[43]

The identification of the African as male here is revealing and speaks for itself.

In 1936 "forced marriages" became an issue after the Liberal MP Eleanor Rathbone raised questions in Parliament about colonial policy and the colonial secretary issued another questionnaire.[44] In his reply, the chief commissioner concluded that women in the Northern Territories enjoyed "only slightly less freedom of choice with regard to their husbands than that to which their sisters in more civilized countries are entitled." If this observation was indicative of the position of women under colonialism, it should be noted that LoDagaa women had probably enjoyed even greater freedom than their "sisters" in Western societies before the start of the colonial project. He correctly noted that

> if [arranged unions] prove unsatisfactory to [women] there are means available for their annulment to which girls are not slow to resort. . . . If a woman seeks to have her marriage dissolved, it is almost certain that she is contemplating another. In that event the new husband would compensate the former husband, which he is generally given ample time to do.[45]

These remarks pertained to the sphere of daily social life, not to what occurred in the sphere of the courts, where disputes were, with the exception of extremely rare cases such as Angmin's, exclusively between men. Officers might have believed that presenting conjugal payments entitled men to have their wives restored to them, but by frustrating their rivals' attempts, officers were restricting women from leaving unions. The only means of "annulment" available to women was the successful formation of another union. The chief commissioner admitted to a preference toward husbands in the courts when he noted, "In the opinion of some officers the native law on divorce is too lax and operates to the advantage of the woman rather than that of the man."[46] This attitude persisted for some time, although individual officers occasionally deviated from the party line. In the annual report for 1938, for example, it was observed that women were only "regarded as vehicles for the production of children, or as mere domestic drudges, privileged to give sexual relief to their husbands."[47]

It was not until 1936 that a record of LoDagaa "marriage laws" was drafted, in response to a circular from the chief commissioner requesting such information, and then only after the Colonial Office had recommended such groundwork as part of plans for more effective administration.[48] As a result, the district commissioner of Lawra codified the marriage and divorce laws of the LoDagaa.[49] While he competently surveyed the views and opinions of the colonial chiefs, he did not determine whether they were the legitimate interpreters of LoDagaa social practices.[50] Under similar conditions men invented marriage laws throughout Africa in response to requests by colonial administrators. The two sets of males had a common interest in asserting control over women in the name of a past that often never existed except in the imaginations of its authors.[51] The district commissioner's report gave the impression that LoDagaa social practices were both definite and formalized. This was not surprising, as its informants were all chiefs. Furthermore, the quality of the information gathered purposively by district commissioners was delimited by the nature of the administrative questionnaires to which they were responding; these played a very important part in what Guyer called the "conceptual normalization" of marriage. As Musisi has argued in the previous chapter of this volume, historians have often overlooked the significance of such paradigmatic forms for the organization and categorization of knowledge about African societies.[52] For example, the following details were requested under the heading of "divorce":

> 1. On what grounds is it obtainable? 2. What repayments, if any, have to be made by the family of the woman? 3. What is the actual ceremony of the divorce (in the Colony the women are marked with white chalk)? 4. What is the position of the woman with regard to marriage after divorce?[53]

Although responses were furnished on each of these points, the questionnaire ignored the more fundamental question of whether or not there was any indigenous equivalent to the concept of divorce, let alone marriage as its inverse.

In response to the same questionnaire, the British anthropologist Meyer Fortes compiled an infinitely more thorough and subtle account of social practices among the Tallensi, a society to the east with striking similarities to the LoDagaa. He argued, "Tallensi ideas about the 'sanctity of marriage' are so different from our own that their attitudes to divorce and adultery cannot be measured by ours."[54] The suggestion that European and Tallensi concepts were incommensurable was not merely a theoretical qualification, but was also of practical relevance to the nature of disputes that emerged in the native courts.

> It should be noted, to begin with, that the term "divorce" is not applicable in the contexts of Tallensi marriage in the sense it bears for us. There are no legal "grounds for divorce"; and there is no legal procedure for obtaining a divorce from a spouse. In fact, legal action arises as a result of ruptured marriage, not as a means to dissolve it.[55]

Although Fortes did describe formal means and contexts for the dissolution of unions, he stressed that these were rare, and that normally these issues were never straightforward. In the report on LoDagaa practices, there were none of the qualifications and distinctions raised in Fortes' report.[56] In 1944, only six years later, a subsequent officer questioned the validity of this codification of laws relating to divorce: "The procedure for local divorce recorded at a Native Authority conference in 1938 . . . is a bit ambiguous, and I have some doubts whether it is correct."[57] When a conference of the chiefs was convened two months later, the district commissioner discovered that the difficulty did not rest with the language of the draft laws, but emanated from a more fundamental difference: "It transpires that there is no definite 'divorce,' the only thing anyone is interested in being the repayment of dowry [conjugal payments]."[58] In the amended version of the "laws" drawn up at the same conference it was stated, "No act, rite, or form of words . . . is necessary to effect a divorce between two persons married according to Native Customary Law."[59]

Administrators again became concerned about women's freedom very briefly in the late 1930s when LoDagaa women, who had begun to convert to Christianity in the early 1930s, began to leave their husbands for the mission station. The concern was ironic because at first the administration was very critical of the freedom that the missions afforded LoDagaa women.[60] At some times they accused the missionaries of inciting women converts to leave their non-Christian husbands, and at others they questioned the "the morals of a woman saving her soul at the expense of her children."[61] The missionaries were reported to have answered that God would provide for the children, but they were less sanguine when women left Christian husbands.[62] From the start, missionaries' attitudes toward non-Christian women were similar to those of early administrators, with complaints about the "vagabond morals" of women.[63] The underlying issue in both these cases—a woman's leaving her pagan husband when she converted, or deserting a Christian marriage for a pagan union—was the autonomy of women in LoDagaa society.

The conference of chiefs held in 1944, where it was ascertained that there was no such thing as formal divorce, had been convened to discuss the issue of women, or "wives," absconding to mission stations. The presiding officer had noted that there was a "good deal of tension on both sides, and it is plain that the local people have been suffering from a sense of grievance. I think the trouble is that the people suspect that unfaithful wives use conversion as a means of changing husbands."[64] Women would only have been doing so if their ability to leave one husband for another had been significantly constrained. Even though there was no commensurable indigenous sanction, the courts had used the idea of divorce introduced by administrators to keep women from leaving unions. Throughout the colonial period officers remained relatively unconcerned about the effects of their rule in restricting the freedom of LoDagaa women, because they generally believed that women already enjoyed too much freedom. This, rather than competition between men for wives, was seen as the cause of most disputes. Women were regarded as having no social agency in the courts, received no recognition, and were assumed to have no inherent rights. However, they had moral responsibilities and duties, namely toward children and husbands as mothers and wives.

Lovers, Adultery, and Male Rivalry

As direct control over women became more difficult to exercise in the 1930s due to the change in attitude of colonial administrators, who were increasingly responsible to external pressures, former and current husbands attempted to constrain the freedom of their wives by bringing their wives' lovers, their rivals, to court. Although there was no indigenous precedent for the charge of seduction in the 1908 case of *Rex vs. Bowo*,[65] there was an indigenous model on which to justify the prosecution of adultery cases before the courts. However, LoDagaa concepts of sexual offenses were very different from the jural concept that was applied by the courts in their various guises—just as different as those concerning the dissolution of conjugal unions were from the idea of divorce. In his response to an administrative questionnaire on "customary law" in 1931, an unusually perceptive officer replied that "adultery such as we understand the meaning of the word did not exist."[66] By this time the statement had to be made in the past tense; litigation for jural adultery had become common before the chiefs' tribunals.

Among the LoDagaa, categorizations of sexual offenses did not accord with Western patterns. Jack Goody, a student of Fortes and the first anthropologist to study the LoDagaa in great detail, noted that in the 1950s there were three types of sexual offences in daily life, known as *paa bume* or "matters of the vagina": "sleeping with a clanswoman, sleeping with the wife of a clansman, and sleeping with other married women." The first type required no payment and was not treated as a serious matter. The second offence "not only requires but demands a sacrifice," whereas with the third whether a sacrifice was required depended on the degree of physical proximity and ritual cooperation between the husband's and rival's households.[67] The latter category of offense, the one most susceptible to public scrutiny, was both ambiguous and contingent, depending on the variables of ever changing social networks. The creation of colonial courts, however, removed some of that uncertainty by establishing an overreaching political network that contracted notions of social distance and extended the physical range of possible offences.

Any transgression of sexual prohibitions was expressed in terms of physical affliction, and therefore did not rely on any moral or political sanction: "It may bring sickness or death on the woman's husband or children or even herself, for it is a serious affront to her husband's ancestors."[68] The sanction was a means of solving the cosmological problems which such actions were seen to create. Adultery was inextricably linked with the way in which indigenous conflicts were defined and resolved within precolonial LoDagaa society. Sanctions, insofar as they existed, did not prevent conflict but provided the means of limiting it and setting it within a context of ritual observances. Captain R. S. Rattray, a colonial officer and ethnographer, provided the following description of the form of resolution:

> The unfaithful wife would prepare beer and the male adulterer be called to come and drink with the husband [after the offense was confessed by the woman and admitted to by the man, and the necessary sacrificial animals supplied] and an agreement entered into, either to terminate the illicit relations between the parties concerned, or to recognize and, as it were, to legalize it, by the husband agreeing to allow his wife to have her lover.[69]

This arrangement, distinct from "taking a wife," was called "'lover enters the house'" (*sen kpe dia*).[70] In these instances a sexual relationship was authorized between a "married" women and her lover through the presentation by the lover of sacrificial items to the husband's household. Prior to colonialism, if the husband's rival (the wife's lover) was too distant, either socially or physically, for the husband to be certain of receiving the necessary sacrificial items, retaliatory action would have been taken.[71] The imposition of colonial judicial structures changed this, by compensating the husband (not his household) and punishing the rival. Goody reported that following the sacrifice of the surrendered animals, the husband did not eat the meat with the rest of his household: "To eat the flesh of an animal killed for a sin committed by one's wife might be taken as condoning the offense, and even profiting from it."[72] If any penalty or punishment was involved outside of prescribed areas, it was effected only through the use of force or retaliatory action. However, these perceptions had changed well before Goody's time in the field.

It would be a mistake, then, to see indigenous sanctions against adultery as having existed to protect conjugal relations. Adultery was not an institutional violation but an offense against the interests of the husband's household, or, more specifically, its ancestors. This could have given rise to the paradoxical situation among the Tallensi where "a woman who while away from home, yields to temptation and commits adultery without wishing to leave her husband, often runs off to marry the adulterer in order to avert the consequences of her lapse." Under these circumstances, if a woman returned to her former husband she did so "as a runaway wife, not as an adulteress."[73] The indigenous distinction between adultery and taking the wife of another man was easily obscured in the courts. Husbands who had succeeded in obtaining the return of their former wives often insisted that their rivals' presentations of conjugal payments were only sacrificial items necessary for what they attempted to reinterpret as adultery, but which, outside the court, would have been perceived only as evidence of rivalry and competition.[74]

The decisions of the district commissioner's court during the first three decades of colonial rule were supported by the definition of seduction as a criminal offense by the *Laws of the Gold Coast*. There are no records of the decisions of the native tribunals of this period. However, it is evident from a tabulation of "seduction fees" recorded in the District Record Book in 1917 that the chiefs' courts were imposing material penalties which internal social practices did not demand, let alone approve.[75] In 1932 seduction was omitted from the new ordinances which were to regulate the jurisdiction of the Native Authority Courts. The colonial administration restored it as a criminal offense in 1935 after complaints by the chiefs. But there had been two dissenting voices. The first was the assistant district commissioner of Zuarungu, an area to the east of Lawra that was ethnographically similar. He argued that seduction charges encouraged forced marriages. "If the Courts are able to force a woman to return as a wife to a man whom she does not want it will mean that the marriage of Frafra girls will become nothing less than a sale by auction."[76] The second voice, Meyer Fortes's, pointed out that what was referred to indigenously as "marrying another man's wife" was clearly differentiated from adultery. If a woman went to stay with a man, "even if it is only for one night, this is not adultery." The courts were denying the indigenous legitimacy of "marrying another man's wife." When the Tallensi brought cases to the court for the restitution of wives, they did so in the "name of the whiteman's law."[77] Litigants sought, not the application of a specific category of offense, but the general principle of male authority over women and the advantage of husbands over rivals afforded by British officers and exercised by chiefs.

A legal concept of adultery, as either a civil offense or criminal charge (e.g., for seduction), was a significant innovation in the repertoire of indigenous social practices. Through its application by the Native Authority Courts, it affected conjugal strategies and also caused indigenous perceptions of conjugal relations to assume jural characteristics appropriate to an institutional conceptualization of conjugal unions as marriages. In the 1940s charges for seduction and adultery were used, not to obtain the restitution of wives, but to punish rivals. The absence of cases for restitution in the Native Authority Court records can be attributed to warnings issued to chiefs in the late 1930s not to enforce unions against the will of women. Such practices did continue, but there were dangers that made them less frequent—not least of which was the knowledge that if women complained to the district commissioner the chiefs would be reprimanded. But in response to this curtailment of their jurisdiction, the Native Authority Courts applied the categories of "abduction" and "detention" to cover circumstances where a man married the wife of another man. These were applied when a woman had "divorced" her husband by entering into another union but the rival had not yet made the necessary conjugal payments, thereby creating a period of ambiguity between the dissolution of one union and the formation of another. In order to win his case, the former husband had to summon his rival to court before he made the conjugal payments.

The language of the former husbands' claims is indicative of a new proprietorial sense of male control over wives that emanated from the courts. In a case from 1942, a husband sought to have his rival fined for seduction, but as the woman denied having been seduced, the court fined the defendant one pound "for keeping the woman for a week as your wife."[78] The amount of damages awarded could not have been claimed according to indigenous practice; they were not even necessary under that system. But the clearest development documented in these records is the inflation of claims from expiatory to compensatory and penal proportions. These increased from one pound, seven fowls, and a sheep in 1943 to nine pounds, nine shillings in 1952 in the Jirapa Native Court, and from two pounds sixpence in 1948 to five pounds, a goat, a sheep, a dog, and ten hens in 1953 in the Lawra Native Court. The grounds for decisions were equally arbitrary, from a defendant's having "sexual relations" with a plaintiff's former wife to his "marrying" her. In the case of *Kyirguu vs. Debdaa* the nonspecificity of indigenous terms, which appears to account for the somewhat contradictory translations found in the records, was revealed in the plaintiff's claim: "I got to know that my wife got married to the above Debdaa, that is why I have come to issue summons against him to get my wife." The court ordered that the woman be returned to him and awarded him eight animals, ten hens, and ten thousand cowries "in order to sustain the woman's life."[79] In the case of *Der vs. Kuunohra,* the plaintiff sought the return of his wife through the Jirapa Native Court. He stated that the defendant had "married" his wife even though he had not "divorced" her. "I have therefore brought this to court that the defendant may explain to me why he has unlawfully married my wife. I want my wife." The defendant explained to the court that he loved the woman and she loved him. The court discovered that the woman did not wish to return to her former husband and so instructed the defendant to return the plaintiff's conjugal payments through the woman's household. However, it noted that the woman had already been residing with the defendant for three months, instituted criminal proceedings for "adultery," and fined him two pounds.[80]

In these adultery and seduction cases from the 1940s and 1950s litigants did not use the court as the medium for the return of their wives, but, instead, employed a more oblique strategy. They brought their rivals to court to preempt the presentation of conjugal payments and, thus, to assert their claims over the women in question as their wives. They also availed themselves of the court to have their interests in their former wives publicly acknowledged by their rivals. This was well illustrated in the clerk's translation of the case of *Boi Dagarti vs. Siekpe Tingani,* heard in 1952 before the Jirapa Native Court, in which the plaintiff explained that the defendant had "stolen" his wife three months ago, adding, "I do not know whether he has married her or he is simply loving her. That is why I have issued summons against him to tell the court the reason he did so."[81] The lack of specificity in such claims was due, not to the poor quality of translation, but to the absence of any indigenous equivalents to the social categories upon which these offenses were predicated—in particular, the lack of an indigenous term for "marriage" as a specific form of conjugal union. Similarly, in the case of *Nahab vs. Tingan,* which came before the Lawra Local Court in 1958, a year after the end of colonial rule, Nahab brought the lover of his brother's wife to court to demand sacrificial items to regularize their relationship, as his brother was at that time working in the south. He explained that once he discovered that the defendant had begun "loving" his brother's wife, he had asked him to provide a fowl to indicate that the woman was still married to his brother, "but the defendant refused and said it would appear shameful to do so."[82] Here it was not the threat of affliction that motivated the action, but the desire to have the court acknowledge the union in case of a later dispute over child custody.

The innovatory jural concept of adultery, first introduced by district commissioners at the turn of the century and applied by the chiefs from 1917 onward, had obvious effects on the nature of conjugal relations and the autonomy of women. In 1951 a committee investigating Native Authority Courts in the Gold Coast reported that even though the courts in the Northern Territories had been empowered to exercise customary law, the only purportedly indigenous offense that had received statutory recognition was "sexual connection with another man's wife." Chiefs had been able to innovate "rules . . . at variance with customary law as it was conceived of two to three generations ago," regardless of "the local people's idea of marriage."[83] This trend toward order and clarity is clearly indicated in a statement on the issue of "marrying another man's wife" by the Jirapa Native Authority Court in 1952: "This has been a practice which continues to entangle people. . . . This is a warning to all. The courting should be done according to customary law."[84] Here "customary law" meant the "conceptual normalization" of foreign "ideological valuations"—or, to put it differently, the invention of marriage and the imposition of a colonial patriarchy through the use of adultery charges.

Conclusion

In 1857, a century before the end of colonial rule in Lawra District, the British Parliament enacted the Divorce and Matrimonial Causes Act. For the first time, husbands could divorce their wives for adultery alone, whereas wives were only entitled to divorce if the adultery occurred along with crimes—e.g., bestiality, cruelty, desertion, incest, rape, or sodomy. This double standard, long part of English culture but never explicitly enshrined in law until this time, was meant to make the consequences of divorce ruinous for women. Keith Thomas has argued that the double standard on divorce had little to do with male concerns over the certainty of paternity, even though these informed Victorian theories about the purpose of marriage. Instead, it was due to the long-held "view that men have property in women and that the value of this property is immeasurably diminished if the woman at any time has sexual relations with anyone other than the husband."[85] The legal reification of the double standard was more the result of commercial considerations than a function of Victorian sexual anxiety. Although the idea of women as property (and as without property) died slowly in Britain after 1857, colonialism gave it new life in Lawra District. There, a transplanted ideology of male proprietorial authority over women became a reality in the courts a hundred years later.

During the colonial period the contextual nature of LoDagaa women's social identity as wives, upon which social practices had been predicated, was replaced by a proprietorial concept of women's belonging to husbands. In the courts women went from being wives *to* husbands to being wives *of* husbands, and conjugal payments, rather than a woman's residence, came to be seen as the significant factor in deciding whose wife she was.[86] In 1908 an administrator commented that LoDagaa women did not make good wives, due to their "unfaithfulness." Women's freedom was blamed for the frequency of disputes between rival males over the custody of children, which, it was claimed (with typical colonial moral exaggeration), were so common that "'it is a wise child that knows his father.'"[87] However, in their efforts to assert greater claims over their wives against rivals, LoDagaa husbands were trying, not to be certain of paternity, but to gain control over women. In the early years administrators regularly returned women to husbands; as this became less common, plaintiffs began to substitute material compensation for physical control. By 1957 husbands came not to demand the return of their wives but to claim damages for their loss—the woman's residence and alleged identity did not coincide.

The indigenous notion of wife (*pog*) had acknowledged women's autonomy and husbands' lack of control over wives, whereas the colonial idea of a wife increasingly allowed husbands to assert ownership through the courts. However, by examining women's behavior outside the courts, albeit through court records, we can see beyond these "ideological valuations." Although husbands increasingly saw wives in a proprietorial way, the history of litigation before the courts from 1907 to 1957 is the story of effective evasion and protracted resistance on the part of women through their choice of residence. This was the heart of Angmin's strategy. For most women it was the choice to leave rather than to stay that was their most effective weapon. This struggle between the conjugal payments of men and the residence of women cannot be fully understood unless we appreciate the intrinsic foreignness of the idea of marriage as an institution and adultery as an offense, and so avoid the "conceptual normalization" of these instruments of colonial patriarchy. Wives were treated as property in the courts in the 1940s and 1950s, but the colonial conceptualization of "wife" that allowed this did not reach beyond the courts. Extracting money from rivals in court was as close as husbands could come to controlling wives outside the courts by this time. Outside the courts women had more control over choosing husbands than husbands had over wives.

Primary Document

1. National Archives of Ghana, ADM 61/4/1, Lawra District Record Book, *Rex vs. Bowo*, 27 April 1908.

> Charge: Assaulting a woman
> *Kabiri states:* The accused caught my wife and slept with her and otherwise, ill treated her.
> *Chila:* I am the King of Zambor and I know this to be true that Bowo took Kabiri's wife and slept with her.
> Bowo   Q. Do you admit taking the woman and using her?
>   A. Yes.
>   Q. Why did you do it?
>   A. I wanted to marry her.
>   Q. You knew that she was Kabiri's wife.
>   A. Yes I knew.
> Sentence: 3 months Impt. HL 24 lashes [Signed DC Lawra 27/5/08]

2. National Archives of Ghana, ADM 61/4/1, Lawra District Record Book, *Kompailah vs. Naiver*, 5 August 1908.

> Charge: Claims his wife
> *Plaintiff:* I went to mines to work & left my wife at home. I paid 50/- & a sheep for her on my return I found deft had taken her so I took out summons against him to recover her.
> *Deft:* I have got no wife so when I saw this woman I took her. I knew she was plaintiff's wife but she said her husband had gone away. I am willing to give up the woman if D.C. says so.
> *Komp:* I am Kompailah's wife. I don't want to go back to either man. I

want to go home my husbands brother flogged me for going after men when my husband went away so I don't want to go back to my husband. I know my husband paid head money for me.

Plaintiff: When I went home I went to my father in law and asked him for my wife. my father said he did not know where woman was gone that I must go defendant and ask him. I did not ask deft as if I had gone he would make row, so I took summons.

Judgment. Kompo to go back to her husband

Kompailah & Naiver the deft to pay 3/6 costs. [Signed for DC Lawra 5/8/08]

3. Jirapa Native Authority Court, Civil Record Book, 18 January 1951.

18th Jan. 1951   In the NATIVE COURT JIRAPA
Der of Jirapa Tampoe vs. Kuu Noba of Dogo

The Plaintiffs [*sic*] as follows: My wife has been taken away and married by the ~~plaint~~ Defendant while I never divorced her. I have therefore brought this to court that the Def. may explain to me why he has un-lawfully married my wife. I want my wife.

Plea: ~~Not~~ Liable

Def: Yes, I married the Plaintiffs wife because love me and I loved her.

Judgement of the Court: Judgement of the Case. Court went through the case asked the woman and she said she does no more wish to marry old husband. In the opinion of the court the Def. no doubt had sexual inter-course with the woman while she was yet under old husband. The woman stayed with the new husband for a month and half; and he failed to pay the dowry.

Order of the Court: Well as the woman said she does no more want you; then the new husband keeps her. Dowries to be paid to the woman's ~~fee~~ parents.

Def. fees detained.

Ref References to Governors of order No. 43 of 1936
This is a criminal case
See opposite page for char charge.

The President
The Sabuli Naa
The Tizza Naa
[Signed by Native Authority Registrar]

In the Native Court of Jirapa . . .
For that you on the 1st of December 1950 did have sexual connection with one Pogpla the wife by native Customary law of one Deri of Tam-poe. When you were aware that she was directly under a husband. Contr. to Gov. order No. 43 of 1936

Plea: Guilty
Finding: Guilty
Sentence: £2 fine or in default of payment 1 month impr.

The President [Signed]
The Sabuli Naa
The Tizza Naa [Signed]
[Signed by Native Authority Registrar]

4. Jirapa Native Authority Court, Civil Record Book, 25 March 1952.
4/52   In the Jirapa Native Authority Court held on 25/3/52.
Boi Dagarti vs. Siekpe Tingani 766077 = 5/- 766078 = £3
Complainant states that my wife went to her fathers house, while I was aware of it, and later on my in-law came and told me that Siekpe Tingani has stolen away your wife to Saawie for about three months. I do not know whether he has married her or he is simply loving her. That is why I have issued summons against him to tell court the reason he did so.
Plea: liable
Findings: liable
Sentence: £3 or 1½ month I.H.L.
Judgement of Court:—Court went through the case and found Def. liable. Def. to pay £3 or 1½ months I.H.L.

The Jirapa Naa President [Signed]
The Tizza Naa Member [Signed]
Tugu Naa Member his mark X

NOTES

1. National Archives of Ghana (hereafter NAG), ADM 61/4/4, *Angmin vs. Tabbere*, 15 July 1944.
2. Ann Whitehead noted the same exclusion of women from litigation among the neighboring Kusasi, where "women are barely represented in 'woman' cases." These cases constituted the majority of litigation before the courts among the LoDagaa just as they did among the Kusasi. Ann Whitehead, "Men and Women, Kinship and Property: Some General Issues," in *Women and Property—Women as Property*, ed. Renée Hirschon (New York: St. Martin's, 1984), pp. 187–88.
3. In a study of court records from the 1930s and 1960s in Akuapim, an area just outside Accra, Dorothy Vellenga noted that the issue of "who is a wife" was always in question. Among the LoDagaa, once a woman left her natal household and lived with a man in his household she became a wife. However, the question of whose wife she was mirrored the question of who was a wife in Akuapim. Dorothy Vellenga, "Who Is a Wife? Legal Expressions of

Heterosexual Conflicts in Ghana," in *Female and Male in West Africa*, ed. Christine Oppong (London: Allen and Unwin, 1983), pp. 144–55.

4. The LoDagaa were the main inhabitants of Lawra District. This ethnic name refers to people who shared a variety of linguistic, cultural, and social affinities, but who did not share a common sense of identity before or during the colonial period. Before colonial rule these agriculturalists lived in decentralized congregations. During colonial rule a sizeable portion of the adult male population became migrant laborers and chiefs were imposed upon settlements, thereby bringing about important social and political changes.

5. Elizabeth Schmidt, *Peasants, Traders, and Wives: Shona Women in the History of Zimbabwe, 1870–1939* (Portsmouth, N.H.: Heinemann, 1992); Diana Jeater, *Marriage, Perversion, and Power: The Construction of Moral Discourse in Southern Rhodesia, 1894–1930* (Oxford: Clarendon, 1993).

6. In their explorations of the effects of colonial rule on gender relations in southern Africa, both Chanock and Jeater have demonstrated how central these issues were to the colonial project. Martin Chanock, *Law, Custom, and Social Order: The Colonial Experience in Malawi and Zambia* (Cambridge: Cambridge University Press, 1985); Jeater, *Marriage, Perversion, and Power*.

7. Chanock, *Law, Custom, and Social Order*, p. 145. Similarly, Kristin Mann and Richard Roberts have observed that "[l]aw was central to colonialism in Africa as conceived and implemented by Europeans and as understood, experienced, and used by Africans." Richard Roberts and Kristin Mann, "Law in Colonial Africa," in *Law in Colonial Africa*, ed. Kristin Mann and Richard Roberts (Portsmouth, N.H.: Heinemann, 1991), p. 3.

8. For examples of this in Ghana see Michel Verdon, *The Abutia Ewe of West Africa: A Chiefdom That Never Was* (Berlin: Mouton, 1983), pp. 164–72; Vellenga, "Who Is a Wife?" p. 145; Lynne Brydon, "The Dimensions of Subordination: A Case Study from Avatime, Ghana," in *Women, Work, and Ideology in the Third World*, ed. Haleh Afshar (London: Tavistock, 1985), pp. 112, 123. Innumerable studies have noted that marriage is extremely ambiguous in sub-Saharan Africa. See especially John L. Comaroff and Simon Roberts, *Rules and Processes: The Cultural Logic of Dispute in an African Context* (Chicago: University of Chicago Press, 1981), pp. 132–74, as well as many of the essays in Caroline Bledsoe and Gilles Pison, eds., *Nuptiality in Sub-Saharan Africa: Contemporary Anthropological and Demographic Perspectives* (Oxford: Clarendon, 1994).

9. *Northern Territories of the Gold Coast: Report for 1907*, Colonial Report-Annual, no. 566 (London: H.M.S.O., 1908), p. 9.

10. Regional Archives, Tamale (hereafter RAT), ADM 430, "Essay on the Peoples of the North West Province," Moutray-Read, PC NWP, 22 November 1908.

11. RAT ADM 514, Annual Report, Lawra District, 1937–38.

12. Stanley J. Tambiah, "Bridewealth and Dowry Revisited: The Position of Women in Sub-Saharan Africa and North India," *Current Anthropology* 30, no. 4 (1989): 419, 424–25.

13. Jane I. Guyer, "Lineal Identities and Lateral Networks: The Logic of Polyandrous Motherhood," in *Nuptiality in Sub-Saharan Africa*, ed. Bledsoe and Pison, pp. 234–35.

14. LoDagaa conjugal payments were economic, but made by men to other men,

and so did not directly impinge upon women except when, following colonization, men could bring rivals and women to court. The LoDagaa made clear distinctions between a wife and a slave; conjugal payments were much more substantial than the cost of slaves, and slaves were not given a proper burial. Edward Tengan, "The Institution of Marriage among the Dagaaba," in *Traditional Marriages*, ed. Edward Tengan (Wa, Ghana: Wa Catholic Press, 1990), pp. 26–28. For a discussion of these issues in a non-African context, see Marilyn Strathern, "Subject or Object? Women and the Circulation of Valuables in Highlands New Guinea," in *Women and Property—Women as Property*, ed. Hirschon, pp. 162–63.

15.   Payments were seen to be made *for* wives, and as representing the transfer of rights *in* or *over* women. For example, Radcliffe-Brown claimed that within a jural interpretation of conjugal payments "a person may be treated as a thing," even though he objected to economic interpretations of conjugal payments. A. R. Radcliffe-Brown, introduction to *African Systems of Kinship and Marriage*, ed. A. R. Radcliffe-Brown and Daryll Forde (London: Oxford University Press, 1950), pp. 12, 47, 50–52. Goody used similarly jural and proprietorial language (rights *in uxorem* and *in genetricem*) in order to analyze the implications of payments among the LoWiili, a particular society within the wider LoDagaa culture, even though he denied that these had connotations of purchase. Jack Goody, *The Social Organisation of the Lowiili* (London: HMSO, 1956), p. 54. Elsewhere, Goody remarked that although he used a jural language of rights in women in his analysis of conjugal payments, "as in the case of many property transactions in non-European societies, the complete alienation implied by our concept of 'gift' or 'sale' is rarely involved." Jack Goody, *Death, Property, and the Ancestors: A Study of the Mortuary Customs of the LoDagaa of West Africa* (Stanford, Calif.: Stanford University Press, 1962), pp. 275–76.

16.   Alice Singer, "Marriage Payments and the Exchange of People," *Man* 8, no. 1 (1973): 80–81.

17.   Anthropological theory's emphasis on the direction of conjugal payments greatly obscured attendant features grounded in their particular ethnographic contexts. Comaroff, criticizing this "unquestioning analytical priority," suggested that other features might be equally significant. "After all, the labels 'bridewealth' and 'dowry' select, as analytical *significata*, only the source and destination of payments, leaving as residual the dimensions of content, context and meaning." John L. Comaroff, introduction to *The Meaning of Marriage Payments*, ed. John L. Comaroff (London and New York: Academic Press, 1980), p. 10. The adherence to a structural perspective is directly related to the jural analysis of conjugal payments. Because anthropologists prioritized the direction of payments, they saw a woman's change of residence in the other direction as both their consequence and their explanation, and so academic interpretation was substituted for indigenous meaning.

18.   RAT ADM 430, "Essay on the Peoples of the North West Province," provincial commissioner, North West Province, 1907.

19.   District Magistrate's Court (Lawra), Court Record Book, vol. 7, L13/7/1966, *Eribari Zambo vs. Tangan Zambo*. For similar statements among the neighboring Lobi, see Madeleine Père, *Les Lobis: Tradition et changement*, vol. 1 (Paris: Éditions Siloë, 1988), p. 381.

20.   Barbara Hagaman, "Beer and Matriliny: The Power of Women in a West African Society" (Ph.D. diss., Northeastern University, 1977), pp. 101–102; P. A. Evans, "The LoBirifor/Gonja Dispute in Northern Ghana: A Study in Inter-ethnic Political Conflict in a Post-colonial State" (Ph.D. diss., University of Cambridge, 1983), pp. 118–19.

21.   Evans, "LoBirifor/Gonja Dispute," 119.

22.   NAG ADM 61/4/1, Lawra District Civil Record Book, 27 April 1908.

23.   Formerly, if Kabiri had been able to convince his wife to return, he would have had to be satisfied with the payment of sacrificial items, and then only if Bowo had lived close enough for a claim for such payment to be effective. Otherwise, Kabiri would have had to resort to uncertain retaliatory action of some kind.

24.   NAG ADM 56/1/50, Reports on Tours of Inspection, North West Province, April–May 1906. Evans noted that the LoBirifor, another LoDagaa subsociety, reacted much the same way to Gonja chiefs in the 1920s when they migrated into areas on the periphery of the chiefs' control. Evans, "LoBirifor/Gonja Dispute," pp. 119–20.

25.   Similar observations were made by Fortes, an anthropologist working for the colonial administration, and Labouret, a colonial administrator turned ethnographer, concerning the respective experiences of the Tallensi and LoWilisi. "The political and legal behaviour of the Tallensi, both commoner and chief, is as strongly conditioned by the ever-felt presence of the District Commissioner as by their own traditions. . . . And always, the District Commissioner, whether actually present or not, was one of the principal sanctions determining the outcome of events." Meyer Fortes, *Marriage Law among the Tallensi* (Accra: Government Printing Department, 1936), p. 27. "The rules that now exist seem to be the result of developments triggered by European occupation. Under the influence of administrative tribunals all local customs tend to be standardized and thus compromised, such that they no longer reflect indigenous practices." Henri Labouret, *Les tribus du rameau Lobi* (Paris: L'institut d'ethnologie, 1931), p. 256 (the translation is mine).

26.   Jane Parpart, "Sexuality and Power on the Zambian Copperbelt: 1926–1964," in *Patriarchy and Class: African Women in the Home and the Workforce*, ed. Sharon B. Stichter and Jane L. Parpart (Boulder, Colo.: Westview, 1988), pp. 199–222.

27.   Roger Thomas, "Forced Labour in British West Africa: The Case of the Northern Territories of the Gold Coast, 1906–1927," *Journal of African History* 14, no. 1 (1973): 79–103.

28.   NAG ADM 61/4/1, Lawra District Civil Record Book, *Kompailah vs. Naiver,* 5 August 1908.

29.   NAG ADM 61/4/1, Lawra District Civil Record Book, *Depang vs. Quiniari,* 5 August 1908.

30.   See Goody, *Social Organisation,* p. 53.

31.   NAG ADM 61/4/1, Lawra District Court Record Book, *Loab vs. Chiapuun,* 24 May 1909.

32.   These were not the only terms, but they were the most generic. See Capt. R. S. Rattray, *The Tribes of the Ashanti Hinterland,* vol. 2 (Oxford: Clarendon, 1932), pp. 54, 91; Bozi Somé, "La parenté chez les Dagari," *Notes et documents voltaiques* 2 (1968): 11; Tengan, "Marriage among the Dagaaba," pp. 10–12;

Gregory Eebo Kpiebaya, *Dagaaba Traditional Marriage and Family Life* (Wa, Ghana: Wa Catholic Press, 1991), pp. 5–10.

33. NAG ADM 61/4/1, Lawra District Civil Record Book, *Rex vs. Zanya,* 18 July 1913.

34. "Once a woman is embarked upon marriage, she remains married for the rest of her life. She is likely to change husbands, but there is never a time when her brideprice is not paid by someone. . . . A woman is never fully integrated into the residence of her husband and remains all her life as mobile as everything in the house which is not dug into the earth." Hagaman, "Beer and Matriliny," pp. 137, 214–15.

35. Barbara M. Cooper, *Marriage in Maradi: Gender and Culture in a Hausa Society in Niger, 1900–1989* (Portsmouth, N.H.: Heinemann, 1997), pp. 62–69.

36. NAG ADM 61/5/6, Lawra District Complaint Book, 18 October 1918.

37. NAG ADM 61/4/2, Lawra District Civil Record Book, quoted in provincial commissioner, North West Province, to district commissioner, Lawra, 12 October 1911.

38. NAG ADM 61/4/2, Lawra District Record Book, acting secretary of native affairs to acting chief commissioner of the Northern Territories, quoted in provincial commissioner, North West Province, to district commissioner, Lawra, 12 October 1912.

39. A. W. Cardinall, *The Natives of the Northern Territories of the Gold Coast: Their Customs, Religion, and Folklore* (London: George Routledge and Sons, 1920), p. 79.

40. Ibid., p. 76.

41. Ibid., pp. 79–80.

42. RAT ADM 3, Female Excision (Circumcision), 1930–33, quoted in commissioner, Northern Province, to chief commissioner of the Northern Territories, 10 June 1930.

43. RAT ADM 3, Female Excision (Circumcision), 1930–33, assistant medical director to chief commissioner of the Northern Territories, 2 June 1931. It would be equally inappropriate to judge administrative attitudes from anything other than a European perspective. From a non-European perspective, administrative officers' sudden toleration of this one aspect of indigenous culture was transparently hypocritical.

44. RAT ADM 259, Rules Made under Section 17 of Native Authority Ordinance, secretary of state to governor of the Gold Coast, 17 August 1936. The matter had arisen following questions in the House of Commons by Eleanor Rathbone, MP, on 22 July 1936. The secretary of state appears to have been less than completely enthusiastic about the whole question, stating that "the extent and evil of the pressure which may be exercised on African girls to marry against their will are capable of exaggeration." The questionnaire asked whether physical coercion was involved and, if it was, whether women were free to bring cases to the notice of officers, what action officers had taken, and whether such steps were sufficient to prevent serious abuses or whether further measures were necessary. See *Correspondence Relating to the Welfare of Women in Africa, 1935–37,* Parliamentary Papers, Cmd 5784 (London: H.M.S.O., 1938). On Rathbone's earlier work to have female circumcision outlawed in Kenya, see Susan Pedersen, "National Bodies, Unspeakable Acts:

The Sexual Politics of Colonial Policy-Making," *Journal of Modern History* 63, no. 3 (1991): 647–80. I have the editors of this volume to thank for this citation.

45. RAT ADM 259, Rules Made under Section 17 of Native Authority Ordinance, chief commissioner of the Northern Territories to the colonial secretary, 21 October 1936.

46. Ibid.

47. RAT ADM 514, Annual Report, Lawra District, 1937–38.

48. RAT ADM 292–93, Record of Native Law and Custom, chief commissioner of the Northern Territories to district commissioner, Northern Territories, 17 June 1936.

49. RAT ADM 514, Annual Report, Lawra, 1937–38, Appendices.

50. Rattray noted that chiefs were particularly unreliable sources of information for the anthropologist. *Ashanti Hinterland,* p. xii.

51. For examples of this see especially Chanock, *Law, Custom, and Social Order;* Jeater, *Marriage, Perversion, and Power.*

52. Jan Vansina, "Knowledge and Perceptions of the African Past," in *African Historiographies: What History for Which Africa?* ed. Bogumil Jewsiewicki and David Newbury (Beverly Hills: Sage, 1986), p. 31.

53. RAT ADM 292–93, Record of Native Law and Custom, chief commissioner of the Northern Territories to district commissioner, Northern Territories, 17 June 1936. The nature of the questionnaire, and not just its lack of congruence with indigenous concerns, also created distortion, because of the difficulty of translating concepts.

54. Fortes, *Marriage Law,* p. 13.

55. Ibid., p. 14.

56. The district commissioner stated that the father-in-law executed the divorce following the return of his daughter by her husband. He admitted that the father-in-law could not refuse to "grant" a divorce, but insisted that he had to be recognized simply because "there is no other competent authority." NAG ADM 292–93, Record of Native Law and Custom, "Marriage Laws of the Lobi/Dagarti Natives Resident in the Lawra Native Authority Area," 1938.

57. RAT ADM 342–43, Informal Diary, Lawra, May 1944.

58. Ibid., July 1944. A generation earlier an officer had made this observation, not as a statement of practice, but as a moral criticism. See NAG ADM 61/5/3, Lawra District Complaint Book 13/15, July 1916. When it appeared that his daughter's husband (a colonial employee) intended to take her south, the chief of Gengenkpe attempted to return the conjugal payments himself. The district commissioner refused to return his grandchildren to the chief, but allowed the woman to be withdrawn from the union. However, he was ambivalent about having done so and commented, "These people seem to think that they can have it both ways and get everything by returning the bridewealth."

59. NAG ADM 61/5/11, Lawra District Record Book, 14 July 1944, p. 394. Further and perhaps more significant amendments were made. It was argued that the father-in-law was not a "competent authority to pronounce or grant divorce," being merely a witness to the dissolution of a union and a "channel through which the bride price is paid by any new husband to the old." Follow-

ing this last point, the amendments stressed, "In the event of a wife effecting divorce, the dowry can be reclaimed by the husband only from a subsequent husband."

60. RAT ADM 247, Informal Diary, Lawra, March and April 1937; RAT ADM 301, Informal Diary, Lawra, January 1938.

61. RAT ADM 301, Informal Diary, Lawra, January and February 1938.

62. Ibid., February 1938. "Called the girl and explained that as she herself had chosen the Christian religion unforced she had no right to throw it over for a love affair. Told the chiefs that the return of dowry, usual in such cases, would not settle the matter in this case as the unfortunate, legitimate husband was debarred from marrying again. Told the girl to return to her father's house as she refused to return to her husband. Probably she will live a spinsters life."

63. *Rapports annuels*, no. 26, 1930–31 (Rome: Pères blancs, 1932), p. 195.

64. RAT ADM 342–43, Informal Diary, Lawra, April 1944.

65. NAG ADM 61/4/1, Lawra District Civil Record Book, *Rex vs. Bowo*, 27 April 1908.

66. RAT ADM 169, Native Administration, district commissioner, Lawra, to chief commissioner of the Northern Territories, 31 March 1931. Writing at the same time, Labouret noted of LoWilisi perceptions that "The effects of this infraction [adultery] are quite different from the ones we attribute to it; it is a serious offence against the Earth, goddess of fertility, and against the guardian gods of the family [rather than a legal offence]." Labouret, *Rameau Lobi*, p. 286 (the translation is mine).

67. Goody, *Death, Property, and the Ancestors*, pp. 204–205, 391–92.

68. Meyer Fortes, *The Web of Kinship among the Tallensi: The Second Part of an Analysis of the Social Structure of a Trans-Volta Tribe* (Oxford: Clarendon, 1949), p. 117.

69. Rattray, *Ashanti Hinterland*, p. 416.

70. Ibid. See also Goody, *Death, Property, and the Ancestors*, p. 139.

71. Fortes, *Web of Kinship*, p. 116.

72. Goody, *Death, Property, and the Ancestors*, p. 392.

73. Fortes, *Marriage Law*, p. 18.

74. See NAG ADM 61/4/2, Lawra District Civil Record Book, *Wor vs. Keyli*, 17 July 1912; NAG ADM 61/5/3, Lawra District Complaint Book, 22 February and 10 June 1916; NAG ADM 61/5/4, Lawra District Complaint Book, 20 February 1929.

75. NAG ADM 61/5/1, Lawra District Record Book, "Satisfaction and Adultery Fees Customary in the Chiefs' Courts," n.d., p. 445.

76. RAT ADM 259, Rules Made under Section 17 of the Native Authority Ordinance, 1934–51, acting district commissioner, Zuarungu, to chief commissioner of the Northern Territories, 20 August 1936.

77. Fortes, *Marriage Law*, pp. 18, 20.

78. Jirapa Native Authority Court, Criminal Record Book, 10 February 1942.

79. Lawra Native Authority Court, Civil Record Book, 4 September 1953.

80. Jirapa Native Authority Court, Civil Record Book, 18 January 1951.

81. Ibid., 25 March 1952.

82. District Magistrate's Court (Lawra), Court Record Book, vol. 1, L18/4/58, *Nahab of Kunyukuo vs. Tingan of Tolibri*.

83. *Report of the Commission on Native Courts,* Gold Coast (Accra: Government Printing Department, 1951), pp. 16–18.

84. Jirapa Native Authority Court, Civil Record Book, 5 December 1952.

85. Keith Thomas, "The Double Standard," *Journal of the History of Ideas* 20 (1959): 209–10. See also George W. Stocking, Jr., *Victorian Anthropology* (New York: Free Press, 1987), pp. 197–208; Susan Kingsley Kent, *Sex and Suffrage in Britain, 1860–1914* (Princeton: Princeton University Press, 1987), p. 29.

86. At the beginning of the colonial period defendants routinely explained that they had taken the wives of plaintiffs because they too wanted "*a* wife." Plaintiffs, most often chiefs and migrant laborers, asked for the return of "*my* wife," but the possessive pronoun found in the court records at this time indicated a sense of desire rather than ownership. Administrators returned the women in question out of their sense of what was appropriate rather than what was indigenously normal or possible. Fifty years later plaintiffs came to the courts of Native Authority chiefs to seek damages for the proprietorial interests they had come to believe they still enjoyed in wives who had left them. This was the product of the assimilation of the "ideological valuations" inherent in the colonial categories of marriage and adultery. These former husbands invariably referred to their former wives as "*my* wife" even though they acknowledged that these women had left them for other men. The shifting meaning of the possessive pronoun in the court records signifies a major shift in the identities of women in the minds of both plaintiffs and court assessors.

87. RAT ADM 430, "Essay on the Peoples of the North West Province," provincial commissioner, North West Province, 22 November 1908.

6 Colonialism, Education, and Gender Relations in the Belgian Congo: The *Évolué* Case

Gertrude Mianda

Recent studies in the field of education throughout Africa document the extent of sexual segregation in the educational system missionaries put in place during the colonial period. Many argue that girls' education continues to lag behind that of boys because girls have been trained primarily for domesticity. As Nakanyike Musisi points out for Uganda, with the complicity of the chiefs, the daughters of aristocrats were trained by missionaries to become the wives and mothers of elite men and to manage the household, while sons were trained for the public sphere. In subsequent years, this type of education was extended to the wider population.[1] In southeast Nigeria, boys and girls were not segregated in school, but fewer girls went to school than boys, and girls' education was limited to apprenticeship, manual work, and homemaking.[2] In the Belgian Congo, education was similarly entrusted to the missionaries, by virtue of the convention concluded between the Catholic Church and the Independent State of the Congo on 26 May 1906.[3] Men were the first to receive instruction, and they received it in French; thus they had access to a prestigious social status. Girls' education, offered in indigenous languages, focused on the acquisition of homemaking skills and the reinforcement of supposedly feminine characteristics, which were defined by Christian morality. As a consequence, the first Congolese elite was made up exclusively of men—*les évolués*. As a group, the évolués brought together in the period between the two wars the first generation of educated people in the Belgian Congo. This chapter focuses on this elite and its vision of gender relations and of the proper place for women.

In many ways, colonization improved some men's gendered positions by according them more privileges than women in political, judicial, economic, and social domains. This was certainly the case with the évolués. As the first to master spoken and written French, they were also the first to produce their own publication—*La voix du Congolais* (The voice of the Congolese).[4] For over a decade (1945–59), this journal served as the undisputed standard-bearer of évolué opinions and, at the same time, the instrument for affirming their social, political, and literary status. Évolués firmly believed that they had attained a level of "civilization" which brought them much closer to whites than to the commoner Congolese. They felt themselves charged, in turn, to propagate this civilization to the wider population.[5] As they sought to make themselves as much like whites as possible,[6] they used La voix du Congolais to circulate their demands for status and to articulate their views about the position of women, among other issues. Through this process, they espoused a new model of gender relations.

In this chapter, I explore the social construction of this new model of gender relations by examining the demands expressed by the évolués in La voix du Congolais. I seek to expose the central features of évolué discourse about Congolese women's position, taking into consideration évolués' education and the representation of women that colonial education produced. To undertake a study of gender using a source that primarily captures the opinions of men might appear to contradict the tenets of feminist scholarship, which foregrounds women's points of view and lived experiences.[7] But it is precisely because women were kept on the margins of social and public discourse in the Belgian Congo that we must begin to write their history by making use of men's writings. Only in this way can we extricate Congolese women from the rubbish of colonization.

The first article written by a Congolese woman did not appear in La voix du Congolais until 1956, and it was translated from Lingala by the male editor, A. F. Bolamba.[8] Even after that date, Congolese women expressed themselves in La voix du Congolais primarily in interviews conducted by men. This is why I draw upon men's discourse, but scrutinize it according to the feminist principle that "gender relations are always power relations."[9] The fact that male évolués demanded the improvement of women's education does not diminish the need to analyze their discourse in terms of relations of power between the sexes. Thus, my analysis foregrounds masculine domination[10] while demonstrating how gender relations are socially constituted, represented, lived, and contested[11] in colonial society.

Gender relations flow fundamentally from the social order and the symbolic meaning of "discourse" (religious, scientific, and legal), as well as from institutions and their practices, cultures, and ways of thought. Thus, the évolués' discourse on gender relations should be understood not as the expression of bad attitudes or false beliefs, but in light of the social order and meanings established in colonial society.[12] In that society, the West and its values were placed on a pedestal as a model to be emulated at whatever cost, and social actors, male and female, used the resources at their disposal in their social interactions. In this chapter, I use a sociological approach (drawn from an ethnomethodological perspective), but add a historical perspective.[13] In the first section, I examine girls' education in the Belgian Congo in order to delineate one area of daily social life—colonial society's system of education. This provides the background necessary to examine, in the second section, évolué discourse about women's situation and gender relations in Congolese society of the period.

Sexual Segregation in Education in the Belgian Congo and the Image of Women in Colonial Society

Education in the Belgian Congo was constituted, first and foremost, on a racist basis by separating blacks and whites.[14] Beyond this, a Christian education was as fundamental for girls as it was for boys.[15] The broad lines of educational policy in the Belgian Congo envisaged a type of professional and agricultural mass education for the purpose of training assistants for the whites;[16] material to be taught to girls and to boys was clearly differentiated.[17] In the minds of colonizers and missionaries, the purpose of school was to make boys into artisans and girls into mothers of families and perfect wives,[18] by inculcating new, Western, Christian values in them.[19]

The colonialists established two educational levels: primary and secondary. The primary level included the *maternelle* (kindergarten) and two more stages. The first stage offered basic training for both sexes, while the second differed according to gender. Boys were trained to be assistant clerks for the whites or tradesmen; girls received practical training in homemaking and an apprenticeship in teaching.[20]

Major changes were introduced by the 1948 reform. Primary education was extended by a year, and the first stage was further distinguished from the second. The first stage, or ordinary training, was for general education and was conducted in local languages;[21] now, certain students were selected for a second stage (*l'enseignment de selection*), given in French, that prepared them for secondary school.[22] Under the new system, girls also received more training in household management.

The 1948 reform also introduced a long cycle of six years of study at the secondary level for students who had received a "selected" education. This secondary education had two sections: a special one, which trained students for a profession, and a general one, which prepared them for future studies with a more intellectual focus. This option offered the Congolese wider training for more prestigious careers in public service or private enterprise. Most importantly, however, it prepared them for post-secondary education. From its conception, this program was intended exclusively for boys and was administered in French. For girls, whose education was entrusted solely to nuns, the reform underlined the necessity of a practical, moral education that would prepare them for their future roles as wives and mothers. Thus, girls were limited, even in "selected" education, to taking the three-year middle school homemaking program or moving on to teachers' training school, which consisted of four years of study following the six years of primary school.[23] This training was to enable girls "to become good wives, informed mothers, and perfect household managers."[24]

As late as 1955, however, there were only six schools for girls in all of the colony that offered the "selected" second degree, and thirty classes that prepared girls for post-primary education.[25] There were seven middle schools of household management and two professional schools for clothing design and sewing, at Elisabethville and Leopoldville. As for normal schools, there were twenty-three girls' schools of teaching apprenticeship and twenty-two girls' teacher training schools, with a combined total of 1,600 students, compared to 7,750 boys enrolled in the same type of institution. French education in girls' classes was less emphasized because, quite simply, its usefulness for girls was disputed. As M. J. Van Hove, the advisor to the colonial minister, noted, "with respect to girls, for whom knowledge of a European language seems of debatable utility, for most of them at least, the teaching of French—while not being removed from the program—will have a reduced place except at the secondary level."[26]

The names of courses in homemaking schools illustrated their goal, namely, to make girls into better wives. They included the following, though they varied somewhat from one institution to another: religion, arithmetic, the metric system, French, one's native language, drawing, geography, the sciences, hygiene, conversation, observation, music, singing, gymnastics, sewing, agriculture, housework, and politeness. This constituted the program's intellectual training, though much emphasis was also placed on practice. Girls were instructed in simple housekeeping, flower arranging, laundering, ironing, sewing, fieldwork, and cooking. In order to know how to beautify a house, girls learned washing, door dressing, home furnishing, and window decorating.[27] The goal of homemaking school was clearly underlined by Mother Van Hove's report about the Mbanza Boma middle school: "Our objective is to train Christian wives and mothers of the future. . . . To train their taste, to develop their aesthetic sense, is to prepare the future woman of the interior, shining center of the home."[28] Thus, girls were introduced to housekeeping, mending and sewing, washing and ironing, cleaning rooms, cooking, and gardening—apprenticeships in orderliness and cleanliness. With the 1948 reform, schools for nurses and nursing assistants (*gardes sanitaires*) were also organized. Here, girls received two years of instruction in nursing and midwifery, followed by practical training.[29]

Clearly, the goal of girls' education in the Belgian Congo was to turn out homemakers trained in Christian religious convictions. M. J. Van Hove expressed this eloquently when he recalled the ideas that guided the 1948 reorganization of girls' education:

> . . . to assure by appropriate means an education for the indigenous female element which, pulling her out of her semi-servile state, permits her to respond to women's eternal calling in veritably every human society, which is not only to give birth to, but also to raise, men.[30]

Because of such ideas, girls' training was considerably delayed in comparison to that of boys. The principal reasons for the delay were considered to be "customs and traditions" which assigned women the role of wife and mother.[31] But the patriarchal ideology which governed education in the Belgian Congo clearly exacerbated the gap between girls' and boys' instruction. In its philosophy, the system was simply an adaptation in the colony of the sexist, patriarchal educational ideology which governed the training offered girls in the colonial metropole, Belgium.[32] The colonial system of education in the Belgian Congo thus consolidated social-sexual roles on the basis of existing sexual discrimination, by offering women a feeble instruction which confined them to the household and fostered activities presumed to correspond to feminine nature.

Yet the 1948 reform was also a response to the desire of évolués, who wanted their wives and daughters to receive a better education and thus attain the same level of "civilization" they themselves had.[33] This desire was highlighted in the report of the Coulon-Deheyn-Renson pedagogical mission established to assess the need for additional reforms:

> One knows the drama of évolué households in which a black has become conscious of his personality as a civilized man and wishes to have others' behavior and relations conform to his, but must in fact spend his life at the side of a *musenji* [a backward person, a savage].[34]

To the degree that the homemaking school program was aimed at évolués' daughters,[35] it proceeded to fulfill this expectation. The reformed education system aimed at producing virtuous Christian women who, as wives and mothers, would be excellent household managers.

Évolué Discourse about Women's Situation: Toward a New Representation of Gender Relations

The évolué demand that their wives and daughters be "civilized" by education requires us to investigate more closely the évolué conception of gender relations. Like most systems of education,[36] that of the Belgian Congo divided the sexes hierarchically, to the disadvantage of women, and this division profoundly shaped the évolué conception of gender relations. One can uncover the évolués' attitudes toward women's issues, as well as the wider issue of gender relations, by analyzing their demands for women's instruction and their debates concerning prostitution and marriage, as well by examining their carefully constructed lifestyle.

In order to understand évolué demands concerning the social condition of Congolese women, it is important to situate the évolués in Congolese society. To be admitted to the évolué class, it was necessary to meet specific criteria: education in a middle school, a normal school, or a seminary;[37] a monthly income of no less than a thousand francs;[38] a professional identity; and, finally, a certain Christian morality, especially with respect to lifestyle. The first two criteria allowed access to a specific socioeconomic position. Those who graduated from the right schools could permit themselves certain material comforts, such as a cement house, a bicycle, or a phonograph.[39] It was thus possible for évolués to display an external appearance which mirrored that of whites. Professional integrity had to be demonstrated by working in conformity to expectations.[40] As for the new morality, it had to be obtained through education.[41] It rested, most notably, on the adoption of monogamy and the denunciation of polygyny; it implied, quite simply, the acceptance of the Western Christian family model.

The intellectual and Christian training the évolués received enabled them to meet these conditions. But it was necessary to maintain good habits and improve them. By virtue of their intellectual training, évolué circles under the colonizers' control were called upon to take up this task.[42] In imitation of the diffusers of modernity, the évolués, for their part, believed themselves charged with positively influencing the rest of the indigenous population:[43]

> In the course of our stay on the school bench, we were subjected to severe discipline, and we received a careful education, which inculcated solid principles in us which must guide us in life. These principles constitute the basis of this Christian civilization toward which we strive. We must not conserve them only for ourselves. It is our duty to communicate them through our private and public conduct, our counsels, and our teachings to those of our racial brothers who have not received them.[44]

Another writer agreed, stating, "The true, the unique évolué is the one who puts his situation to the service of the mass in order to be a precious assistant to his civilizers."[45] Another concurred: "The évolué is like a reservoir who receives in order to pour out afterwards to others."[46] The évolués considered themselves to have undergone a cultural conversion which assimilated them to whites. Their most important demands, therefore, were for recognition of a status different from, and above, that of the masses of Congolese.[47] And they justified their claims to superiority by frequent reference to women's position and the nature of the family, notably to the monogamous family model with its matrimonial regime and patrilineal succession. They also articulated ongoing struggles against polygamy, prostitution, and the high cost of bridewealth. These themes filled the pages of *La voix du Congolais* and provide extraordinary insight into the évolués' conception of gender relations.

Évolué Demands regarding Girls' Education: A Struggle for Women's Emancipation?

Father Vermeersch was among the first to demand education for Congolese women. The évolués in turn clamored insistently for the instruction of their daughters and demanded that this be done in French.[48] For them, the French language denoted social promotion and prestige; it was a sign of "civilization."[49] But the évolués, although demanding French education for girls, were not beginning to favor women's emancipation and gender equality:

> We are not demanding that our wives acquire profound and special knowledge which would place them at a level which is not naturally reserved to them. We wish only that our wives be brought closer to our degree of evolution and understand us. . . . In households in civilized countries, women have also been men's best counsel.[50]

> Also we demand that true homemaking schools be created where our daughters can be prepared for domestic life by developing in them intellectual skills and solid moral qualities. . . . it is necessary to teach them how to take care of a household

in the most perfect way possible. If domestic work isn't accomplished with order-liness and cleanliness, a man won't stay at home.[51]

The paradox revealed in these demands undercuts any illusion that évolués might have supported the liberation of women. They desired education in French for their daughters, but they opposed their wives' involvement in salaried work,[52] though some favored women's limited salaried employment on the grounds that a wife with a salary could contribute to household income.[53] *La voix du Congolais* often hosted an engaging debate on these issues:

The Congolese Woman at Work

We read with lively interest M. G. Mukelebwe Ebwe's article in the July issue of *La voix du Congolais* about the possibility of letting Congolese women work for the administration or in private companies.

It is certainly time that the authorities examine this question.

However, we do not agree with all the opinions M. G. Mukelebwe Ebwe expressed and we *think it best* that single rather than married women work in one organiza-tion or another, the *proper place* of the latter being at home with her children, if she has any.

In *grounding our argument* on these facts, we are persuaded that it is absurd to let a married woman work for a company to which she will have to return in the afternoon, thus neglecting her children's and husband's care.

On the one hand, it is necessary for a single woman to work even if she does not save the money that she earns by the sweat of her brow. Working will permit her to support herself honestly, respecting her body at the same time, rather than selling it at the risk of contracting and propagating venereal diseases.

On the other hand, if married women work, we will see that little by little they will lose respect for their husbands. The percentage of divorces will augment pro-portionally.

It is very true that it is the Christian family that will lead our country, the Congo, in the future and that it is through work that a country earns its merit.

Our intention is far from disallowing the right to equality which must remain between husband and wife—what we envision is that our daughters acquire a very profound moral education and that they collaborate with their husbands with respect to household management so that they educate their children suitably, cradle of a prosperous Congo.

Gabriel Sulet Ekongo

N.d.L.R.—A married woman must remain at home—I agree. If a supplementary salary is necessary (to build or improve the house, for example), the wife must be able to find work to do at home. A single woman need not necessarily go to work "for the administration or in a private company" although, however, a livelihood is desirable in the case of prostitutes.

Also, it would be desirable to create workshops for learning feminine trades (cutting-up and making clothes, knitting, sewing, etc.).

A.R.B.[54]

In fact, for the évolués, a wife's working outside the household conflicted not only with woman's role in society, but also with the man's duty to provide for the needs of the household.[55] As for the woman, the évolués expected her to be a wife, good household manager, and mother:

In effect, the father, head of the family, or still better, its protector, has only one care, that of working to earn the money necessary to feed and maintain his own.[56]

The husband owes protection and assistance to his wife. He must watch over the security and interest of his family. He owes protection to his wife against her weakness and her moral failures. He will be her legitimate support in her listlessness and fatigue. Through his work, he assures the subsistence of his entire household and avoids compromising its security through excessive and extravagant personal spending.[57]

What we expect is to have educated women in our homes, in our country villages, that is to say, women who know how to wash clothes, to press them in the right way, to replace lost buttons, to mend torn clothing, to shine shoes, to cook suitably and properly, and above all to educate our children.[58]

The true function of the wife consists in devoting herself to the needs of the household, bringing to it her devotion, her spirit of orderliness and of economy. But her role is not limited to being the steward of household resources; she must also be a counselor, aid, support, and devoted collaborator who knows how by well-chosen words to calm her husband's anxieties and fortify his courage.[59]

These were not just empty words in magazine columns. The colonial administration reinforced this idea that a woman belonged at home by placing her under male guardianship, by requiring, through legislation, a husband's authorization before his wife could work. Marital authorization for work indicates the very different places in society that the colonial administration accorded to women and men—places which corresponded to the training they received—and reveals the ways in which the patriarchal ideals of colonial administrators, missionaries, and male évolués overlapped and reinforced one another.[60]

In the évolués' mind, a wife had to be economically dependent on her husband, who would earn money to support the family. Women's primary responsibility was to maintain the household in such a way as to reflect the couple's level of education. The image (see figure 6.1) published in La voix du Congolais and titled "The Congolese woman's place is in the home, near her children" is a clear expression of these gender relations.[61] In their desire to take on a white lifestyle, the évolués aspired to converse with their wives and children in French and to entrust the raising of their children to women "civilized in children's education."[62] They wanted women's education to consist of an apprenticeship in their roles as mothers and wives by way of training in homemaking, which was to be offered in French,[63] and practical education offered through social centers.[64]

Although they supported girls' instruction, the évolués also understood edu-

Figure 6.1. "The Congolese woman's place is at home, near her children."
From *La Voix du Congolais* 88 (July 1953): 475.

cation to be a threat; it might result in their daughters' sexual liberation. In order to guard against this danger, they wanted girls' education to take place in a controlled location, such as a boarding school. This, they believed, would ensure young girls' moral training and preserve their nature.[65] Yet girls' instruction remained in constant tension with fears about sexual liberation,[66] to the point that many saw a direct, causal link between girls' education and the dissolution of morality.[67] And the rising rate of prostitution in the urban centers only intensified évolués' concerns and their insistence that girls' morality be developed through carefully monitored educational systems.

Beyond the Debate on Prostitution, Marriage, Matrilineal Kinship, and Bridewealth: Évolués' Vision of Gender Relations

Hoping to contain urban prostitution and under the influence of the missionaries, in the 1930s the colonial administration decided to require travel permits (*permis de mutation*) for healthy indigenous women who, in theory, were living alone.[68] For the missionaries, and particularly for Catholics, the city was a place of depravity[69] and the évolués favored the adoption of judicial measures to fight prostitution.[70] Indeed, the évolués' vehement opposition to such practices as prostitution provides crucial insight into their evolving vision of gender relations and into the impact of Christian education on their world-views. For example, in the 1940s, the évolués demanded that the system of travel permits be extended to wives and young girls in order to control their migration to the city and preserve their moral integrity.[71] The Legislative Ordinance of 20 July 1945 required officials to refuse a travel permit to wives and minor daughters who did not have a husband's or father's authorization. Thus a woman could enter a city only with the permission of a man.

The évolué position on marriage was equally unequivocal. Polygamy went against Christian morality: "Polygamy is un-Christian," J. E. Mupenda emphasized.[72] "A polygamist is an exploiter of black women," reiterated E. Ngandu.[73] Because polygamy was perceived as immoral, and all manner of nefarious effects attributed to it,[74] the évolués demanded its abolition, particularly after a supplementary tax failed to stop its expansion.[75] The Decree of 4 April 1950 then forbade polygyny for all marriages contracted after the first of January, 1951. The évolués' rejection of polygyny, though couched in language that suggested support for women's emancipation, merely demonstrated their willingness to impose a Christian morality on others and to hold up the monogamous family as a sign of civilization. Monogamous marriage was adopted by the Legislative Ordinance of 10 July 1945, and it served to reinforce men's position as family heads. The colonialists perceived the Congolese conception of marriage as retrograde. They believed it was necessary to rupture the wife's relationships with her natal lineage and her husband's lineage and to render her dependent solely on her husband. P. Coppens expresses this clearly:

> Hasn't the time come for a married woman to distance herself partially from belonging to her natal family to devote herself more to her European-style family—to husband and children? Clan solidarity is good in itself, but can be tempered by the content of new notions about the family, not incompatible, giving an honorable place to the respective rights and duties of the spouses as well as the natural parental vocation vis-à-vis their children, even after the dissolution of the marriage. This would be a question of proper and wisely measured adaptation, in each patri- or matrilineal milieu, to the new times.[76]

Similarly, the évolués favored the establishment of a marriage regime based on patrilineal succession, and men belonging to matrilineal kinship systems found that this alternative form of marriage accorded them power that they did not have under customary law.[77] Under it, they were able to become veritable family heads with rights over their wives and children: "According to the Christian conception of the family that we have adopted," wrote one contributor, "the family is composed of the father, mother, and children; its head is the father and not the maternal uncle."[78] Another elaborated:

> The European conceives of the family in a restrained, but reasonable and social way. For him, the family is made up of the father, the mother, and the children. In marrying, the wife really leaves her former family in order to found a new one with her husband, and she takes her husband's name. The children which issue

from this union belong in fact and in law to the father and mother. They are naturally members of the family. And all of them, wife and children, live together
under the father's authority. . . . A married woman must not be under her brother's
[authority]. She must belong to her husband, author of the home that he founded
with his wife and in which they join both their efforts, sharing pain and difficulties in order to raise their children.[79]

Some more tolerant évolués did not require the radical suppression of the matrilineal system, especially among non-évolués.[80] And some, especially those from
patrilineal groups, expressed reserve regarding monogamy and its system of
succession because it deprived men of certain rights, particularly to custody of
the children in case of divorce.[81] In the end, however, the law against polygyny
and the system of patrilineal succession adopted by the colonial administration
legitimated the Western conception of marriage and the family.

In contrast to their opposition to polygamy, the évolués did not wish to completely eliminate bridewealth, but to drastically reduce its cost.[82] As they sought
a way to do this, they always referred to the colonial model.

> Bridewealth is the goods that a woman brings to marriage. But this is not the case
> in the Congo. For the Congolese, bridewealth is wife purchase, from which comes
> the abuse. . . . It is true that bridewealth is still necessary for family stability but, as
> évolués, we must devise a bridewealth strategy for ourselves. Instead of relatives
> benefiting from bridewealth, it would be equitable for the money to be put aside in
> a bank for the future children of the couple.[83]

The évolués, then, wanted to eliminate bridewealth, not in order to liberate
women from the exploitation which could result from it, but only to unite
couples in the Western manner. But while it was necessary to accept Western
values and to reject all the customs and traditions perceived as "primitive," they
were clearly selective with regard to gender relations. With few exceptions, they
preserved those "traditions" which accorded them privileges as men vis-à-vis
women, and they adopted those of white "civilization" which favored their indisputable role as head of the nuclear family.

Évolué Lifestyle as a Reflection of the New Model of Gender Relations

While much can be discerned about évolué gender relations from the
pages of *La voix du Congolais*, there is also much to be learned by looking at
lifestyle choices, especially at dress and interior decoration. These elements,
among others, were the outward, distinctive signs of "civilization" and évolué
status. At certain periods, wearing a suit with a tie and sometimes a melon hat
identified an évolué.[84] Photos of the interiors of évolués' households, moreover,
sharply reveal their views about women's status and gender relations (see figures
6.1 and 6.2). An important focal point of the interior, which distinguished the
évolués from other Congolese, was the family dining table. Any évolué worthy
of his name had to eat at a table in the company of his wife and children.[85] It

Figure 6.2. "The family in its narrow sense (father, mother, children), the very image of Christian civilization." From *La Voix du Congolais* 90 (September 1953): 617.

was the responsibility of the wife to organize this time. Homemaking schools administered by Catholic missionaries, as well as social centers, trained women to create and orchestrate family meals, to preserve order, and to maintain the home's interior. The degree to which women fulfilled these roles as wives and mothers, creating well-appointed interiors, clean and well-organized, demonstrated their success.[86]

Women Reply

What was women's response to Christian moral education and to the image it produced of them? Much of the evidence suggests that, in general, Congolese women did not contest this type of colonial education, because in many ways it reproduced indigenous sexual divisions of labor to which they had been socialized. Moreover, it was presented to them as the way to become "civilized," and, if nothing else, speaking French assured social prestige. Madame Thomas Nkumu, née Josephine Siongo, the first Congolese woman to sit on Leopoldville's city council, emphasized that domestic responsibilities were women's natural duty:

[T]he role of a black woman is to aid her husband to promote the household economy. In this same order of ideas, I cannot tolerate my husband having any other washerwoman than myself. The order and cleanliness of the home and parcel of land devolve upon me personally.[87]

Another woman, who attended a women's social center (*foyer social*), made a similar point:

> I learned many new things at the social center, but what interested me most was the way to raise and educate children, to put a cloth on the table, and to eat at the table with my husband and all our children. . . . I was enchanted with that. Because a woman who maintains her home well and accomplishes all the duties of a homemaker honors her position.[88]

In whatever language it was given, women's education socialized them to conform to their "nature" and thus to accept their social role as natural.[89] Évolués' wives and daughters did not oppose social hierarchy in the household. Yet they demanded, in turn, that men also conform to the Christian morality to which "civilized" people should aspire. Louise Efolio, the first woman whose voice appeared in *La voix du Congolais*, abruptly turned the tables on men by insisting that they were the ones who were failing to live up to a Christian morality:

A Congolese Woman Speaks to You

Louise Efolio, translated from Lingala into French by A. R. Bolamba[90]

We always hear men say: We are civilized; our women are not yet civilized. We do not deny that men have attained a certain degree of evolution but, on the whole, men spoil their reputation by engaging in behavior which does not conform to the demands of civilization. Some examples—there are more than a thousand. But we will deal with only one, which is the most general.

In order to live peacefully and for the security of his family, a man builds a comfortable house. Why does this man leave his wife and children alone in the house and go elsewhere to drink? Can we say that this man is civilized? To whom does the house that he built belong? Only to his wife and children? That is not serious. And to say that this man can sleep elsewhere and forget his household . . .

The fact that the husband wastes money everywhere which he ought to reserve above all to feed and clothe his wife and children has given rise to numerous household discussions.

Another man said, "I am civilized, thus, I am like a white." But who is the serious white man who would go drinking all night, leaving his wife and children alone at home?

When whites want to drink, they buy a bottle of beer and talk of serious things while they relax. As for our husbands, they buy drinks for a hundred, even two hundred francs. They drink to get drunk. The whites, they don't want that; at least it is not a matter of being improvident.

We do not believe that, when they begin to drink, our male compatriots discuss serious things or speak about problems which concern our Congo's evolution. Thus, can they make us believe that they are civilized? Is civilization in alcohol? Rather, on the contrary, civilization is revealed by a person who respects himself, by a man who maintains his prestige in order to distinguish himself.

Certain husbands claim that they leave their wives at home because they don't want to give them more children. But why is it that one meets fathers of families who do everything elsewhere, who neglect, as it is said, their family? By going off to drink, they make their wives and children die of hunger. This is not civilization, is it?

One other thing:

Numerous times one finds men who have important occupations (nurses, judges, what more can I say) who act impolite toward women with whom they must deal. They are arrogant and sometimes discourteous toward old women. These men must not pretend to be civilized.

We can say that many of our men have not yet acquired anything of true civilization, as meant by the Europeans. We will admit that a man is civilized when he gives proof of a true evolution, when he abstains from the irregular maintenance of two or three women, and when he no longer frivolously dissipates money which is indispensable for the maintenance of his household.

If men want to imitate whites, they'd better do a good job of it.

The colonial system of education distanced women from salaried work at the same time that it prepared men for it. A minority of women were trained to hold jobs that fell within the realm of "feminine work": nursing, elementary school teaching, and infant care. But, as we have seen, it is necessary to look beyond Congolese customs and traditions to explain the feeble representation of women in the labor market revealed in colonial documents and in Western literature in general. "Tradition" certainly had and still has a considerable influence, but women's minimal numbers in the salaried workforce also reflect the combined effect of Christian education and colonial legislation which restrained wives' freedom to work outside the home. As stipulated in the work contract between *indigènes* and *maitres civilisés*: "a woman married through civil ceremonies or religiously or following indigenous custom cannot legally work without the formal or tacit authorization of her husband."[91] Thus married women could not legally hold public service jobs without their husbands' permission. "[W]ith my husband's consent, I will continue to work," explained a young woman who was educated at Mbanza-Mboma School.[92] The words of Suzanne Freitas, one of the first Congolese women to become a journalist, reveal similar sentiments: "Once married, the only freedom I asked my husband for was permission to continue to write newspaper articles. Journalism is a profession I adore."[93]

Demonstrating the processes of cultural conversion through an example from the Centre extra-coutumier d'Elisabethville, V. Y. Mudimbe notes that, beginning in the 1930s, the goal of colonization appears to have been the invention of a new cohesive culture whose constitutive traits were the French language, monogamous marriage, and patrilineal succession. Following Mudimbe, it is clearly important to place the new gender relations that emerged among évolués in the Belgian Congo in the wider context of cultural transformation.

The évolués participated in the conversion of gender relations in a game of interaction with the colonial order in which feminine nature became a "strategic field," in the sense intended by Michel Foucault.[94] The colonizers condemned Congolese women to an inferior level of education corresponding to their so-called feminine nature in order that women could fill their natural roles as mothers. The évolués appealed to this same feminine nature in demanding that women be taught in French, in order to be able to fill their roles as wives, counselors, and mothers of the family. Thus, strategically, the évolués made use of the resources put at their disposal by the system of education, colonial law, and Christian morality to consolidate their position and subordinate women in the name of protecting feminine nature. As Michel de Certeau clearly expresses it, they manipulated the possibilities available in their environment.[95]

Congolese men and women who went through these colonial institutions internalized the values given to them and adopted a model of gender relations which they viewed as similar to that of whites. The resulting cultural transformation was the product of a system which engendered a new form of social hierarchy between the sexes for the évolués themselves, who, in their quest for "civilization," wanted to assimilate to the whites' way of life at whatever cost. In this new conception of gender relations, women were not only economically dependent on men, they were completely under a husband's jurisdiction in legal matters. Their legal subordination to men—a common characteristic of colonial law—was reproduced by the Second Republic through the Family Code of 1988.[96]

There is no doubt that the évolués took part in the construction—or invention, to use V. Y. Mudimbe's term[97]—of a new model of gender relationships. The évolués participated in the processes of cultural conversion despite the fact that those processes had been imposed on them. They produced a discourse, as well as behavior and opinions about women, which conformed to the totality of understandings produced and circulated by the colonizers (the administration and the church) in a context of domination. For its part, this totality of information drew its legitimation from the colonial episteme which gave the order to "civilize" in the Western mode. Thus, the educational system in the Belgian Congo introduced a Western type of patriarchy and reinforced male domination with a new form of women's alienation encoded in a new model of gender relations.

NOTES

I would like to thank York University for awarding me a Social Sciences and Humanities Small Research Grant, and Glendon College for a travel grant. This support permitted me to go to Brussels to undertake archival work for this paper, which is preliminary to a larger project on women's education and gender relations during the colonial period in the Belgian Congo. I would also like to thank Jane Turrittin for translating this text and for useful discussion.

1.	Nakanyike Musisi, "Colonial and Missionary Education: Women and Domesticity in Uganda, 1900–1945," in *African Encounters with Domesticity,* ed. Karen Tranberg Hansen (New Brunswick, N.J.: Rutgers University Press, 1992), pp. 172–94.

2.	Estelle Pagnon, "'Une oeuvre inutile'? La scolarisation des filles par les missionnaires catholiques dans le Sud-Est du Nigeria (1885–1930)," *CLIO* 6 (1997): 35–59.

3.	E. de Jonghe, "La question des subsides scolaires au Congo belge," *Zaïre, Revue congolaise* 1, no. 5 (1947): 35–42; M. J. Van Hove, *L'éducation et l'évolution de la société indigène en Afrique belge,* Extrait du cahier no. 1, Cahiers de l'institut de sociologie Solvay (Bruxelles: Les editions de la librarie encyclopedique, S.P.R.L., 1951), pp. 4–5.

4.	*La voix du Congolais* was a bimonthly periodical born of the demands of the évolués for a tool of their own so that they could take responsibility for their own cultural and intellectual growth. Other analyses of *La voix du Congolais* exist, notably Annick Vilain, "Essai de définition du statut des évolués à travers les éditoriaux de la revue *La voix du Congolais,*" sous la direction de Marc Quaghebeur et Philippe Nayer, *Papier blanc, encre noire: Cent ans de littérature au Zaire. Regards croisés* (Kinshasa: Centre Wallonie-Bruxelles, 1996), pp. 333–46; and Joseph Lisobe, "Analyse de contenu de *La voix du Congolais,* 1945–1959," *Cahiers congolais de la recherche et du développement* 15, no. 3 (Kinshasa: ONRD, 1970): 46–70.

5.	Isidore Ndaywel è Nziem, *Histoire du Zaïre: De l'héritage ancien à l'âge contemporain* (Louvain-la-Neuve: Duculot, 1997), pp. 448–49.

6.	Ibid.

7.	Dorothy Smith, "Le parti pris des femmes?" in *Femmes et politique: Sous la direction de Yolande Cohen* (Montréal: Le jour, 1981), pp. 139–44.

8.	This article, written by Louise Efolio, is titled "La femme congolaise vous parle." *La voix du Congolais,* no. 124 (July 1956): 477–78.

9.	Sandra Harding, "Gendered Ways of Knowing and the 'Epistemological Crisis' of the West," in *Knowledge, Difference, and Power: Essays Inspired by* Women's Ways of Knowing, ed. Nancy Rule Goldberger et al. (New York: Basic, 1996), pp. 435–36.

10.	Jane Flax, "Postmodernism and Gender Relation in Feminist Theory," in *Feminist Theory in Practice and Process,* ed. Micheline R. Malson et al. (Chicago and London: University of Chicago Press, 1989), pp. 39–62.

11.	Joan Scott, "Genre: une catégorie utile d'analyse historique," *Les cahiers du Grif* 37–38 (1988): 125–53.

12.	Harding, "Gendered Ways of Knowing," pp. 435–36.

13.	Pierre Bourdieu, *Esquisse d'une théorie de la pratique* (Genève: Droz, 1972).

14.	*L'enseignement au Congo: Rapport du Bureau du comité permanent du congrès colonial national* (Bruxelles, Goemaere: Imprimerie du Roi, 1922), pp. 1–52; Leo Mundeleer, *L'enseignement au Congo,* Rapport présenté à la journée des amis de l'enseignement public (Service des publications de la ligue de l'enseignement, 1939).

15.	*L'enseignement au Congo,* pp. 14–29; G. E. Jambers, *L'enseignement au Congo belge* (Leopoldville: Imprimerie du courrier d'Afrique, 1947), pp. 31–37.

16.	E. de Jonghe, "L'instruction publique au Congo belge," *Congo* 1, no. 4 (April

1940): 503–504; Oswald Liesenborghs, "L'instruction publique des indigènes du Congo belge," *Congo* 1, no. 3 (March 1940): 233.

17. National Colonial Congress, twelfth session, *La promotion de la femme au Congo et au Ruanda-Urundi*, Assemblées Générales des 23 et 24 novembre, Rapports et compte rendus (1956), pp. 106–13.

18. F. Gabriel, *Essai d'orientation de l'enseignement et de l'éducation au Congo: Education professionnelle* (Bruxelles: Librairie Albert Dewit, 1922), p. 33.

19. de Jonghe, "L'instruction publique," p. 501; Liesenborghs, "L'instruction publique," p. 246.

20. Van Hove, *L'éducation et l'évolution*, pp. 6–7; Association des intérêts industriels du Congo, Léopoldville, *Rapport sur les travaux de la commission pour l'étude de l'éducation des masses indigènes* (His Majesty's Stationery Office, Colonial No. 186, 1945), pp. 45–82.

21. M. J. Van Hove, *L'oeuvre d'éducation au Congo belge et au Ruanda-Urundi*, Extrait de l'encyclopedie du Congo Belge (Bruxelles: Editions Bieleveld, 1953), p. 757; F. Scalais, "La réorganisation scolaire au Congo belge," *Zaïre, Revue congolaise* 4 (1950): 421–28.

22. Van Hove, *L'éducation et l'évolution*, pp. 4–8.

23. Ibid.; Van Hove, "*L'oeuvre d'education*," pp. 734–36.

24. Van Hove, "*L'oeuvre d'education*," p. 20.

25. Theoretically, girls were admitted into all the secondary institutions in the 1950s. However, very few girls were enrolled in secondary schools by 1958.

26. Van Hove, *L'éducation et l'évolution*, p. 21.

27. Xavier Noel, "Les écoles ménagères: L'enseignement au Congo et au Ruanda-Urundi," *Grands Lacs*, no. 2 (or no. 156): 27–29.

28. Mère Van Hove, "L'éducation de la jeune fille noire évoluée au Congo," *EPSI* 16 (1950): 155. Mother Van Hove was a nun of the order of the Sacred Heart of Jesus.

29. National Colonial Congress, twelfth session, 1956, pp. 109–13. Parallel to this formal training, informal training was provided in social centers, which targeted housewives, in particular, in order to offer them appropriate homemaking training. Van Hove, *L'oeuvre d'éducation*, pp. 787–89.

30. Van Hove, *L'éducation et l'évolution*, p. 28.

31. Sohier Brunard, "L'impréparation de la femme indigène du Congo aux tâches que la vie a notre contact lui impose" (Extrait du Cahier No. 1 des cahiers de L'institut de sociologie Solvay, Bruxelles, Les éditions de la librarie encyclopedie, 1951), p. 2. Many documents also mention black girls' "mental retardation" among reasons for this delay.

32. Schools for whites in the Belgian Congo also gave differe   training to girls, as was done in Belgium. See the Ministry of the Colonie. (for the) Belgian Congo, *La réforme de l'enseignement au Congo belge* (Bruxelles: Mission pédagogique Coulon-Dehheyn, 1954), p. 234.

33. G. Van Buick, "La promotion de la femme au Congo belge et au Ruanda-Urundi: À propos de la XIIè session du Congrès colonial national, 23–24 novembre 1956," *Zaïre: Revue congolaise* (Bruxelles: Editions Universitaires, 1956): 1067–74; Van Hove, "L'éducation et l'évolution," p. 20.

34. Ministry of Colonies, *La réforme*, p. 235.

35. M. A. Prignon, "Les programmes scolaires et la promotion de la femme indigène," National Colonial Congress, twelfth session, 1956, 423.

36. Pierre Bourdieu and J. C. Passeron, *Les héritiers* (Paris: Minuit, 1964).

37. Ndaywel è Nziem, *Histoire du Zaïre*, p. 448; A. R. Bolamba, "Opportunité de créer un statut spécial pour les évolués," *La voix du Congolais* 3 (May–June 1945): 77–81.

38. Bolamba, "Opportunité de créer un statut spécial," p. 77.

39. Ndaywel è Nziem, *Histoire du Zaïre*, p. 448.

40. Louis Mutonkole, "Conscience professionnelle," *La voix du Congolais* 25 (April 1958): 158–59.

41. Léon Bongongo, "De l'évolué—Réflexion," *La voix du Congolais* 24 (March 1948): 110.

42. Ndaywel è Nziem, *Histoire du Zaïre*, p. 449.

43. A. R. Bolamba, "La position sociale des évolués," *La voix du Congolais* 24 (August 1948): 319–21; Eloise D. Mulengamungu, "Qu'est-ce donc qu'un évolué," *La voix du Congolais* 123 (June 1956): 406–407.

44. Mathieu Goma, "Nos devoirs d'évolués," *La voix du Congolais* 18 (September 1947): 769.

45. E. Ngandu, "La polygamie était-elle la règle des mariages Africains?" *La voix du Congolais* 28 (July 1948): 291.

46. Michel Colin, "Le rôle de l'évolué vis-à-vis de la masse," *La voix du Congolais* 109 (November 1954): 791.

47. Ndaywel è Nziem, *Histoire du Zaïre*, pp. 450–51; A. R. Bolamba, "La politique indigène d'après-guerre," *La voix du Congolais* 8 (March–April 1946): 298–300.

48. A. R. Bolamba, "L'enseignement des révérendes dames chanoinesses de St. Augustin à Léopoldville," *La voix du Congolais* 20 (November 1947): 857; L. Moraes, "L'avenir des filles de chez nous," *La voix du Congolais* 21 (December 1947): 919; Bernard Kabesa, "La jeunesse féminine noire, élément important de notre civilisation," *La voix du Congolais* 64 (July 1951): 358; Yoka Mampunga, "Comment peut-on faire évoluer la femme congolaise?" *La voix du Congolais* 74 (May 1952): 284.

49. V. Y. Mudimbe, *The Idea of Africa* (Bloomington and Indianapolis: Indiana University Press, 1994), p. 132.

50. F. Wassa, "Education de la femme noire," *La voix du Congolais* 59 (January 1951): 81.

51. Pierre Kangudi, "Des écoles ménagères pour nos filles," *La voix du Congolais* 37 (April 1949): 141.

52. Gabriel Sulet Ekongo, "La femme congolaise au travail," *La voix du Congolais* 82 (January 1953): 718.

53. Ebwe Mukelebwe, "Aujourd'hui ou demain, la femme congolaise au travail," *La voix du Congolais* 88 (July 1953): 476.

54. Gabriel Sulet Ekongo, "La femme congolaise au travail," *La voix du Congolais* 37 (April 1949): 141.

55. A. M. Mobé, "À propos des devoirs des évolués," *La voix du Congolais* 34 (January 1949): 14, and "Pour la paix dans le ménage," *La voix du Congolais* 69 (December 1951): 662.

56. Lombolo, "La femme, base de toute évolution d'un peuple," *La voix du Congolais* 28 (July 1948): 296.

57. F. Wassa, "Le mariage," *La voix du Congolais* 64 (July 1951): 537.

58. Lombolo, "La femme," p. 297.

59. Wassa, "Le marriage," p. 538.

60. Direct collaboration between the church and the colonial administration goes back to the epoch of the Independent State of the Congo under Leopold II. See Mudimbe, *The Idea of Africa,* pp. 105–10. It became officially effective with the signing of the Decree of July 16, 1890. Nancy Rose Hunt calls attention to missionaries' influence on the colonial administration's adoption of certain regulations bearing on women. See Nancy Rose Hunt, " 'Le Bébé en Brousse': European Women, African Birth Spacing, and Colonial Intervention in Breast Feeding in the Belgian Congo," *International Journal of African Historical Studies* 21, no. 3 (1988): 401–32.

61. Mukelebwe, "Aujourd'hui ou demain," p. 475.

62. Moraes, "L'avenir des filles," pp. 918–19; A. R. Bolamba, "À propos des internats pour les enfants Congolais," *La voix du Congolais* 60 (March 1951): 129–30.

63. Kangudi, "Des écoles ménagères," pp. 141–43; Albert G. Bukasa, "L'éducation de la femme noire," *La voix du Congolais* 61 (April 1951): 176.

64. F. Wassa, "Liberté de la femme noire et prostitution," *La voix du Congolais* 23 (February 1948): 72.

65. Louis Ilonga, "La femme et le ménage indigène," *La voix du Congolais* 30 (September 1948): 375; Moraes, "L'avenir des filles," pp. 918–19.

66. Louis Agwandunga, "L'enseignement et l'éducation des jeunes filles noires à Léopoldville," *La voix du Congolais* 18 (September 1947): 77.

67. Lomami-Tshibamba, "À propos de l'inscription de la protection du mariage monogamique indigène," *La voix du Congolais* 8 (March–April 1946): 306; Wassa, "Liberté," pp. 71–72.

68. Hunt, " 'Le Bébé en Brousse,' " pp. 488–93.

69. Charles D. Gondola, "On, rio-Ma! Musique et guerre des sexes à Kinshasa, 1930–1990," *Revue française d'histoire d'outre-mer* 84, no. 314 (1996): 54.

70. Antoine J. Omari, "Remèdes contre la prostitution," *La voix du Congolais* 59 (February 1951): 59–63.

71. E. Ngandu, "La prostitution ronge le Congo," *La voix du Congolais* 6 (November 1945): 210; Ilonga, "La femme," p. 375.

72. Jean Ernest Mupenda, "Prostitution et polygamie," *La voix du Congolais* 19 (October 1947): 822.

73. E. Ngandu, "La polygamie et ses méfaits sociaux," *La voix du Congolais* 19 (October 1947): 811.

74. Ibid., pp. 808–14.

75. E. Ngandu, "Faut-il des machines agricoles pour réduire la polygamie?" *La voix du Congolais* 25 (April 1948): 150–53; E. Manono, "Quelques commentaires sur l'article 'La polygamie et ses méfaits sociaux' de Monsieur E. Ngandu," *La voix du Congolais* 22 (January 1948): 30–33.

76. "La promotion de la femme au Congo," Archives du Musée royal de l'Afrique centrale, Papiers Coppens, 56.11.5.

77. P. Nimy, "La polygamie et le matriarcat, coutumes à combattre, parce qu'elles vont à l'encontre de la saine notion de la famille," *La voix du Congolais* 43 (October 1949): 417–20; Raphaël Batshikama, "Qui est le chef des enfants dans le Bas-congo? Le seul problème, le seul effort," *La voix du Congolais* 58 (January 1951): 26–28; Th. Dimbany, "Sous le joug du matriarcat, que sera l'avenir de nos enfants?" *La voix du Congolais* 85 (April 1953): 50.

78. K. Kanza, "Qui est le chef des enfants dans le Bas-Congo?" *La voix du Congolais* 49 (April 1950): 205.

79. Nimy, "À propos du matriarcat," *La voix du Congolais* 35 (February 1949), pp. 58–59.

80. J. Kasa-Vubu, "À propos de la suppression du matriarcat," *La voix du Congolais* 64 (July 1951): 374–75.

81. Pascal-M. Luanghy, "À propos du statut de la population congolaise civilisée," *La voix du Congolais* 41 (August 1949): 297–307.

82. Daniel Perrin Kande, "Les mariages sans dot," *La voix du Congolais* 120 (March 1956): 176–77; Pierre Kangudi, "La famille congolaise marche vers sa destruction," *La voix du Congolais* 45 (March 1950): 155–57. Bernard Kabesa was probably the first évolué to marry off his daughter without accepting bridewealth.

83. Silvain Zinga, "Le noir évolué," *La voix du Congolais* 8 (March 1946): 313.

84. Many of the wives and daughters of évolués continued to wear skirtcloths and appeared less willing to mimic Western styles than their husbands or fathers. See Gondola, "On, rio-Ma!" 38; Michel Massoz, *Les femmes bantoues du XXe siècle* (Liège: Michel Massoz, 1991), pp. 204–205. A widespread style in the West, a long skirt open along its entire length and attached at the hips, shows some evident similarities with skirtcloths. Overall, however, Congolese women seem to have resisted Western styles more than the men.

85. Lomboto, "La femme," p. 297.

86. During the interviews he carried out for the benefit of *La voix du Congolais*, Michel Colin gave special attention to a home's interior in order to have an idea of the behavior of and the training received by his interviewees.

87. J. F. Lyeky, "Un pas de plus vers la promotion de la femme noire," *La voix du Congolais* 129 (December 1956): 862. The quotation is taken from an interview with Madame Nkumu by Michel Colin.

88. Michel Colin, "Trois femmes congolaises," *La voix du Congolais* 119 (February 1956): 131.

89. Ibid.

90. Efolio, "A Congolese Woman."

91. *Bulletin officiel du Congo belge*, vol. 15, no. 4 (15 April 1922).

92. Michel Colin, "Quelques instants avec Mlle Georgine Zimbu," *La voix du Congolais* 137 (August 1957): 605.

93. Michel Colin, "Vingt minutes avec Suzanne Freitas," *La voix du Congolais* 134 (May 1957), p. 349.

94. Michel Foucault, *Dits et ecrits*, vol. 4 (Paris: Editions Gallimard, 1994), p. 123.

95. Michel de Certeau, *L'invention du quotidien I: Arts de faire* (Paris: Gallimard, 1990), pp. 87–88.

96. Gertrude Mianda, *Femmes africaines et pouvoir: Les maraicheres de Kinshasa* (Paris: L'harmattan, 1996), pp. 26–27.

97. V. Y. Mudimbe, *The Invention of Africa: Gnosis, Philosophy, and the Order of Knowledge* (Bloomington and Indianapolis: Indiana University Press, 1988).

7   Virgin Territory? Travel and Migration by African Women in Twentieth-Century Southern Africa

Teresa Barnes

It is a truism that the study of the past helps us understand the present. In post-1994 southern Africa, however, an observer seeking to understand the gendered demographics of urban areas, the presence of women from neighboring countries working as urban hawkers, or the growing discourse of xenophobia would be hard-pressed to find detailed historical studies which can assist in the search for understanding. A major reason for this lacuna is the power of the intellectual paradigm of regional labor migration, which is universally invoked to explain the movement of large groups of Africans into urban spaces in colonial southern Africa and the contemporary legacies of that movement.[1] This paradigm was a ringing achievement of revisionist Marxist scholarship in southern Africa in the 1970s and 1980s. Eschewing the previous economic histories centered on white settlers, it brought African workers into focus, thereby mapping a (generally) southward movement of black labor away from "reserves" toward areas of relatively higher wages, and the mechanisms erected by national states to both coerce and obstruct this movement. Metaphors of blood and water were often used to describe the aggregated journeys of these workers: trickles, flows, floods, hemorrhages.

The writing of this essay has been prompted by three related problems with the dominant paradigm of southern African labor migration studies. The first is that there is no room in the above set of concepts for the mobility of African women. As will be explored below, despite the androcentric nature of the paradigm, the urban areas of southern Africa were marked by the presence of women from the earliest colonial days. This essay thus attempts to take women seriously as economic agents, with motivations and experiences either similar to or different from those of their male counterparts. The second problem is the differential manner in which white and black travelers are described in regional historiography. While whites are explorers, pioneers, or tourists, blacks are simply and universally migrants. This is partly due to the different focal lengths used in biography and class-based economic history; nonetheless, such stereotypes of difference should be investigated rather than perpetuated. Finally, as an immigrant in both Zimbabwe and South Africa, I have witnessed a general acceptance of immigrants in the former in the 1980s but a widespread xenophobia in the 1990s, at both popular and governmental levels, in the latter. After the end of formal apartheid and the 1994 elections, as citizens of neighboring countries arrived in "the new South Africa," they were quickly demonized by many South Africans—white and black—as only being interested in "taking our jobs and stealing our women and selling drugs on our streets." Investigating the roots of international migration in the region may help us understand this contemporary South African phenomenon.

From these three directions, therefore, comes the question stated in the title of this essay: "virgin territory?" How did African women come to be in the colonial-era towns of southern Africa, and how did they get there, if they did not travel in roughly the same manner as men? The central tenet of this essay is that although labor migration was dominated numerically by men, African women's presence in colonial towns, mines, and farms was far from negligible and must therefore be historicized. When historians follow the dominant model and consider mobility, travel, and migration a priori as male preserves, African women are automatically consigned to mass immobility. They are barred from center stage and frozen in perpetual economic childhood.[2] Historiography which is built on these inaccuracies ignores the life experiences of many individual African women and, in a larger sense, of gendered dimensions of twentieth-century social experience in southern Africa.

An intriguing example of the kind of information which cannot be explained by the migration paradigm is provided by a set of figures compiled by the Southern Rhodesian Department of Labour. In the 1950s, the Southern Rhodesian government offered free round-trip bus services as an inducement to workers from colonial Malawi (Nyasaland) and Zambia (Northern Rhodesia) to seek employment in its larger, stronger but labor-poor economy. Although historiography and conventional wisdom would have led us to expect buses exclusively filled with men, figures from 1958 and 1959 show significant numbers of migrant women on the "Ulere" service. In 1958, 1,733 women and 17,813 men from Nyasaland took the bus into Southern Rhodesia; 100 women and 2,925 men from Northern Rhodesia did the same. The following year 1,305 women and 15,726 men from Nyasaland and 56 women and 1,144 men from Northern Rhodesia used the service to travel to Southern Rhodesia. Large numbers of children also rode the "Ulere" buses.[3] Of course, these figures do not tell us nearly enough—were families traveling together? Were the women dependent on or independent of the men? How long did they stay in Southern Rhodesia? But they do at least suggest that the terms "migrants" and "women" should not be seen as mutually exclusive.

In addition, as recent studies have pointed out, the correspondence of colonial-era officials was often replete with images of migrant and mobile women. "Towns full of women," native commissioners grumbled; "flows of women" to towns, they unhappily noted.[4] As Karen Jochelson's excellent recent review article points out, "We need to ask why women became migrants, and how their communities, the state and they themselves viewed migrancy."[5] Recent scholarship has also begun to investigate how the capitalist transformations of African life were also constituted through domesticity.[6] These fields of study can be enriched by setting a firmer theoretical foundation for the very existence of African women in towns, and also on mines and farms—destinations of travel and migration. I hope that this discussion of women's mobility (primarily between South Africa and colonial Zimbabwe) and of the racialized historical difference between travel and migration will assist in chipping away at a deadening, but pervasive, historiographical image of African women as "faceless subsidizers of cheap male labour in the rural reserves."[7]

Women Absent

Labor migration "has been one of the most important demographic features of the African continent."[8] Charles van Onselen's *Chibaro* (1976) was the first real model for studies of migration across the Limpopo River, setting the parameters of men, mining, and the strategies of labor control and resistance all firmly within the context of class struggle.[9] The accuracy and usefulness of the paradigm has meant that although it has been challenged on a number of grounds, and despite the intervening "linguistic turn" in historiography over the course of the 1990s, it has remained a dominant conceptual force in southern African studies. The 1970s labor migration studies almost completely ignored the agency of African women and were written before issues of gender became matters of widespread scholarly concern. However, even grafting "gender" onto these studies in the 1990s has not changed their fundamental assumptions: changing "migrants" to "male migrants" as a way to satisfy the "gender lobby" has left the androcentric logic of the paradigm untouched.[10] General overviews of migration in southern Africa which have been built on the model reproduce its flaws and therefore continue to substantively relegate African women to the shadows. Thus, for example,

> Colonial labour migration was selective along gender and age lines. The migratory process drew exclusively productive males from rural areas. The labour of African women was not widely valued; thus women were not an important source of wage labour and were not actively sought by recruiting agencies. . . . The colonialists wanted the rural areas to be labour-producing areas while those who remained continued their traditional economies. Thus, the rural areas lagged behind in development.[11]

Similarly, the UNESCO survey history of Africa tells us that migrant labor in South Africa and Southern and Northern Rhodesia was (at least until 1935) exclusively restricted to adult males because of white fears about African urban settlement and pressures from white trade unions.[12] Thus, studies which mention women in the context of migration often merely "explain" that there were so many obstacles in the way of women's migration that it did not occur.[13] These works, and the paradigm to which they subscribe, provide a normative illusion which has practically become conventional wisdom: African women were "passive rural widows" who stayed put somewhere, practicing subsistence and, later, cash crop agricultural production while their men departed, perhaps never to return.

Upon examination, the contradictions inherent in this paradigm are readily apparent. As I have argued elsewhere, at least in colonial Zimbabwe, where they were not required by law to carry identity documents, African women were less burdened with restrictions on their physical mobility than were African men, and many made use of this freedom.[14] Secondly, it is difficult to reconcile passivity with agricultural production in a region where, for ecological and political reasons, farming has been a challenging occupation requiring skill, imagination, and foresight. And finally, if African women waited passively in the regions of southern Africa, which after the imposition of colonialism became construed as "rural," how was it that the "urban" areas were full of women? As Walker has pointed out, in the early decades of the twentieth century African women made up 19 percent of the African urban population of South Africa, and women's rate of urban settlement increased markedly faster than men's into the 1940s.[15]

In fact, southern African women's experience of regional mobility is so common that, upon reflection, any number of colloquial tales come to mind: so-and-so's Xhosa auntie in Bulawayo; so-and-so who went with her employers to Cape Town as a domestic worker; so-and-so who lived in Zambia for many years.[16] The South African missionaries who were among the first African foreigners in Southern Rhodesia brought their wives with them.[17] Decades later, many of the Southern Rhodesian African men who had been educated in South Africa—pioneering lawyers, nationalist politicians, and businessmen—came home with South African wives.[18]

Women Marginalized

Even studies which take the mobility of African women seriously tend to conceptualize and theorize the "migrant experience" according to male criteria, making women's meaningful entry into and participation in the paradigm impossible. One such study, which surveys all of Africa south of the Sahara, distinguishes categories of migrant women and discerns patterns in their rural-urban migration. This study, however, subscribes to the underlying idea that urbanization in colonial Africa was primarily a male phenomenon, and that only in its later colonial phases, when wives who had been previously left behind in rural areas came to towns to join husbands, did urbanization take on a gendered dimension.[19] Thus the "passive rural widow" creeps again into studies of African migration, and once again black women are semantically trapped in a world where they make no choices and are rooted in the earth. In another example, although the presence of women in migrant worker hostels in contemporary South Africa is acknowledged, "the migrant experience" is defined as that of an essentially "free peasant," shielded from the full impact of market forces by virtue of continued customary access to rural land (regardless of that land's high degree of impoverishment).[20] But customary access to rural agricultural land is only granted to men in South Africa; women's access to it is entirely mediated through men.

Other studies in the 1980s, focusing on male mine workers in South Africa, admitted that this model had some deficiencies, among which were its failure to investigate either African agency or conflict inside the South African capitalist system between employers, recruiters, and branches of the state and between South Africa and supplier states.[21] Patrick Harries took up these issues in a study which follows migrants from southern Mozambique to the South African gold mines, mainly on the Witwatersrand, and back again.[22] While abandoning a Marxist paradigm, Harries keeps as a central theme workers' struggle with their environment (broadly defined, including their employers) to fashion lives which would satisfy their cultural and personal needs. He delineates a "tramping system" of male workers walking many hundreds of kilometers from Mozambique to Kimberley, Durban, and Johannesburg. This study brings a welcome human touch to the historiography of migrant labor in the region, as Harries salutes the heroism and tenacity of the early pioneers of migrant labor.[23] He also focuses on male migrants, although he mentions women in passing, and includes a fascinating section on how an elaborate system was constructed to indoctrinate young boys into performing the submissive tasks required by older men who, in the compounds, were deprived of the physical, domestic, and emotional services of already socialized women.[24] Harries makes brief mention of the fact that Mozambican female immigrants to the Rand tended to congregate in Johannesburg itself, and that there were about ninety women there in 1896, rising to perhaps 6,500 by the 1930s.[25] Interestingly, he does not cite Bonner's observation that "women from Mozambique were initially the most prominent practitioners of the [beer] brewing craft [on the Rand]," and that a group of Mozambican men complained in 1921 of the "large-scale movement of Mozambican women" to the Rand. They requested the repatriation of two thousand such women.[26]

Mobile Women, but No Big Picture

A generation of feminist scholarship ago, Christine Obbo pointed out that African women used various strategies, including migration, to achieve their goals of "power, wealth and status."[27] In this spirit, the view that women in Southern Africa simply could not and therefore did not migrate is being challenged by a number of scholars through tightly focused case studies of women's mobility and migration, generally inside national boundaries. The strongest statement comes from Julia Wells, whose examination of women's pass resistance logically includes the topic of mobility. Although she, too, generally takes the term "migrant" to mean "male," she makes the important point that urbanization in South Africa was a complex and far from uniform process, and that the segregated locations of the platteland[28] towns were settled by both African male and female workers. Her study shows "[African] women [who were] sought after and coerced as workers in their own right; women fighting to preserve other income-generating options; a huge preponderance of urban family units over migrant labourers and institutionalized black social stratification." This description of African women as adult, valuable workers is an important corrective to the more prevalent view which incessantly records them, as Wells notes, as victims of the "migrant's widow syndrome."[29] Hilary Sapire similarly mentions the women who settled in the East Rand town of Brakpan who had run away from the "patriarchal controls and poverty of the Reserves" or had come to town with their families from white-owned farms.[30] Generally, however, African women in migrant historiography are first ignored and last, if ever, counted.

Gina Buijs discusses contemporary African women migrating from Pondoland in the Transkei to work in the sugar fields of Natal, noting that nothing less imperative than the sheer threat of starvation could send women out from their rural homes to look for work.[31] Some were recruited by agencies and participated in the formal structures of migrant labor, while others bypassed these structures and simply went to find work wherever they could. Historically, she relates the phenomenon of women's migration from colonial Basutoland and Bechuanaland to the impoverishment of rural economies caused by the imposition of colonial labor policies.[32] Here her major source is Bonner's study of the virtual exodus of Basotho women to Johannesburg in the first half of the twentieth century.

This well-known work is perhaps the first to deal with African women as migrants who found work in the interstices of the urban economy even though formal employment was, for a variety of reasons, largely closed to them. Bonner's study is important for this reason, although, paradoxically, he almost overlooks the fact that the women he is discussing were actually international migrants, as he draws attention to what he terms the merely "notional barrier" of the Basotholand/South Africa border.[33] Belinda Bozzoli's examination of the lives of women migrants from a homeland area to the Johannesburg area makes the vital point that migrancy can be seen, not so much as a response to immediate financial crisis, but as a measured effort over the course of a woman's lifetime to directly contribute to her own and her family's well-being.[34] A work which to some extent incorporates issues of women and gender into the discourses and paradigms of African labor migration is Frederick Cooper's recent magnum opus on debates and changes in colonial labor policy.[35] African women move through Cooper's narrative of the ways in which French and British officials tried to comprehend, cope with, and (ultimately unsuccessfully) shape an answer to "the labor question" in colonial Africa. Cooper does not quantify female migrancy, but he acknowledges that it did exist.[36] On a larger scale, the very crux of the issue was whether, and how, male workers would be "stabilized" by being allowed to live with women and children rather than as perpetual urban bachelors. The presence or absence of women as wives and urban workers was thus crucial to the strategic shape of colonial labor policy; and that policy was constantly having to cope with the fact that there were more women in urban areas than any set of regulations permitted. Finally, once in town, such women rarely behaved as docilely as African or European men would have wished.[37]

Women on the Move: Migration vs. Travel

> We have tried to assemble a diverse body of work that charts feminism, over close to three hundred years, through women and their journeys. . . . We regret the absence of more multicultural voices. It is our hope that in the future both the gender and racial gaps will be bridged, but for now the voices we present are those we found.[38]

Central to the construction and perpetuation of the stereotype of the "passive rural widow" is a two-fold conceptual investment in the immobility of African women. Women have been given no room in the labor migration paradigm; but they have also been excluded from discourses and investigations of travel. Migration implies some kind of coercion, pushing and pulling; travel, on the other hand, is movement voluntarily undertaken. Travel, and the images it evokes of sightseeing, danger, excitement, adventurousness, discovery, and touring—such as those collected in the book from which the above quotation was taken—are rarely associated with African people, or even with people of African descent. They are the objects of the gaze, not subjects with sight. Even landmark autobiographical monographs by women of color are generally ignored in the "intrepid lady traveler" literature.[39]

Studies of colonial culture are beginning to explore how traveling was a crucial element not only in the ideological construction of colonial empire, but in the construction of "whiteness" itself.[40] Inderpal Grewal's marvelous study of the travels of upper-class Indian women to Britain in the penultimate phases of the Raj discusses the complex interplay between women's desires for equality inculcated by British education and the emerging, perceived dichotomy between the "unfreedom" of the immobile Indian woman in India and the women's "freedom" of movement in Britain.[41] For these members of the Bengali elite, traveling abroad was a crucial element in the construction of concepts of Self and Other, home/abroad, modern/traditionalist, freedom/sequestration. According to Grewal, however, these concerns were not shared by all mobile Indian women. Thousands of female indentured laborers who, like their male counterparts, were taken to work in many British colonies "were not concerned with constructing a Self or a history and . . . were also outside the framework of either anti-colonial, reformist or nationalist discourse."[42] This class-based dichotomy thus approximates the division made in this chapter between traveling women—those for whom mobility was mainly voluntary—and migrant women, for whom economic necessity was a primary motivation.[43]

Regional scholarship has yet to come to grips with the travels of southern African women who approximate Grewal's Bengali sophisticates. The ultimate goal of upwardly mobile black colonial Southern Rhodesians was a post-primary education in South Africa.[44] Traveling south for educational purposes was an unmistakable marker of distinction, and one which a few select African women shared as early as the 1940s.[45] Increasing numbers of teachers and nurses were educated in South Africa through the 1950s. Paeans of praise were heaped upon the first male graduates of South African institutions who returned to Southern Rhodesia; it was written of one that "his acquaintance with the English tongue is perfect and his taste exquisite. . . . He has had the best European learning and his feet have been placed on a very high rung of the ladder to progress and civilisation. He has returned to Southern Rhodesia to lend a hand to those of his people who are still on the ground."[46]

Another aspect of regional travel in which women participated was international visits. Gertrude (Moeketsi) Shope, past president of the ANC Women's League and now a member of the South African parliament, grew up in the Salisbury area of colonial Zimbabwe.[47] The Moeketsi family had migrated north from South Africa before 1925. Mr. Moeketsi's father and brother were already Methodist missionaries in Salisbury; he joined them with his family when he found work there as a motor mechanic. Gertrude Shope's recollections of her childhood include vivid memories of traveling, as a member of a group of people who lived in one country, had family in another, and might send their children to school in a third. For example, according to Mrs. Shope,

[In the 1930s] there were some people who came [to Harare] from South Africa. Some of them were women who came from . . . [South Africa] who married Zimbabwean men, but others [were] men and women who [were] of Xhosa-speaking origin, but who had settled in Zimbabwe, different places. So some of them were in Salisbury, in town. So we used to go and visit them. . . . Nearly every December [when she was a girl] we came back to South Africa. We either came to South Africa or went to Botswana or Lesotho.

In another instance, international travel also marked female members of a budding African middle class in Southern Rhodesia in the 1950s. In June 1955, the main newspaper of Southern Rhodesia's capital city published the obituary of Mrs. Helen Mangwende, the popular wife of a modernizing rural leader who had been instrumental in forging alliances with white women to set up an African women's club movement in the rural areas.[48] Among her accomplishments the newspaper saw fit to record that

[d]uring the Royal Tour in 1953 [Mrs. Mangwende] was introduced to Queen Elizabeth the Queen Mother, and Princess Margaret laid the foundation stone of the club hall in Mrewa which she had been instrumental in obtaining for the locality. Last year she spent some months in England. It is thought that she was only the second African woman ever to have visited that country from Rhodesia [Mrs. Savanhu, wife of one of the first African members of the Federal Parliament, being the first].[49]

These participants in "royal tours," both actual and metaphorical, were the exceptions who proved the truth of the rule, however. The mass of African women was considered immobile, stagnant, and hide-bound both by nature and by circumstance.

Zimbabwean Women in South Africa

As Harries points out, regional migration did not begin with the imposition of colonial demands for tax and labor.[50] Schmidt documents the precolonial mobility of Shona women who worked during community hunting and gold-panning expeditions, and perhaps also as porters.[51] Similarly, Bhila's study of precolonial trade and politics mentions women trading with the Portuguese in markets in the sixteenth century.[52] While this movement was qualitatively different from the individualized migration which came after the colonial rupture of rural African society, these sources do reveal that African women's autonomous mobility for gain (as opposed to their movement as the objects of capture and trade) was not completely a colonial invention.

More recently, Martin Murray's study of migration across the Limpopo River in the early years of the twentieth century has pointed out that the four-hundred-mile border between South Africa and Southern Rhodesia was so poorly policed that it "presented no obstacle to anyone with even the slightest determination to cross it."[53] When this observation is added to an earlier study, which suggests that the people on both sides of the Limpopo in this area worked together, intermarried, and formed large, mobile hunting parties which included men and women,[54] it becomes almost impossible to imagine that the opportunity to join "the relentless, silent march southwards"[55] to labor centers in South Africa was not taken up by African women from Southern Rhodesia.

We turn next to sources of empirical evidence of women's international migration: early to mid-twentieth-century census data from South Africa and Southern Rhodesia. This data, though structurally flawed by racist colonial ideas about which people were important enough to be enumerated (employed urban Africans) and which were not (the rest of the African population), does give an indication of the migration streams.[56]

The first census after the union of all of South Africa's provinces in 1910 shows that African women from north of the Limpopo had indeed been traveling southward in the two decades since the imposition of the British South Africa Company's rule in colonial Zimbabwe. In fact, the 1911 census of the Union of South Africa indicates that there were more Southern Rhodesian women than men in the country: 5,178 women and 5,078 men. Most were in the Transvaal: 5,035 women and 4,594 men.[57] This is an intriguing, even startling, statistic, and one which I am unable to explain on the basis of my current research. What was happening that brought more women than men to the Transvaal? Was the economic situation in rural colonial Zimbabwe so dire that, fourteen years after the crushing of the first anti-colonial rebellion, women simply flowed off the land? Did the mines briefly try to stabilize labor, allowing men to move southward with female family members?[58] In these last years before the passage of the infamous South African 1913 Land Act, African peasant farmers in the Transvaal fared fairly well despite a period of general drought, leaving white farmers chasing labor again.[59] Perhaps, then, many women came to farms in the south to work as laborers. Whatever the combination of factors, if the 1911 census statistics are not simply due to a technical error, they indicate that in one historical era women possessed greater need, willingness, or ability to cross international borders than did their male counterparts.

Unfortunately, the changes in census categories make it impossible to follow this story over time. The 1936 Union census[60] did not give the absolute numbers of African women from Southern Rhodesia. In South Africa as a whole, there were 72,641 women who had not been born there;[61] of these, 4,350 African women had been born in neither Basutoland (now Lesotho) nor Portuguese East Africa (now Mozambique). By a process of elimination, one can surmise that most of these women, listed as coming from "elsewhere," were actually from Northern and Southern Rhodesia. Of these African women from "elsewhere" who lived in the Transvaal, nearly 60 percent were to be found in the province's rural areas. In 1946 the South African census classified the African population by "language groups." In greater Johannesburg, there were 1,724 African women and 15,650 African men who spoke non–South African languages as their mother tongues. For the sake of comparison, there were a total of 139,900 African women and 247,275 African men in Johannesburg.[62] The 1960 census classified Africans, not by nationality or language, but by birthplace. In what one would now consider to be greater Johannesburg (Johannesburg, the East Rand, and Germiston), in a total African population of 1,100,587, there were 313 women and 7,709 men between the ages of fifteen and sixty-five who had been born in Northern or Southern Rhodesia. There were no such women over the age of sixty-five. For the sake of comparison, there were 13,908 African women and 28,190 African men from Basutoland counted in greater Johannesburg.[63]

The little that one can glean from South Africa's census records on this issue, therefore, suggests that the formal, enumerated population of African women from colonial Zimbabwe in South Africa fell both relatively and absolutely over the course of the twentieth century. Whether this was a merely statistical phenomenon, fed by the political imperatives of a South Africa hardening into apartheid, or evident in actual experience will only be ascertained by further research. Given, however, that census counts of African people were far more likely to err on the side of undercounting, especially as the apartheid-era government was at pains to whiten South Africa by any means necessary, it can be assumed that there were far more black women from colonial Zimbabwe in South Africa than official records reveal. At any rate, international migration southward was clearly not an exclusively male preserve.

South African Women in Colonial Zimbabwe

It is slightly easier to discuss travel and migration in relation to black South African women, since their mobility is much better documented. Charlotte

Maxeke, one of the founders of the ANC Women's League and one of modern South Africa's most accomplished women, traveled to Britain, Canada, and the United States as early as the 1890s in a choir in which she was accompanied by several other black women singers.[64] Maxeke remained in the United States to complete her university education;[65] Sibusisiwe Makhanya was a student in the United States from 1927 to 1930.[66] We have already seen women of the Moeketsi family undertaking extensive regional travel. These women were travelers more than migrants, with better educations and more social and economic options than the vast majority of black South African women. Nonetheless, they shared a common purpose with poorer female compatriots: to move as their needs required.

The first black South African woman whose presence is recorded in colonial Zimbabwe is Martha Ngano, a teacher and missionary who traveled north just after the 1896–97 anti-colonial rebellion, played a prominent role in the establishment of the first national African political organization in Southern Rhodesia, and founded a "Bantu Women's League" in the 1930s.[67] Another prominent immigrant was Edith Opperman-Mfazi, remembered by residents of Harare, a segregated township in the capital city of Salisbury, as the first nurse, and the first South African nurse of several, to work in the local clinic.[68] In later years, the presence of a number of South African women in the Salisbury townships led to their setting up their own women's club.[69] Another South African woman in Southern Rhodesia was Mary Moeketsi, the mother of Gertrude Shope. The family lived on the grounds of Epworth Mission outside Salisbury; Mrs. Moeketsi raised her children and did not work for wages, although she did participate in the trade of homegrown produce—flowers, in her case—to Salisbury. The family moved to the more elite township of Old Highfield around 1943.[70]

But there were other South African women in Salisbury who were not respectable wives, teachers, or nurses. Their stories were recorded, not in biographies, but in police files. For example, two Basotho women appear in the Salisbury police files of 1920 as being involved in small-time prostitution and gambling.[71] One, Mary Nyrenda, had been identified as embodying all the worst vices of urban black women: she illegally brewed and sold beer, engaged in interracial prostitution, and even, as a madam, traveled with groups of prostitutes around the mines of Mashonaland.[72] Interestingly, by the 1930s, Nyrenda reportedly had become "queen" of the respectable Manyika Burial Society in Salisbury while still dominating the local "underworld."[73]

Nyrenda was not alone in the police files. In 1932, only six of the thirty-one women whose given names appeared on a list of "native females alleged to be prostitutes in the location" were born in South Africa or Zambia.[74] Another set of police records holds the following statement from a woman in July 1920:

I am a Baralong native girl. I am single and aged 21. I was 21 years of age last year. I was born at Bloemfontein. My parents are dead and I am alone in this country.

I have neither friends or relations in Rhodesia. I was baptised in the Church of England at Bloemfontein. Before I came to Rhodesia I was at school near Francistown. I was there 18 months. Then I came up to Salisbury. I came up to the Rev. Webster. I think he wrote for me to come up from Francistown. I came up as [a] nurse girl.

According to the statement, this woman met a man who promised to marry her, but he deserted her when she became pregnant. The statement ends with sentiments that many a southern African migrant must have shared: "I don't know what to do. I have no where [*sic*] to go to."[75]

It is impossible to say whether the African women from South Africa who migrated to Southern Rhodesia were of the ilk of Martha Ngano or of Mary Nyrenda, but the Southern Rhodesian censuses are surprisingly helpful in counting them. The 1901 census did not count Africans from Southern Rhodesia, but it did count so-called "colonial natives" from South Africa; in that year in the two provinces of Mashonaland and Matabeleland there were 1,188 African women and 2,540 African men from South Africa. Of the women, 705 were over the age of sixteen, and most were in rural rather than urban areas.[76]

The 1904 census was the first to display the Rhodesian bias for Africans as workers, not as people per se; only those who were formally employed, and not those merely resident, in various areas were counted. Until 1961, therefore, these censuses are employment surveys rather than population counts, from which it is impossible to tell the total number of Africans of any nationality who lived in the country. The returns do, however, give some indication of the magnitude of employment for foreign women. In 1904 there were 62 adult African women from south of the Limpopo working in the urban areas of Southern Rhodesia, and 54 in the rural areas. There were also, for the sake of comparison, 473 such men in the urban areas and 460 in the rural areas.[77] The 1911 census did not divide the African population by birthplace; but the report of the census director did note that the employed African women professionals listed were "nearly all teachers of alien [i.e., foreign] race"—women who most probably were South Africans.[78]

According to the 1921 census there were 8,557 Southern Rhodesian African women and 52,527 Southern Rhodesian African men in urban employment in the colony. There were also 5,904 employed African women who were not from Southern Rhodesia. Of these, 602 were from South Africa and Bechuanaland, 3,172 from Nyasaland, 924 from Northern Rhodesia, 1,189 from the Portuguese colonies, 12 from Kenya and Tanganyika, and 5 from other, unidentified places.[79] The large numbers of women coming into Southern Rhodesia from the north became a topic of correspondence between branches of the Native Department (the branch of colonial government charged with administering all aspects of African life) in 1921–22. The text of one of these letters is reproduced as the primary document at the end of this essay. After reading it, the chief native commissioner (CNC) was of the opinion that the majority of women migrants "come down with one object, namely prostitution," which they tried to disguise by contracting marriages with local men once they arrived in the country. Since, as explained above, there were no census statistics on the African population, this conclusion was completely subjective. The CNC also believed that rural commissioners should refuse to register such marriages unless corroborating evidence of the women's sincerity was available, given their "immorality" and the difficulties of later finding them due to their "constantly changing abode(s)."[80] Another official pointed out that economic desperation drove many people out of colonial Mozambique in 1922, and reported that they had told him "that the 'hunger' in that Territory is appalling and many people are dying."[81]

The census taken in May 1926 recorded 383 African women from the Portuguese colonies, Northern Rhodesia, Nyasaland, and "other sources" who were formally employed in Southern Rhodesia as a whole, compared to 1,245 African women from Southern Rhodesia itself.[82] In 1932, information from another source illustrated the presence of foreign women in Salisbury—importantly, these were the numbers of residents, not only of workers. Out of a total adult population of 679 women and 2,352 men, there were 4 African women from South Africa, 72 from Nyasaland, 119 from the Portuguese colonies, and 58 from Northern Rhodesia. Foreign women made up 37 percent of the location's female population. The situation was reversed in the case of men, of whom the majority, 56 percent, were foreigners.[83] The 1936 census called foreign workers "alien natives" and recorded that 367 such women and 144,901 such men were employed in the colony. The vast majority of the women were employed in agriculture. The census director's report noted that 20 percent of all the African women who were formally employed were foreigners.[84] Similar results were reported in the 1941 and 1946 censuses.[85]

The 1951 census went into a useful degree of detail regarding African women employed in Southern Rhodesia. It should be remembered that these statistics were only kept on women who had formal employment, not on the women residents of any part of the country. (See table 7.1.) Thus, in Salisbury, the largest cohort (108) of employed foreign women were domestic workers from Malawi. South Africa was not listed as a separate point of origin for the foreign female workers, but there were 44 women from "other territories" in Salisbury (and 91 in Bulawayo) who were employed as domestic workers. These women probably came from South Africa.

Virgin Territories Breached

As incomplete as they are, and even though it is maddeningly impossible to directly compare figures from different censuses, let alone from two different countries, the statistics cited above indicate that African women from all the countries in the region were traveling and migrating across borders from at least the very beginning of the twentieth century. The difficulties with these statistics do not obscure the fact that the term "migrant" did not necessarily mean "male"

Table 7.1. African women in Salisbury/Bulawayo from Southern Rhodesia, Portuguese East Africa, Northern Rhodesia, Nyasaland, and other territories in formal urban employment, 1951*

Industry	SRh women	PEA women	NRh women	N women	OT other women	Total
Agriculture	56/24	20/0	12/4	28/5	0/1	126/34
Mining	0/5	0/0	0/1	0/1	0/0	0/7
Manufacturing	188/721	37/1	36/10	39/4	0/29	300/765
Construction	9/25	8/0	2/3	6/4	1/0	26/32
Electricity and water	5/2	0/0	0/0	4/0	2/0	11/2
Commerce and finance	27/35	1/0	0/0	7/0	1/4	36/39
Transport and communications	1/17	0/0	0/0	0/0	0/0	1/17
Private domestic service	942/1,432	71/14	23/57	108/46	44/91	1,188/1,640
Other services	172/163	1/0	2/1	21/1	10/9	206/174
Total	1,400/2,424	138/15	75/76	223/61	58/134	1,894/2,710

*Report of the 1951 Census (Salisbury: Government Printer, 1953).

in southern Africa. Also, because of the enormous gaps in census-taking methodology, it can be reliably assumed that there were significantly more women living in the towns than were recorded either as employed or as resident by the census enumerators. For example, while Harries's contemporary source estimated 6,500 Mozambican women on the Rand in the 1930s, the 1936 census listed only 4,917 Mozambican women in all of South Africa.

What significance can be ascribed to these foreign women in the towns of Southern Rhodesia and South Africa? Perhaps we must first discuss why women traveled to foreign towns in the first place. The dominant paradigm of women's mobility is that of escape from the rural areas and from patriarchal control.[86] But Deborah James cautions that this perspective may be more dependent on historians' reading of sources from colonial officials and irate patriarchs than on the intentions and experiences of women migrants themselves. Further, the conventional wisdom and recent scholarship which explains male migrant ideology as devoted not only to keeping the land but to keeping control of women often simply perpetuate the rendering of women as silent objects of history. This perspective, James argues insightfully,

tacitly excludes women as the possible initiators of ethnic ideologies, or as the members of migrant groupings. If they are the objects of control through these [ethnic] ideologies or by these associations, they are unlikely also to be active subjects initiating or perpetuating them.[87]

James's observation suggests that Elizabeth Schmidt's conclusions regarding the reasons that women did not migrate in colonial Zimbabwe, and why the ranks of domestic workers in European homes were therefore primarily filled by African men, should be reexamined. Schmidt writes of all the factors which relegated African women to the rural areas: the undermining of male and chiefly authority, the unwillingness of African women to replace their own marriage and reproduction with long stints of caring for European children, the loss of male control of women's labor and bridewealth payments, and older women's fear of losing the younger women who did the bulk of agricultural and household production. These factors were certainly important, but say more about why African women did not become domestic servants than about why they did not migrate. Schmidt does point out that women migrating to the towns usually found informal employment (as beer brewers and sellers, and as hawkers of grains and vegetables), which could be combined with childcare responsibilities and allowed more freedom of movement, to be more attractive.[88] Because there were many more African women living in Southern Rhodesian towns than were formally employed,[89] it is among this class of migrants, rather than those formally employed women who so conveniently, but misleadingly, appear in formal statistics, that new research may find the dominant dynamic of women's migration.

Luise White's study of prostitutes in Nairobi has provided one enduring distinction between the strategies of urban migrants. Some undertook short-term work in order to raise cash to send back to the rural areas, while others dug in, made capital investments, and used their earnings to try to set themselves and their descendants up permanently in town.[90] This distinction may correlate with that between formally and informally employed women. White's observation is enormously helpful because it treats women as subjects making economic and personal decisions. But then there should be a myriad of reasons why women migrated to towns and a myriad of responses to their various predicaments, which new research should also probe.

The histories and experiences of Mary Nyrenda and Mary Moeketsi, for example, were probably very different. Yet both were South African women living in the Salisbury area at roughly the same time. Because the published statistics are so unreliable, it is impossible to say whether there were more respectable wives and mothers like Mrs. Moeketsi or more independent operators like Mary Nyrenda in the migrant stream. Respectable women like Mrs. Moeketsi have received much better historiographical attention, having perhaps left precious written records and literate offspring. Even a cursory look into Terence Ranger's recent book, based on the records of one such prominent African family in Southern Rhodesia, shows that South Africa was firmly implanted in the consciousness of the Southern Rhodesian proto-elite. It was their lodestar, the source of education, of, in all senses of the word, mobility itself. For the first generation of conquered, yet unbowed, Africans in Southern Rhodesia, there was guidance on how to stand up as human beings, and it came from fellow Africans in the south. The speech from which Ranger takes the title of his book illustrates the spiritual, practical—and gendered—impulses of unity among peoples in the region:

> We must unite and speak with one voice we black people making a great cry which shall be heard in every place in South[ern] Africa so that it will get into the heart of those who form the Government. . . . We have seen that the European Missionaries are united together, well then, what stops us black people from being like the whites? Are we not also men born with the spirit of manhood within us? Let us stand together.[91]

People migrate to the areas which offer them the best opportunities, and it would seem, on the evidence of the censuses, that rural areas often claimed the majority of female migrants to South Africa. These women became either farm workers or domestic workers for white farm families. Bonner's study of the exodus of Basotho women does not record, for example, that in the 1936 census (admittedly a year before the start of what he calls an "unprecedented influx" of Basotho women to the Rand), 52 percent of Basotho women in South Africa were to be found in the rural areas of the Orange Free State, employed "in domestic service and seasonal operations in agriculture," compared to 12 percent in the urban areas of the Transvaal.[92] Similarly, of the African women from "elsewhere" (the majority of whom, as noted above, must have been from Northern and Southern Rhodesia) in 1936, nearly 58 percent were in the rural Transvaal, compared to 21 percent in Transvaal towns. This suggests that for female migrants, employment on white farms fairly close to their national borders was more likely than urban employment. Male migrants were more likely to be recorded as present in urban South Africa than were their countrywomen.[93]

But what, then, of the women who did go to the Rand, to Bloemfontein, to Salisbury and Bulawayo? A minority of a minority, what roles did they play, and what niches did they carve out? These questions can only be answered with more research. However, this preliminary investigation shows that foreign women must have contributed to the heterogeneity of southern African urban spaces.[94] Perhaps they were agents of the new, perhaps the unconventional, sometimes the outrageous. In this regard, mention can be made of provocative Basotho women on the Rand in the 1950s flinging up their skirts at men and crying derisively, "Take and eat!";[95] of Mary Nyrenda taking over the Manyika Burial Society; of the Mozambican women expelled from Johannesburg for beer brewing in 1920.[96] However, the new and the unconventional were not necessarily notorious: the immensely powerful and respectable *manyano* movement of African churchwomen spread from South Africa to Southern Rhodesia on the lips of the wives of African missionaries.[97]

Thus, foreign women's activities were not necessarily incompatible with respectability. Mrs. Loice Muchineripi, a Zimbabwean woman who spent many years living in Lusaka with her husband in the 1950s and 1960s, recalled, rather condescendingly, that in the days when she was one of the few Zimbabwean women in Lusaka,

> Then in Lusaka, we were selling fish. The people there were stupid. They would go without relish, when things were so near. I had a *musika* [market] of fish . . . I had a musika for fish. The people didn't know anything. . . . You could do what you wanted in selling fish, selling firewood—you did what you wanted! Ah! I never stopped working! Yes! I would get fish and meat and sell them outside my house. Some fish came from Bechuanaland. [The people in Zambia] didn't know anything. They ate poor things; everything they did was poor. There was no musika for vegetables, they didn't know vegetables. They called spinach rape [i.e., they did not know which vegetable was the Zimbabwean staple called rape]. When we formed clubs that's when they knew—these vegetables are called rape. Yes.[98]

Aside from Mrs. Muchineripi's brand of vegetable imperialism, if there is any truth to her statement, it may lie in the fact that she and the few women like her brought to (or perhaps imposed on) local communities changes that could not have been suggested by other outsiders.

Finally, one of the advantages of studying women's regional migration and travel is sometimes being able to tap into the comparative sense that they developed about people's lives. Historians are slow to come to regionally comparative work, but the same certainly cannot be said of the women who regularly crossed borders. For example, Gertrude Shope had strong—and surprising—views on the disadvantages of Johannesburg's African townships compared to those in Salisbury:

> You know it's a bit difficult to compare [conditions for] the people who lived in townships in Zimbabwe and people who lived in the townships in South Africa, because there were these two systems. In our system, people were deliberately denied everything, and therefore it was difficult for them to, to compare with the people in Zimbabwe. Who, even at that time, had lights, you know. Whereas in South Africa we were using candles, or lanterns, even for studying, because first and foremost we didn't have electricity. If ever there was electricity at all, it was just one, and another [far away], right along the roads. But very, very few. Even now, where we live, even now in the house we use candles! There was no question about that one.
>
> [The houses were small here,] but not only that, the house I occupied before I left [South Africa, to go into exile in 1966] was made of bricks, but not red bricks. And I'm telling you about Soweto now, what they call central Jabavu. To be very honest, you know, I'm not joking, when you were inside, because of the type of bricks that were put together, the way they were put together, just one single brick on top of another, you could see light coming in through, between the bricks. We used to laugh at that, you know? . . . Red bricks were better, stronger. Our townships were mass production. They would finish about twenty or thirty houses per day. So you can imagine.
>
> . . . You see, the difference came up in this way. The Rhodesians had always been under the British. Even their education was higher. That is why when they said they were building people small houses, but [even so] they were red bricked.

But other people here, our white people here, especially after '48, when the Nationalist Party took over, these new houses that we are talking about, they were very cheap quality. Very, very cheap quality.[99]

Mrs. Shope's statement touches on interesting issues of comparative colonial economic analysis: the relationship between British and Afrikaner capital and electrification of townships, for example. A more whimsical aspect of comparative consciousness was that South African women who went to Southern Rhodesia as wives in the 1940s and 1950s faced anxious relatives back home who thought that the lands to the north were so wild that their migrant daughters probably had to regularly fend off lions in their travels.[100]

The following statement by a Zimbabwean woman, Cornelia Ndhlovu (not her real name), illustrates the legacy of decades of women's international migration in the region, and some of the new (post-Leonine) perils they face in the 1990s. Mrs. Ndhlovu was born in 1955 in Kezi, a rural area of Matabeleland in southwestern Zimbabwe. By 1993 she was a divorcee with nine children, and in that year she decided to cross into South Africa in search of employment. She borrowed some South African currency, said good-bye to her children, and set out alone, on foot, without passport or visa, for the promised land. She paid a South African guide to get her through the border fences;[101] she then made her way to Johannesburg, where she lodged with members of a network of distant relations until she found employment. After about a year she found a good job in a daycare center in central Johannesburg. Her employers did not ask for South African identification documents and she did not bring the subject up. She has since settled down, found a boyfriend, and acquired identity documents. In 1995 she gave birth to her tenth child.

This is what I will never forget in my life. To be a Zimbabwean Citizen and why I'm here in South Africa and How.
Zimbabwe is [a] quiet country but there are no jobs that's why people left the place to [go] to other countries but crime is less than here; the only thing is money that's why we came here in S.A. although some of us came by passports and those who got no passports are crossing, jumping the boder fencies until they reach South Africa and its not easy to cross because you will be having no transport no money for the journey—no money for food on your way or if you got money but no passport you will take otherwise two weeks travelling begging lifts on the road and you will be sleeping in the bush no blanket no food or either you can be arrested because there are more policemens guarding some farms we sleep in the farms on our way and we are not suppose to be seen and you must be careful and clever wherever you are on the way . . .[102]

The standard paradigm of regional labor migration in southern Africa tells us that capitalism was constructed by millions of African male international travelers and migrants in twentieth-century southern Africa. Recent scholarship has brought African women into this narrative to some extent, as people who "stayed at home." Thus, the paradigm does not tell us about the mobility of African women in the colonial era, domestically or internationally. The aim of this chapter has been to use statistical, documentary, and oral evidence to critique the paradigm's simplification of this complex social equation by always representing the African woman as "the one left behind," the "passive rural widow." This construction of a gendered binary opposition in the physical and economic mobility of African people has been a founding and integral image in late-twentieth-century southern African historiography. Echoing in some ways the very colonial discourses which it is meant to contest, this historiography often renders women as hapless residents of a twilight world of perpetual social childhood. In order to provide an alternative view of the historical scope and potential of this topic, this chapter has cited examples of many women engaged in travel and migration, mainly between South Africa and colonial Zimbabwe. The current, limiting view of African women's socioeconomic immobility in southern Africa should be fundamentally challenged by further research into why and how, as Mrs. Ndhlovu might say, women were "on the way."

Primary Document

National Archives of Zimbabwe, File N3/22/7, "Influx of Foreign Native Women."
Native Commissioner's Office
Shamva (Rhodesia)
NO.N.C.526/21
3rd March, 1921
The Native Commissioner
MAZOE

Influx of Foreign Native Women.

In consequence of a number of native marriages, involving alien women, having been registered at this Office recently, and owing to an increasing number of disputes and complaints concerning alien women, enquiries have been made with the object of ascertaining the extent of the influx of foreign native women, and the result leads one to believe that there is a steady and increasing influx of these women into the Territory.

There are now approximately 500 resident in this sub-district, the majority of whom are resident in Mine compounds as the wives or reputed wives of mine labourers.

Enquiries have elicited the fact that these women come down with gangs of men from the north, but avoid Native Commissioner Stations in order to escape observation. As they are exempt from the provisions of the Pass Laws, it follows that Native Department officials have no opportunity of interrogating them or of observing the extent of the influx.

Disputes have proved that these women are extremely fickle, and desert from one man after another, which accounts for the number of disputes and complaints. There is consequently an increasing tendency to conform to local Marriage Laws, and a number of marriages have recently been registered with apparently satisfactory results. The lobola custom is not observed by these people, and this probably has the effect of restricting the intermarriage of Alien men with women of indigenous tribes.

In so far as the large Compounds are concerned, the advent of these women is more or less welcomed, as the labourers are now more contented, and remain in employment for longer periods. The opinion is also freely expressed that the presence of these women has the effect of minimising the danger of "black peril" cases. On the Shamva Mine certain restrictions are enforced, and, inter alia, marriages must be legally registered before women are allowed to reside in the Compound.

It would appear, in so far as one can judge from short experience, that the advent of these women is an advantage, but it is a question whether the unchecked influx might not lead to serious problems. There is no doubt that a large number of the women come down with only one object, namely, prostitution, and there is reason to believe that a number are exploited by men in this respect, or purpose of gain, which is an easy matter in view of the extremely low moral tone of the women. Owing to the extent to which prostitution is practised, there is a danger of a serious spread of venereal disease or syphilis. Four Alien natives suffering severely from Syphilis are at present detained here for treatment by the District Surgeon, and the source of infection in each case has been traced to Alien women. Efforts to locate these women, with a view to deporting them, have failed, as I am informed that they travel about the country and their names are not known.

In conclusion, it would appear to be desirable, amongst other things, that the entry of these women should be compulsorily brought under the observation of the Department, in order to enable Native Commissioners to observe the extent of the influx, and to exclude undesirable characters.

(signature illegible)
ASSISTANT NATIVE COMMISSIONER

NOTES

Versions of this chapter were presented at two conferences: Africa's Urban Past, University of London, June 1995, and the Twelfth International Economic History Congress, Madrid, Spain, August 1998. For discussion of immigration to South Africa in its press, see *The Star* of 9, 26, and 30 January and 7 February 1995; *The Sunday Times* of 29 January 1995; and the *Mail and Guardian* of 20 March 1998. Thirteen thousand illegal immigrants were repatriated to Zimbabwe from South Africa in 1994. For a discussion of the contemporary migration of Zimbabwean women to South Africa, see A. P. Cheater and R. B. Gaidzanwa, "Citizenship in Neo-patrilineal States: Gender and Mobility in Southern Africa," *Journal of Southern African Studies* 22, no. 2 (1996): 189–200.

1. Another is a growing disinterest in the study of history generally in southern Africa.

2. This is ironic, of course, because under colonial law, African women *were* perpetual minors.

3. "Migratory Labour Carried by Southern Rhodesia Government Migrant Labour Transport (Ulere)," file S 2239. This and all other file numbers refer to the collection of the National Archives of Zimbabwe (hereafter NAZ).

4. For discussions of this discourse in colonial Zimbabwe, see Elizabeth Schmidt, "Negotiated Spaces and Contested Terrain: Men, Women, and the Law in Colonial Zimbabwe, 1890–1939," *Journal of Southern African Studies* 16, no. 4 (1990): 622–48, and "Patriarchy, Capitalism, and the Colonial State in Zimbabwe," *Signs: Journal of Women in Culture and Society* 16, no. 4 (1991): 732–56; Teresa Barnes, "The Fight for Control of African Women's Mobility in Colonial Zimbabwe, 1900–1939," *Signs: Journal of Women in Culture and Society* 17, no. 3 (1992): 586–608.

5. Karen Jochelson, "Women, Migrancy, and Morality: A Problem of Perspective," *Journal of Southern African Studies* 21, no. 2 (1995): 323.

6. See contributions to Karen Tranberg Hansen, ed., *African Encounters with Domesticity* (New Brunswick, N.J.: Rutgers University Press, 1993).

7. Jonathan Crush, "Cheap Gold: Mine Labour in Southern Africa," in *The Cambridge Survey of World Migration*, ed. Robin Cohen (Cambridge: Cambridge University Press, 1995), p. 172.

8. Hamilton Sipho Simelane, "Labour Migration and Rural Transformation in Post-colonial Swaziland," *Journal of Contemporary African Studies* 13, no. 2 (1995): 207.

9. Charles van Onselen, *Chibaro: African Mine Labour in Southern Rhodesia, 1900–1933* (London: Pluto, 1976).

10. To my mind, the clearest statements of these two alternatives remain Joan Scott, "Gender: A Useful Category of Historical Analysis," in her *Gender and the Politics of History* (New York: Columbia University Press, 1988), and Belinda Bozzoli, "Marxism, Feminism, and Southern African Studies," *Journal of Southern African Studies* 9, no. 3 (1983): 139–71.

11. Nsolo Mijere and A. Chilivumbo, "Development Policies, Migrations, and Their Socioeconomic Impact in Zambia," in *Migrations, Development, and Urbanization Policies in Sub-Saharan Africa*, ed. Moriba Toure and T. O. Fadayomi (Dakar: Codesria, 1992), p. 282.

12. A. Adu Boahen, ed., *Africa under Colonial Domination, 1880–1935*, volume 7 of the UNESCO *General History of Africa* (London: James Currey, 1990), p. 205.

13. See, for example, D. Gelderblom and Pieter Kok, *Urbanisation: South Africa's Challenge*, vol. 1, *Dynamics* (Pretoria: Human Sciences Research Council, 1994), p. 74; Cheater and Gaidzanwa, "Citizenship," pp. 191–92.

14. Teresa Barnes, "'Am I a Man?' Gender and the Pass Laws in Urban Colonial Zimbabwe," *African Studies Review* 40, no. 1 (1997): 59–81.

15. Cherryl Walker, "Gender and the Development of the Migrant Labour System, c. 1850–1930: An Overview," in *Women and Gender in Southern Africa to 1945*, ed. Cherryl Walker (Cape Town: David Philip, 1990), pp. 187–88.

16. In fact, all these stories can be found in Irene Staunton, ed., *Mothers of the Revolution* (Harare: Baobab, 1990).

17. Terence Ranger, *Are We Not Also Men? The Samkange Family and African Poli-

tics in Zimbabwe, 1920–64 (Portsmouth, N.H.: Heinemann, 1995), p. 40. One such family, the Moeketsis, are mentioned below.

18. Sibongile Mhlaba, "South African Women in the Diaspora: The Case of Zimbabwe," paper presented to the Women's History Workshop, biennial conference of the South African Historical Society, Rhodes University, Grahamstown, July 1995.

19. Joseph Gugler and Gudrun Ludwar-Ene, "Gender and Migration in Africa South of the Sahara," in *The Migration Experience in Africa,* ed. Jonathan Baker and Take Akin Aina (Uppsala: Nordiska Afrikainstitutet, 1995), pp. 257–68, especially p. 260.

20. Mahmood Mamdani, *Citizen and Subject: Contemporary Africa and the Legacy of Late Colonialism* (Princeton: Princeton University Press, 1996), p. 219.

21. Crush, "Cheap Gold," p. 172.

22. Patrick Harries, *Work, Culture, and Identity: Migrant Laborers in Mozambique and South Africa, c. 1860–1910* (Portsmouth, N.H.: Heinemann, 1994).

23. Ibid., pp. 28–34, 115–200.

24. Simone de Beauvoir's famous comment that women are made, not born, was never better illustrated.

25. Harries, *Work, Culture,* pp. 114, 280 n. 34.

26. Philip Bonner, "Desirable or Undesirable Basotho Women? Liquor, Prostitution, and the Migration of Basotho Women to the Rand, 1920–1945," in Walker, *Women and Gender,* pp. 227–28.

27. Christine Obbo, *African Women: Their Struggle for Economic Independence* (London: Zed, 1980), p. 5.

28. This is an Afrikaans term; its closest English equivalent is "prairie." The platteland is generally considered to include the agricultural high ground of the old South African provinces of the Transvaal and the Orange Free State.

29. Julia C. Wells, *We Now Demand! The History of Women's Resistance to Pass Laws in South Africa* (Johannesburg: Witwatersrand University Press, 1993), pp. 13, 11.

30. Hilary Sapire, "African Settlement and Segregation in Brakpan, 1900–1927," in *Holding Their Ground: Class, Locality, and Culture in Nineteenth and Twentieth Century South Africa,* ed. Phillip Bonner et al. (Johannesburg: Ravan, 1989), p. 145.

31. Gina Buijs, "Women Alone: Migrants from Transkei Employed in Rural Natal," in *Migrant Women: Crossing Boundaries and Changing Identities,* ed. Gina Buijs (Oxford: Berg, 1993), pp. 179–94.

32. Buijs, introduction to *Migrant Women,* p. 17.

33. Bonner, "Basotho Women," p. 229.

34. Belinda Bozzoli with Mmantho Nkotsoe, *Women of Phokeng: Consciousness, Life Strategy, and Migrancy in South Africa, 1900–1983* (Portsmouth, N.H.: Heinemann, 1991).

35. Frederick Cooper, *Decolonization and African Society: The Labor Question in French and British Africa* (Cambridge: Cambridge University Press, 1996).

36. Ibid., p. 28.

37. Ibid., p. 46. See also Teresa Barnes, " 'So That a Labourer Could Live with His Family': Overlooked Factors in Political and Economic Strife in Colonial Zimbabwe, 1945–1956," *Journal of Southern African Studies* 21, no. 1 (1995): 95–113.

38. Mary Morris, ed., with Larry O'Connor, *The Virago Book of Women Travellers* (London: Virago, 1994), pp. xxi–xxii.

39. Despite their supposed search for "multicultural" voices, for example, Morris and O'Connor completely ignored black Briton Mary Seacole's book *Wonderful Adventures of Mrs. Seacole in Many Lands,* which was written in 1857 but was republished in 1985 and again (by Oxford University Press) in 1988. See also a brief review of this kind of literature in Angela Woollacott, "'All This Is the Empire, I Told Myself': Australian Women's Voyages 'Home' and the Articulation of Colonial Whiteness," *The American Historical Review* 102, no. 4 (1997): 1006 n. 15.

40. Morris and O'Connor, *The Virago Book.*

41. Inderpal Grewal, *Home and Harem: Nation, Gender, Empire, and the Cultures of Travel* (Durham, N.C.: Duke University Press, 1996).

42. Ibid., pp. 142, 160–61.

43. A comparison between colonial India and southern Africa does reveal differences, however: in the latter, the issue of African women's mobility was not only within the framework of anti-colonial and nationalist discourses, but was intricately bound up in them. To a significant extent, women's mobility was the medium through which many of these battles were articulated. See Teresa A. Barnes, *"We Women Worked So Hard": Gender, Urbanization, and Social Reproduction in Colonial Harare, Zimbabwe, 1930–1956* (Portsmouth, N.H.: Heinemann, 1999); and Timothy Scarnecchia, "Poor Women and Nationalist Politics: Alliances and Fissures in the Formation of a Nationalist Political Movement in Salisbury, Rhodesia, 1950-6," *Journal of African History* 37, no. 2 (1996): 283–310.

44. The first government high school for Africans in Southern Rhodesia was not opened until 1946, and the first university only opened its doors in 1957.

45. Ranger, *Are We Not Also Men?,* pp. 50–51. See also Michael O. West, "African Middle-Class Formation in Colonial Zimbabwe, 1890–1965" (Ph.D. diss., Harvard University, 1990), chapter 2.

46. The first male graduate was Tennyson Hlabangana, followed by Stanlake Samkange, for whom these words of praise were written (quoted in Ranger, *Are We Not Also Men?,* p. 53). I have been unable to discover the name of the first Southern Rhodesian woman to graduate from a South African university; the first African woman from colonial Malawi to do so, however, was a Miss Vida Mungwira, who attended Fort Hare and graduated in 1954. *The African Parade,* March 1955.

47. Shope was a prominent leader of the ANC in exile and was elected head of the revived ANC Women's League in 1991. This information and quotation are taken from my interview of her in Johannesburg, 22 March 1996. See also Shelagh Gastrow, *Who's Who in South African Politics,* vol. 4 (Johannesburg: Ravan, 1992), p. 280.

48. See Timothy Burke, *Lifebuoy Men, Lux Women: Commodification, Consumption, and Cleanliness in Modern Zimbabwe* (Durham, N.C.: Duke University Press, 1995). For a short biographical sketch of Mrs. Mangwende, see Sita Ranchod-Nilsson, "'Educating Eve': The Women's Club Movement and Political Consciousness among Rural African Women in Southern Rhodesia, 1950–1980," in Hansen, *African Encounters,* pp. 202–203.

49. *The Rhodesia Herald,* 21 June 1955, quoted in Terri Barnes and Everjoyce Win,

To Live a Better Life: An Oral History of Women in the City of Harare, 1930–70
(Harare: Baobab, 1992), p. 158.

50. Harries, *Work, Culture,* chapter 2.

51. Elizabeth Schmidt, *Peasants, Traders, and Wives: Shona Women in the History of Zimbabwe, 1870–1930* (Portsmouth, N.H.: Heinemann, 1992), pp. 47, 50–51.

52. H. H. K. Bhila, *Trade and Politics in a Shona Kingdom* (London: Longman, 1982), p. 77.

53. Martin Murray, "'Blackbirding' at 'Crooks' Corner': Illicit Labour Recruiting in the Northeastern Transvaal, 1910–1940," *Journal of Southern African Studies* 21, no. 3 (1995): 380.

54. Patrick Harries, "'A Forgotten Corner of the Transvaal': Reconstructing the History of a Relocated Community through Oral Testimony and Song," in *Class, Community, and Conflict: South African Perspectives,* ed. Belinda Bozzoli (Johannesburg: Ravan, 1987), pp. 97, 99.

55. Murray, "Blackbirding," p. 379.

56. The census categories were often changed, and so the results for different years are never exactly comparable to each other. Until 1961, for example, because of the colonial view that Africans were important only when they were performing labor for settlers, the Rhodesian census only counted urban Africans who were formally employed; others were dismissively classified as "vagrants" and "loafers."

57. Union of South Africa, Report of the 1911 Census (Pretoria: Government Printing Office, 1913; U.G. 32/1912), p. 10. These figures are not supported in breakdowns by province and by urban and rural areas in subsequent tables in the census report, however.

58. This may have been the case; see the discussion of the early stabilization policies of mines in the Johannesburg area in Alan Jeeves and Jonathan Crush, "The Failure of Stabilisation Experiments on South African Gold Mines," in *Crossing Boundaries: Mine Migrancy in a Democratic South Africa,* ed. Jonathan Crush and Wilmot James (Cape Town: Institute for Democracy in South Africa, 1995), pp. 3–6.

59. Charles van Onselen, *The Seed Is Mine: The Life of Kas Maine, a South African Sharecropper, 1894–1985* (Cape Town: David Philip, 1996), p. 38; Luli Callinicos, *Working Life: Factories, Townships, and Popular Culture on the Rand, 1886–1940* (Johannesburg: Ravan, 1987), p. 82; Colin Bundy, *The Rise and Fall of the South African Peasantry* (Cape Town: David Philip, 1988), pp. 209–12; Timothy Keegan, *Rural Transformations in Industrializing South Africa: The Southern Highveld to 1914* (Johannesburg: Ravan, 1986), pp. 170–72.

60. Union of South Africa, Sixth Census, 1936, vol. 9. (Pretoria: Government Printing Office, 1942; U.G. No. 12/42).

61. This is in comparison to 261,136 African men who had not been born there, and a total African female population of 3,284,038. Ibid., pp. x–xi.

62. Union of South Africa, Population Census, 1946, vol. 4 (languages and literacy), (Pretoria: Government Printing Office, 1949; U.G. 51/1949), vol. 4, table 31, p. 146.

63. Republic of South Africa, Population Census, 1960, vol. 2, no. 9 (Pretoria: Government Printing Office, 1966), table 57, p. 148. This table lists the birth-

places of Southern Rhodesia, Northern Rhodesia, and "Rhodesia (so stated)." For the sake of argument I have grouped them all together, although the numbers of women seem ridiculously low, which I would attribute to the exigencies of the apartheid census bureaucracy.

64. Margaret McCord, *The Calling of Katie Makanya,* abridged edition (Cape Town: David Philip, 1997).

65. Gail Gerhart and Thomas Karis, *From Protest to Challenge: A Documentary History of African Politics in South Africa, 1882–1964,* vol. 4 (Stanford, Calif.: Hoover Institution Press, 1977), p. 81.

66. Shula Marks, ed., *Not Either an Experimental Doll: The Separate Worlds of Three South African Women* (Pietermaritzburg: University of Natal Press, 1987), pp. 32–33.

67. Terence Ranger, *The African Voice in Southern Rhodesia* (London: Heinemann, 1970).

68. Barnes and Win, *Better Life,* p. 183. "Nurse Opperman-Mfazi enjoys the rare privilege of being the only African lady after whom a street in an African township is named in Southern Rhodesia." *African Weekly,* 26 April 1944, quoted in ibid., p. 185. The segregated municipal compound for African workers slowly grew in the township of Harare; following the achievement of independence in 1980, the township was renamed Mbare and Salisbury as a whole was renamed Harare.

69. Mhlaba, "South African Women."

70. Shope, interview. Regarding this trade, see Barnes and Win, *Better Life,* pp. 113–16.

71. Statement taken by officer of the Criminal Investigation Department, Bulawayo, 9 September 1920, S 1222.

72. Tsuneo Yoshikune, "Black Migrants in a White City: A History of African Harare, 1890–1925" (Ph.D. diss., University of Zimbabwe, 1990), pp. 139–40. In all fairness to Nyrenda, it should be pointed out that these sins were essential elements of the demonizing mythology which settler society leveled against independent African women.

73. Ibid., p. 179 n. 25.

74. "List of Native Females Alleged to Be Prostitutes in the Location," typewritten with handwritten notes by R. Lanning, Bulawayo Native Commissioner, 23 February 1932, S 1222.

75. A "nurse girl" took care of her employer's children. Typed statement of "Jeanie Sarah," Bulawayo, 24 July 1920, S 1222.

76. In Mashonaland, 16 out of 79 were in urban townships; in Matabeleland, 60 out of 626 were in towns. 1901 census, reported in *Southern Rhodesia Census Reports, 1901–1936* (Salisbury: Government Printer, 1944).

77. These people were actually listed as "natives from territories south of the Zambezi other than Southern Rhodesia," so I have recorded them as coming from south of the Limpopo. 1904 census, tabulated results, table 2, "Classification of Natives of Central and South African Origin Enumerated on Householder's Forms," NAZ file C 3/2/5, p. 16.

78. Report of the director of the 1921 census, p. 26, Southern Rhodesia Census Reports, 1901–36. This census was undertaken in conjunction with the counting of people throughout the British Empire; the question of votes for women had become a hot issue, and in Britain suffragettes declared, "No votes for

women, no information from women" and spent census night driving and walking around in order to be absent from home during the enumerators' visits. NAZ file C 5/10/1.

79. Report of the 1921 Southern Rhodesian Census, "Native (Bantu) Population, in Employment and in Urban Areas (That Is, Not under Tribal Control, but Returned on Householders' Forms)," p. 19, Southern Rhodesia Census Reports, 1901–36. The age of these "females" was not given in the report.

80. Chief native commissioner, Salisbury, to superintendent of natives, Salisbury, 17 March 1921, NAZ file N3/22/7.

81. Native commissioner, Mazoe, to superintendent of natives, Salisbury, 1 December 1922, NAZ file N3/7/2.

82. Report of the director of the 1926 census, "Natives Employed on 4 May 1926," table 54, p. 47, Southern Rhodesia Census Reports, 1901–36. Women who were traders or informally employed would not have been enumerated in the census.

83. Testimony of the location superintendent to the Commission of Inquiry into the Salisbury Municipal Location, NAZ file S 85.

84. Report of the director, 1936 Census (Salisbury, cyclostyled, 1938?), p. 107.

85. In 1941 there were 654 employed African women in Southern Rhodesia who had not been born there; 595 worked in agriculture and domestic employment. This was in comparison to 168,106 men. Five years later there were 3,552 foreign women working in the colony, of whom 3,302 were in agriculture and domestic employ; there were 202,412 foreign male employees. Report of the 1946 census, table 3, p. 21 (Salisbury: Government Printer, 1947).

86. See Barnes, "African Women's Mobility"; Buijs, *Migrant Women*, pp. 16–17; Walker, "Gender and the Migrant Labour System"; Bonner, "Basotho Women"; Schmidt, *Peasants, Traders;* Jane Parpart, "Class and Gender on the Copperbelt: Women in Northern Rhodesian Copper Mining Communities, 1926–1964," in *Women and Class in Africa*, ed. Claire Robertson and Iris Berger (New York: Holmes and Meier, 1986), pp. 141–60; Diana Jeater, *Marriage, Perversion, and Power: The Construction of Moral Discourse in Southern Rhodesia, 1894–1930* (Oxford: Oxford University Press, 1993).

87. Deborah James, "Bagagesu/Those of My Home: Migrancy, Gender, and Ethnicity," paper presented to the Institute for Advanced Social Research, University of the Witwatersrand (13 March 1995), p. 4.

88. Elizabeth Schmidt, "Race, Sex, and Domestic Labour: The Question of African Female Servants in Southern Rhodesia, 1900–1939," in Hansen, *African Encounters*, pp. 223–24.

89. See Terri Barnes, "African Female Labour and the Urban Economy of Colonial Zimbabwe, with Special Reference to Harare, 1920–39" (M.A. thesis, University of Zimbabwe, 1987); and Barnes, "*We Women Worked So Hard*," chapters 2–5.

90. Luise White, *The Comforts of Home: Prostitution in Colonial Nairobi* (Chicago: University of Chicago Press, 1990).

91. Ranger, *Are We Not Also Men?*, p. 15.

92. Bonner, "Basotho Women," p. 232; Union of South Africa, 1936 census, p. ix–x.

93. Union of South Africa, 1936 census, p. x.

94. See Philip Bonner, "African Urbanisation on the Rand between the 1930s and 1960s: Its Social Character and Political Consequences," *Journal of Southern African Studies* 21, no. 1 (1995): 128.

95. Bonner, "Basotho Women," p. 231.

96. Harries, *Work, Culture,* p. 280 n. 34.

97. Ranger, *Are We Not Also Men?*, p. 40.

98. Mrs. Loice Muchineripi, interview by the author and Everjoyce Win, 8 March 1989, Mbare, Zimbabwe.

99. Shope, interview.

100. Mhlaba, "South African Women."

101. Some of South Africa's international borders are "protected" by electrified fences. According to one estimate, between 1986 and 1990, approximately eight hundred to a thousand people were electrocuted trying to cross these fences. In comparison, seventy-eight people were killed trying to cross the Berlin Wall in its twenty-eight-year existence. Crush, *Beyond Control,* pp. 100–101, 125.

102. This is a handwritten statement in my possession. Mrs. Ndhlovu wrote it in 1994, for her own edification and, I think, as a way of recording her triumph over the adversities of "illegal" international migration. She was the aunt of a woman whom I met in Johannesburg; when she heard that I was interested in Zimbabwean women who had come to South Africa she proudly offered this statement of her own history. For discussions of the illegality of the kind of venture she undertook, see Cheater and Gaidzanwa, "Citizenship," and Jonathan Crush, ed., *Beyond Control: Immigration and Human Rights in a Democratic South Africa* (Cape Town: Southern African Migration Project and the Institute for Democratic Alternatives in South Africa, 1998).

8 "When in the White Man's Town": Zimbabwean Women Remember *Chibeura*

Lynette A. Jackson

The compulsory venereal disease examinations imposed on single African women who traveled to urban and industrial spaces in colonial Zimbabwe (Southern Rhodesia) are an example of how gender violence and violation were formalized as official state policy. By discussing the history of these campaigns, uncovering women's memories of them, I set out to decenter (but not marginalize) male-centered nationalist narratives of the past, of pain, struggle, and contest, and deprivatize female-centered narratives. Uncovering women's memories of being forced to open their legs and allow themselves to be "inspected" by agents of colonial authority adds an important gendered dimension to existing discursive paradigms of colonial experience. The fact that African women were subjected to these examinations when they traveled to towns or near sites of production speaks volumes to the distinct ways in which they were mapped (or remained unmapped) in the political, economic, and sociospatial order of Southern Rhodesia. Unattached and mobile African women in towns were suspected of being both disreputable and diseased. They were inscribed into colonial space as "stray women" who, according to the colony's medical director from 1896 to 1929, were responsible for "spreading disease all over the country."[1]

Outside and Unmapped

Spatial metaphors like "mapping" and "stray" reflect geographical, as well as social and ideological, inscriptions and boundaries. In his work on nationalisms, Benedict Anderson employs mapping as a metaphor for the ways in which states and nations imagine and attempt to concretize the human landscapes under their control—to make their domains visible. He writes, "[T]he condition of visibility was that everyone, everything, had a serial number."[2] But, in Southern Rhodesia, African women were not numbered; they were not formally charted on the official, albeit often imaginary, grids of public space. Instead, they were expected to be yonder, in the reserves set aside for the reproduction of African male labor power. One of the earliest pieces of influx control legislation in Southern Rhodesia, Ordinance 16 of 1901, provided for only African males to be registered and issued passes, stating, "No native, not being a married woman whose husband is in employment in the township, shall remain within the limits of any township to which this Ordinance applies" without a pass or registration certificate. African women were not issued passes or registration certificates. In essence, they were not "natives." This was not necessarily a bad thing. It did give African women, as Teresa Barnes demonstrates in the previous chapter, more room than their brothers in which to maneuver. But it also made their legal presence in the towns contingent upon having a husband "in employment in the township" and on being able to prove it. And, while African men were poorly accommodated and African families were rarely accommodated, unattached African women were almost never legally accommodated. Furthermore, the lack of sanctioned accommodation for such women fortified the jural minor status of African women, which was being codified in the Southern Rhodesian constructions of "native customary law."[3]

The 1913 Native Pass Consolidation Ordinance made African women's position off the colonizer's map even clearer. The fact that the term "native" referred only to African males "above the age of fourteen years, both of whose parents are members of some aboriginal race or tribe of Africa," was made explicit.[4] As late as 1958, African women were not technically included under the term "native."[5] The condition of African women in the colonial public sphere throughout most of the colonial period was thus akin to that of what Gayatri Spivak calls the "unaccommodated female body," which, while "displaced from the empire/nation negotiation," ultimately contests that displacement by imposing itself bodily upon that space, by reinscribing space with itself.[6] One example of this process is that African women were the first to make the municipal locations their permanent homes. In fact, during the first decades of the century, they were the chief homeowners. For example, at the outbreak of World War I, African women owned 106 of the 115 rented stands on the Bulawayo (Makokoba) Location. This caused growing tension between the women, particularly those who were single, divorced, or widowed, and the African men who inhabited the location.[7]

One outcome of the dominant construction of "unattached" and mobile African women and the lack of sympathy for these women among African respectables was the compulsory venereal disease exams. Called "inspections" by agents of colonial authority, they were first introduced on the compounds of large mining concerns like the Shamva, Globe, and Phoenix and Falcon mines, in the early 1920s.[8] Women in Fort Victoria, Shabani, and Gwelo (now Masvingo, Zvishavane, and Gweru) referred to the examinations as *chibeura,* meaning to open something, often with force.[9] Women in different locales referred to the exams by different names; for instance, women in the Makokoba and Mzilikazi locations of Bulawayo called them Town Pass exams.[10] But, for clarity's sake, I will call them *chibeura* here.

African men holding or seeking employment were also required to submit to medical examinations, but theirs included checks for tuberculosis, scabies, leprosy, scurvy, and ringworm.[11] While the examinations for neither male nor female Africans should be viewed as wholly altruistic, there were differences between them, and these differences are instructive. Compulsory medical examinations of African men seeking employment were an extension of a whole range of regulatory practices that had been directed at African male bodies since they first started to work and die on the mines and farms of Southern Rhodesia.[12] These exams focused on ascertaining a man's suitability for labor, on determining whether or not he was suffering from a communicable disease, and on ascertaining the least costly means by which general health among laborers could be maintained and labor power reproduced. Thus these practices were imposed in the interests of capital accumulation and performed on African men as units of production. African women were not formally incorporated into the colonial political economy as units of production until much later. In the early twentieth century, they were treated as extensions of these African male bodies. In essence, their bodies were regulated for their potential to infect African men with venereal disease and, to a lesser degree, for their potential to infect European men (who, everyone knew, consumed their sexual services) and, when Europeans began hiring African women as nursemaids, European children. Mobile African women and girls were equated with immorality and disease.

From the late 1910s, the state, mining capital, European landowners, and various categories of African men became increasingly concerned about regulating the bodies of mobile and unattached African women. In general, policy makers and spokespersons for mining and agricultural capital sought the regulation, but not the prohibition, of such women in urban space. They sought the regulation of their genitalia. Vocal segments of the urban African male community, on the other hand, sought state assistance to prevent these women from migrating to towns and compounds in the first place, unless they were under the strict supervision of fathers or husbands. One group, the Matabeleland Home Society, proposed that the government "shut the gates into the Town Locations and in Compounds" by regularly inspecting the marriage certificates of African women.[13] The Loyal Matabele Patriotic Society resented the fact that single women were allowed to rent stands and build houses on the location, stating that "nearly all of the huts are occupied by single women who should not be there at all, for the reason that these Locations are established for male servants who are working in town."[14] Another group of concerned men, members of the compound police at Railway Block Mine in Selukwe who were organized in the Keeper of Life Society, requested that "Every native female even to those who have been well experienced of running everywhere from place to place should have husbands without that should not be allowed to go in the compounds, until they wish they get married." The men also wanted the two-day passes given to women visiting the locations and compounds to be eliminated, believing that they gave women too much freedom to visit persons other than their relatives, which could lead to their "spoliation."[15] In essence, these men wanted the colonial state to help them prevent women from migrating to the towns and compounds unless under the strict watch of fathers or husbands. While there was a degree of collaboration between colonized and colonizer men, between the two contesting patriarchies, in their desire to control African women's sexuality, it was only provisional.

Scholars like Teresa Barnes and Elizabeth Schmidt have effectively discussed contestations of African women's mobility during the colonial era. It is not necessary for me to review this literature here.[16] With the exception of an earlier paper I wrote on the topic, there have been no extensive treatments of compulsory venereal disease examinations in Southern Rhodesia, and certainly none which makes African women's memories of these examinations central.[17] This chapter explores the nature and experience of chibeura from the divergent perspectives of colonial authorities, African respectables and patriarchs, and the "inspected" women themselves.

Memory Lapses

The public memory of colonialism in Zimbabwe, and in other parts of Africa, for that matter, has its roots in male experience. As Cynthia Enloe has observed, nationalisms spring from "masculinized memory, masculinized humiliation and masculinized hope," and so for that matter do national historical memories.[18] The system of contract migrant labor (*chibaro*) and white fear of the black male as sexual predator (the Black Peril) are examples of such memories in the history of central and southern Africa. Both have been presented as sites of national pain and as signs of national humiliation. Invariably, they have been represented as exclusively masculine outrages. Indeed, in the most well known work on the subject, Charles van Onselen's *Chibaro* (1977), women are scripted as "parasites within the Black working class," as saps on its already depleted blood supply. They are "purveyors of sex in a sexually deprived community . . . simply one more level of social control" on the black labor force. They owe their "only allegiance to the highest bidder [and act] as the catalyst of conflict among poorer workers."[19]

Just as the masculinization of colonial memories rendered African women urban parasites, so too did it marginalize them in any critical examinations of the so-called Black Peril, which is most commonly presented as a site of the colonizer's war against black manhood. The term referred to the rape or attempted rape of a white woman by a black man and reflected a perceived omnipresent sexual danger posed by black males. As I will argue here, it also highlights African female supra-marginality in both colonial discourse and postcolonial memory.[20]

Colonial "perils" were products of anxieties, stereotypes, and perceived interests of settler groups, rarely of objective reality. As a result, the Black Peril could thrive even within an environment in which actual cases of black-on-white rape were surprisingly rare. This is because the underlying ideological foundation for the discourse of the Black Peril was white supremacy and the commitment to the preservation of whiteness. In one rather infamous case of Black Peril in Southern Rhodesia, the Umtali rape case of 1910–11, the death sentence for an African male defendant accused of raping a white woman was commuted to life in prison by the high commissioner in Cape Town. White males from Salisbury to Cape Town were outraged by this decision and threatened to lynch the defendant, Alukuleta, themselves. One group wrote from South Africa expressing its solidarity with the outraged white settlers of Southern Rhodesia, proclaiming that there must be "no extenuating circumstances, the native must be shewn at all costs that the honour of the white woman is to be held sacred, and any attempt at rape must be punished with death." A group of ex-Rhodesians resettled in South Africa wrote, "[N]othing that can be advanced by humanitarians and negrophilists will prevent [us] from insisting that the Native must be taught at all costs, that the person of a white woman is to be held sacred and inviolable."[21] The notions of the vulnerable white female and the sexually dangerous black male were central in colonial cultures and, according to Anne Stoler, legitimized restricting the liberty of both black males and white females in the process of enhancing white male supremacy.[22]

What about black womanhood? One could argue that where Black Peril is strong, White Peril is either weak or nonexistent, because Black Peril is a specific assertion of white male supremacy. In Southern Rhodesia, when one heard of White Peril at all, it was rarely in reference to what one might think, i.e., it did not refer to the rape or attempted rape of black women by white men. Instead, according to Sergeant Brundell of the Criminal Investigation Department (CID) in Bulawayo, it referred to "white females who prostitute themselves with natives for the purpose of monetary gain or otherwise, such prostitution coupled invariably with the illicit sale or supply of liquor to natives."[23] Sex between white men and black women, consensual or nonconsensual (except in the most brutal cases), while known to occur, was not a criminal offense.[24]

The focus upon sexual relations between European women and African men, and the exclusion of relations between European men and African women, created regulatory contradictions that were not lost on the parties involved. In 1916, when the legislative council of Southern Rhodesia was deliberating over legislation regulating sexuality, the Loyal Matabele Patriotic Society complained in a petition to the administrator of "the evils of promiscuous sexual intercourse between male whites and female natives, and the neglect by the parent of the results of such miscegenation." They also warned that "the racial danger is not the only one following on this intercourse of black and white, the risk of the spread of syphilis is great."[25] Around the same time, 1,600 white women signed a petition to include white men in the 1916 Natives Adultery Law. They wanted those white men who were having sexual relations with the wives of black men to be punished. But the all-white male legislative council opposed any such inclusion, claiming that it might lead to efforts by black females to blackmail white males. The council did decide, however, to include white females within the framework of the Immorality and Indecency Suppression Ordinance. This ordinance made it illegal for white women to make "indecent" suggestions to black men and vice versa, and made such acts punishable by three and five years in jail respectively.

When a portion of the white female population (those whose husbands met the property requirement) gained the right to vote with the Women's Franchise Ordinance in 1919, they again sought to address the issue. Throughout the 1920s and into the 1930s, white women tried to criminalize white male sexual liaisons with black females, but to no avail, as challenges to such a fundamental element of white male privilege were assiduously guarded against. But while it was not a crime for a white man to have sex with a black woman, the CID did keep watch for cohabitation between the two, which could lead to Yellow Peril, the children produced through their miscegenation. European men who were known to cohabit with African women were sometimes refused licenses to trade in African areas. In some cases, these men were deported as "undesirables."[26]

Failing in their efforts to place checks on European men's sexual relations with African women, European women turned their attention toward African women. Endeavoring to make fraternizing with African women as difficult as possible for their husbands, they opposed the African women's employment as domestic workers in European homes.[27] In evidence given to the 1932 Native Domestic Labor Committee, many European ladies submitted opinions similar to that of Mrs. Chattaway: "Our [African] girls in Southern Rhodesia are mentally inferior to other natives. They are merely accustomed to be regarded as goods and chattels. It would take a long time to develop sufficient self respect to enable them to be employed with safety."[28] White men clamored to remove black men from domestic service, in order to protect white women from the Black Peril. Meanwhile, white women were exercised by the peril of black female proximity to the white male for whom miscegenation was no crime.

While there is ample evidence of how at least some white women, black men, and white men thought about black women's sexuality, we know little of how black women felt about their own sexuality or, more to the point, what they thought about being relegated to the role of "loose women." Indeed, in colonial discourses, black women were objects only, never subjects. While scholars have paid considerable attention to their sexualization and, most recently, to their historical reduction in Western medical science to the genital, very little has been written to date on their subjectivity, what it meant to be so rigidly stereotyped and to have one's sexuality so scrutinized. Scholars like Alexander Butchart and Dunbar Moodie have recently examined the policing and punishing of black men's bodies,[29] but there have been few efforts to examine women's similar experiences,[30] and fewer still which enlist women's own stories and place them into the broader social and cultural historical context.

Genital Influx Control

Compulsory venereal disease examinations were a component of colonial regulations intended to control the influx of natives. The discourse surrounding their imposition is expressive of the ways in which African women

196 *Lynette A. Jackson*

were formally incorporated into Southern Rhodesian influx controls, genitals first. The fear of "the venereal native" grew rapidly during World War I. As with the Black Peril, this fear fluctuated between a sustained murmur and occasional hysteria until the arrival of penicillin following World War II.

From the beginning of the twentieth century, annual reports on public health contained accounts of the extent to which Africans, particularly employed Africans, were infected with venereal diseases. By 1917, mine owners had been medically examining their African male workers for many years, and the various border agents and native labor authorities conducted examinations at points of entry as well. During the First World War, the concern about the "venereal native" grew, and discussion began on how to ensure that no African infected with a venereal disease could come into contact with a European.[31] In the aftermath of the influenza epidemic, the colonial authorities and the medical community grew even more concerned about the presumed role of the native as disease carrier and passed legislation to make it easier to regulate and inspect African bodies. In 1918 an amended Native Registration Act provided for

> compulsory vaccination and medical examination of natives applying for certificates of registration under the "Native Registration Ordinance, 1901" or during the period of employment under such certificates, for the prevention of natives entering or remaining in employment when found to be suffering from such contagious or infectious diseases.

Those examined received a health certificate which was valid for three months, after which they would require another examination. Further,

> Any native refusing to allow himself to be vaccinated or examined in accordance with the regulations or to submit to such treatment as may be directed by the medical officer shall be liable for a fine of £10, or in default of payment to imprisonment with or without hard labour, for a period of not more than three months.

These provisions relied on the Native Registration Ordinance of 1901 which, as stated above, excluded African women from the definition of "native."

With the growing perception that the problem of venereal disease lay in the unattached and uncontrolled African women on the locations and on the compounds, the exclusion of women from the definition of "native" created glaring problems for colonial officials. What legal means were available to apprehend and inspect these women?[32] Dr. Andrew Fleming, for one, saw women as the crux of the colony's venereal disease problem and was joined in this opinion by some vocal members of the urban African male community. In 1921, a group of African men, calling themselves the "leaders of the Christian missions at work on the Falcon Mine and the township of Umvuma," sent an appeal to both the medical director and the Loyal Women's Guild of Salisbury clamoring for the inclusion of "loose women" in the compulsory anti–venereal disease measures facilitated by the 1918 legislation. They warned,

> For some time we have considered that there is something wrong with a people to give rise to the great amount of quarreling, fighting and burning of houses, and

also the vast amount of venereal disease. All those happenings are interfering with the morals and welfare of the man in employment and the only cause of the trouble is the number of loose women who are permitted to roam about without hindrance. . . . Men have evil communication with them, the result is that the men are stricken with foul disease.

Then, using the same tactic that the Loyal Matabele Patriotic Society had used a few years earlier, they hit the colonizer where he lived by stating that "many of these loose women are decaying the white people when taken on as nurses to white babies."[33]

But the desires of the colonizers were much more ambiguous than those of these African Christian leaders. The Christian leaders wanted assistance in preventing African women from traveling to towns in the first place. They wanted them to have to show marriage certificates or documents attesting to parental consent before being allowed onto urban locations and compounds. Government officials and industrial capitalists, on the other hand, resisted this form of control because women contributed to the "daily reproduction" of the African male wage labor force.[34] Moreover, many state and municipal authorities were candid about what they thought were the prophylactic benefits of the single African woman in town, even if she was suspected of disease transmission. According to one officer of the British South Africa Police, "the acknowledged prostitute is somewhat of a safeguard to native men's instincts."[35] In other words, they protected white women against the Black Peril. Thus the mine managers continued to allow single women to live on their compounds even though, or precisely because, they believed many to be prostitutes.[36]

Labor historian Brian Raftopoulos has recently pointed out that, until the mid-1940s, the colonial state's efforts to deal with the increasing number of African women in the cities were not part of any comprehensive response, and that African patriarchs often complained about the ad hoc approach to dealing with "unruly women." Indeed, Raftopoulos observes that, from the point of view of mobile women, "migrating was a transgressive modality through which women entering the city escaped the authoritarian structures of father and husband." Not surprisingly, African fathers and husbands were, at times, more agitated by this phenomenon than their patriarchal sometimes-allies.[37]

While the colonial authorities gave only lip service to the preservation of African patriarchy, they did take the protection of the white household seriously. And, insofar as the unattached and mobile African woman was a threat to this sanctuary of whiteness, they tried to regulate her. They were also concerned about the productivity of the African male workforce and how the rapid spread of venereal disease could sap its vitality. In response to this combination of factors, a government notice was issued in 1922 stating that all African men and women were to be medically examined before being issued passes to seek work, and at three-month intervals thereafter.[38] But again, as the ruling only applied to African women in or seeking employment, it failed to cover many others. Furthermore, there was no provision for the treatment of those found infected, e.g., no funds were set aside by the state to hire additional medical officers or establish venereal disease clinics and lazarettos. As long as the British South Africa Company administered the colony, public health expenditures would remain conservative and oriented toward short-term economic expediency. It was not until after the granting of responsible government, or settler rule, in 1923 that policies extending beyond the direct relationship of capital and labor were seriously contemplated.

The issue of compulsory examinations of African women for venereal disease was hotly debated in 1923. At the request of the Chamber of Mines, a Mr. Moffat moved that "in view of the increase in V.D. among Natives," it was necessary for the government to take action "to deal with this serious menace to the welfare of the natives of this country and danger to the white population" by proposing that "immediate steps be taken to deal with it by compulsory medical examination on mines and by treatment of all native men and women found to be infected." Delegates from various mining concerns spoke of how the prevalence of venereal diseases was growing at their respective sites, and several native commissioners told the legislators how birth rates and the stamina of the adult male worker were affected. Of the mines with representatives present for the debates, the Falcon and Shamva mines were the only ones to report a decrease in the prevalence of venereal diseases. This was said to be the result of the system Falcon Mine had instituted whereby "all natives on engagement [were] medically inspected, and native women [were] similarly dealt with and compelled to carry a medical certificate" if found free of disease. Women found with the disease were sent away. According to a Shamva Mine representative, the same was done on his mine: African men were examined before employment and every six months thereafter (later it was every three months), and were also inspected, specifically for venereal diseases, when "seeking permission to live on compounds." He stated, moreover, that the women were examined by "a committee of native women" and that they did not mind this at all.[39]

Perhaps the fact that African women inspected other African women led historian Charles van Onselen to attribute the mine venereal disease inspections to African initiative.[40] This conclusion would seem to be supported by the various petitions from African societies during the period. But, as the evidence and testimonies of the examined women will show, it was far more complicated. Were women self-appointed inspectors or were they hired or even compelled to do the work? Did they examine women because they wanted the examinations to take place, or did they volunteer to avoid having the exams conducted by persons whom they considered entirely inappropriate, e.g., men or very young women? Were the examiners married women, examining unmarried women to protect themselves, for fear that their husbands might sleep with such women and infect them?

With responsible government, the state was able to pass more encompassing legislation, such as the Public Health Act of 1925. This act gave authorities more power than ever to apprehend those considered public health risks. Part 3, section 47 made it an offense for anyone with a venereal disease to knowingly continue in employment "in or about a factory, shop, hotel, house or other place in any capacity." What is more, employers who knowingly allowed persons with venereal diseases to remain in employment were to be penalized. Section 52 of the act required medical examination of inhabitants in areas where venereal disease was believed to be prevalent, stating that "any person who refuses to comply with such order or with any lawful instructions shall be guilty of an offense." Further, section 53 specified that the examination of females should be done by a female medical practitioner if one was available. Thus the exams were no longer confined to those in or seeking formal employment, and the government was committed to the provision of spaces in which medical observation, segregation, and detention could take place. In 1925, both Salisbury and Bulawayo opened African lazarettos on their municipal locations.[41]

Providing even greater latitude to the campaign against venereal diseases, a government notice was issued in 1929 mandating that "no native female servant be allowed to accept a post as general servant, housemaid, nurse or children's attendant except she be in possession of a clean bill of health signed periodically by a suitable medical attendant."[42] Thus, with the new act and government notice, the menace supposedly posed by African women in or seeking employment, or by those inhabiting areas prone to venereal disease, was addressed. However, there was still nothing to prevent African women from moving from place to place and thus circumventing detection and inspection.

The perception that mobile African women were a problem grew exponentially and within a variety of constituencies during the late 1920s and 1930s. This was in no small part a response to the fact that the mobility of these women had actually increased. Between 1929 and 1944, for example, the African female population of the Bulawayo Municipal African Location rose from 750 (and 4,500 men) to 2,178 (and 6,816 men).[43] It is instructive to note that other places were similarly mobilizing public health machinery to confront a perceived disorder of women out of place during this period.[44]

In 1928, the Rhodesian Landowners' and Farmers' Association organized a conference with government officials and community leaders to discuss the problem. Dr. Andrew M. Fleming attended the conference.[45] He continued to emphasize the "problem" of floating or stray African women while, at the same time, stressing that the actual rate of venereal infection was comparatively low. In 1929, Fleming compiled the following chart:

Examination of Natives: Bulawayo
returns for month ended May 31, 1929

number examined:	684
number of cases of V.D.:	4
percentage:	0.5%

These statistics did not, however, prevent Fleming from seeking better ways to regulate the flow of unmarried African women into the vicinity of the mining compounds, which he considered "a growing menace [which] should be combated to prevent a serious problem from developing."[46] He made his point even clearer in a letter to the colonial secretary a few months later. The venereal disease problem, he wrote, was the problem of "stray women . . . spreading disease all over the country."[47] Others of his peers attributed the "problem" to "girls on the move," or to the "traveling prostitutes who changed their names" as they traveled from compound to compound and were thus difficult to track down.[48] The language employed by these men is telling, particularly their use of words like "stray" and "floating" to describe African women as they came and went. The words are striking because they deny social agency. Women are equated with domestic farm animals who unknowingly roamed out of their places, or with a virus which floats into the bloodstream to wreak havoc.

The issue of compulsory venereal disease exams was integrally linked to the issue of influx control. As long as African women were not a regulated group, they could not be regulated as disease vectors. Since there were many loopholes in the legislation, different municipalities and different locations developed their own mechanisms in the multipurposed campaign against venereal disease. Johanna Scott, who lived in the Harare Location in the 1930s, remembers frequent raids on the homes of women suspected of illegal beer brewing and on the bodies of women suspected of housing the *treponema pallidum* spirochete.[49] And indeed, the superintendents of the African locations in both Salisbury and Bulawayo staged sporadic raids for "unmarried women," who were rounded up and examined. Like the medical officer of health at Shamva Mine, the superintendent of the Bulawayo Native Location, a Mr. Collier, insisted that the women did not mind. But the raids only maintained a precarious situation by criminalizing unattached women. They did not prevent these women from traveling to the location. Superintendent Collier himself estimated that in 1931, 135 single women and girls arrived on the location. Although he sent them away, they simply returned. He complained that there was very little that he could do about this, as they were not covered under influx control regulations and thus could only be sent away, not fined or imprisoned.[50]

If found to be free of venereal disease, the women were issued certificates of health. This document became, in effect, their *situpa* (the authorizing document that African men were made to carry, their "pass"). While Collier insisted that African women did not mind these exams, his own evidence suggests that many did and, as a result, they frequently evaded them. African protests against the raids as early as the mid-1920s are further indications that the exams were disliked. In one such protest, Martha Ngano of the Rhodesia Bantu Voters Association Women's League challenged the colonial authorities to force white women to submit to examinations for venereal diseases so that they could see what it felt like to have to submit to such an intimate intrusion as the price of admission to town.[51]

The Land Apportionment Act of 1930 gave authorities somewhat greater powers to group all African women, employed or not, together and subject them to greater controls.[52] Other acts of legislation, particularly during the 1930s, made the situation of non–wage earning African town dwellers more precarious by the day. They, along with their rural compatriots, felt the burden of legislation passed during the Depression years, legislation which sought to preserve the economic strength of the European settler population. A crucial example was the 1936 Native Registration Act, a formal effort to deal with the "influx of young women who evaded parental control." This act was partly an effort to appease an African patriarchy which had been clamoring for controls on the mobility of African women, and partly an effort to appease the rapidly expanding European population, which was increasingly in competition with all levels of African petty entrepreneurialism. The act was a serious blow to all Africans operating in the "informal" economic sector as keepers of rooming houses, beer brewers, wood sellers, and food hawkers, many of whom were women, and made such activities more difficult and, in most instances, illegal.[53]

Following the Second World War, "the problem of the urban native" loomed in settler consciousness. There were many reasons for this, including the growth in both African and European urban populations, the rise in secondary manufacture, and the desire to restructure the labor force. Tighter controls were placed on the urban African population in general and, what is more, African women became more formally incorporated into the colony's influx control discourse because of their increased rates of migration, the changing nature of their economic involvement, Europeans' desire for stabilization, and the growing number of African women in formal employment:

Africans in Employment
(based on annual census returns)[54]

Year	Males	Females
1921	139,676	628
1926	171,970	1,628
1931	179,092	1,066
1936	252,482	1,815
1941	299,450	3,778
1946	363,344	13,524

When Bulawayo was declared a proclaimed area under the Native Urban Areas Act of 1946, all African women "not in employment or seeking work," except those who were wives, were directed to submit to a medical exam. This act had even broader application than the Public Health Act of 1925, as it targeted the informal sector as well. Any African woman who was not known to be married by the person making the inquiry, e.g., women who were visiting from a neighboring reserve, could be compulsorily examined. But the potential of the act and the reality were two different things, and African women continued to evade the procedure.

In 1949, a venereologist, Dr. Willcox, was commissioned by the government of Southern Rhodesia to look into the venereal disease problem and address it using the most modern methods available. Like his predecessors, Willcox singled out African women as the major culprits. He wrote, "Girls on the move frequent the road camps and infect the transport drivers while in transit." He provided many examples of the centrality of African women as carriers of venereal disease to support his rather draconian remedies, after he observed the "routine examinations" of African employees at the Bulawayo Municipal Lazaretto and personally examined a group of African nannies and food handlers seeking town passes. In the exams of women, he admitted that, while both urethral and cervical smears were ideal, "sometimes only a vaginal smear [was] taken by a native nurse," which would be tested in a laboratory. In one testing of thirty-four women secured in a single raid at the Railway Compound in Umtali (Mutare), he reported that "no less than sixteen were detained in hospital, ten with sores and six with gonorrhea." In a sample of 554 women and 29,618 men undergoing "routine" employment examinations at the Bulawayo Lazaretto, 60 of the women (10.8 percent) and 253 of the men (0.8 percent) were retained at the lazaretto. In Salisbury, a routine examination of cervical smears of 742 nannies produced 19 positive reactions, 2.6 percent. Less frequently, blood and spinal fluid were tested using the Wassermann and Kahn Reaction tests.[55]

While the technology for detecting and treating venereal disease had improved vastly, the problem of "floating" African women who evaded the inspections persisted. Even with periodic raids, Willcox complained that women managed to slip by. He thus felt that it was necessary to take advantage of the opportunities created when "these women come under the official eye" for vagrancy and trespass offenses to compulsorily examine them: "It should be said that any mass raids on locations or industrial sites, undertaken with the object of securing large numbers of infected women, should be arranged in advance to alleviate the potential displeasure of examining doctors caught unaware."[56] Unlike Collier and others, Willcox was completely unconcerned about whether or not the women—or men, for that matter—minded these intrusions. By the late 1940s and into the 1950s, compulsory exams were in operation in the largest urban locations, on mine and other compounds, and at border posts. They were conducted on employed African men and women and on unattached women, whether employed or not.

I contend that these compulsory examinations should be viewed as similar to influx controls, or to chibaro contract labor for men. Institutionalized access to and control over African male bodies have come to be nationally and publicly remembered and generalized, while comparable experiences of African women under colonialism have gone largely unrecorded and remain unincorporated into the dominant national historical narrative. Like so many other examples of violations of African women's bodies, chibeura has been largely consigned to the private spaces of women's memories.

Memories of Chibeura

The discussion thus far has explored the different attitudes and interests reflected in the discourse around the regulation of black women's bodies, specifically through the imposition of compulsory venereal disease "inspections" or chibeura exams. Location superintendents and medical officers of health insisted that women did not mind these exams. Deputations of African men often wanted the exams imposed on all unmarried women. Everyone seems to have had views about the danger of mobile African women and what to do about them—everyone except the women. What follows is an attempt to uncover some of the thoughts of the women who knew chibeura, the women who could not travel into town without opening their legs for inspection. Through a series of interviews conducted by myself, several Ndebele- and Shona-speaking interpreters/research assistants, and a colleague in 1991 and 1998, I attempt to uncover some of the thoughts and memories of women who knew chibeura intimately.

Mrs. Furiana Gosa left Mozambique with her husband sometime during World War II, "Hitler's war," to escape forced labor. They chose Southern Rhodesia because Mrs. Gosa had a brother in Salisbury who she hoped would be able to get work for her husband, who was a mechanic. The couple crossed the border into Southern Rhodesia at Mt. Darwin. They were medically examined at the border post. After successfully passing the "test," as Mrs. Gosa called it, the couple received passes: her husband, a situpa or registration certificate, and Mrs. Gosa, a medical certificate verifying that she had no venereal disease. When asked what the examination consisted of and what the experience was like, Mrs. Gosa responded,

> Before one was given an identity card one had to undergo a medical examination. It was only after the examination that I knew that the doctors and nurses were checking whether we had any sexually transmitted diseases. What happened was men and women went into separate rooms where there was a doctor and a nurse who was African. The doctor was male and a white man. Can you imagine they even touched, poked, and looked at our private parts? It was very embarrassing.
>
> I got into the room and I was asked to take off my skirt. Those days we did not wear any panties at all. So I was asked to lie on the bed and open my legs. Then, wonder of all wonders, this white man began touching and poking at my private parts. It was the worst experience that had ever happened to me. Even my husband had never looked at my private parts like that. I just wished the earth would open up and swallow me. The black nurse was just standing there mum. I had to close my eyes tight to stop myself from crying because of the shame that I felt. You see, I was still in that age where women gave birth to their children at home with traditional midwives attending, not a foreign male doctor like what you have in hospitals right now. So you can imagine how I felt when this white man was looking at me naked.

We asked whether the doctor had explained the purpose of this exam, or whether she had inquired:

> No. Those were the days when you could never ask a white man anything for fear of being thrown into prison. I could not ask the black nurse either because she also looked like someone who was also afraid of the white doctor. Every time he said something she jumped. In any case, I was not yet fluent in Shona and she could not

have understood me because my mother tongue is Chikunda. So I just suffered in silence.

She did not tell her husband what had happened to her while she was in the clinic.

> You know in life there are things that those close to you are better off not know-ing. Can you imagine what telling him about the rigorous examination would have done to him? I just told him I had been examined and I had passed the test and it ended there. He died without knowing, I thought we were better off without him knowing.[57]

She only experienced the examination once. This may be because she was known as a "respectable" married woman by the authorities and didn't travel to different places within the colony often, or because she was already middle-aged by the time she and her husband traveled to Southern Rhodesia. Others, however, were not so fortunate.

Ambuya Madzingirwa recalls the exams as a regular feature of town life dur-ing her frequent visits to the Shabani (Zvishavane) Asbestos Mine compound in the 1940s and 1950s. I interviewed her twice, once in 1991 and once in 1998.[58] During the 1991 interview, she was considerably more willing to condemn co-lonial practices like chibeura than she was in 1998. The reason for this discrep-ancy is unclear. However, it does seem to reflect the ambiguities within African public opinion—ambiguities and contradictions.

Like Mrs. Gosa, Ambuya Madzingirwa first came to the Southern Rhodesian towns during World War II. She and her husband lived on the reserve, but Madzingirwa regularly traveled to shop at the Shabani Asbestos Mine com-pound. According to several informants, this compound was run like a very tight ship by a white man named John Bera. The consummate paternalist, Bera instituted schools and training programs for women who lived on the mines, and encouraged them to learn crafts, cooking, sewing, and knitting. He also exercised strict control over the bodies of those women who visited the com-pound, even if they were married, like Ambuya Madzingirwa.

According to Madzingirwa, every time she traveled to the compound, she was sent to the place where the exams were conducted: "when you arrived with lug-gage, first thing you did" was submit to a chibeura exam.[59] "Outside women" were feared because they were thought to bring disease to the compound. Thus, all "outside women" and unattached women were subjected to monthly inspec-tions by nurses known as "the people of John Bera."[60] These examinations in-volved entering a bath, a shelter with cement floors and little in the way of fur-nishings. The women were instructed to lie down and open their legs; they would be examined and a vaginal smear taken. If the doctor did detect signs of venereal disease, they would be either chased from the compound or sent to the clinic for treatment. If deemed free from venereal infection, they were issued certificates which functioned as passes. While these exams were meant to pro-tect the compound's inhabitants from "bad" or "loose" women and their supposed diseases, and thus were rhetorically directed at *mahure* (prostitutes) and single women from outside, all women who were not "grown-up women," e.g., quite old, were examined. According to Ambuya Madzingirwa, "they couldn't distinguish between prostitutes and married women," and "John Bera wanted everyone to be checked."[61]

Madzingirwa was ambivalent about assigning blame or an unequivocally negative value to the exams. Whom she found more guilty, the colonizers for conducting the intrusive exams or the "loose women" who would infect other women's husbands, is hard to tell from her testimony. For one thing, it seems that when blame was being assigned for the spread of sexually transmitted disease, women were the natural targets. This was not true only among the colonizers. Africans in Southern Rhodesia, like those in many other African countries in the past and the present, refer to sexually transmitted diseases as "women's diseases."[62] In Zimbabwe, as recently as the early 1990s, HIV was assumed to be transmitted largely from women to men and from mothers to children.[63]

Perhaps it is that contemporary context—of AIDS and HIV transmission—which shaped Ambuya Madzingirwa's more recent recollections. In the 1998 interview, Ambuya Madzingirwa stated that it was a good thing for women to be checked "so that our husbands wouldn't get sick." A wife who feared that her husband slept with other women would want these women examined. She said that there were certain types of women who dressed provocatively and that she "was so happy that they were tested." Interestingly, she stated that the only ones who were unhappy with the exams were those who were infected with sexually transmitted diseases. When pressed about how it felt to be assumed a mahure, she explained that, as modernity was just coming and changing morals, people wanted protection. The coming of new structures was linked to new diseases which people feared would destroy their communities. Thus she implied that the protection was worth the intrusion. "If you don't like it, don't come. . . . If you go to mines, you obey their rules." But this support for the exams is contradicted at various points in her testimony. For instance, she recalled that women often felt that "[i]t was a mistake to walk next to a man," since a woman who did so would be suspected of prostitution and sent for chibeura.[64]

A fascinating aspect of the reaction to chibeura is the way it was associated with traditional ways of controlling virginity. Many sought to domesticate the colonial practice by likening it to the traditional Shona practice of kuchenurwa, the "to be proved innocent" exam.[65] The notions of innocence and guilt were very prevalent in Madzingirwa's testimony. Her insistence that only the infected, the guilty, disliked the exams suggests that the exams had both public health and social control (morals policing) functions and intersected with different and often opposing agendas. The two tests are similar in that they place the onus on the female to prove that she is pure. The exams might be said to have fitted into a "moral economy" of the compounds and locations which arose in the circumstances which Madzingirwa has equated with "occupation." According to Mrs. Johanna Scott, who lived in Harare Location, near Salisbury, from the

1930s, the kuchenurwa exams were conducted by old women on unmarried girls to ensure virginity, and the compulsory VD exams were for the same purpose.[66] But Mrs. Scott was pained by the fact that these exams were sometimes carried out by European male doctors. Other informants, including Ambuya Madzingirwa, complained that the exams were often conducted by younger women who were employed as "nurses." This also went against the grain. She said that "there were some who resented this because they didn't feel that it was appropriate." Mrs. Munyoni, who, like Ambuya Madzingirwa, lived in Shabani during the 1940s, recalls that

> We were inspected once a month especially those who were [not?] married. . . . Young women used to bring disease from other neighboring mines. . . . Married women traditionally got the disease from their husbands. . . . The single or the new neighbors, unmarried women, were inspected more often. . . . Us [married] women were at times happy of that because it lessened diseases from our husbands, although it was harassment.

Mrs. Munyoni was deeply hurt by the fact that "young ladies [were used to] inspect old ladies"; "in our tradition," the opposite was the case. But she said that "we couldn't resist because of fear of being chased from the mine."[67] Mr. Banda, who worked on the Shabani Asbestos Mine during the same time, similarly indicated that young girls examining older women was one of the more offensive aspects of chibeura.[68] According to him, "the only consoling thing was that women were looked at by women and not men." But, as Mrs. Gosa's evidence suggests, this was not always the case, particularly not at the police camps and border posts. Mr. Banda also felt that the exam was unfair to men, as their wives were also examined: "Women, especially those from rural areas, were resistant because they believed that it was an intrusion of privacy. But they didn't resist for a long time because if the bosses found out that they were resisting they could be chased out of the mine so they had no choice but to do what they were told."[69] Ambuya Madzingirwa recalled how embarrassed she felt when the African police would parade through the compounds and locations shouting "Chibeura, chibeura, madzimai, chibeura."[70] This was a bit like yelling "Open your legs, open your legs; come, women, and open your legs!" Mrs. Scott also remembers how these raids were conducted every several months: "the [black] police would walk on foot (no shoes). They would come early in the morning, three A.M."[71]

One way women passively resisted was by avoiding the towns. Because older women did not like the idea of younger women from the same village examining them, they would send others to go and shop for them. Ambuya Madzingirwa said that "others just wanted to do their own shopping, so they just dealt with the exam" as the price to be paid. "It was a bit ridiculous, but there was nothing else." When asked what the husbands thought, she said, "When you went home, your husband would ask, have you been checked?"[72] suggesting that there was a general concern about venereal diseases and, it seems, some degree of support for the exams because of fears of male infertility, infant sickness, or even death. But Mr. Banda's evidence suggests that many husbands did mind. Mrs. Scott refers to protest actions organized by husbands particularly because married women were being netted in the raids. Indeed, in the 1950s nationalist parties like the Rhodesia Industrial and Commercial Workers Union and the Southern Rhodesian African National Congress, along with their respective Women's Leagues, actively protested these examinations as outrages.[73] However, they protested only insofar as they were outrages committed against respectable women.

Probing for memories of resistance and expressions of outrage among women exposes ambiguities, tensions, and competing obligations, even in the testimonies of one woman. For example, Ambuya Madzingirwa both endorsed the compulsory exams and recalled, "[T]here was no way out; if you protested, you would be sent to the hospital." And the "hospital" to which she referred in one account was a place she herself described, on another occasion, as an overcrowded and messy oversized bathroom. The nurses there wore gum boots and gloves; patients were made to wear boots, as well, because of all the mess on the floors. Perhaps the recollection of this space had jolted some old feelings when she admitted, "We suffered." The fact is that chibeura became one of the banalities of urban African colonial life. When one considers that Ambuya Madzingirwa associated colonialism with a state of siege, with being under occupation, this is perhaps more readily understood. Under such abnormal circumstances, chibeura could be normalized. "It's obvious women did not like being looked at, but there was nothing we could have done," she said.[74]

But Africans were increasingly attracted to the life offered on the compounds, because they were hungry and were unable to prosper in the rural areas. Mr. Phiri was originally from Malawi and traveled to Shabani in the 1930s. He said that many people were attracted to the mines at the time because food was available there. He also claimed that many single Shona women went to the mines in search of husbands because men from Zambia and Malawi had a reputation for staying with their women until death. The transient nature of life in the mine and railway compounds, however, led to the fear that venereal disease was prevalent. And indeed, by the late 1940s, when Willcox conducted his study, this would appear to have been the case.[75]

According to Mr. Phiri, women's role on the mine was to keep their husbands healthy by cooking good food. He recalls that

[t]hose without a marriage certificate were more prone to chibeura. The single ladies were given a passbook and in the mine they had a register. The passbook was a record to show your progress or your record of health on chibeura. . . . If you had no VD and the record showed it, you were usually allowed into the mine. . . . This passbook was demanded on entry into each and every mine. You had to produce it to show that you were clean. Even men who hired prostitutes asked for the passbook so as to see that the person they were dealing with was clean and to make

sure that they were dealing with a clean person because this could make them lose their monthly allowance.[76]

Mrs. Ndongo, who is currently matron at the Zvishavane (previously Shabani) Asbestos Mine hospital, recalls that married women would sometimes resist the exams by returning to the rural areas just a day or so before the inspection round-ups. Like Ambuya Madzingirwa, she attributes the end of chibeura to developments in African politics: "People were made aware that this was an invasion of privacy by the politicians."[77] But as opposition rose by the 1950s to the "raiding approach" to public health, articulated outrage at chibeura was generally couched in the language of the innocent, respectable, married female victims of such raids. As is seen in the Willcox Report, colonial public health campaigns were often insensitive to questions of human rights and cultural sensibilities. The venereal disease campaign was discontinued in 1958 because of the growing political sophistication identified by Mrs. Ndongo and Madzingirwa and the changing needs of capital. To paraphrase Frederick Cooper here, these campaigns and, more particularly, the working and living conditions which made them necessary were incapable of reproducing the type of labor force desired by manufacturing capital, i.e., a stabilized, permanent labor force.[78]

Never, however, did the opposition to chibeura encompass a critique of patriarchy, of its ability to criminalize and pathologize single and mobile women. Perhaps this is why, as late as the early 1990s in Zimbabwe, public health campaigns continued to single out mobile African women or "single mothers at growth points" as the key transmitters of HIV. Single women remain the scapegoats, and public health the objectifying discourse. In both colonial and postcolonial Zimbabwe, discourses of public health and social order, of gender, space and disease, intersect. The fact that chibeura occurred daily and was one of the banalities of urban colonial life, certainly from the mid-1940s to the late 1950s, renders the continued shroud of silence all the more surprising. African women were consistently located at the intersections of colonial discourses of disease, control, and regulation, and this chapter has been an effort to recover African women's memories of those intersections—of times and places erased from the national, postcolonial memory.

Primary Document

"Notes of a Conference Held in the Committee Room, Municipal Offices, Bulawayo, Saturday, October 6th, 1928," National Archives of Zimbabwe, S1173/ 220.

> *Mr. Hay:* . . . There was a point I would like to put to Dr. Fleming which has not been mentioned up to date. He made a number of suggestions, but the most important was on the question of the examination of native women. Men, as far as I can understand, may be examined, but are there

no facilities in any way for the examination of women? Is there no way of having women examined either in the town or in the rural districts? I think that that is a most important point. The women are much more dangerous than the men in this matter of disease.

Mr. H. R. Barbour: . . . Some of the native women do go to the hospital to be examined voluntarily; but it should be compulsory. The employers of labour in Bulawayo, if they were in earnest about this matter, should so arrange it that they would not employ women unless they had some sort of certificate to show that they had undergone some kind of examination. I agree with Mr. Hay in that the women present the greater danger. In a town where the men are in very much larger numbers than the women, you are bound to have this sort of thing happening. . . . They [the women] should not be allowed to remain in the location unless they have certificates from the medical officer of health. I believe that is happening to-day. Up to a little over a year ago I was Mayor of Bulawayo, and I had heard a good deal about venereal disease and how it was spreading. I became alarmed and went to see our medical officer of health, and his figures greatly reassured me. It really was not as bad as it was made out to be. Those figures included natives who had been examined over and over again, as they are supposed to be examined every three months by the medical officer of health. . . .

I am rather bucked with the medical officer of health's statement with regard to the small percentage of natives who are suffering from this disease, which we all thought was so rampant. I think we might take the assurance of the medical officer that the Government is going to tackle this thing on a larger scale than ever before, and this [*sic*] relieve the apprehension. There is no doubt but that when one or two cases are discovered in a small place, they are magnified enormously. . . .

Mrs. Bloomhill: A very important point raised by Dr. Fleming is the ratio of the native population to the white. The very fact that it is in such a very large ratio means that the percentage of the incidence of the disease among the natives is very much greater than it would otherwise be. The natives are 20 to one when compared with the whites. You take the percentage of the incidence among the natives who come into contact with the whites. If it is .4, then, considering that there is such a small percentage of white people, the seriousness of the thing is magnified more than statistics lead one to believe.

Mr. Fleming: What Mrs. Bloomhill means is that, if it is .4 per cent among the natives in employment, if we take it for the whole country it would be very much greater.

Mrs. Bloomhill: No, the danger to the Europeans would be twenty times greater if whites and blacks were equal in numbers.

Dr. Fleming: I do not want to discuss the incidence among Europeans, but if you went into European figures, you might find them worse than those of the natives.

NOTES

1. National Archives of Zimbabwe (hereafter NAZ) S 1173/221, Dr. Andrew Fleming to colonial secretary, Salisbury, 11 May 1929.
2. Benedict Anderson, *Imagined Communities: Reflections on the Origin and Spread of Nationalism,* 2nd ed. (New York: Verso, 1991), p. 185.
3. Numerous scholars have discussed colonial inventions of "customary law" in central and southern Africa. See, for example, Martin Chanock, *Law, Custom, and Social Order: The Colonial Experience in Malawi and Zambia* (New York: Cambridge University Press, 1985); Joan May, *Zimbabwean Women in Colonial Customary Law* (Harare: Mambo, 1983); Marcia Wright, "Justice, Women, and the Social Order in Abercorn, Northeastern Rhodesia, 1897–1903," in *African Women and the Law: Historical Perspectives,* ed. Margaret Jean Hay and Marcia Wright (Boston: Boston University, African Studies Center, 1982), pp. 33–50; Terence Ranger, "The Invention of Tradition in Colonial Africa," in *The Invention of Tradition,* ed. Eric Hobsbawm and Terence Ranger (New York: Cambridge University Press, 1983), pp. 211–62; M. F. C. Bourdillon, "Is 'Customary Law' Customary?" *Native Affairs Department Annual* 11, no. 2 (1975): 142–43; Elizabeth Schmidt, *Peasants, Traders, and Wives: Shona Women in the History of Zimbabwe, 1870–1939* (Portsmouth, N.H.: Heinemann, 1992), pp. 106–10.
4. NAZ H 2/9/2, Department of Public Health, Re: Medical Inspections.
5. In the report of the Urban African Affairs Commission of 1958 (the Plewman Commission), Appendix 1, it was recommended that the term "native" include African women as well. This was a component of the commissioners' overall belief that, in response to the changing needs of industry for a stabilized workforce, African women, as wives, should be formally recognized as members of the urban and employed community of the colony.
6. Gayatri Spivak, "Women in Difference: Mahasweta Devi's 'Douloti the Bountiful,'" in *Nationalisms and Sexualities,* ed. Andrew Parker et al. (New York: Routledge, 1992), pp. 112–13.
7. Stephen Thornton, "The Struggle for Profit and Participation by an Emerging African Petty-Bourgeoisie in Bulawayo, 1893–1933," *Societies of Southern Africa* 9 (1980): 70.
8. Southern Rhodesia, Legislative Council Debates, 30 May 1923.
9. In a recent conversation, I was informed that "chibeura" is also used colloquially to refer to loose women, i.e., those who are "open," those to whom one can gain easy sexual access. There is apparently a popular song in which a female vocalist harangues a chibeura for taking her man. Personal communication with Norman Mlambo, 4 October 1998.
10. Mrs. N. Ncube, interview, Mashumba Beer Garden, Bulawayo, 23 July 1991. All interviews were conducted by me unless noted otherwise.

"When in the White Man's Town" 211

11. Evan Tsouroulis, "The Compulsory Medical Examination of African Workers in Harare, 1923–1939" (M.A. thesis, Department of Economic History, University of Zimbabwe, 1988).

12. For a detailed discussion of the health conditions of African labor migrants in Southern Rhodesia, see I. Phimister, "African Labor Conditions and Health in the Southern Rhodesian Mining Industry, 1898–1953," in *Studies in the History of African Mine Labour in Colonial Zimbabwe*, ed. I. Phimister and C. van Onselen (Gwelo: Mambo, 1978), pp. 102–49.

13. NAZ S 1227/1, The Matabeleland Home Society, Bulawayo, minutes from meeting on 12 April 1935, Re: Native Marriage Ordinance.

14. NAZ N3/21/1–10, petition from the Loyal Matabele Patriotic Society to town clerk, Bulawayo, 30 August 1916.

15. NAZ S1227/1, re: "Immorality of Native Girls," The Keeper of Life Society, Selukwe, to Chief Native Commissioner C. L. Carbutt, n.d.

16. Elizabeth Schmidt, "Negotiated Spaces and Contested Terrain: Men, Women, and the Law in Colonial Zimbabwe, 1890–1939," *Journal of Southern African Studies* 16, no. 4 (1990): 622–48; Schmidt, *Peasants, Traders, and Wives*, chapter 4. See also Lynette A. Jackson, "Uncontrollable Women on an Urban African Location: Bulawayo Location, 1894–1958" (M.A. thesis, Columbia University, 1987).

17. See Lynette A. Jackson, "'Stray Women' and 'Girls on the Move': Gender, Space, and Disease in Colonial and Postcolonial Zimbabwe," in *Sacred Spaces and Public Quarrels: African Cultural and Economic Landscapes*, ed. Paul Zeleza and Ezekiel Kalipeni (Lawrenceville, N.J.: Africa World, 1998), pp. 147–70.

18. Cynthia Enloe, *Bananas, Beaches, and Bases: Making Feminist Sense of International Politics* (Berkeley: University of California Press, 1989), p. 44.

19. Charles van Onselen, *Chibaro: African Mine Labour in Southern Rhodesia, 1900–1933* (Johannesburg: Ravan, 1977), pp. 179, 182, 180.

20. For general discussion of the Black Peril, see Dane Kennedy, *Islands of White* (Durham, N.C.: Duke University Press, 1987); Tsuneo Yoshikune, "Black Migrants in a White City: A History of African Harare, 1890–1925" (Ph.D. diss., University of Zimbabwe, 1990); and John Pape, "Black and White: The 'Perils of Sex' in Colonial Zimbabwe," *Journal of Southern African Studies* 16, no. 4 (1990): 699–720. An interesting yet problematic analysis of the Black Peril can be found in Charles van Onselen's "Witches of Suburbia," in his *Studies in the Social and Economic History of the Witwatersrand, 1886–1914* (Johannesburg: Ravan, 1982). Van Onselen links Black Peril hysterias with periods of economic insecurity. He also, in my opinion, perpetuates the notion that the rape of the colonizer's or master's woman is an act of revolt against the system of oppression. Rape of the master's woman, while not presented as acceptable, is presented as reaffirming of manhood.

21. Bulawayo Records Center, Location 23/3/6R, Box 6435, Re: Umtali Rape Case, Jan.–Feb. 1911.

22. Anne Stoler, "Making Empire Respectable: The Politics of Race and Sexual Morality in Twentieth Century Colonial Cultures," *American Ethnologist* 16, no. 4 (1989): 642.

23. NAZ 1227/2, Re: Black and White Peril in Southern Rhodesia, n.d.

24. NAZ S 1222/2, Re: Immorality Files: Personal, 1913–25. Many such liaisons

and even relationships were under the surveillance of the CID and compiled as immorality cases.

25. NAZ N 3/21/1–10, Native Associations, Re: The Loyal Matebele Society Petition to His Honour the Administrator, September 20, 1916. The LMS complained that white fathers did not take responsibility for their mixed-race offspring.

26. NAZ S1222/1, Criminal Investigation Department, Re: Immorality: Personal, 1917–30.

27. Elizabeth Schmidt, *Peasants, Traders, and Wives,* p. 177.

28. NAZ S 235/594, Notes of Evidence, Committee Appointed to Inquire into Employment of Native Female Domestic Labour, 1932, pp. 112–16.

29. Alexander Butchart, *The Anatomy of Power: European Constructions of the African Body* (New York: Zed, 1998); Dunbar T. Moodie, *Going for Gold: Men, Mines, and Migration* (Berkeley: University of California Press, 1994).

30. One such effort is found in Karen Poewe, *The Namibia Herero: A History of Their Psychosocial Disintegration and Survival* (Lewiston, N.Y.: Edwin Mellen, 1985).

31. NAZ H2/9/2, town clerk's office, Salisbury, to the administrator, 11 May 1917.

32. Southern Rhodesia, Report on the Public Health for the Year 1914.

33. NAZ A 3/12/7, Appeal from the Leaders of the Christian Missions at Work on the Falcon Mine and the Township of Umvuma to the Medical Director, 21 April 1921.

34. This concept of "daily reproduction" was developed by Luise White in "A Colonial State and an African Petty Bourgeoisie," in *Struggle for the City: Migrant Labor, Capital, and the State in Urban Africa,* ed. Frederick Cooper (London: Sage, 1983), pp. 167–94.

35. NAZ S 1227/1, Immorality: Native Girls, 1931.

36. Van Onselen, *Chibaro,* p. 48.

37. Brian Raftopoulos and Ian Phimister, eds., *Keep on Knocking: A History of the Labour Movement in Zimbabwe, 1900–1997* (Harare: Baobab, 1997), p. 31.

38. Government notice no. 512, 10 November 1922.

39. Re: Venereal Diseases among Natives, Southern Rhodesia Legislative Council Debates, 30 May 1923.

40. Van Onselen, *Chibaro,* p. 51.

41. Muriel Horrell, "The 'Pass Laws': A Fact Paper," South African Institute of Race Relations, 1960, p. 71.

42. NAZ S241/531, office of the colonial secretary, Re: "Anti-Venereal Disease Clinics in Urban Areas," 6 May 1929.

43. Southern Rhodesia, Report of the Committee to Inquire into the Control and Welfare of the Native Population in Bulawayo, 1930, p. 3; Percy Ibbotson, "Report on a Survey of Urban African Conditions in Southern Rhodesia," *Africa* 16, no. 2 (1946): 74.

44. Hazel Carby has discussed how the state enacted policies of "policing black women's bodies" in the United States. See Hazel V. Carby, "Policing the Black Woman's Body in an Urban Context," *Critical Inquiry* 18, no. 4 (1992): 738–55.

45. NAZ S1173/220, Minutes from the Conference on Venereal Diseases, Bulawayo, 6 October 1928.

46. Southern Rhodesia, Report on the Public Health for the Year of 1914.

47. NAZ S1173/220, A. M. Fleming to colonial secretary, Re: Anti-Venereal Clinics, 6 May 1929.

48. These comments were made several years latter by R. R. Willcox in his Report on Venereal Diseases, Survey of the African in Southern Rhodesia. Southern Rhodesia, Department of Public Health, 1949. This document will be discussed further below.

49. Mrs. Johanna Scott, interview by myself and Joseph Derere, 17 August 1991.

50. NAZ S235/594, Native Domestic Labour Commission Evidence, 1932. See also Charles van Onselen and Ian Phimister, "The Political Economy of Tribal Animosity: A Case Study of the 1929 Bulawayo Location 'Faction Fight,'" *Journal of Southern African Studies* 6, no. 1 (1979): 1–43.

51. NAZ S 138/37, superintendent, Criminal Investigation Department, Bulawayo, to native commissioner, Bulawayo, 17 May 1925.

52. E. Tsouroulis, "The Compulsory Medical Examination," p. 39.

53. The criminalization of African women in the Bulawayo Location is discussed in Thornton, "The Struggle for Profit," and Jackson, "Uncontrollable Women."

54. Southern Rhodesia, Report of the Commissioner of Native Labour for the year 1947, p. 39.

55. Southern Rhodesia, Report on a Venereal Diseases Survey of the African in Southern Rhodesia, prepared by R. R. Willcox, October 1949, pp. 2–4, 11, 47, 8.

56. Ibid., 48.

57. Mrs. Furiana Gosa, interview by Joyce Chadya, Mbare, Harare, 19 August 1998.

58. Ambuya Madzingirwa, interviews by Lynette Jackson and Elizabeth Ncube, Harare, 16 July 1991, and by Lynette Jackson and Isabel Mukonyora, Harare, 10 September 1998.

59. Madzingirwa, interview, 16 July 1991.

60. Madzingirwa, interview, 10 September 1998.

61. Madzingirwa, interview, 16 July 1991.

62. Michael Gelfand, *The Sick African* (Cape Town: Juta, 1943), p. 47; Lewis Wall, *Hausa Medicine: Illness and Well-Being in a West African Culture* (Durham, N.C.: Duke University Press, 1988), p. 186.

63. See Never Gadaga, "AIDS: What Others Say," *Sunday Mail* (Harare), 15 September 1991. In this article, the "others" were single mothers living in growth points: small towns or "nodes" of development located next to rural areas, established at independence as part of Zimbabwe's efforts to decentralize infrastructure and extend it into the rural areas. These single mothers, the "others," were presented as synonymous with AIDS/HIV transmission. See also Never Gadaga, "Anatomy of AIDS in Mashonaland," *Sunday Mail*, 8 September 1991. For discussion of the scapegoating of women in Zimbabwe's early anti-AIDS campaign, see Mary Bassett and Marvellous Mhloyi, "Women and AIDS in Zimbabwe: The Making of an Epidemic," *International Journal of Health Services* 21, no. 1 (1991): 143–56.

64. Madzingirwa, interview, 10 September 1998.

65. Dr. Isabel Mukonyora defined this term for me. For more on traditional virginity inspection, see S. Holland, "Sexually Transmitted Diseases in Rhodesia," part 2, *Central African Journal of Medicine* 22, no. 11 (1976): 219.

66. Mrs. Johanna Scott, interview by Lynette Jackson, Harare, 2 September 1991.

67. Mrs. Munyoni, interview by Daphne Mpofu, Zvishavane, 27 September 1998.
68. Mr. Banda, interview by Daphne Mpofu, Zvishavane, 26 September 1998.
69. Banda, interview, 26 September 1998.
70. Madzingirwa, interview, 16 July 1991.
71. Scott, interview, 2 September 1991.
72. Madzingirwa, interview, 10 September 1998.
73. Scott, interview, 2 September 1991.
74. Madzingirwa, interview, 10 September 1998.
75. Mr. Phiri also recalls that the place where women were inspected was called *kwa John Bera*.
76. Mr. Phiri, interview by Daphne Mpofu, Zvishavane, 27 September 1998.
77. Mrs. Ndongo, interview by Daphne Mpofu, Zvishavane, 27 September 1998.
78. Frederick Cooper, "Urban Space, Industrial Time, and Wage Labor in Africa," in Cooper, *Struggle for the City,* p. 32.

Part Three. *Power Reconfigured/ Power Contested*

Though spanning the entire colonial period and a diverse range of historical experiences—from the queen mothers of late-nineteenth-century Buganda to women guerrillas in Zimbabwe's war of liberation—the five chapters in this final section share a concern for the ways in which women were excluded from the public politics and public discourses of colonial rule, while they struggled to retain control over their productive and reproductive labor in monetized colonial economies. That women's rank and status profoundly shaped their experiences of political marginalization and economic subordination is brought into sharp relief by the range of lived experiences explored. The chapters illustrate how women used and adapted preexisting forms of collective mobilization as they challenged the legitimacy of colonial rule and contested new configurations of patriarchy.

Queen Mothers and Good
Government in Buganda:
The Loss of Women's Political
Power in Nineteenth-Century
East Africa

Holly Hanson

Drastic transformations in East African societies occurred in the decades preceding the imposition of European colonial rule. As a consequence partly of new kinds of long-distance trade and partly of the violence that accompanied the introduction of slave trading, rulers lost authority, political institutions took new forms, and ordinary people revised their expectations of what leaders might do for them. In the kingdom of Buganda, located on the northern shore of the great East African inland sea now known as Lake Victoria, the queen mother lost her power to enthrone or depose a king and to restrain the actions of the king in power. The queen mother in Buganda had participated in a system of gendered political power in which the mother of the king had autonomous authority, which she used to check his excesses and protect the nation. By the 1890s, when Ganda chiefs began to negotiate with the British officers who became their allies, the queen mother's political influence had already diminished. After briefly outlining forms of women's authority in other precolonial African societies, this chapter explores the role of queen mothers in the government of Buganda and shows how the turmoil caused by Buganda's involvement in long-distance trade in ivory, guns, and enslaved people undermined the Ganda political order, including the institution of the queen mother.

Gendered Forms of Authority in African Societies
before 1875

Autonomous queens and influential queen mothers are the most obvious evidence that women in precolonial Africa had significant political power, but in order to comprehend that power, it is essential to pay attention to characteristics of precolonial African governments.[1] In many African societies in the past, ruling involved maintaining a balance among competing interest groups, and political structures allowed multiple participants to work out their relative strengths and develop working compromises. Gendered forms of political power were often part of these systems.[2] Just as a gendered division of labor involved the idea that women "naturally" did some kinds of work and men "naturally" did others, a gendered system of political power was based on the idea that some aspects of governing were the appropriate responsibility of women and others were the appropriate responsibility of men.

Queen mothers were not just women rulers; they were women who ruled by doing for kings the things that mothers did for their sons, which included "supporting, advising, defending, protecting, punishing, and nurturing."[3] In a gendered system of political power, a mother's work translated into a queen mother's responsibilities for the nation. Other institutions that expressed a gendered division of political power included women's title societies, women's councils, market associations, age-set organizations, and forms of spirit mediumship.[4] Observing the extent of women's office-holding in sub-Saharan African societies, Sandra Barnes calls African women "one of history's most politically viable female populations."[5]

African women wielded political power in many different ways. In the royal family of Dahomey, female dependents of the king served as "ministers of state and counselors, as soldiers and commanders, as governors of provinces, as trading agents and as favored wives."[6] The Asante queen mother was co-ruler with the ruling chief; she participated in state councils not as a representative of women but as a preeminent authority in the state, and she determined who had the right to claim leadership.[7] In Asante, Dahomey, Lagos, and many other African polities, queen mothers built up political coalitions that brought their sons to power; in the political turmoil of nineteenth-century West Africa, a queen mother's ability to protect and provide refuge for her son among her own people became crucial.[8] As Misty Bastian demonstrates in a subsequent chapter, women also exercised considerable political power in less hierarchical societies. Igbo women's title societies and market associations controlled important aspects of community life.[9] Women's age-set organizations and councils among the Kikuyu and other East African peoples also played a role in government.[10] *Kubandwa* spirit mediums had tremendous influence in many societies in the East African great lakes region, not only among women seeking assistance with fertility and healing, but also in the courts of kings seeking to harness (or at least, not to alienate) the spiritual forces marshaled by mediums.[11]

What happened to women's political power in Africa? One valid explanation for its decline is that colonizing Europeans effaced women's political institutions because they could only see and comprehend the political power of men.[12] Sometimes the drawn-out process of conquest brought Europeans into direct conflict with women's forms of authority: queen mothers were banished and activities of spirit mediums that involved whole communities were criminalized.[13] It is important to keep in mind, however, that newly arrived European colonial officers were not the only historical actors who shaped political and social life. My argument regarding Buganda draws attention to processes that consolidated power in men's hands before colonial rule.[14] The unusually rich evidence for Buganda provides a picture of the power of a queen mother inside an African kingdom, and how one East African people met the challenge of social and political turmoil that preceded the imposition of direct colonial rule.

The Queen Mother in the Buganda Kingdom

In Buganda, as in many European and African kingdoms, political institutions developed when lords or chiefs who controlled land and people gradually gave up some of their autonomy to an emerging monarch with central power. This happened in Buganda between five hundred and seven hundred years ago, after people in the region gradually switched from growing grains and yams, fishing, and raising cattle to intensive cultivation of *matoke* (cooking bananas).[15] Ganda origin myths say that Kintu, the first man, and Nambi, the first woman, arrived in the land that became Buganda with the first shoot of a banana tree. Banana cultivation enhanced the nation's prosperity because relatively small amounts of effort (compared to what was required for grain crops) produced large amounts of food, the population increased, and people had time to devote to activities beyond subsistence. The Ganda people developed a pattern of life in which women cultivated bananas and men produced cloth and fine handcrafts and built houses, roads, and the elaborate fences and buildings that marked the compounds of chiefs and the king. Ganda men also participated in military expeditions, and, under the kings who ruled in the late eighteenth and early nineteenth centuries, Buganda was aggressively expanding into the territory of neighboring peoples.

It is impossible to discern from oral tradition whether the first kings obtained power through conquest, through negotiation with existing leaders (such as lineage heads, the leaders of groups of people descended from a common ancestor), or through the gradual accretion of power by one regional leader, but kingly authority was established in Buganda by approximately 1500.[16] The structure of the Ganda kingdom, from the beginning, included limitations on the power of the king; a fundamental element of this structure was the balancing power of the queen mother.[17]

The queen mother's authority mirrored that of the king. The king appointed ministers of various kinds, allocated land to them, and collected taxes.[18] The queen mother appointed her own ministers (who matched those of the king), placed them on lands that were exclusively under her control, and received a portion of all taxes collected.[19] Each of these aspects of the queen mother's royal prerogatives reinforced her autonomous power. The queen mother's prime minister, second-in-command, and other appointed chiefs did not have to obey the king or his ministers. For example, when the explorer John Hanning Speke stayed in the Ganda capital in 1862, he was astonished to receive a visit from the *Sabaganzi*, the brother of Queen Mother Muganzirwaza. The king had forbidden anyone to visit Speke, and no other Ganda person had broken the rule, but the Sabaganzi was exempt, as he was the queen mother's minister.[20] The queen mother's lands, located in every part of the kingdom, gave her a material base independent of the king: the people who lived on these lands served her and not the king. As one resident of a queen mother's land later explained, "we have always been fishermen for the *Namasole* [queen mother] from time immemorial."[21] The queen mother's lands were exempt from taxation by the king and from plundering by his men. Speke noticed in 1862, as he traveled away from the capital, that his guides took care never to lodge the travelers in a village owned by the queen mother, as that would have obligated residents to provide food, which would have created "disagreeable consequences with the king."[22]

The queen mother's place in the kingdom, and the organization of the kingdom as a whole, can be discerned from maps of eighteenth- and nineteenth-century capitals of Buganda. Wide, well-maintained roads led straight to the *kibuga* (capital) from each of the ten provinces. At the top of each road was the residence of the chief of that province, and at the very center was the king's palace. His court was a large open area where ministers and people gathered to greet him. In these gatherings, chiefs presented gifts of barkcloth, crafts, beer, and other products to the king, and the king redistributed these things to the followers he favored.

The palace of the queen mother had to be on a different hill, separated from the kibuga hill by a stream of running water. In her court, the queen mother received the same kinds of tribute and made the same kinds of redistributions. In the mid–nineteenth century the leading mediums of the *Chwezi* spirit medium cult lived with the queen mother; her palace was therefore one of the centers of spiritual power in the kingdom.[23] Speke described the queen mother's palace in 1862:

> Every thing looked like the royal palace on a miniature scale. A large cleared space divided the queen's residence from her *Kamraviona's* [prime minister's]. The outer inclosures and courts were fenced with tiger-grass; and the huts, though neither so numerous nor so large, were constructed after the same fashion as the king's. Guards also kept the doors, on which large bells were hung to give alarm, and officers in waiting watched the throne-rooms. All the huts were full of women, save those kept as waiting rooms, where drums and harmonicons were placed for amusement.[24]

The queen mother never entered the kibuga; instead, the king regularly came to her palace to visit her.[25] The stream of running water signified the need to keep the king's power separate from the queen mother's.

Ganda queen mothers acted as king-makers: a woman obtained the position of queen mother by mobilizing her lineage and its allies to support her son as the next king, rather than one of the previous king's sons by a different wife. Since one extended set of lineage relatives (called a clan, *ekika*) did not provide enough supporters to win the throne, the would-be queen mother had to create broad-based support in order for her son to come to power.[26] Once her son be-

222 *Holly Hanson*

came king, she used the resources of the coalition she had built, and the land and people attached to the position of queen mother, to protect her son and to ensure that his actions as king benefited the people who put him in power.

Ganda oral traditions, written down at the turn of the century, contain many stories of queen mothers acting to protect their sons when they were vulnerable. When Kabaka Ndawula, who probably ruled around 1700, became ill, he conferred with the queen mother, the Sabaganzi (his mother's brother), and the prime minister about the advisability of following a particular cure; the queen mother and these two ministers decided the cure would be good for him, took the necessary steps to bring him back from the forest when the cure was to have taken effect, and averted a potential insurgency caused by his withdrawal. Kabaka Suuna's queen mother likewise moved to protect her son after he got into a conflict with Kigemuzi, a famous spirit medium who had challenged some unfair rulings. Kigemuzi was captured and imprisoned, but refused to back down. The king became furious and ordered a soldier to stitch up Kigemuzi's lips. The spirit medium answered, "Yours will also be stitched." When he was hit for being impudent he said, "You will also be struck." That night, as Kigemuzi was languishing in prison, awaiting a certain execution the next day, King Suuna himself was struck by lightning. The king immediately sent for the spirit medium, who told him, "Did I not warn you that you would also be burnt? But to strike a child is not to kill it, you will recover soon." Kabaka Suuna acknowledged his debt to Kigemuzi by giving him women and cattle; his queen mother attempted to neutralize the harm done to Suuna's reputation by giving land to Kigemuzi and arranging for her people to take him to his new estate. One generation later, Queen Mother Muganzirwaza sought to protect her ailing son Kabaka Mutesa against his rivals by having all but three of the sons of her former husband, Kabaka Suuna, starved to death.[27]

At least one queen mother used her resources and influence to withdraw support from the reigning king and assist another son in taking the throne. Kabaka Junju, who ruled in the late eighteenth century, lost the throne because his queen mother, Nanteza, turned against him. Nanteza directed the rebellion of her second son, Semakokiro, when Kabaka Junju took actions which displeased her. Prince Semakokiro had attracted many people to his estates, partly because of his innovations in making hunting nets. He had saved Junju in an earlier battle, and his people did not respect the Kabaka. Sensing that he was making his brother angry, Semakokiro sent some of his wives to the king with gifts of maize. Kabaka Junju killed one of the wives because she refused to sleep with him, pleading pregnancy. When Semakokiro told the Queen Mother Nanteza what had happened, she switched her allegiance to him. She tricked her first son, the king, into banishing his brother to a distant forest area by saying to him,

> In order that you avoid quarrelling among yourselves always, expel Semakokiro from his estate of Ttula and give him another one in the forests of Namwezi. While he is there, the *Mbwa* flies will bite him and he may die. This will ensure that you do not quarrel.[28]

In this distant area, Semakokiro amassed a large following, including a contingent of fighting men sent to him by the queen mother. He eventually succeeded in overthrowing Junju. (A translation of parts of this narrative appears at the end of this chapter.)

The Ganda system of gendered political power extended a mother's role in influencing her son's behavior to a kingdom-wide role of constraining the potentially excessive power of a king. Ham Mukasa, a Ganda chief who rose to power in the nineteenth century and who continued in office after the imposition of colonial rule, explained that a king had to have a queen mother to prevent him from being too violent and that, without a queen mother, "there would be no one to check him if he behaved too evilly."[29] To fulfill this responsibility, the queen mother had the same resources as the king: land, material resources, subordinate chiefs, and people who owed her allegiance. She wielded formidable political influence because she represented the coalition of groups that had put the king in power. Her palace was the headquarters in the Buganda kingdom for spirit mediums of the Chwezi cult, revered and feared throughout the region for their ability to make people and communities productive and prosperous.[30] Using these multiple resources, the queen mother balanced the power of the king.

Although it is almost impossible to trace how the institution may have developed over the centuries or how the prerogatives of queen mothers may have changed from generation to generation, the Ganda queen mothers observed by foreign visitors in the nineteenth century had a clear and fundamental role in the government of Buganda. The Ganda people advising Speke suggested that he appeal to the queen mother to intercede with the king on his behalf in 1862, and the queen mother herself responded to his request—for accommodation closer to the palace—by saying that, as she "influenced all the government of the country, she would have it carried into effect." Speke's attempt to play the queen mother against the king to enhance his own position backfired drastically, however: both courts withdrew from a conflict over him, and Speke was left without food or patrons.[31]

Queen Mother Muganzirwaza exercised a visible influence over her son Mutesa. One of the missionaries who arrived at the court of Kabaka Mutesa in the 1870s observed that "the King respected and feared her. He used to say that no one would dare to displease her."[32] The queen mother consistently acted to reduce the influence of foreigners on the king. She had been amused by wearing imported cloth during Speke's visit in 1862, but as long-distance trade and its negative effects on Buganda increased (see below), she refused to wear any imported cloth.[33] At the time when Mutesa observed Ramadan and Friday prayers, the queen mother blamed a drought on "Arabs hanging down their heads as they sat" and forced Mutesa to remove all the donkeys (which were owned by Arab traders and one missionary) from the capital.[34] When Mutesa showed interest in the teachings of both Catholic and Protestant missionaries, she insisted that he accept treatment by the medium of the Ganda god Mukasa. Alexander

Mackay, of the Church Missionary Society, complained to the king about preparations for the spirit medium's arrival at the palace, but Mutesa told Mackay he was obliged to do what the queen mother wanted:

> Mutesa said that he did not know what to do, as his mother and her friends were the main advocates of the *lubare*, and it was they who first advised his [Mutesa's] being carried to see the wizard; and when he declined, on the ground of sickness, they got him to have the wizard brought here. He did not know how to get out of the fix, for he knew that it was wrong, yet his mother's people wished it.[35]

The missionaries, and some later commentators, took this as evidence that the queen mother was committed to Ganda religion, but it is also possible to interpret her actions as intended to protect the power of the king. Mutesa's queen mother asserted the validity of Ganda religion and political order at a time when missionaries and Arab traders were challenging it. When Mutesa's son Kabaka Mwanga ordered the execution of Christians and Moslems, his queen mother refused to allow Christians among her followers to be killed.[36]

The queen mother was not the only person in the Ganda political order who acted as a counterweight to the power of the king. The most powerful leader of lineages, the *Mugema*, also had his residence separated from that of the king by a stream of running water. As the "prime minister" of the deceased kings, the Mugema could speak with a voice of authority that challenged the reigning king. He was the only chief who remained standing, rather than kneeling, in the presence of the king, and neither the queen mother nor the Mugema ate food prepared by the king's cooks, demonstrating that, unlike most of the nation, they did not depend on the king for sustenance.[37] The prime minister and a second important chief with religious responsibilities controlled land independently of the king, and received a portion of taxes: these chiefs could compel the king to consider their point of view and served as foci for coalitions of chiefs with particular interests.[38] Each king also had a queen sister, a princess who participated with him in the ceremonies that made him king: the queen sister had her own palace, chiefs, and estates throughout the country.[39] Although the queen sister's influence on the king is not obvious in sources for Ganda history, the recorded oral traditions of Buganda show that dissent and rebellion against a king sometimes crystallized around other princesses.[40]

Oral traditions, patterns of tribute, maps of earlier capitals, and memories of people who were chiefs in the nineteenth century suggest that good government in Buganda came from the interaction of a powerful king with leaders who had the authority to influence him. Until the turmoil of the late nineteenth century, Buganda was a society with a very definite center—all roads led to the palace of the king—but it also had diverse, overlapping, multiple locations of power. The Ganda said that the king "ate" the country, and he had the power of life and death over his subjects, but a king could only continue to rule as long as he satisfied the queen mother and the leading chiefs. These partially autonomous leaders could compel a king to take action, hold him accountable, and foment rebellion if a king failed to meet their demands. In the structure of the kingdom evident in the allocation of land and the organization of the capital, the queen mother was the most important counterweight to the king.

The End of the Queen Mother's Power

The turmoil that encompassed most of East Africa in the nineteenth century fundamentally transformed Ganda institutions, and the political order described above ceased to function. When long-distance trading caravans, seeking to exchange imported goods for ivory, reached the interior, rulers like the Ganda king lost control of the exchange of commodities, and this undermined their authority. Provincial chiefs and other lesser rulers bought goods from caravan traders which they had previously received only as gifts from the king. These goods, such as imported cloth, were symbols of authority: for a chief to obtain them on his own was like a European lord appearing with the crown and scepter that signified royal power. Access to these symbols disrupted established power relationships; thus the ability to trade allowed some chiefs to collect followers and wield power independently of the king.[41]

This tumultuous situation was even more volatile because the caravan trade led to slavery.[42] A substantial amount of the trade, as it extended into the East African interior, was in ivory. Traders acquired slaves to carry ivory tusks to the coast, and the existence of a market for human beings, together with the established practice of using the labor of war captives, led to deliberate raiding for slaves.[43] Elephant hunting required guns, and after the elephants in a region were exterminated the hunters still had guns and used them to hunt people. The slave trade intensified in this region with its abolition internationally, because slaves began to be used on the Swahili coast to produce commodities for export in the "legitimate trade."[44] The caravan trade undermined the authority of rulers for two reasons: first, because redistribution of goods had been the sole prerogative of rulers, and second, because enslavement utterly effaced the rulers' legitimacy with their people.[45]

At first, goods from the coast flowed exclusively to and from the king. In 1861, after Speke's visit, Kabaka Mutesa killed a chief, the Mutongole of Karema, for acquiring cloth in Karagwe which he did not turn over to the king.[46] Foreign traders were met at the borders of the kingdom and escorted to the capital, and food was provided to them in order to prevent them from trading on their own.[47] Gradually, however, chiefs began to trade on their own, and the king could not stop them. Caravan traders sought to break the king's monopoly in order to obtain better terms, and chiefs benefited from the goods and guns they obtained through independent trading. The huge volume of the trade overwhelmed the king's efforts to stay in control: Speke's gun was a wonder in Buganda in 1862, but there were five hundred guns in 1875, and two thousand in 1882.[48]

The existence of a market for slaves and the enticement of new kinds of trade goods dramatically changed the nature of war. Buganda had been expanding aggressively against neighboring states since the middle of the eighteenth century. Raiding Ganda chiefs had asserted control over territory, in the process capturing large numbers of women and cattle.[49] These wars, however devastating for captured people and groups who lost goods, family members, and autonomy, were intended to incorporate the conquered people into an enlarged Buganda state. The violence of the mid–nineteenth century was different because its goal was to generate wealth for the perpetrator. The missionary Mackay wrote in 1881, "One army has been sent east to murder and plunder. Not even the natives themselves can call it war, they all say it is for robbery and devastation."[50] Kabaka Mutesa and Kabaka Mwanga tried to control the dangerous possibilities of trade by creating special chiefships for wealth, for hunting elephants, and for carrying guns. But these new chiefs, and others who could obtain guns, began to act more and more independently. They made raids outside Buganda without the king's permission, they started to withhold the goods they captured, and they began to raid inside Buganda.

One sign of deteriorating order was that Kabaka Mutesa attacked lands within Buganda which had been protected from raiding "from time immemorial." These included areas dedicated to the worship of particular deities, and also areas controlled by the queen mother.[51] Chiefs, trading independently and collecting their own followers, threatened the power of the king, and the king, attempting to maintain control in a volatile situation, violated Ganda concepts of social order which limited his power in relation to spiritual forces and to the queen mother. The dissolution of authority is also evident in the drumbeat of the chief of elephant hunters, which appropriated the language of the king's power and asserted this chief's independence from moral limits:

I eat what I choose:
I eat what I find:
I eat whatever does not belong to me.[52]

Kabaka Mwanga appointed chiefs who raided other chiefs and enslaved their followers. Mwanga himself, when he went on the customary royal tour intended to show the new king to his people, captured his own followers in three provinces and sold them. People in Buganda had a high tolerance for cruel behavior on the part of their kings, but Mwanga's actions exceeded their limits. Chiefs refused to support a king whose actions were so destructive of the kingdom, and Mwanga was overthrown in 1889.[53] Although the chiefs who removed Mwanga installed one of his brothers as king, Ganda institutions did not function in the new circumstances, and for the next five years factions supporting various potential kings fought for control of Buganda. Each momentary victory was an opportunity for another faction to start the conflict again, because out of it came war booty in the form of slaves that could be sold.

In Buganda the king had been the embodiment of the kingdom, but long-distance trade allowed chiefs to trade independently, to obtain cloth that denoted power, goods that attracted followers to them, and guns that gave them the capacity to force their will on others. All the roads in the kingdom still led to the palace of the king, but, by 1888, chiefs with guns and followers had absorbed much of the power that had belonged to him in the past. The chiefs in the center of the kingdom and the chiefs of provinces were the first to trade independently and amass their own armed followings. When the king on the throne was seen as weak and ineffectual, the gatherings of these chiefs in the courtyard of the king became more important.

Ganda institutions still existed, but their meaning shifted radically. The king became a figurehead, carrying out the will of coalitions of chiefs with military power. The queen mother ceased to have a meaningful role in politics, because a queen mother had always exercised authority in relation to a powerful king. In relation to a weak king, the queen mother's ability to influence affairs of state was severely diminished. Stanislaus Mugwanya, one of the most powerful chiefs during the late-nineteenth-century turmoil and the early colonial period, remarked on the queen mother's loss of power in relation to the chiefs: "The *Namasole* or king's mother got estates, and originally was a person of more consideration and honour than the *Katikiro* [prime minister]."[54] When the center of Ganda political struggle shifted to the relationships among warlord chiefs, the balancing power of the queen mother became less significant.

The rise of leaders who maintained themselves by armed force was a disaster throughout East Africa. Below Lake Victoria, in what is now Tanzania, many societies had been much less hierarchical than Buganda. There, the upheaval caused by trade in ivory, guns, and enslaved people caused chiefs whose authority came from their ability to protect their followers to be replaced by chiefs who ruled through terror. "Rugaruga" were followers of a powerful "big man" who broke the rules of social interaction and exerted power over others through military force.[55] The way people lived in their environment changed in response: they grouped themselves into large defensive settlements, behind walls of stone and spiny cactus, whose ruined outlines are still sometimes visible in the rural landscape. This social upheaval undermined the political power of women in nonhierarchical societies just as it had undermined the gendered system of power in hierarchical Buganda. For example, Kikuyu women ceased to be able to travel to trade with the Kamba and Masai because women traveling alone were at risk of being captured and sold.[56] Women lost not only the responsibility for intergroup exchange but also the profit they had realized from these ventures.[57] Women had been able to build networks of social obligation and influence through their control of food stores and beer brewing for work parties; the caravan trade undermined this dimension of women's social power directly when crops were stolen or commandeered by caravans seeking supplies, and indirectly when violence impeded people's abilities to sustain agricultural production.[58]

In Buganda, the consequence of social, political, and economic turmoil was "wars that would not let go."[59] Using the structures of Buganda's well-developed bureaucracy, coalitions of armed chiefs fought each other for control of the kingdom. The confusion caused by the deterioration of central power and the new autonomous power of chiefs was compounded by the fact that many chiefs had converted to Islam, Catholicism, or Protestantism: these new religions gave people reasons to keep fighting, and each group had its own sources of military supplies. Some battles left fields where "skulls are as numerous . . . as mushrooms"; the famine and plague that accompanied the war killed large numbers of people, and many others emigrated to neighboring countries.[60] The Ganda institutions that might have resolved conflict in the past were no longer effective. Ganda spirit mediums were not acceptable mediators to chiefs who adhered to new religions; the queen mother's authority functioned in relation to the king, not to sets of fighting chiefs; and the central chiefs who had had responsibilities related to the whole kingdom were in the middle of the fight. Although Ganda chiefs struggled to reimpose order on their nation by incorporating new religions into the logic of chiefship and control of land, none of their efforts succeeded in quelling the violence.[61]

This was the situation in Buganda at the time when European powers began to compete over spheres of influence in East Africa. Ganda chiefs responded to the overtures of both British and German imperial entrepreneurs. At one point, two Ganda chiefs were dispatched to Zanzibar to learn how European rulers had decided Buganda's future. Groups of Christian chiefs made several appeals to England for military assistance, and missionaries in Buganda mobilized British public opinion in favor of that nation's involvement in Buganda.[62] Partly as a result of the extremely close collaboration of leading Ganda chiefs and Protestant missionaries, Buganda came into the British "sphere." The coterie of chiefs who had assumed the power of the king in the previous decade consolidated their control over the nation for the next half century through the alliance they made with the Imperial British East African Company for the conquest of Buganda's neighbors. The dilemma of the functional powerlessness of the king was neatly resolved by placing an infant on the throne. The Ganda chiefs, especially in the first decades of the British presence, thought of themselves as the leaders of their country and the British Protectorate officials as their guests. The Katikiro admonished the British High Commissioner for accepting gifts that demeaned his dignity.

The established Christian chiefs and newly arrived British authorities together created a hierarchical political order in which instructions, demands, and punishments flowed out from the center and dissent was not allowed. People continued to hold titles that indicated positions in the Ganda political order, but the practical importance of these positions had been eliminated. The queen mother's influence over the king had no meaning when the king himself was actually a figurehead, and although chiefs spoke in the gathering at the king's court, the leading chiefs did not feel obliged to listen.[63] A system that had been complex and multilayered, and had held rulers accountable, became more and more centralized. This change had already taken place by the time British overrule began in the 1890s.

The trend toward a simpler and more hierarchical government intensified under the British. Some important positions in Buganda disappeared because the leading chiefs gave the land of the authority figure to someone else at the creation of private land ownership in 1900. Other leaders got excluded from the rank of chiefs when British officers became more involved in tax collection and "rationalized" the system. Other positions, such as that of the Sabaganzi, the brother of the queen mother, ceased to have meaning in the new order of power and disappeared in all but name at the death of the person who had been holding the title in 1900. The Sabaganzi had had estates all over the country as an agent of the queen mother, and he had acted as a defender of the king, or sometimes as the promoter of an alternative king. The new order established by the leading chiefs in 1900 and their British counterparts made no place for either the queen mother or the Sabaganzi. In 1924, the proper Sabaganzi still held the estates related to his position, but as privately owned land which, when he died, would be inherited by his children. The Sabaganzi estates, which had a distinct and important political purpose, would cease to exist. Any future Sabaganzi would have to settle on land of the Kabaka, completely undermining the independent authority the position had once implied.[64]

The queen mother and other royal women received the estates related to their positions as privately owned land in 1900, but the hierarchy of administrative chiefs established by the leading chiefs and the British ignored them. The form of political authority wielded by royal women in Buganda was so different from forms of authority familiar to British colonial administrators that they perceived the newly formed chiefly hierarchy (with no gender-doubled institutions) as "traditional." The absence of royal women's power was never remarked upon in colonial documents; it is only because these relationships were inscribed in land ownership that they can be discerned.

There was clearly no place for royal women's authority in the colonial era, when government was shaped to meet British officials' needs for labor, cash crop profits, and compliance. After 1900, the queen mother owned as private property the large amount of land that had been the material basis for her autonomy in the past, but she was no longer the king-maker, or the protector, defender, and regulator of the king's power. Royal women did not disappear— they still mattered intensely to Ganda people, as Nakanyike Musisi's chapter in this volume demonstrates—but, in a way, they did not make sense. Ganda princesses had always been the foci of political dissent, but, stripped of its political implications, their beyond-the-bounds behavior appeared to be nothing but rowdy disorderliness. A speaker in the Buganda parliament complained in 1907, "[T]hese princesses are also very cheeky. When they come visiting they stay a whole month or a full week all the time drinking beer and without any thought of returning to their homes."[65] If we look carefully at Buganda history, we can see that it was not a European presence that diminished the power of the queen mother. Rather, the multidimensional arrangements of power and authority that had cemented the Buganda kingdom ceased to function in the violent crises of the nineteenth century.

Recognizing the crisis in authority in Buganda that preceded the arrival of formal colonial rule provides a context for understanding the social, economic, and political changes that took place in the following decades. As African communities struggled to meet the bizarre demands and intriguing opportunities presented by colonizers and cash economies, they dealt not only with the shock of the new—new rules, new ideas, and new productive possibilities—but also with the pervasive loss of deeply useful dimensions of social life, such as the presence of powerful queen mothers and a gendered system of political power.

Primary Document

Sir Apolo Kaggwa, *Basekabaka be Buganda* (Kampala: Uganda Bookshop, 1901). Translated by M. S. M. Kiwanuka as *The Kings of Buganda* (Nairobi: East African Publishing House, 1971), from which this excerpt (pp. 91–92) is taken.

Junju became king when he succeeded his father Kyabaggu. After completing the mourning rites, he left Lubya and built himself a capital on Mugongo hill. A few months afterwards, he returned to Kanoni to fetch his belongings. He spent the night at Kavule, near the river Koba, and while he was there, he learnt that Prince Mukuma was making an attack on him. Junju attacked Mukuma at once, and the latter defeated the king. But while part of Mukuma's army was chasing Junju, Mukuma himself was attacked from the rear by Semakookiro, who was a full brother of Junju because their mother Nanteza was the same. Because Mukuma himself had only four divisions remaining with him and because Semakookiro had very many, he fought his opponent and even killed him. Mukuma's death was the origin of the song, "Abatta Mukuma bamusambya nnya" -"Those who killed Mukuma did so with four" (meaning the number of divisions he had). At the end of the war, Junju built his capital at Migo in Singo. . . .

Junju lived at his capital of Migo for a long time during which he gave the estate of Ttula in the county of Kyaddondo to his brother Semakookiro. As soon as he settled at Ttula Semakookiro made hunting nets which he used for trapping game. He attracted many followers and when their number increased, they used to boast: "We, the boys of Katasa (Semakookiro), we rescued the goat from the leopard." The reason why they made this boast was that it was Semakookiro's army which had saved Junju when he fought against Prince Mukuma. However, when the king learnt of these boasts, he became very angry. As soon as Semakookiro realized that he was falling out of the king's favour, he thought of the following plan. He started growing maize and used to send his wives to take some to the king; [one day] when the wives took the maize, Junju wanted to sleep with one who was the most beautiful of them all. But when she came before the king, she declined, pleading that she was pregnant. The king, however, insisted and even claimed that the baby was his. The wife also continued to resist firmly which enraged the king. Hence he told the soldiers: "Go and execute that woman, disembowel her and find out whether the baby is a boy or a girl." Forthwith the soldiers executed the woman and removed the baby. On seeing that one of them had been executed, Semakookiro's wives hurried home and broke the news to their husband: "One of our friends has been executed and had a baby removed from her," they reported. When he heard that, Semakookiro sent this report to Nanteza the queen mother, that Junju had executed his pregnant wife. "If he killed your wife," said the queen mother, "I shall go and ask him to give you an estate in the Mabira district. Separation will stop you from quarrelling among yourselves. As soon as you have attracted enough fighters, you will come and fight him. He really did a dreadful thing to kill your child especially as he himself is barren: he has only two children, Prince Semalume and Princess Nakabiri." Semakookiro on the other hand had many sons who became the Princes of Emituba.

Having made a plan for Semakookiro, the queen mother sent this request to Junju: "In order that you avoid quarrelling among yourselves always, expel Semakookiro from his estate of Ttula and give him another one in the forest of Namwezi. While he is there, the *Mbwa* flies will bite him and he may die. This will ensure that you do not quarrel." On hearing his mother's words, Junju accepted the plan and sent Kinyolo to go and help Semakookiro to pack his belongings and also to escort him to Namwezi. Hence on his arrival where Semakookiro was, Kinyolo said: "I have dismissed you from Ttula and I am taking you to Namwezi." Semakookiro accepted at once and calling his men together, he told them to build twenty houses for storing in his nets. The men built twenty huts at once and as soon as they were finished, he hung in them his nets and set off for Namwezi. During his stay at Namwezi, Semakookiro attracted a very large number of followers and at the same time, his mother who loved him dearly, sent him seventy fighting men with the following challenge: "If you are a woman, get married to these men." The reason why the queen mother sent those men to Semakookiro was the great shock she had felt at Junju's murder of the baby. When Semakookiro himself saw that his mother had sent him fighters, he worked even harder to attract more followers. . . .

[Junju sent a messenger to determine whether Semakookiro had really started a rebellion.] When he [the messenger] reached the capital, he confirmed that Semakookiro had really rebelled. Junju acted swiftly and appointed Nakyejwe, the Sekibobo, to attack Semakookiro. . . . [After several battles, Junju was killed while fleeing, which made Semakookiro angry because he had not wanted his brother killed.]

. . . Semakookiro sent one of his men called Galifumita to go and break the news to the queen mother. But when Galifumita came where the queen mother was, he did not tell her that Junju had been killed, for fear that she might execute him. He therefore deceived her that Junju had been captured. But after Galifumita had gone away, those people who were with the queen mother, told her the real truth that King Junju had been killed. Hearing this, Nanteza burst into tears and wept bitterly for her eldest son. After that Semakookiro handed the body to the Mugema who took it to Merera and put it in a house as the custom concerning all the kings was. The jawbone was taken to Luwunga, decorated with beads and stored in a wooden bowl. Junju was a very bad king because he executed many people. These were his important chiefs with whom he ruled the kingdom. . . .

NOTES

1. Catherine Coquery-Vidrovitch surveys histories of powerful women rulers in *African Women: A Modern History* (Boulder, Colo.: Westview, 1997), pp. 34–44; and Joseph C. Miller describes the career of one well-known African queen in "Nzinga of Matamba in a New Perspective," *Journal of African History* 16, no. 2 (1975): 201–16.

2. As Beverly Stoeltje has pointed out, the idea that political power is concentrated "in one figure at the top of a hierarchy" makes it difficult for foreigners to grasp an African dual-sex political system, and African women rulers have often been interpreted as auxiliaries of men. Beverly Stoeltje, "Asante Queen Mothers: A Study in Female Authority," in *Queens, Queen Mothers, Priestesses, and Power: Case Studies in African Gender,* ed. Flora Edouwaye Kaplan, Annals of the New York Academy of Sciences, vol. 810 (New York: New York Academy of Sciences, 1997), p. 44.

3. Sandra T. Barnes, "Gender and the Politics of Support and Protection in Precolonial West Africa," in Kaplan, *Queens,* p. 13.

4. Annie Lebeuf, "The Role of Women in the Political Organization of African Societies," in *Women in Tropical Africa,* ed. Denise Paulme (Berkeley: University of California Press), pp. 93–120.

5. Barnes, "Gender and the Politics of Support," p. 2.

6. Edna G. Bay, "Servitude and Worldly Success in the Palace of Dahomey," in *Women and Slavery in Africa,* ed. Claire C. Robertson and Martin A. Klein (Madison: University of Wisconsin Press, 1983), p. 340.

7. Agnes Akosua Aidoo, "Asante Queen Mothers in Government and Politics in the Nineteenth Century," in *The Black Woman Cross-culturally,* ed. Filomina Chioma Steady (Cambridge, Mass.: Schenkman, 1985), pp. 65–77.

8. Barnes, "Gender and the Politics of Support," 10–12.

9. Nina Emma Mba, *Nigerian Women Mobilized: Women's Political Activity in Southern Nigeria, 1900–1965* (Berkeley: University of California, Institute of International Studies, 1982), p. 27; and Bastian, this volume.

10. Tracy Colleen Baton, "Women, Work, and Social Change: Kikuyu Women in the Late Nineteenth Century" (unpublished paper, University of Florida, 1992).

11. Iris Berger, "Fertility as Power: Spirit Mediums, Priestesses, and the Precolonial State in Interlacustrine East Africa," in *Revealing Prophets: Prophecy in Eastern African History,* ed. David M. Anderson and Douglas H. Johnson (Athens: Ohio University Press, 1995), pp. 65–82.

12. Judith Van Allen, " 'Sitting on a Man': Colonialism and the Lost Political Institutions of Igbo Women," in *Perspectives on Africa: A Reader in Culture, History, and Representation,* ed. Roy Richard Grinker and Christopher B. Steiner (London: Blackwell, 1997), pp. 536–49.

13. Aidoo, "Asante Queen Mothers," p. 75; Barnes, "Gender and the Politics of Support," p. 7; Berger, "Fertility as Power," p. 68; Philip Curtin et al., *African History: From Earliest Times to Independence,* 2nd ed. (New York: Longman, 1995), pp. 493–94.

14. These processes have been observed by other historians as well: Edna Bay

considers the diminishing power of the queen mother of Dahomey in the nineteenth century, and Tracy Baton documents curtailment of Kikuyu women's roles in the same period. Edna Bay, "The Kpojito or 'Queen Mother' of Precolonial Dahomey: Towards an Institutional History," in Kaplan, *Queens,* pp. 19–40; Baton, "Women, Work, and Social Change."

15. David Lee Schoenbrun, *A Green Place, a Good Place: Agrarian Change, Gender, and Social Identity in the Great Lakes Region to the Fifteenth Century* (Portsmouth, N.H.: Heinemann, 1997), pp. 72–74, 80.

16. M. S. M. Semakula Kiwanuka, *A History of Buganda: From the Foundation of the Kingdom to 1900* (New York: Africana, 1972), pp. 32, 39–41; Benjamin Ray, *Myth, Ritual, and Kingship in Buganda* (New York: Oxford University Press, 1991), p. 101; Christopher C. Wrigley, *Kingship and State: The Buganda Dynasty* (Cambridge: Cambridge University Press, 1996).

17. See Schoenbrun, *Green Place,* pp. 192–93, for the antiquity of queen mothers, and David L. Schoenbrun, "Gendered Histories between the Great Lakes: Varieties and Limits," *International Journal of African Historical Studies* 29, no. 3 (1996): 461–92, for a nuanced exploration of gender in the creation of Ganda social forms before the fifteenth century.

18. This interpretation of the Ganda political system differs from the explanation provided by Karen Sacks and others because I have drawn on a different set of sources. I have argued elsewhere that documents generated in the 1920s Butaka controversy led historians (including those cited by Sacks) to focus on conflicts between clans and the king in ways that obscured the significance of other important dimensions of the Buganda polity. Holly Hanson, "When the Miles Came: Land and Social Order in Buganda, 1850–1928" (Ph.D. diss., University of Florida, 1997), pp. 285–89; cf. Karen Sacks, *Sisters and Wives: The Past and Future of Sexual Equality* (Urbana: University of Illinois Press, 1982).

19. John Roscoe, *The Baganda: An Account of Their Native Customs and Beliefs* (London: Frank Cass, 1911), p. 237.

20. John Hanning Speke, *Journal of the Discovery of the Source of the Nile* (Edinburgh: Blackwood and Sons, 1863), p. 359.

21. Entebbe Secretariat Archives of the Uganda Protectorate, Secretariat Minute Paper, No. 6902, *Transcript of the Butaka Land Commission,* p. 428.

22. Speke, *Journal,* p. 416.

23. J. F. Cunningham, *Uganda and Its Peoples: Notes on the Protectorate of Uganda, Especially the Anthropology and Ethnology of Its Indigenous Races* (London: Hutchinson, 1905), p. 184; Speke, *Journal,* p. 376.

24. Speke, *Journal,* pp. 294–95.

25. Cunningham, *Uganda and Its Peoples,* 182.

26. Martin Southwold has pointed out that the necessity of finding broad-based support for one woman's son over another's gives Ganda succession democratic elements and "some of the virtues of both a monarchy and a republic." Martin Southwold, "Succession to the Throne in Buganda," in *Succession to High Office,* ed. Jack Goody (Cambridge: Cambridge University Press, 1966), pp. 96–97.

27. These stories are found in Sir Apolo Kaggwa, *The Kings of Buganda,* trans. M. S. M. Kiwanuka (Kampala: East African Publishing House, 1971), pp. 60, 118–19, 168.

28. Ibid., p. 92.

29. Ham Mukasa, "Some Notes on the Reign of Mutesa," *Uganda Journal* 1, no. 2 (1934): 128.

30. Berger, "Fertility as Power," pp. 66, 68; Speke, *Journal,* p. 376.

31. Speke, *Journal,* pp. 300, 305–307, 339, 409.

32. Cunningham, *Uganda and Its Peoples,* p. 184.

33. Speke, *Journal,* p. 295; Cunningham, *Uganda and Its Peoples,* p. 189.

34. Cunningham, *Uganda and Its Peoples,* p. 194.

35. Alexander M. Mackay, *A. M. Mackay, Pioneer Missionary of the Church Missionary Society in Uganda* (London: Hodder and Stoughton, 1891), p. 162.

36. Robert Pickering Ashe, *Chronicles of Uganda* (New York: Randolf, 1895), p. 8.

37. Roscoe, *The Baganda,* p. 253; Cunningham, *Uganda and Its Peoples,* pp. 197–98.

38. Hanson, "When the Miles Came," pp. 44–51.

39. Laurence D. Schiller, "The Royal Women of Buganda," *International Journal of African Historical Studies* 23, no. 3 (1990): 455–73.

40. Kaggwa, *Kings,* pp. 63–65.

41. Richard Waller, "The Traditional Economy of Buganda" (M.A. thesis, University of London, School of Oriental and African Studies, 1971), pp. 28–32.

42. This analysis relies on Richard Waller, "The Traditional Economy of Buganda," and Steven Feierman's analysis of the consequences of long-distance trade for a kingdom with a tribute-based economy in *The Shambaa Kingdom: A History* (Madison: University of Wisconsin Press, 1974).

43. Curtin et al., *African History,* pp. 352–76, 354.

44. "Legitimate trade" implied the attempt to replace international trade in slaves with trade in commodities produced in Africa, such as rubber, palm oil (in West Africa), spices, and ivory (in East Africa). The term has an ironic ring not only because the commodities were often produced by enslaved people, but also because the foreign powers involved forced terms of trade that strongly disadvantaged the African trading partners.

45. This argument is developed in Hanson, "When the Miles Came," pp. 55–100.

46. Kaggwa, *Kings,* p. 64.

47. Mackay, *Pioneer Missionary,* pp. 216–17; Speke, *Journal,* pp. 326–27.

48. Waller, "The Traditional Economy of Buganda," p. 29.

49. Kabaka Semakokiro, who initiated the period of expansion, acquired over 8,500 female dependents; his predecessor, Kabaka Junju, had 600. Nakanyike B. Musisi, "Women, 'Elite Polygyny,' and Buganda State Formation," *Signs: Journal of Women in Culture and Society* 16, no. 4 (1991): 757–86, especially table 1, p. 769.

50. Mackay, *Pioneer Missionary,* p. 185.

51. Kaggwa, *Kings,* p. 175.

52. Michael Twaddle, *Kakungulu and the Creation of Uganda* (London: James Currey, 1993), p. 21.

53. Mwanga's alleged plan to maroon his Christian and Moslem chiefs, which is often considered to be the cause of their rebellion, needs to be considered in its larger social and political context. The outrage chiefs felt at Mwanga's actions is evident in Ashe, *Chronicles of Uganda,* p. 90; also James S. Miti, *A Short History of Buganda,* n.d., an unpublished manuscript in the Makerere University Library, Africana Collection, pp. 252–97 (pagination of this document is unreliable).

54. "Enquiry into Native Land Tenure in the Uganda Protectorate," Uganda (Kingdom), Rhodes House, Bodleian Library, Oxford; shelfmark MS Africa S 17.

55. John Iliffe, *A Modern History of Tanganyika* (Cambridge: Cambridge University Press), p. 75.

56. Baton, "Women, Work, and Social Change."

57. L. S. B. Leakey, *The Southern Kikuyu before 1903* (New York: Academic Press, 1977), p. 491, cited in Baton, "Women, Work, and Social Change."

58. Baton, "Women, Work, and Social Change."

59. E. M. K. Mulira, *Sir Apolo Kaggwa, K.C.M.G., MBE* (Kampala: Buganda Bookshop, 1949), unpublished translation by Dr. John Rowe, which he was kind enough to let me see, p. 2.

60. Twaddle, *Kakungulu,* p. 52.

61. Hanson, "When the Miles Came," pp. 86–99.

62. D. Anthony Low, *Buganda in Modern History* (Los Angeles: University of California Press, 1971).

63. Hanson, "When the Miles Came," pp. 257–69.

64. Entebbe Secretariat Archives, S.M.P. 6902, p. 457.

65. Lukiiko [parliament] of Buganda, Records translated into English by the East Africa Institute of Social Research, 24 January 1907, p. 74, seen by courtesy of Dr. John Rowe.

10 Marrying and Marriage on a Shifting Terrain: Reconfigurations of Power and Authority in Early Colonial Asante

Victoria B. Tashjian and Jean Allman

In the 1910s and 1920s, a British government anthropologist, R. S. Rattray, devoted considerable effort to making sense of marriage in the former West African forest kingdom of Asante, a state just to the north of the Gold Coast Colony which had only come under British rule at the turn of the century. Rattray was especially confounded by conjugal relations in this matrilineal society, particularly by what he saw as the ambiguous position of a "wife":

> [T]he wife retains her own clan identity and name and transmits both to her offspring. . . . At first sight, when we consider all that this means, and the possible results socially, the innovation seems in the nature of a revolution. . . . Her position (apart from the contract she has entered) appears to be one of almost complete isolation and independence, among strangers, for the very children she may bear will not belong to her new lord. . . . To her husband she does not appear to be bound by any tie that—in Ashanti—really counts. . . . Such appears to be the status of a wife in Ashanti in relation to her husband.[1]

In this chapter, we seek to show that, at the very moment Rattray drew these puzzled conclusions and pondered their "revolutionary" implications, Asante women were being more closely bound to husbands by new kinds of ties that increasingly counted. As a result of the monetization of the economy, the rapid expansion of cocoa production, and the "customary" interventions of indirect rule, the meanings and makings of conjugal relations in Asante were being substantially rewritten. If "independence" could aptly describe the conjugal positionings of the free mothers and grandmothers of the first generation of women born under colonial rule, it proved more and more elusive for those born after 1900, who lived in the ever-expanding shadow of cocoa production.

A highlife song popular in the 1950s captured in lyrical ways the salience of cocoa in the lives of twentieth-century Asante women and men:

> If you want to send your children to school, it is cocoa,
> If you want to build your house, it is cocoa,
> If you want to marry, it is cocoa,
> If you want to buy cloth, it is cocoa,
> If you want to buy a lorry, it is cocoa,
> Whatever you want to do in this world,
> It is with cocoa money that you do it.[2]

Indeed, cocoa transformed the landscape of Asante following its arrival around the turn of the century. It is certainly central to the reminiscences of women who came of age during those years. Afua Dufie of Oyoko, born around 1906, remembered, "Cocoa came at my time. When I was a small girl my father went to the coast to buy cocoa seedlings, six of them, and gave them to my mother to plant. . . . I saw it come."[3] As Akua Ababo of Mamponten, born around 1918, explained, "cocoa was the work of the day. Everybody took to it; it was profitable."[4] And historians and anthropologists who have focused specifically on cocoa, as well as those who have written more broadly on nineteenth- or twentieth-century Asante, are no less attentive to cocoa's impact, arguing that it was absolutely transformative in giving a broad range of rural commoners access to cash and the cash economy—access that ushered in a host of related social, as well as economic, changes.[5] One of the most profound of those changes occurred on the conjugal terrain with the increased demands husbands made upon the productive labor of their wives.

Because of the pioneering work of numerous women's historians over the past two decades, we have a much better understanding of the myriad ways in which changes in production—like those which occurred in Asante with the spread of cocoa—affected African women's daily lives during the colonial period.[6] Clearly, in some cases, particularly where white settlers were present, tax burdens were heavy, and land was expropriated, male wage-earners migrated out and, as a result, women's status declined substantially, while their labor burdens increased. In other cases, where women were active as producers of cash crops, their status often increased, as long as they were able to "retain control over the products of their labor." Yet "over time," as Schmidt has written, "the position of the vast majority of women deteriorated, as strategic resources such as land, labor, and cash income increasingly concentrated in male hands."[7] Scholars have posited numerous reasons for this deterioration—among them, patterns of land ownership, colonial taxation, and male migration and wage earning. Yet in colonial Asante many of those factors were not present. There was no large white settler population, land was not expropriated, hut or poll taxes were nonexistent, and there was no substantial out-migration of Asante men. The "cocoa revolution," as it was called, was the product of Asante farmers' commercial initiative on Asante-owned land. Still, women's work burdens increased, though perhaps not to the degree they did in parts of southern Africa.

This chapter explores how and why women's status in Asante deteriorated and their labor burdens grew heavier during cocoa's expansion, even though domestic economies included both husbands and wives and the factors usually associated with African women's declining status were conspicuously absent.[8] It is based upon a broad range of sources: customary court cases, early anthropological writings, colonial government documentation, and the oral reminiscences of the first generation of Asante women and men born under British colonial rule (roughly 1900–20), a generation that came of age with cocoa. Because agricultural production in Asante for domestic consumption, as well as for the market, has long been organized around and through conjugal relationships, our strategic entry point into the gendered past of early colonial Asante is marriage. Like Cooper, we have found that a focus on marriage allows us "to bring together political economy and cultural analysis, for marriage is both a fundamental principle organizing productive and reproductive arrangements and a key element of . . . cultural and social life. . . . [I]t serves well as a point of entry into a consideration of how gender shapes and is shaped by broader processes."[9] It is to Asante marriage, then, that we first turn.

Defining Asante Marriage: Early Anthropological Perspectives

Unfortunately, much of the secondary literature on Asante marriage that might help us make sense of cocoa's impact on conjugal relations, especially on women's experiences of marrying, is not particularly attuned to change, even though it was based on research undertaken during years of social, political, and economic transformation in Asante (1910–50) and even though the researchers themselves were fully cognizant of the changes occurring around them. Rattray, the author of three classic ethnographies in the 1920s, conceived of his mission as securing "before it was too late a record of Ashanti customs and beliefs." He was convinced that had his work been delayed at all, "it is doubtful whether much information would have been obtained."[10] Though aware of change, Rattray was more concerned with capturing an increasingly elusive past than with exploring the magnitude of social change around him. Thus, for Rattray, marriage in Asante neatly fell into six discrete categories: marriage between a free man and a free woman (*adehye awadie*); concubinage or, as he termed it, "the mating of lovers" (*mpena awadie*); marriage between a free man and a pawn (*awowa awadie*); marriage between a free man and a slave (*afona awadie*); levirate marriage (*kuna awadie*); and sororate marriage (*ayete awadie*).[11]

The vast majority of women who shared their reminiscences with us had marriages which fall roughly within the first three categories described by Rattray, so it is upon those that we will focus here. Marriage between a free man and a free woman, according to Rattray, was a union formalized by the "giving and acceptance of *aseda* by the contracting parties," thereby forming a "strictly legal marriage."[12] Such a marriage conferred certain rights and responsibilities on the spouses, the most important of which Rattray understood to be the husband's right to claim adultery fees (*ayefare sika*) or monetary damages from any man with whom his wife had a sexual relationship. (This right derived from a wife's obligation to provide her husband exclusive sexual access.) In the less formal mpena awadie (concubinage), aseda had not been presented to formalize the union, but the couple lived in a relationship that was "based on mutual voluntary consent, intended to be permanent, and carried out openly." Once again Rattray focused upon the question of sexual rights and obligations; it was his understanding that the most significant distinction between full marriage and concubinage lay in the fact that concubinage did not give men the right to collect adultery fees. Rattray added that the absence of aseda, "while rendering a union in a sense irregular, did not . . . brand a couple who lived together openly as man and wife with . . . [any] stigma." Consequently, he wrote, "I have included it among regular marriage formalities because I think that in olden times it constituted a more or less recognized form of union" which had been considered a "strictly regular" relationship.[13]

The third type of conjugal union discussed by Rattray, marriage between a free man and a pawned woman (awowa awadie), occurred when a man took as his pawn a woman whom he had already married, or when a man married a woman already held in pawn by him.[14] Rattray suggested that pawn marriages were most likely to occur when a free wife became her husband's pawn, since a married woman was the family member most likely to be pawned by a family in need of cash.[15] When a family decided to pawn a married woman to raise money, they first offered her in pawnship to her husband, and it was considered very bad form for her husband to refuse what was essentially a firm request for a loan from his in-laws. Though a husband who took his wife as a pawn lost the use of the money he loaned to his in-laws, he also gained substantially in this arrangement since his marital rights increased quite dramatically. Among other things, he gained far greater control over the use of his now-pawn-wife's labor. Rattray explained that a pawn-wife was under a definite obligation "to rise up when called upon and accompany the husband to his farm, to cook for him, and to perform the household duties. Hitherto she would ordinarily have carried out these tasks, but she was apparently under no legal obligation to do so."[16] Rattray's writings thus leave us with a highly structured understanding of what marrying meant for women in early colonial Asante. Either they were in a formalized or nonformalized marriage with a free man, the primary difference being the right of the husband to collect adultery compensation, or they were in a marriage in which they were both wife and pawn and were subject to greater control by their husbands.

Meanings and Makings of Marrying: Perspectives from Asante's First Colonized Generation

Rattray's structuralist account of marriage in Asante is challenged by the reminiscences of Asante women and men who came of age during the very years the government anthropologist was conducting his research. For women of Asante's first colonized generation, marriage was clearly not a state of being, but a series of multiple, often overlapping processes—processes which do not fit easily into Rattray's rigid typology. Indeed, most described conjugal relationships along a continuum of what can best be described as "degrees of knowing." That marrying was a process involving numerous stages of becoming better and more formally "known" to the couple's families is evident not only in the oral reminiscences of this generation but in Thomas E. Kyei's singularly insightful written account, *Marriage and Divorce among the Asante.*[17]

Born in Agogo in 1908, Kyei worked with the anthropologist Meyer Fortes during the Ashanti Social Survey of the 1940s and the results of his research, which were shaped profoundly by his own experiences in colonial Asante and his position as a cultural insider, were published by the African Studies Centre at Cambridge University in 1992. In a richly detailed description of marriage, Kyei explains that initially the husband-to-be gave small presents, called "seeing things" (*ahudee*) or "door-knocking things" (*aboboom-bo-dee*), to the woman's family and father. Presentation of these gifts gave formal notice of the couple's desire to marry, while acceptance of them indicated that the woman's family approved of the proposed marriage. The presentation of knocking gifts also gave the couple the right to an open sexual relationship or, as Kyei put it, the right to "live as . . . concubines."[18] In the second stage of marrying, the husband-to-be presented marriage gifts to the woman, her family, and her father. The man's family became involved in the third stage of marrying, when the man's senior relatives formally asked the woman's family for permission for the marriage to take place. This step was followed by the central act which, according to Kyei, indisputably formalized the marriage: the presentation of thanksgiving drinks, called *tiri nsa* (literally "head drinks") or, less commonly, *tiri aseda* ("thanks for the head"), to the woman's family and father.[19] Next the newly married woman prepared an elaborate meal for her husband in order to showcase her domestic skills. Finally came the payment of *anyame-dwan* (literally "god sheep"). This final step recognized that the spiritual protection which a daughter had received from her father from conception until puberty would now be forthcoming from her husband. Kyei identified one additional stage, which occurred in only some marriages. If, at some time following a marriage, a woman's family found itself in financial difficulty and in need of a loan, her relatives might turn to her husband as a potential creditor. They could ask him to loan them the sum they needed, with the understanding that his wife would then become his pledge or pawn. If the husband agreed to the family's request, he made them the loan, the sum of which was known as *tiri sika* (literally "head money"), and with that the woman became his pawn, as well as his wife.[20]

In describing processes of marrying, Kyei reveals a crucial point which Rattray missed: marriage occurred in stages, and moreover in stages that could be spread over a period of years. Thus, at the fully formalized end of the continuum, marrying (*awaree*) was signified by the payment of tiri aseda in the form of drinks or money by the husband and his family to the family of his wife. The husband was fully known to and recognized by the wife's family as her husband, and she, likewise, as his wife. But because tiri aseda was usually accompanied by a large number of gifts, which could make marrying quite costly for a man and his family, there were other ways of initiating the process, while postponing, as it were, the payment of tiri aseda. Less formal or less "known," therefore, might be a relationship based on ahudee or aboboom-bo-dee, which were often drinks. In these cases, a man was known to his wife's family. The process of marrying was recognized as being underway, with the expectation that tiri aseda would formalize the relationship in the future. Other conjugal relationships along the continuum fell within the range of what has been loosely and unfortunately translated as "concubinage."[21] In these relationships, the man and woman were lovers (mpena). The lovers might be known to both families, but the woman's family would not have been formally approached; typically, only the woman's mother was informed of the relationship, and this knowledge was transmitted by either her daughter or her daughter's lover. In some cases, however, lovers kept their relationship private and families remained ignorant of the connection. With the exception of these more furtive relationships, the crucial factor differentiating conjugal relationships was the degree of knowing: the level of formality with which the couple's families had been made aware of the union. What constituted marriage then was very much a family affair, open to the interpretations of the parties involved. Indeed, many to whom we spoke viewed door-knocking (aboboom-bo-dee) relationships as legitimate marriages precisely because the families had formal knowledge of them. Consequently, many people said of a man who had presented only the knocking fee, "He is called a husband. He has gone to the house," and, "It is taken into account that you are a husband. They have seen you."[22] Families thus retained the power to define the status of any known conjugal relationship, at any point in time, as they saw fit. If families considered a door-knocking relationship or a relationship between two lovers a marriage, marriage it was.[23]

Shifting Rights and Obligations in Conjugal Relationships

Although men and women of Asante's first colonized generation remembered marrying processes that probably differed little from those of earlier generations, in that they were fluid and dialogical, their stories of the rights and obligations in conjugal relationships reveal seismic shifts in the makings of marriage. While Rattray emphasized as the most significant rights and obligations of a formal marriage a wife's duty to provide her husband with exclusive sexual access and a husband's right to collect adultery compensation, those who shared their memories with us spoke far more broadly of a wife's responsibility to work for her husband and of a husband's responsibility to provide care. Their reminiscences also lend incomparable insight into the ways in which obligations to labor were gradually transformed with the arrival of cocoa and the increased monetization of the Asante economy. At the center of these processes of transformation was the very meaning of conjugal labor.

Although descent in Asante was (and still, for the most part, is) determined through the matriline, the production of marketable goods, such as gold, kola, and, later, rubber, has been organized around and through conjugal relationships. A reliance on conjugal labor has also characterized agricultural production in the area since long before the formation of the Asante state at the end of the seventeenth century.[24] It was a system of conjugal production distinguished by a high degree of reciprocity—a salient feature of marriage in Asante. For example, Asante men had the right to call on the labor of their wives and expected them to provide a broad range of domestic services, including fetching water, cooking, cleaning, and looking after children. In turn, women expected to receive from their husbands care or maintenance, in the form of meat, clothing, and food crops. Kyei defined a husband's primary duty as *obo no akonhama* ("he maintains her with food").[25] Additional reciprocal obligations linked husbands to the families of their wives, and wives to the families of their husbands, in a series of ongoing transactions and interactions. If either partner failed to meet any of the myriad reciprocal responsibilities fundamental to Asante marriage, divorce could be initiated quite easily by either spouse. That marriage was centered on ongoing reciprocal obligations and responsibilities meant that it was an institution continually renegotiated and reaffirmed between families, rather than a state of being that was entered or exited by two individuals at single points in time.[26]

As a central feature of the marrying process in the eighteenth and nineteenth centuries, partners provided mutual assistance in cultivating their farms. In most marriages between free commoners, men and women both had access to plots of their own family's land on which they grew the staple root crops, plantains, and vegetables which formed the basis of the Asante diet. Spouses helped each other farm. Joint labor was mutually beneficial, and producing crops together helped ensure a steady supply of food to the couple and any dependents. Although spouses jointly produced a reliable supply of foodstuffs, joint labor did not give rise, over time, to jointly held property. Instead, as is the case in most matrilineal societies, property was owned by one spouse or the other—a circumstance which accounts for the very high value Asante women have historically placed on economic independence. Consequently, if divorce came, as it frequently did, division of conjugal property was virtually a nonissue, since both spouses had benefited equally from conjugal labor, and since each retained access to the farms located on his or her *abusua* (matrilineal family) land. Moreover, any food farms the spouses had created together were of limited value. First, the crops were produced primarily for consumption rather than for sale, and so did not possess a significant monetary value.[27] Second, the farms were of value over a limited period of time only, since the nature of tropical forest agriculture, with shifting plot cultivation, meant any particular farm was productive for only one to three years before being fallowed.

In addition to jointly producing foodstuffs, husbands and wives produced for the market. European observers of the Asante economy in the eighteenth and nineteenth centuries regularly commented on rural commoners being engaged during the agricultural off-season in panning and mining for gold and in the collection and sale of first kola and later rubber. Once again the primary source of labor was the conjugal family, which was supplemented by any dependent pawns or slaves. Though the majority of Asante worked primarily in subsistence agriculture during the eighteenth and nineteenth centuries,[28] market-oriented roles were, as La Torre recognized in his masterful dissertation, "roles temporarily played by ordinary farmers" on a regular, indeed annual, basis.[29]

With the rapid spread of cocoa cultivation in the early twentieth century, however, conjugal labor aimed at production for the market was no longer a temporary state of affairs. Increasingly, it was the primary form of conjugal production, and the implications for the meaning and makings of marriage were profound. While the spread of cocoa farming in Asante is well documented,[30] only recently have scholars been concerned with gender and the exploitation of unpaid labor in the initial years of cocoa's expansion. As Austin has shown, the labor necessary for the rapid spread of cocoa came "very largely from established, non-capitalist sources."[31] Initially, these sources included the "farmowners themselves, their families, their slaves and pawns, cooperative groups of neighbors and, in the case of chiefs, corvée labor provided by their subjects."[32] However, with the abolition of slavery and the prohibition of pawning in Asante in 1908, wives' labor became, for most men, absolutely essential, particularly to the initial establishment of the farm. Wives' provision of labor in the initial creation of cocoa farms flowed logically from the pre-cocoa productive obligations between spouses described above. Wives commonly grew food crops on land cleared by their husbands—crops which both fed the family and provided a surplus which wives were entitled to sell. When cocoa farms were first established, the pattern differed little. In the first three to four years of their existence, the only returns from cocoa farms were the food crops, such as plantain or cocoyam, which were planted to shade the young trees during their first years. After that point, however, food crops, which were the wife's only material and guaranteed return on her labor investment in the farm, diminished. The main product of the farm now became the cocoa beans, which belonged, in whole, to the husband. Any labor invested by a wife after a cocoa farm became mature was directly compensated "only in the continued obligation of her husband," as Penelope Roberts writes, "to provide part of her subsistence from his own earnings."[33]

Yet Rattray's elderly informants, reflecting on rights and obligations in late-nineteenth-century marriages, painted a very different picture for the anthropologist. While a husband did gain a legal right to "profit by the fruits of . . . a wife's labor and later that of her children," Rattray concluded, "Such a right does not by any means entitle the husband to order about either wife or children like slaves, and in reality amounts only to the mutual assistance that persons living together and sharing a common menage would naturally accord to each other."[34] By 1922, however, as he reflected on the duties of wives, J. B. Danquah argued that wives had to "do all domestic and some of the farm work."[35] The picture had changed even more dramatically two decades later; in the 1940s, Kyei described a radically different state of affairs: "On the farm a wife must assist her husband by doing any work that she feels her strength would permit. In particular she is expected to plant food crops, to clear weeds growing in a new farm, and to lend a hand in cocoa harvesting operations."[36]

In the reminiscences that were shared with us, it is clear that during the childbearing years of this first colonized generation, husbands began to assert an increasingly unfettered right to draw on the labor of their wives. And the ramifications of this profound shift in obligations shook the domestic economy of conjugal production to its foundations. Men's assertion of increased rights to their wives' labor was facilitated by the particular circumstances of cocoa's expansion. Because all of the suitable lands in central Asante rapidly came under cultivation, men traveled to new areas in order to obtain land on which cocoa could be grown. With travel, both the balance and the significance of conjugal labor changed dramatically. Spouses no longer resided in a village where both held rights to family land, land on which they produced foodstuffs to which each alone held indisputable claim. Instead, the couple often traveled to vacant land far afield, and once there, in the vast majority of instances, only the husband obtained rights to land. In theory, both husband and wife could gain access to separate plots of individually owned land, a right effected by paying an annual fee to the local ruler. In practice, however, this was not done, and overwhelmingly the husband was the only one who acquired use rights to land. This resulted in farms that belonged to him and him alone, but on which both he and his wife labored.

In this setting, where spouses did not both retain use rights to land, husbands' rights to wives' labor took on entirely new meanings. Conjugal labor as mutual assistance on each other's farms did not exist on the cocoa frontier, and was instead replaced by a unidirectional flow of labor from wives to their husbands' farms. Travel thus eroded the reciprocal nature of conjugal agricultural labor and disrupted a woman's independent agricultural production. Since a wife usually did not gain farmland herself, and since she was often too far from family land in her home village to make use of it, she no longer had her own farms, and with them the indisputable right to their crops. Travel to a husband's distant cocoa farms also meant that a woman was unlikely to continue any income-generating activities of her own, for cocoa cultivation is highly labor-intensive in its early stages and allows little time for other activities such as soap making, pot making or petty trading. Furthermore, the sheer quantity of time women spent on agricultural labor rose dramatically with cocoa farming because the labor requirements of food farms remained constant alongside the new labor demands of cash cropping. In short, all of the work of cocoa farming was simply added to preexisting agricultural responsibilities, with the result that women worked markedly longer hours in farming than they had previously, and thus had less time to engage in income-producing pursuits of their own.

The profound shifts in conjugal production and the pervasive burdens born by women on the cocoa frontier are brought into stark relief by the life stories of women like Akosua Mansah. Born in the first decade of the century, Akosua married shortly after her nubility rites and traveled with her husband to Ahafo.

Initially she focused her attention on selling *kenkey* (fermented corn meal, often rolled into small balls), while her husband "went for a piece of land to farm on." After he acquired the farm, they settled near it, outside Boma, and Akosua devoted all of her labor to assisting her husband on his farm. Over the course of the years, she gave birth to thirteen children. Because they were located far out on the cocoa frontier, Akosua did not have access to a midwife nor to any other female birth attendant, so her husband helped her deliver the children. "No one was around," she remembered. "We were the first people at the place." When she and her husband went to work on the farm, they brought their young children with them. "We would put down plantain leaves and they would lie on them and I would work." Akosua's husband passed away in the 1980s. Although he gave her some of the farm they had jointly worked, she recalled with great bitterness that "his family members got it away from me because I did not pour drinks to . . . signify the gift."[37]

Clearly, the effects of this new pattern of conjugal farming were profound and enduring. Because many wives traveled with their husbands in order to farm cocoa, they were distanced from their families, from family land that might provide alternative economic security, and from female kin who could share childcare responsibilities. In marked contrast to conjugally worked farms, moreover, cocoa farms created through a couple's joint labor were not entities from which both necessarily derived benefits, since only the owner of a property had a right to its fruits. Thus, a woman had no incontrovertible right to any portion of her husband's cocoa farm or its profits, as Akosua Mansah and many others discovered. Most significantly, cocoa farms were valuable in ways that food farms simply were not: cocoa was a cash crop with monetary value, produced for the global market, in marked contrast to foodstuffs grown primarily for use. That cocoa farms were productive for many years more than were food farms created a long-term financial interest in these properties which simply had not been at stake with food farms. These multiple factors led to obvious problems in cases of divorce. Leaving a husband now meant a woman was walking away from properties of considerably greater and longer-term value than had been the case with food farms. Besides, a woman who accompanied her husband to his distant cocoa farms often no longer had access to food farms of her own to turn to in the case of divorce, increasing even more the costs of leaving her husband. In short, conjugal labor in the production of cocoa severely eroded the reciprocity which had previously been a defining element of Asante marriage. The long-standing right of Asante husbands to the labor of their wives did not create gross inequalities in a subsistence economy, so far as can be determined. But it created increasingly unequal and inequitable financial rewards for husbands and wives in the more fully monetized economy of the twentieth century. Cocoa and the expansion of the cash economy, then, with their reliance on conjugal labor aimed at production for the market, had profound repercussions for what had heretofore been the fluid, dialogical underpinnings of Asante conjugal relations.[38]

The Changing Content and Meaning of
Marriage Payments

Men's increased access to and control over the labor of their wives was articulated in the changing content and meaning of marriage rituals. Money, even in small amounts, became so central to the rituals between a man and a woman's family that the line between tiri aseda (the thanksgiving drinks presented at marriage) and tiri sika (a husband's loan to his wife's family, for which the wife stood as a pledge or pawn) grew increasingly blurred. The long-term result, we argue, was a gradual conflation of, or collapse of the historical distinctions between, the statuses of free and pawn wife. As we have seen, the giving and receiving of aseda was the one event which indisputably created a fully regularized marriage. Before the heightened monetization of the rural economy, aseda in marriage took the form of drinks: tiri aseda or tiri nsa. People with fewer assets presented palm wine, a relatively inexpensive drink tapped and sold locally, while people who could afford it might give more prestigious imported alcohol, generally schnapps or gin. Formalizing a marriage, then, required only the presentation of drinks, which were shared among both matrilineal families and fathers in order to render them all legal witnesses to the marriage.

In the first half of this century, the composition of tiri nsa underwent significant changes. As Asante became progressively more monetized, so did tiri nsa. Rattray made no mention in *Ashanti Law and Constitution* of the presentation of anything other than drinks in his legal discussion of the process of marrying.[39] However, in a passage in an earlier book which also addressed marrying, he noted a schedule of fees to be paid at the time of marriage, ranging from nine shillings for a slave, to 10/6 for a commoner, to £8 for royals. He also suggested that such payments had previously been unnecessary, drinks alone or even the simple consent of the families and parents being sufficient to effect a marriage.[40] In his research several decades later, Kyei found that while drinks alone might still be accepted in some localities, increasing numbers of families now required cash (*sika*), from £1 3/ to £2 7/, along with drinks.[41] According to Manuh, who gives a very useful overview of tiri aseda in the town of Kona for the entire first half of this century, the tiri nsa intrinsic to marrying involved a cash payment either in addition to, or in lieu of, drinks by the 1920s. The amount presented rose from ten shillings in the 1920s, to as much as £3 by the 1940s, to more than £8 in the 1950s.[42] Manuh connects the large jump in aseda in the 1950s to an increase in cocoa prices, which caused an "increased demand for wives" (and their labor) among men who wished to grow cocoa.[43] Arhin has also concluded that during the twentieth century money became an important part of the aseda presented in marrying.[44] Those who shared their recollections with us recalled that while drinks alone had sufficed to formalize marriage in their childhoods, by the time they themselves married money had become a common component of the marriage aseda, required by most, if not all, families. Although cash came to replace or accompany drinks in the formalization of marriage, it retained the name "tiri nsa." It was not generally referred to as tiri sika, or "head money," the term used for the loans made by men when they took a pawn-wife. Yet the monetization of tiri nsa would gradually work to obscure earlier distinctions between the two types of marriage payments.

That tiri sika continued as a marriage payment, even though pawnage was abolished in 1908, only served to render those distinctions all the more blurred. And as one marriage payment faded, in substance and meaning, into the other, the differences between the status, rights, and obligations of a free wife and those of a pawn-wife grew increasingly ambiguous. Marrying and pawning thus became overlapping systems of exchange, and the implications of this were substantial. As female pawnage was subsumed within the colonial category of "wife," it disappeared from the colonial gaze,[45] and as both Austin and Grier have argued, wives-as-pawns were absolutely crucial to the expansion of the cocoa economy both before and after 1908. Indeed, Austin writes of the "feminization of pawning" and Grier of a "coercive and exploitative precapitalist relationship [becoming] relegitimised and harnessed to . . . accumulation."[46] Yet the blurred distinctions between free and pawn-wife had profound implications not only for pawnage—allowing it to persist, gendered female, long after its legal abolition—but for marriage generally. As female pawnage was collapsed into the now singular category of "wife," women's rights and obligations in marriage, across the board, shifted dramatically.[47]

Let us look first at the relative incidence of free and pawn-wives over the course of the first five decades of this century. Clearly, wives-as-pawns were relatively common during the first two decades of the cocoa boom, 1900–20—the period during which men relied heavily upon unfree conjugal labor, among other forms of labor, to work their emerging cocoa farms. Both Fortes and Kyei, working from the same data collected during the Ashanti Social Survey of the 1940s, found that in the "haphazard sample" of 608 marriages, 227 "involved the payment of tiri sika."[48] Kyei concluded that pawn-wives constituted close to 50 percent of the women who, given their age, were likely to have been married during the initial establishment of the Asante cocoa industry. Among women born between 1890 and 1909, a group that would have begun marrying between 1905 and 1924, on average 45 percent were pawn-wives. Kyei's findings then indicate a gradual decline in the incidence of wives-as-pawns among women born between 1910 and 1919, who would have begun marrying from about 1925 to 1934; 28 percent of this cohort were pawn-wives. The decline continued for women born between 1920 and 1929, who would have begun marrying around 1935 to 1944: this group became pawn-wives only 14 percent of the time.[49]

Austin has posited that the decline in tiri sika, and thus of female pawnage, can be connected to women's increased economic autonomy after the 1920s, as women moved to become cocoa farmers in their own right or to enter the cash economy through trade or production of foodstuffs for the market. In this changing context, "*tiri sika* was less worth paying because the wife felt less obliged to her *abusua* to respect the marriage on the terms that her elders had accepted on her behalf."[50] This argument, while compelling in many ways, needs to be set against the evidence in the previous section—gleaned both from life stories and from the observations of scholars like Rattray, Danquah, and Kyei—that demonstrates a trend toward husbands' demanding and obtaining increased labor from their wives. The "mutual assistance" required in the free marriages described by Rattray for the 1910s had clearly given way by the 1930s to a set of obligations that eerily mirror Rattray's description of late-nineteenth-century and early-twentieth-century pawn marriage (awowa awadie):

> Half of any "treasure trove" found by the pawn was to belong to the husband; . . . the husband [was] to have authority to take the wife on trading expeditions without consulting any of her *abusua;* the wife henceforth [was] to have no alternative but to reside in her husband's home; the wife was now under a definite obligation "to rise up when called upon and accompany the husband to his farm; to cook for him and to perform the household duties." Hitherto she would ordinarily have carried out these tasks, but she was apparently under no legal obligation to do so; a man's mother often cooked for him.[51]

Rattray's description clearly captures the life experiences of many women in Asante's first colonized generation who, as free wives, found themselves more obligated to, and more under the control of, their husbands than their free mothers had ever been. It is because the clear distinction between pawn- and free wives had collapsed, beginning in the 1930s, that tiri sika began to disappear, and it is not simply coincidence that, as it disappeared, tiri aseda (or tiri nsa) carried a growing monetary component. The conflation of pawn-wife and free wife simply rendered the separate payment of tiri sika meaningless. Since free wives had to labor for their husbands as fully as did pawn-wives, men lacked any incentive to incur the additional expense which gaining a pawn-wife entailed. It is thus not surprising that in 1945 Kyei remarked, "*tiri-sika* is not paid in many marriages these days."[52] In some instances it may not have been worth paying because "a wife felt less obliged to her *abusua*." In others, however, it may not have been worth paying because a wife, with the simple payment of tiri nsa, was already fully obligated to her husband.

You Either Are or You're Not: Defining Who Is Married in the Colonial Courts

Asante's first colonized generation grew up in a world which viewed marrying as a fluid, dialogical process largely defined by the families involved. But the changes set in motion by cocoa and cash meant that marriage did not and could not remain a family affair. The presence of native courts, particularly after 1924, meant that defining marriage, as we have seen in Sean Hawkins's chapter in this volume, was also an affair of the colonial state, as mediated by the evolving structures of indirect rule. With the monetization of the economy and with the financial stakes in conjugal relationships dramatically higher, there was little room for ambiguity or for recognition of process. Either you were married or you were not. Thus, in case after case from the late 1920s on, Asante's native courts struggled to assert a singular definition of marriage by focusing on tiri aseda as its defining component. Only unions in which tiri aseda had been presented were considered true marriages, and all other conjugal relationships were consigned to the category of "mere" concubinage.[53] As the defining of marriage moved from the family to the native court, therefore, marrying was quickly transformed from fluid process to state of being.

Not atypical was the case of *Kofi Pipra vs. Ama Agyin*, which was heard on 18 July 1927 in the native tribunal of the Kumasihene. The case involved a dispute between the couple, who had separated some time previously. When they first decided to marry, and in recognition of this intention, Kofi Pipra presented gin to Ama Agyin's parents as a door-knocking drink. Everyone who testified agreed that he presented nothing else in recognition of the marriage, and that he never followed up the door-knocking drinks with tiri aseda. Nonetheless, all of the witnesses, as well as Kofi and Ama themselves, considered the couple fully married. Kofi Pipra's description of their relationship reads, "I saw defendant we agreed to marry. I went with two bottles of gin to see defendant's parents. . . . They agreed, drank the gin and defendant and I lived together as wife and husband awaiting to pay dowry or headrum." Ama Agyin described the nature of their relationship in greater detail: "Plaintiff is my husband still and he can claim satisfaction [that is, an adultery fee] should anyone have carnal connection with me."[54] The testimony in the case indicates that although this couple never formalized their marriage with the presentation of tiri aseda, they and their families considered the relationship a marriage. The native court, however, understood the relationship as a concubinage, not as the marriage described by the litigants and their families, and thus refused to hear the dispute as a marriage case.

The recollections of rural Asante, as well as the testimony of many of the individuals who came before the courts as litigants or witnesses in court cases, demonstrate that the strict definition of marriage adhered to by the courts continued to diverge significantly from the views of the majority of Asante, who lived their lives and settled most of their conflicts outside of the court system. There, many couples (and their families) never bothered to formalize a marriage with the presentation of tiri aseda, yet all involved still considered it a true marriage. Their fluidity of interpretation stands in stark contrast to the courts' far more rigid view of monies and drinks as serving a fixed and unchangeable purpose. The point is not that ordinary Asante believed conjugal relationships defined as marriages and conjugal relationships defined as "mere concubinages" were one and the same. As we have seen, they acknowledged openly that a conjugal relationship accepted as a valid marriage did differ from a conjugal relationship understood as a concubinage. However, they parted company with the courts in their continued willingness, for a variety of reasons and under a variety of circumstances, to extend conjugal status to many relationships which the courts recognized only as concubinages.

The marked divergence between the court's theory of marriage and the practice or process of marrying, as defined particularly by those who could not afford the growing costs of tiri aseda, finally led the Ashanti Confederacy Council to intervene in 1942. After lengthy discussion, the council ruled that spouses married according to "native law and custom" should register their marriages, so as to streamline the courts' ability to differentiate actual marriages (as they understood them) from more informal conjugal relationships:

> It was suggested . . . that marriages should be registered, "to enable the Native Courts to decide without any waste of time as to whether the union between the man and the woman is strictly in accord with native law and custom, when another man is accused of adultery with the woman," and the husband claims the adultery fee. The Council resolved that "registration of native marriages be adopted," and a fee of 5/-be charged in each case (reduced to 2/6 the next year.)[55]

While native court and council definitions of marriage did not immediately or uniformly affect those outside of the court system, they constituted a state-generated definition, a counter-discourse on marriage, that would increasingly shape definitions and processes of marriage in the years to come. A husband who had not paid tiri aseda in years past, though in a less secure position than a husband who had, could still count on his wife's family to recognize his status, if he met his obligations to his wife and their children. His wife, moreover, could expect and demand full husbandly care. But as family affairs became affairs of state, transactional marrying processes were legally characterized as concubinages and no conjugal rights, claims, or obligations were recognized; more importantly, they could not be enforced. Because virtually every conjugal contest that made its way to the native courts in the colonial period—divorce, inheritance, child or spousal maintenance, adultery—hinged directly or indirectly on verifying the legality or illegality of the conjugal relationship, the transformation of marrying processes into a single act of marriage broadly reshaped the terrain of social reproduction in Asante.

"What Would Be the Sense of Marrying?" Women's Reactions to a Shifting Conjugal Terrain

In the first decades of this century, women of Asante's first colonized generation were drawn into the cash economy on terms that were largely not of their own making. For wives, investing labor in a husband's cocoa farm or any other cash-generating enterprise had very different implications than did investing labor in a food farm. It might mean benefits in the short term, but almost always serious liabilities in the long run. It certainly did not provide for future economic autonomy or security. For this reason, as Okali observed, "wives working on new and young farms were always aware that they were not working on joint economic enterprises. They expected eventually to establish their own separate economic concerns."[56] And the evidence suggests that this is precisely what many did after the initial establishment of cocoa in an area. As Austin has recently argued, it was exceedingly rare for women to own cocoa farms in Asante during the first two decades of this century. After that, it became far more common, in direct correlation to the length of time cocoa had been cultivated in the area.[57] Thus, by the third decade of this century, women in Asante began to establish their own cocoa farms—an option which provided far greater long-term economic security than did laboring on a husband's mature farm. And establishing a cocoa farm was only one among a number of options that opened to women in areas where the cocoa economy was fully in place. "The growth of male cocoa income," according to Austin's recent account, "created economic opportunities for women in local markets, both as producers (for example, of food crops and cooked food) and as traders."[58]

During the 1920s, then, with cocoa well established in many parts of Asante, women's roles in the cash economy were both changing and diversifying. Many wives, who had been the most common form of exploitable labor during the initial introduction of cocoa, began to themselves exploit the new opportunities for economic autonomy and security presented by the established, though still rapidly expanding, cocoa economy. Adwoa Addae, of Effiduasi, recalled this time as an era in which women asserted a great deal of autonomy and independence, much of it linked to the establishment of cocoa farms or to trade in foodstuffs. "In those days," she recalled, "women were hard-working, so we could live without men . . . we were independent. We could work without the assistance of men."[59]

Women's efforts to seize economic opportunities in the years after cocoa's initial expansion are evident not just in the statistics documenting the increasing number of women owners of cocoa farms or in descriptions of the growing market in foodstuffs, particularly in towns like Kumasi and Obuasi, but in the crisis in conjugal production, in marriage itself, which is so well documented in customary court cases and in life histories. In this critical transition period, many women appeared quite prepared to divorce husbands who refused to set up a farm for them. Others routinely divorced men who did not provide them with at least the basics of a housekeeping allowance, clothing, and support of the children. Drawing on his research in the 1910s and 1920s, Rattray argued that "[r]efusal to house, clothe, or feed her properly" was common grounds for divorce.[60] And divorce many did. As Afua Fosuwa explained, a husband's care "is why we marry."[61] And if proper care was not forthcoming, then divorce was the solution. "I will not use my money when he can provide," said Yaa Akom, of Mamponten. "What would be the sense of marrying?"[62]

And as some women increasingly turned to divorce, others turned to customary courts to challenge matrilineal inheritance, demanding portions of a divorced or deceased husband's cocoa farm in recognition of labor invested.[63] Still others sought to avoid marriage altogether or, at the very least, to insist, as their mothers and grandmothers had, on its fluidity and on the mutuality of conjugal obligations.[64] These conjugal struggles, which seemed to engulf Asante between the two world wars, were about control over women's productive and reproductive labor and about the very definition of conjugal obligations at the moment women were negotiating their own spaces within the colonial economy. The changes unleashed by the movement of women into the cash economy, not as wives but as producers in their own right, would combine with a host of other factors—urbanization, Western education, Christianity, and British colonial courts[65]—to produce nothing short of widespread gender chaos throughout the interwar years. It was chaos engendered by cash and cocoa, by trade and transformation.

Women and men of Asante's first colonized generation witnessed profound transformations in the meanings and makings of commoner marriage as they moved from childhood to adulthood. As children, they came to understand the marriages of their parents and grandparents as largely family affairs—fluid, processual, and dialogic. They carried that understanding into their own adult lives, but it was an understanding that quickly proved to be at odds with the harsh realities of an increasingly monetized world. With the expansion of the cash economy, seismic shifts remapped the conjugal terrain. By the time this generation married, a free wife was obliged to provide far more labor to her husband than her mother or grandmother had. She quickly discovered, moreover, that the value of her conjugal labor in a monetized economy was mediated through and realized solely by her husband. As the changing content and meaning of marrying rituals like tiri aseda and tiri sika evidenced, a free wife, despite her free status and despite the abolition of pawnage, was subordinated to her husband much as a pawn-wife had been. But women were not simply victims of this shift. Beginning in the 1920s, many sought economic security and autonomy by entering the cash economy on their own terms and in their own right, as cocoa farmers, produce farmers, or traders. Over the next decades, their actions would present a profound challenge to the underpinnings of conjugality in colonial Asante—a challenge that their daughters and granddaughters would continue to mount in women's ongoing struggles to maintain control of their productive and reproductive power.

Primary Document

Abena Kwa, excerpts from interviews by Victoria Tashjian, Oyoko, 2 and 12 November 1990. Abena Kwa was born in Oyoko, a village approximately fifteen kilometers south of Kumasi, around 1907.

My first husband was Atta Kwasi. He was from Oyoko. We were farming here in Oyoko. We were cultivating cocoyam and plantain. But when we went to the forest, we cultivated cocoa. He said that he was going to cultivate cocoa and I should accompany him, so I did. He needed money, and cocoa was very lucrative. I helped him a lot. When he sowed the cocoa seeds, I also sowed cocoyam and plantain alongside, and when we came back from the farm, I cooked for him. I was not trading or anything; that was all I was doing. The work was so strenuous that we couldn't do any work in addition. Before we went to Ahafo, I was making pots. Oyoko was a center for cooking pots and drinking pots.

We divorced. After we had done the cocoa farming, he wasn't taking care of the children so I divorced him. Also, he only gave me a small portion of the cocoa farms. He should have given me more, but he only gave me a small piece. So it was the accumulation of these things, that is, his not taking care of the children, and his not giving me a proper share of the farms, that finally paved the way for my divorce. Before we divorced he gave me a small portion. It was because of that that I divorced him, because he would not give me a bigger one, and the annoying thing of it all was that it was for me and the children. He should have given me a bigger share because what we did was bigger, and I had done the farming with the children, so proportionately it should have been bigger. He should not necessarily have given me one half, but he should have given me something reasonable. I had made nineteen acres of farm with him, and if he had even given me, say, two acres, I would have been pleased. He gave me roughly an acre. I would not have divorced him if he had given me two acres. It was not the practice here that you are given half of what you did with your husband, but some people did proportionately well. Some, when they farmed with their wives, say farmed three acres, would give their wife one, and if they farmed five acres with their wife, could give her three. If the man was good, he will even give you some of the farm in the initial stages. It depends on the man. Some men were very good. They wouldn't be prompted before they give you some.

My second husband was Kwaku Akyeampong. About a year after the marriage I accompanied him to Ahafo to start another cocoa farm. At first I declined to accompany him, but he went and pleaded to somebody that he will give me some of the farms. He went to my mother's senior sister, and I didn't want to show disrespect, and the man had promised seriously to give me some. At first I didn't want to go because of what I had experienced with my first husband. Once I have been cheated by an earlier marriage and divorced, if I happen to marry again and the husband wants to make farms with me, I will enquire, and if I sense cheating that will come from the man, I wouldn't go; I would rather divorce.

NOTES

1. Robert S. Rattray, *Ashanti Law and Constitution* (London: Oxford University Press, 1929), p. 22.
2. Quoted in Dennis Austin, *Politics in Ghana* (London: Oxford University Press, 1964), p. 275. According to Austin, "the song was written in *Twi* by Fred Sarpong, a journalist and trader and NLM [National Liberation Movement] member."

3. Afua Dufie, interview by Victoria Tashjian, Oyoko, 31 October 1990.
4. Akua Ababo, interview by Victoria Tashjian, Mamponten, 10 September 1990.
5. See Gareth Austin, "The Emergence of Capitalist Relations in South Asante Cocoa-Farming, c. 1916–33," *Journal of African History* 28, no. 2 (1987): 259–79; Beverly Grier, "Pawns, Porters, and Petty Traders: Women in the Transition to Cash Crop Agriculture in Colonial Ghana," *Signs: Journal of Women in Culture and Society* 17, no. 2 (1992): 304–28; Gwendolyn Mikell, *Cocoa and Chaos in Ghana* (New York: Paragon House, 1989) and "The State, the Courts, and 'Value': Caught between Matrilineages in Ghana," in *Money Matters: Instability, Values, and Social Payments in the Modern History of West African Communities*, ed. Jane I. Guyer (Portsmouth, N.H.: Heinemann, 1995), pp. 225–44; K. A. Busia, *The Position of the Chief in the Modern Political System of Ashanti* (London: Frank Cass, 1968); David Kimble, *A Political History of Ghana: The Rise of Gold Coast Nationalism, 1850–1928* (Oxford: Clarendon, 1963); William Tordoff, *Ashanti under the Prempehs* (London: Oxford University Press, 1965).
6. A full listing is not possible here, but see, for example, Claire Robertson and Iris Berger, eds., *Women and Class in Africa* (New York: Africana Publishing, 1986); Belinda Bozzoli with Mmantho Nkotsoe, *Women of Phokeng: Consciousness, Life Strategy, and Migrancy in South Africa, 1900–1983* (Portsmouth, N.H.: Heinemann, 1991); George Chauncey, Jr., "The Locus of Reproduction: Women's Labour in the Zambian Copperbelt, 1927–1953," *Journal of Southern African Studies* 7, no. 2 (1981): 135–64; Barbara Cooper, *Marriage in Maradi: Gender and Culture in a Hausa Society in Niger, 1900–1989* (Portsmouth, N.H.: Heinemann, 1997); Grier, "Pawns"; Margaret Jean Hay, "Luo Women and Economic Change during the Colonial Period," in *Women in Africa: Studies in Social and Economic Change*, ed. Nancy J. Hafkin and Edna G. Bay (Stanford, Calif.: Stanford University Press, 1976), pp. 87–109; Allen Isaacman, *Cotton Is the Mother of Poverty: Peasants, Work, and Rural Struggle in Colonial Mozambique, 1938–1961* (Portsmouth, N.H.: Heinemann, 1996); Margot Lovett, "Gender Relations, Class Formation, and the Colonial State," in *Women and the State in Africa*, ed. Jane L. Parpart and Kathleen A. Staudt (Boulder, Colo.: Lynne Rienner, 1989), pp. 23–46; Elias Mandala, "Capitalism, Kinship, and Gender in the Lower Tchiri Valley of Malawi, 1860–1960," *African Economic History* 13 (1984): 137–70; Elizabeth Schmidt, *Peasants, Traders, and Wives: Shona Women in the History of Zimbabwe, 1870–1939* (Portsmouth, N.H.: Heinemann, 1992); Cherryl Walker, "Gender and the Development of the Migrant Labour System, c. 1850–1930: An Overview," in *Women and Gender in Southern Africa to 1945*, ed. Cherryl Walker (Cape Town: David Philip, 1990), pp. 168–96; Luise White, *The Comforts of Home: Prostitution in Colonial Nairobi* (Chicago: University of Chicago Press, 1990); Marcia Wright, "Technology, Marriage, and Women's Work in the History of Maize-Growers in Mazabuka, Zambia: A Reconnaissance," *Journal of Southern African Studies* 10, no. 1 (1983): 71–85.
7. Schmidt, *Peasants, Traders, and Wives*, p. 5.
8. This chapter is based on research we conducted separately on different aspects of gender and colonialism in Asante between 1989 and 1995. In 1997, it became increasingly clear to both of us that we each had pieces of a very large and complex puzzle, and that by putting our respective pieces

together we could develop a more comprehensive understanding of Asante women's lives during the colonial period than either of us could ever hope to achieve alone. The end product of those efforts is *"I Will Not Eat Stone": A Women's History of Colonial Asante* (Portsmouth, N.H.: Heinemann, 2000). This chapter presents an abridged discussion of the conjugal themes explored in that longer, co-authored work, especially in chapter 2. It also draws from several sections of Victoria Tashjian, "'It's Mine' and 'It's Ours' Are Not the Same Thing: Changing Economic Relations between Spouses in Asante," in *The Cloth of Many Colored Silks: Papers on History and Society, Ghanaian and Islamic, in Honor of Ivor Wilks*, ed. John Hunwick and Nancy Lawler (Evanston, Ill.: Northwestern University Press, 1996), pp. 205–22.

9. Cooper, *Marriage in Maradi*, p. xvii.

10. Robert S. Rattray, *Ashanti* (London: Oxford University Press, 1923), p. 6.

11. Rattray, *Ashanti Law*, pp. 22–32. "Awadie" is Rattray's spelling of what is more commonly rendered "awaree." Because his perspective was androcentric, missing from the list were marriages between free or royal women and men of a lower standing or of a different ethnicity. For example, queen mothers could marry servants, craftsmen, or slaves. See Dorothy D. Vellenga, "Who Is a Wife? Legal Expressions of Heterosexual Conflicts in Ghana," in *Female and Male in West Africa*, ed. Christine Oppong (London: Allen and Unwin, 1983), p. 145.

12. Rattray, *Ashanti Law*, pp. 24–25. Aseda, or "thanksgiving," played an important role in formalizing any transaction in Asante. Historically, aseda was presented in the form of an alcoholic beverage (*nsa*). Giving aseda on the one hand, and receiving it on the other, meant that both parties agreed to a transaction, and that the transaction had become legally binding on each. Everyone who witnessed the giving of aseda received a share of the drinks, and upon accepting them became legal witnesses to the transaction, obligated to testify to its occurrence should any dispute arise.

13. Ibid., pp. 22–32.

14. Marriage could also occur between a pawned woman and a man other than the individual who held her in pawn. Pawning was a common arrangement in precolonial Asante whereby, in lieu of cash interest on a loan, a creditor received the use of a pawned person's labor for the duration of the loan. For a thorough investigation of the history of pawning in Asante, see Gareth Austin, "Human Pawning in Asante, 1800–1950: Markets and Coercion, Gender and Cocoa," in *Pawnship in Africa: Debt Bondage in Historical Perspective*, ed. Toyin Falola and Paul E. Lovejoy (Boulder, Colo.: Westview, 1994), pp. 121–59.

15. Rattray, *Ashanti Law*, p. 49.

16. Ibid., pp. 49–51.

17. T. E. Kyei, *Marriage and Divorce among the Asante: A Study Undertaken in the Course of the Ashanti Social Survey (1945)*, Cambridge African Monographs 14 (Cambridge: African Studies Centre, 1992).

18. Kyei, *Marriage*, p. 27.

19. Very frequently men worked on their in-laws' farms, in addition to providing tiri nsa. See Kwame Arhin, "Monetization and the Asante State," in *Money Matters*, ed. Guyer, p. 101, and "The Pressure of Cash and Its Political Conse-

quences in Asante in the Colonial Period," *Journal of African Studies* 3, no. 4 (1976): 460.

20. Kyei, *Marriage,* pp. 26–39. For another description of the stages of marrying, which adds much interesting detail to the outline sketched above, see Takyiwaa Manuh, "Changes in Marriage and Funeral Exchanges in Asante: A Case Study from Kona, Afigya-Kwabre," in *Money Matters,* ed. Guyer, pp. 190–92.

21. The translation of "mpena" as "concubine" is unfortunate because in English usage "concubine" is clearly gendered female and describes a woman who cohabits with a man outside of marriage. In Asante, "mpena" is used to describe both men and women. Moreover, it carries no pejorative connotation, as it tends to in the Western context.

22. Adwowa Fodwo, interview by Victoria Tashjian, Mamponten, 9 October 1990; and Peter Danso, interview by Victoria Tashjian, Oyoko, 25 October 1990.

23. The concept of "widow" could also be contingent upon degrees of knowing or familial recognition. Vellenga argues that "widow" can refer to any woman recognized as a wife by the deceased man's family, even if no formal marriage had occurred. Dorothy D. Vellenga, "The Widow among the Matrilineal Akan," in *Widows in African Societies: Choices and Constraints,* ed. Betty Potash (Stanford, Calif.: Stanford University Press, 1986), pp. 224–25.

24. Ivor Wilks locates this transition in the sixteenth century. For a fuller discussion, see "Land, Labor, Gold, and the Forest Kingdom of Asante: A Model of Early Change," in his *Forests of Gold: Essays on the Akan and the Kingdom of Asante* (Athens: Ohio University Press, 1993), pp. 41–90. See also T. C. McCaskie, "Marriage and Adultery in Pre-colonial Asante," *Journal of African History* 22, no. 4 (1981): 483–85, and *State and Society in Pre-colonial Asante* (Cambridge: Cambridge University Press, 1995), pp. 25–26.

25. Kyei, *Marriage,* p. 40.

26. See Manuh, "Changes in Marriage," p. 188, and Vellenga, "Who Is a Wife?" p. 145.

27. Joseph R. LaTorre, "Wealth Surpasses Everything: An Economic History of Asante, 1750-1874" (Ph.D. diss., University of California, Berkeley, 1978), pp. 31, 357; see also Ivor Wilks, *Asante in the Nineteenth Century: The Structure and Evolution of a Political Order* (Cambridge: Cambridge University Press, 1975), p. 668; Ray A. Kea, *Settlements, Trade, and Polities in the Seventeenth-Century Gold Coast* (Baltimore: Johns Hopkins University Press, 1982), pp. 196–97; Kwame Arhin, "Trade, Accumulation, and the State in Asante in the Nineteenth Century," *Africa* 60, no. 4 (1990): 525–26.

28. Exceptions included people engaged in craft production and in hunting and fishing, as well as large-scale and long-distance traders. See LaTorre, "Wealth Surpasses Everything," pp. 20–56, and Gareth Austin, " 'No Elders Were Present': Commoners and Private Ownership in Asante, 1807-96," *Journal of African History* 37, no. 1 (1996): 8–10.

29. LaTorre, "Wealth Surpasses Everything," p. 68. LaTorre identifies hunting and snail collecting as other seasonal activities (p. 24). Because commoner participation in the market economy was "discontinuous," Austin prefers to characterize nineteenth-century commoners as "supplier[s]" rather than "trader[s]" or "producer[s]." Austin, " 'No Elders,' " p. 20.

30. Among the most easily accessible sources are Austin, "Capitalist Relations"; John Dunn and A. F. Robertson, *Dependence and Opportunity: Political Change in Ahafo* (Cambridge: Cambridge University Press, 1973); Grier, "Pawns"; Polly Hill, *Migrant Cocoa-Farmers of Southern Ghana* (Cambridge: Cambridge University Press, 1963); Mikell, *Cocoa and Chaos;* Christine Okali, "Kinship and Cocoa Farming in Ghana," in *Female and Male,* ed. Oppong, pp. 169–78; Dorothy D. Vellenga, "Matriliny, Patriliny, and Class Formation in Two Rural Areas of Ghana," in *Women and Class,* ed. Robertson and Berger, pp. 62–77.

31. Austin, "Capitalist Relations," pp. 260–62.

32. Austin, "Human Pawning," p. 140.

33. Penelope Roberts, "The State and the Regulation of Marriage: Sefwi Wiawso (Ghana), 1900–1940," in *Women, State, and Ideology: Studies from Africa and Asia,* ed. Haleh Afshar (Binghamton: State University of New York Press, 1987), p. 54.

34. Rattray, *Ashanti Law,* p. 25.

35. Joseph Boakye Danquah, *Gold Coast: Akan Laws and Customs and the Akim Abuakwa Constitution* (London: Routledge, 1922), p. 153. Also cited in Kyei, *Marriage,* p. 41.

36. Kyei, *Marriage,* p. 41.

37. Akosua Mansah, interview by Jean Allman, Kumasi, 3 June 1992.

38. Claire C. Robertson came to similar conclusions with regard to marriage and Ga women traders in Accra, to the southeast of Asante, in *Sharing the Same Bowl? A Socioeconomic History of Women and Class in Accra, Ghana* (Bloomington: Indiana University Press, 1984), pp. 177–88.

39. Rattray, *Ashanti Law,* p. 24.

40. Robert S. Rattray, *Religion and Art in Ashanti* (London: Oxford University Press, 1927), pp. 81, 82, 84.

41. Kyei, *Marriage,* pp. 29–30. In Tashjian's research the specific cash amounts people mentioned accorded closely with those recorded by Kyei; £2 10/ was the amount most frequently named.

42. Manuh, "Changes in Marriage," pp. 189, 193.

43. Ibid., p. 194. Manuh also gives the amounts of money which changed hands in marriages contracted in Kona, a rural town outside Kumasi, between 1900 and 1955.

44. See Arhin, "Pressure of Cash," p. 460, and "Monetization," pp. 98, 101. Along with *tiri nsa,* other transactions that had formerly not involved cash became monetized at this time. For example, the *aseda* that formalized *abusa* sharecropping contracts was increasingly rendered as drinks or money. See Vellenga, "Matriliny," p. 68. The *nto* or tribute paid by strangers in return for use-rights to land, which had been paid in meat or foodstuffs, has more recently become a cash payment. Arhin, "Pressure of Cash," p. 455.

45. Austin, "Human Pawning," p. 139.

46. Ibid., 137; Grier, "Pawns," p. 182.

47. Barbara Cooper's work on Maradi suggests a parallel process in Niger. "The abolition of slavery," she writes, "set in train a series of redefinitions of marriage as slave-owning families attempted to recast master/slave relations onto the intra-household hierarchies of women." See Cooper, *Marriage in Maradi,* pp. xliv–xlv, 1–16.

48. Cited in Austin, "Human Pawning," p. 157 n. 150. See also "Ashanti Marriage Statistics," Meyer Fortes Papers (Cambridge: African Studies Centre, n.d.).
49. Kyei, *Marriage,* p. 99.
50. Austin, "Human Pawning," p. 143.
51. Rattray, *Ashanti Law,* p. 49.
52. Kyei, *Marriage,* p. 99.
53. Cf. John Comaroff and Jean Comaroff, "The Management of Marriage in a Tswana Chiefdom," in *Essays on African Marriage in Southern Africa,* ed. Eileen Jensen Krige and John L. Comaroff (Cape Town: Juta, 1981), pp. 44–45. In contrast to Asante courts, whose singular definition of marriage diverged markedly from popular commoner definitions of marrying as process, Tshidi courts continued to recognize the "pervasive reality—that all Tshidi may engage in the strategic management of affinity."
54. Manhyia Record Office, Kumasi: Native Tribunal of Kumasihene, Civil Record Book 2, *Kofi Pipra v. Ama Agyin,* dd. Kumasi, 18 July 1927, pp. 593–94, 598–601.
55. J. N. Matson, *A Digest of the Minutes of the Ashanti Confederacy Council from 1935 to 1949 Inclusive and a Revised Edition of Warrington's "Notes on Ashanti Custom Prepared for the Use of District Commissioners"* (Cape Coast: Prospect Printing, n.d. [about 1951]), p. 23.
56. Okali, "Kinship and Cocoa Farming," p. 170.
57. Austin, "Human Pawning," p. 141. Okali has also argued that women began to withdraw their labor from the cocoa farm once it matured. See her "Kinship and Cocoa Farming," p. 172; also Arhin, "Monetization," p. 103.
58. Austin, "Human Pawning," pp. 142–43.
59. Adwoa Addae, interview by Jean Allman, Effiduasi, 30 June 1993.
60. Rattray, *Religion and Art,* pp. 97–98.
61. Afua Fosuwa, interview by Victoria Tashjian, Oyoko, 28 November 1990.
62. Yaa Akom, interview by Victoria Tashjian, Mamponten, 11 October 1990.
63. Countless numbers of such cases can be found in the record books stored at Manhyia Record Office in Kumasi. See, particularly, the records of the Kumasihene's Native Tribunal, 1926–35; the Asantehene's Divisional Native Court B, 1935–60; and the Kumasi Divisional ("Clan") Courts, 1928–45 (consisting of Kyidom, Kronti, Gyasi, Ankobia, Oyoko, Benkum, Akwamu, and Adonten).
64. See Allman and Tashjian, *"I Will Not Eat Stone,"* chapter 4. Roberts noted a similar pattern in Sefwi Wiawso. See her "State and Marriage," pp. 54–55.
65. For an important discussion of the ways in which women to the south of Asante used the British justice system during this period, see Roger Gocking, "British Justice and the Native Tribunals of the Southern Gold Coast Colony," *Journal of African History* 34, no. 1 (1993): 93–113, esp. pp. 108–10.

11 "Vultures of the Marketplace": Southeastern Nigerian Women and Discourses of the *Ogu Umunwaanyi* (Women's War) of 1929

Misty L. Bastian

> The Chairman: Is that it?
> Witness [Ogatu of Ahiara]: Yes, sir.
> The Chairman: Does any Counsel wish to ask questions?
> Counsel: No.
> The Chairman: Thank you.
> Witness: I have not started yet. (Laughter.)[1]

During the last two months of 1929, groups of singing, dancing, and militant women began, in their own parlance, to "move" about the eastern countryside of what was then—at least to British colonial officials—the Southern Nigerian Protectorate. These women sometimes gathered around the compounds of so-called warrant chiefs and demanded the red felt caps given to the "chiefs" by the British administration as markers of their attachment to colonial authority.[2] In those instances where the warrant chiefs rendered up their caps without a fight, the women (who numbered, in later reckonings, between five hundred and five thousand strong) generally extracted a fine, heaped verbal abuse upon the heads of compound inhabitants, and left, satisfied, to add the cap to their growing collection, a collection that would soon be offered to perplexed district officers and assistant district officers in Bende, Okigwe, Ikot Ekpene, and other regional headquarters.

When warrant chiefs attempted to retain their caps and their dignity, more severe consequences could follow. The women's actions might escalate, culminating in property damage and even, on rare occasions, bloodshed. However, most of the blood shed in southeastern Nigeria during November and December 1929 was that of indigenous women, not men.[3] On those occasions when fights broke out between the women's movement and its objects, women were at a disadvantage, since they usually carried nothing but palm fronds and used their bare hands and bodies in their demonstrations, while their antagonists were armed with everything from sticks and whips to rifles and the mechanized Lewis guns.

Ohandum, or Women of All Towns (as Igbo women called themselves during the movement),[4] also engaged in actions directed against nonhuman opponents, notably the hated government roads, cars and trucks, railroad stations, fences surrounding public areas, mercantile buildings like the "factories" (warehouses) that housed the palm oil and foreign commodities trade, and the most obvious sites of colonial work, including native court buildings, colonial administrative headquarters, and jails. Ohandum blockaded the roads and, in some locations, tried to collect tolls from passing motorists. They tore at the very fabric of buildings with their fingers and the weight of their bodies (in some cases breaking down not only doors but whole walls). They were also accused of looting goods from destroyed shops and warehouses, although this is a matter of some debate even in the colonial record.[5]

The women sang "abusive songs" to colonial officials and their interpreters and clerks, even going so far as to "slap their tummies" in a derisive fashion at the officials and their uncomfortable African collaborators.[6] Whether these were the same abusive songs that were directed toward warrant chiefs, court messengers, and the like, it is difficult to say—although, knowing contemporary Igbo women's oratorical and harmonic prowess, I suspect that the songs were appropriate to the circumstances in which they were sung, and hence were at least modified to take into account the fact that colonialists were their objects. The subtle qualities of Igbo, Ibibio, Efik, Ijo, Ogoni, Andoni, Qua, and other women's rhetoric, not all of it verbal, appear to been drained away by the "factual" or "evidentiary" nature of the colonial reports we read to reach back to this moment. Only T. O. Echewa's novel *I Saw the Sky Catch Fire* is necessarily exempt from the charge, but that remains a work of extraordinarily well researched and powerful fiction.[7]

One of the reasons for revisiting this justly famous case, a case that has been extensively written about in the African and Africanist historical literature during the last three decades,[8] is to try to think about the loss of those rhetorical flourishes and gestures. Michel-Rolph Trouillot tells us, "Silences are inherent in history because any single event enters history with some of its constituting parts missing."[9] For the *Ogu Umunwaanyi,* so well known because of the Aba Commission of Inquiry's extensive, publicly distributed *Notes of Evidence,* I would argue that one of the missing parts has been a close reading of southern Nigerian women's speeches and nonverbal displays.[10] This short chapter is meant to reopen our debate about the Women's War, concentrating on what most of us can actually study of those events: what southern Nigerian women said and how they acted during the Aba Commission hearings, and what both African and European men did and said about women in the same hearings. This close reading is meant to help us understand how all of the documented historical actors together, if asymmetrically, reconstructed the Women's War into a coherent narrative about taxation and colonial administration that nonetheless maintained a subtext about women's power, as well as their socioeconomic and religious responsibilities in the southeast, potentially subverting what was required by colonial evidentiary (and more material) disciplines.

Retrospective Significances: Recreations of the Women's War

Retrospective significance can be created by the actors themselves, as a past within their past, or as a future within their present.[11]

What is the smell? Death is the smell.[12]

Women who were called upon to testify at the Aba Commission of Inquiry's hearings were generally those who were supposed to know something about the "disturbances" of late 1929 and to be willing to relate their information to a group of men appointed to listen to them impartially and freely.[13] These men, whose motivations may not have always been as impartial as their mandate suggested, were a mixed group of British government functionaries and Nigeria-based European merchants, as well as African and European lawyers. Each of these commissioners brought his own experience to the hearings and asked his questions based upon that experience. Hence, former European military officers tended to focus on military actions and colonial administrators wanted to know about local politics, while the mainly Sierra Leonean or Lagosian barristers claimed a privileged knowledge of "African" culture, frequently asking the women before them to justify their actions on the grounds of indigenous gender roles. The African men who testified before the commission, as we can see from their own reports, came from all walks of southeastern Nigerian life. They were agriculturists, warrant chiefs, traders, clergy and catechists, clerks and other colonial functionaries. Most of these African and European men, judging from the remarks preserved in the commission testimony, shared a rather uncritical understanding of women's position in southeastern Nigerian social life, often appearing surprised when the women's testimony or activities during the hearings contradicted that understanding.

From their own accounts of themselves, the women who testified appear to have been those who freely admitted to taking part in the Ogu Umunwaanyi, who claimed they knew women who took part, or who came to the hearings in an attempt to settle old scores with warrant chiefs and other colonial officials. Some women, like Nwanyeruwa of Oloko (who was credited with beginning the Women's War, on or around 23 November 1929), were required to give testimony, but the majority seem to have come voluntarily to the various towns where the commission met, to speak directly, as they thought, to those in authority. Most of the women who testified were not asked about their employment, since the commissioners were predisposed to think of them all as "housewives," but many seem to have been involved with trade, some did domestic labor in and around mission or other European compounds, and there was some discussion of prostitution, although no woman declared herself a prostitute during the hearings. Other urban occupations were possible (for instance, one woman who testified was a baker in a southeastern town), but these were not discussed at any length by the commissioners, nor by those women who testified before the Aba Commission. These women were generally older, married, and illiterate in both English and the local languages (called, in the *Notes*, "the vernacular"); they were sometimes Christians but were more often identified as practicing indigenous religion.

This last distinction was carefully inscribed in the *Notes* during oath-taking. Self-identified Christian women were sworn in "on the Bible," while others swore "on the sword." For example, Nwanyeruwa, an elderly Igbo woman, was sworn in "on the sword." Her Oloko male antagonist, the warrant chief Okugo, proudly proclaimed himself a Christian and was sworn in accordingly on the Bible. The choice of sword (sometimes the more contemporary bayonet) or Bible is an evocative one in itself, and the insistence of some more militant women, like Nwanyeruwa, on the sword is only one gesture of many that need further interrogation in an extensive study of the *Notes*.[14]

Women who volunteered to testify before the commission were given a chit and asked to stay outside the meeting with other potential witnesses until they were called. From their testimony we know that members of Ohandum were often delegated by women in their marital towns to speak for the group.[15] This strategy echoed one often seen during the Ogu, when spokeswomen would stand up and give the message of the collected women to colonial officials, warrant chiefs, or other interested parties. These delegates would also take responsibility for crowd control and tended to keep their fellows calm in difficult situations.[16] Unlike those women who were viewed by the British as leaders and potential troublemakers, were required to testify, and were sometimes brought to the hearings under duress or from incarceration, the delegate witnesses tended to avoid talking about their personal experiences of the Ogu in favor of a statement of principles. Indeed, commissioners had a difficult time convincing such delegated women to give any details of the Ogu or to depart from what appeared to be their set verbal texts.

Just as young palm fronds had circulated with a "message" attached during November 1929 and brought together thousands of women to march against warrant chiefs and to destroy colonial and mercantile institutional sites around the southeast, women during the Aba Committee hearings brought a unified and coherent message—one they felt that the colonialists would understand—to the hearings. When speaking as "Ohandum" (itself a *nom de guerre* and more during the Ogu),[17] delegated women made a single, simple set of demands. One particularly clear and eloquent example of these demands comes from the testimony of Ahudi of Nsidimo:

> I want to tell you that these disturbances will go on perhaps for fifteen years unless these Chiefs are decapped. All the Chiefs, when they appear before you, say all

sorts of things to impress you that they are good men. . . . New Chiefs whom the women say are good men, such are the people we want. . . . We ask you to bring peace to the land. You may take evidence for many days, but unless you come to a conclusion which will satisfy the women, we will follow you wherever you go. Formerly we never made demonstrations in this manner, but we do so now in order to show you that women are annoyed. . . . No doubt there are women like ourselves in your own country. If need be we will write to them to help us. We will continue fighting until all the Chiefs have been got rid of, but until then the matter will not be settled.[18]

Besides expressing a desire to be rid of chiefs altogether, or for women to be given a voice in choosing new chiefs, Ohandum delegates constantly demanded that women were not to be taxed and that bridewealth payments should be lowered. Statements like this, consistently presented, are probably why Mba suggests that there was no (or very little) religious content to the Ogu Umunwaanyi.[19] I have emphatically disagreed with her elsewhere,[20] noting that a real continuity exists between Igbo and other southern women's demands in the 1925 *Nwaobiala* ("Dancing Women's Movement"), which she sees primarily as a women's purification movement,[21] and the demands made in 1929. To find this continuity we have to look at some older women's testimony, as well as to the actions of Ohandum during the Ogu.

Following the Nwaobiala, a movement whose protests seem to have been directed largely toward southeastern Nigerian male elites, a number of events appear to have convinced women in the region that the colonial administration was the new power in the southeast. These events included the implementation of the household census, taxation of men, the extension of government roads and lines of rail, the development of "modern marketplaces" (which meant, among other things, fencing in heretofore unrestricted market areas without the permission of their female "owners"), unchecked colonial monetization, and the rising price of imported commodities and bridewealth, coupled with the falling value of produce. Continued colonial expansion into every facet of southeastern life clearly showed that indigenous male leaders had not comprehended the ritual and material significance of women's earlier *egwu* (song, dance). The Nwaobiala's inward focus on warrant chiefs and *ndi ezeala* or *ezeani* (a term meaning "kings of the land," and a group that the Aba Commissioners desperately wanted to make contact with) was evidenced by the fact that most colonial officials only discovered the egwu's presence in their district by accident or informant's report. In direct contrast to the tactics of the Nwaobiala dancers, Ohandum in the Ogu Umunwaanyi went directly to the colonized and colonial sources of their affliction. They not only sang and danced their demands, they tried to act upon the physical spaces and material objects that represented the new order. Although egwu of protest and deep religious meaning continued to be at the center of women's actions, Ohandum does not appear to have thought its Aba Commission interrogators capable of understanding their former poetic subtleties.

As I read the lyrics quoted above from Margery Perham's study of the Nigerian colonial administration, for example, the women of the Opobo movement were preparing themselves for physical confrontation with the authorities and for their possible deaths in that confrontation, but also commenting on the moral condition (death) of the land.[22] Smell is often evoked in contemporary Igbo women's egwu. I heard lines chillingly similar to this in 1987 at a funeral in Onitsha, where they preceded an accusation of poison and sorcery. Gestures that were both threatening and solemn accompanied the song, and the music was difficult even to listen to. A couple of younger women became so agitated at the sound that they clapped their hands over their ears and ran inside the house. The fact that only remnants of what were probably very complex songs and dances remain to us from the colonial archive demonstrates, among other things, how correct Ohandum were to believe that their deeper meanings and understandings of the issues at hand would be beyond their auditors' power to comprehend—or, conversely, how little Ohandum cared to display their poetic and kinesthetic prowess before the commissioners. Nonetheless, it is clear from some of the (African and European) men's testimony that the emotional quality of the egwu could be felt, even if only as an irritating "noise" for colonial soldiers or as an ominous "singing and roaring" for colonized clerks.[23] Some warrant chiefs, better versed in the power of women's egwu than their male counterparts from outside the southeast, ran away rather than (literally) face the music when Ohandum arrived in their towns.

Throughout the Ogu, Ohandum also demanded material tokens of their mastery over men. During the movement of 1925, they had requested that small sums of cash and other fines be given to them for their egwu labors, but by 1929 they had progressed to more substantial requirements. They took caps from warrant chiefs, then tore down the colonized men's houses with their bare hands, even going so far as to take up the chiefs' yams and roast them over fires built of the mats that once roofed chiefly yam barns. In one memorable instance, members of the Ibibio women's association *Iban Esong* in the village of Ukam pelted a European census taker and his Igbo assistant with stones, then confiscated the European's topee, or pith helmet, and the assistant's fountain pen and record book.[24] There could hardly be a clearer representation of women's distaste for the forms of European colonial bureaucracy and mission education than this. The topee was an object associated closely with every sun-fearing, pale colonial official, and the fountain pen and record book represented expensive and opaque technologies associated not only with the hated census and taxation but with every young man who graduated from mission schools and used his new knowledge to lord it over his seniors.[25] Women during the Ogu would eventually attempt to dominate the colonial bureaucracy itself by means of performance art, demonstrating the absurdity of bureaucratic forms by parodying them:

> I addressed the crowd and told them that unless they kept quiet I could not hear what they had to say to me. During this time I was standing close to the fence with my hands on it. As they raised their points one by one, the women asked me to

make a note of them in writing. I did so and I wrote myself with pen and ink all they wanted to say. . . . When I had written this the women asked for my copy and to write one copy for myself. I did so, standing by the fence and writing it under their own eyes. When I was about to hand it over to them they made further demands. First, they wanted it typewritten—then one copy, then two, then four, then five, then six copies, i.e., one each for the women from Opobo town, Bonny, Andoni, Qua, Ogoni and Nkoro. They wanted it witnessed first by my interpreter and then by a clerk. I asked them which clerk and they could not tell me. They also wanted my office stamp fixed on each copy. I told them I would do all these things when I had them typed. . . . By this time the typewritten documents were completed and I proceeded to hand them over to their respective representatives. They again made frivolous demands, one woman wanted them put in envelopes, another wanted a two-shilling stamp on each copy.[26]

During the Nwaobiala, southeastern women had walked on their own pathways (*ama*), appearing quietly inside the markets of towns they wished to cleanse, and had, indeed, demanded that colonial roads be abandoned because the road "brought or causes death."[27] During the Ogu, Ohandum took to the British-constructed roadways, even putting up roadblocks and clogging the major thoroughfares between colonial towns with their bodies, making it difficult for truck drivers and motorists to move safely. The first deaths of Ohandum also occurred at the hands of the colonialists during one of these road protests. William Hunter, the medical officer for Aba, confused by the masses of women surrounding his vehicle and evidently concerned for the safety of a European nursing sister, himself, and his car, ran into two women, Nwanyioma and Ukwa, while trying to escape from the crowd.[28] After the death of their compatriots, Aba women became extremely angry and began to destroy colonial and mercantile property throughout the town, giving rise to the colonial name for the Ogu, the "Aba Riots."

Ohandum also made it clear that they were not pleased with the continued intrusion of men into *afia* (trade, the marketplace). Market spaces that remained under female domination were left untouched during the Ogu and often served as meeting places, campgrounds, and sites for women's oratory. However, male-dominated trading stations, enclosed "modern markets," and fenced-in market areas were targeted for Ohandum's rougher attentions. Colonized Nigerian men's attempts to control markets were particularly disliked by southeastern women, and the African clerks who ran warehouses for imported European goods or tried to "rationalize" women's market practices were targets for Ohandum. For instance, Rosanah Ogwe of Azumini told the Aba commissioners that she had a special statement to make about the problems she and her fellow townswomen were having in this regard:

The Chairman: . . . (To witness) What do you want to say about markets?
Witness: As regards markets, we had five markets from time immemorial and they were going well but to-day none of those markets are functioning. If articles are taken to the market for sale, Court messengers would only throw 4d. on the

ground for an article which should fetch, say, 3s. and go away with that article. If the owner resists or talks in any way about the matter he is assaulted by the Court messengers.[29]

After Ogwe's testimony, one of her colleagues, Rachel Nenenta, forced her way into the witness box and declared that she, too, had something to add in relation to markets:

I agree in the main with what the last witness said but she did not touch on all I should like to touch on. Market is our main strength. It is the only trade we have. When market is spoiled, we are useless. . . . The five markets that my sister, the last witness, mentioned here are the markets where we used to attend in order to live and our parents attended these markets. All those five markets have been closed on account of Government employees, Court messengers. If you have property—it may be property you acquired yourself or property given to you by your parents or husband—and you take it to the market for sale, it is seized by Court messengers and taken away without payment. . . . If a woman is strong enough to catch hold of the Court Messengers and say "Let us go to the Chief in order that I may report to him what you are doing," all that the Chief will say when they go to him is "Go away, I cannot do anything in the matter." You return home crying. You cannot get redress even if you take out a summons against the Court Messengers. If your case is heard in the Court and you are not satisfied with the judgement and you ask for a review or appeal, the case is left for the District Officer to review it. When the District Officer comes to review the case, he will not ask you what you have to say in the matter but he will simply say "Let the judgement of the Chiefs stand."[30]

This evidence of male oppression of women traders (itself only one example of many in the *Notes*) in the changing southeastern market helps to explain why women during the Ogu tended to react most violently to men whose positions in the social structure gave them ready access to women at work. As Nenenta succinctly describes above, the men who made up the colonial administration— African and British alike—supported one another by refusing to recognize women's market rights and claims. Small wonder, then, that these women began to understand themselves, by the late 1920s, as a gendered category which had been singled out for abuse, or that they would begin to see colonial and colonized men as another monolithic group to be remonstrated against. Men who did not interfere with the women's purposes, either before the Ogu or during it, were never hurt and rarely even verbally assaulted; indeed, many of them seemed unaffected by the women's activities.

It appears that part of Ohandum's rhetorical strategy during the Ogu was to demonstrate, by reinscribing them on the landscape of the Nigerian southeast, their desires for a more equitable and culturally appropriate social and economic order. Since men and some colonized women had not heeded the earth deity's message in 1925, Ohandum had to make a more direct set of gestures, putting their own bodies on the line to illustrate what social life ought to be. Igbo women complained to the Church Missionary Society official (and amateur anthropologist) George T. Basden, at the beginning of the disturbances, "that there was no margin of profit at all [in women's market trade], and as they could not make a living, they might as well make a stand, and if they were to become slaves again, they might as well die."[31] Think of this "stand" as a kind of larger sign language, if you will, an attempt to communicate across what Ohandum had learned were abysmal gaps of understanding, using not just their hands but the totality of masses of female signifying bodies. When the colonial administration answered with rifle butts, the stocks, prisons, and, finally, machine guns (techniques already perfected on unruly civilian bodies in Ireland),[32] Ohandum were forced to regroup and recognize that their status as women would not protect them from colonial violence. In the final section of this chapter, I will examine how women represented themselves verbally to the various commissioners and administrative functionaries they met during and just after the Ogu, as well as how they attempted to demonstrate the special status of being *oha nd'inyom* (the active, motivated female public) in words, as well as deeds.

Some Conclusions about Being a Vulture and a Colonial Second-Class Subject

Our grievances are that the land is changed—we are all dying. Our object in coming here is because the news we heard last year has never been heard before. That is what we sang about. We sang so that you might ask us what our grievances were. We had cause for grievances before the taxation was introduced. It is a long time since the Chiefs and the people who know book and the Nkwerre people have been oppressing us. We said that we thought that white men came to bring peace to the land. We were annoyed because men are born by women and they marry women. All the towns were opened so that people might enjoy peace and you now suggest that tax should be paid. . . . We meet you here so that we might settle matters. We are telling you that we have been oppressed. If this oppression continues, how are we to praise you?[33]

From the Aba Commission's *Notes of Evidence,* it seems as if Ohandum were forced to resort to another, lower level of communication—almost as if they had to speak in words of only a few syllables, as to infants, in their set speeches to the commissioners. The testimony quoted above, given by a woman named Nwoto, is a good example. In this speech, the woman "warrior" posits some basic issues for her colonial interlocutors and poses some rhetorical questions, not to gain answers, but strictly for these powerful men to consider: the land is changed; certain kinds of transformation bring death instead of life; southeastern Nigerian women sang to those like you in hopes of receiving your attention; the colonial administration said it would bring peace, yet it engages in warfare against us; oppressed people do not praise their oppressors; is this what you want to be known as? Nwoto's call is for action, not for yet another sterile "meeting."

Ohandum in 1930 clearly still believed in the power of words, but they had become more interested in the proof of deeds, and colonial deeds had been very unsatisfactory. Bridewealth had increased under enforced monetization, making it less possible for women either to marry or to divorce. Male census-taking had clearly led to taxation, a monetary burden that was borne more by women than the British claimed to understand. Missionization was not only bringing Western education, but was exacerbating social fissures between young and old, as well as between the genders. And as women's socioeconomic power decreased under an emerging social system that was doubly patriarchal, they also found themselves with fewer supports to turn to in hopes of any redress.

The Ogu Umunwaanyi might be seen, then, as a determined effort on the part of southeastern Nigerian women to seize and hold the attention of a set of masculine persons, both African and European, who seemed to have forgotten the importance of women's work—conceptual as well as material—in the world. After all, as Ohandum felt compelled to remind the Aba commissioners, they themselves could not have existed without the previous existence of women.[34] This constant female insistence on the importance of women finally led Commissioner Graham Paul to interject into the questioning of a British colleague, "Do you think in pursuing their pretense to destroy, these women were any more actuated by logic than the women suffragettes in England, or was it just a general way of showing their dissatisfaction?" Demonstrating, perhaps, a lack of comprehension of gender questions on two continents, the witness, Fergus Ferguson, district officer of Bamenda, offered a simple response: "I don't know."[35]

Ohandum called themselves many things during the course of their testimony: "useful women," "the trees that bear fruit," even "vultures of the marketplace." These poetic phrases were meant to describe how southeastern Nigerian women saw themselves as active participants in their own societies. Women recognized that they were no longer dealing only with the familiar men of their natal and marital lineages, but with European, as well as African, strangers who were becoming a permanent part of their social milieu. Indeed, even "familiar" men were becoming strangers under colonial conditions: entering women's afia (marketplaces) as traders; being educated in an increasingly alienating fashion; and becoming mobile as few men (outside of specialized long-distance trader groups like the Aro) had previously been. These new men—whether British district officers from Manchester, repatriated Yoruba missionaries from Sierra Leone, jumped-up ndi kotima (court messengers) from Orlu and Aba, or truck drivers from Port Harcourt—understood women's lives and women's work in the rural southeast much less intimately than had the men of Ohandum's collective youth. By describing themselves in deceptively simple terms (the truncated terms, as we will see, of aesthetic and didactic southeastern Nigerian proverbial speech), the women may have also been testing these "new" men in hopes of eliciting some reciprocal understanding of who the British and their collaborators thought Ohandum were. In this regard, we might see the Ogu as a contest of gender categories, with each side attempting to situate and stabilize local concepts of femininity and masculinity in the rapidly transforming context of high colonialism.

Proverbs in Igbo are, as Boadi notes for Akan proverbial speech, representative of "all the aesthetic and poetic values of language use."[36] They are condensed, allusive, and not easily translatable epistemes that are most often used by elders who have a rich command of *asusu igbo* (Igbo language) and wide, historically based personal experience. Like other Igbo rhetorical devices, however, proverbs and proverbial phrases are used differently depending on their audience. That is to say, proverbs can be simply didactic or much more complex speech performances, meant to dazzle the ears and minds of their auditors. Looking at how Igbo and other southeastern Nigerian women named themselves to their audience both during the Ogu and in its aftermath, it seems to me that their proverbial (or self-praise name) performances were meant to work on several levels: as female elders to their male and female counterparts, as female elders to youth of both genders, and as female elders to people whose social understanding was barely childlike (i.e., Europeans and other, outsider Africans). Let us take as our examples the three phrases quoted above, having to do with usefulness, fruit trees, and the "vultures of the marketplace."

To begin with, Ohandum represented themselves as "useful," people who worked in the world and gave something back to their societies. One of the most eloquent female witnesses, Enyidia of Mbiopongo, connected this usefulness directly to the metaphor of "trees that bear fruit."[37] Useful women were, in this formulation, like fruit trees, suppliers of products that enable social interaction. Just as palm kernels were used to make the rich, red, fatty oil that served as one of southern Nigeria's culinary staples and which is still associated with fertility, sustenance, and blood in the region today, in Enyidia's metaphoric trope of women's fruitfulness and usefulness "fruit" and "use" obviously referenced a contemporary link between women's productivity and reproductivity.

At the same time, the metaphor was expanded (for those who could parse it) to reference the multitude of complaints about the devaluation, not only of palm kernels in the local and world markets, but of southeastern women's social position and, indeed, of southeastern women's selves. It was surely no accident in the fine-tuned rhetoric of the Ohandum spokeswomen that the evils of falling produce prices and rising bridewealth were frequently mentioned together. Human fertility was perceived to be at risk, as the women note again and again in their testimony, and as they had sung and danced earlier in both the Nwaobiala and the Ogu Umunwaanyi. If men took it upon themselves to impoverish and kill women rather than to work with them for mutual ends, then the balance of the world was out of kilter and, as Nwoto argues above, "changed" beyond all recognition. Palm fruits without consumers or a market in which to sell them, or women without proper marriages or access to trade, could not develop relations between people. Since exogamously married southeastern Nigerian women historically represented the ties among groups, the discourse seems to imply, it was women's duty to establish continuity or create new versions of these ties. And if the rupture between people had been radical, then the solution must be equally radical.

The radical solution is, I would argue, encoded in Ohandum's rhetoric about being "vultures of the marketplace." The most moving representation of this trope, for me, is to be found in the first commission's evidence. Here is Emena Okpopo witnessing the scene of carnage at Utu Etim Ekpo in December 1929:

> We assembled together that night at Utu Etim Ekpo square to march in to District Officer to tell him we were not to pay tax. The square is not far from Chief Akpan Umo's house but not too near. We heard that we were to pay tax. We never asked Chief Akpan Umo about tax. The reason we did not go to him was that there were too many women and they said if we delayed they would burn our houses. Yes I know he is the right person to ask but we did not go to him; we remained there the whole night and played and sang songs. In the morning we started to come down here there were many and women did not hold sticks and no gun and suddenly we heard the sound of shots. I was not in front nor in the rear I was about the middle, there was no guns, no machetes and no sticks, there were some piccins [children] brought to prevent them crying. I was surprised to see the soldiers fire as we were women we call ourselves vultures as we did not think soldiers would fire at us. Vultures go to market and eat food there and nobody molests them, nobody will kill a vulture even in the market, even if it kills fowls. We only fling sticks at them if they take our chop, and so we thought soldiers will not harm us no matter what we may do. . . . It was the women who came from Aba and Izumini who told us we were to pay tax. They said they had looted Aba and Izumini and no woman had been touched there. When the firing took place some women fell on the road and I thought they were playing and I ran into the bush. I ran to bush and when I went back to my house I found it had been burned. I don't know who burned my house. Men are never called vultures.[38]

These were the "vultures of the marketplace," the scavengers who clean the market and with whom no one interfered, even if they acted disgracefully now and again by stealing fowls. They are, in a sense, much like *ndi afia* (people of the marketplace, both traders and customers); they belong in the space and perform a useful function there. Although they are not beautiful and do not clean themselves, they help to beautify and cleanse the space for others and are respected for that work. Here I think Ohandum and Emena Okpopo may be referring to continuing southeastern Nigerian ideas about the market that are encapsulated in an old Igbo proverb that suggests that all the world is a marketplace, and all who inhabit it must take part in and contribute to exchange. Being a vulture implies being willing to take on the responsibility for that market exchange, picking up the dirt (*alu,* sometimes translated "pollution") that is left behind and ingesting it, if necessary, so that other ndi afia can come to a fresh, cleared space. To kill a vulture who is such a responsible, useful being is tantamount to saying that you would rather live in filth and abandon the market, thereby ending the exchange that enables the circulation of persons, goods, and ideas in the world. Such an action was incomprehensible to Emena Okpopo and her fellow southeastern women, at least until they were forced to witness it happening and were confronted bodily with the violent reality of how much the land had changed in their lifetimes.

The Ogu Umunwaanyi was therefore a seemingly contradictory event, from the perspective of those who witnessed or participated in it peripherally: a "war" to make peace and establish its combatants' right to be responsible for the "good of the land." Many Europeans found it "frivolous," nonsense or a nuisance, except when it affected their purses or caused them major inconvenience. No Europeans and only one African man died in the events of late 1929; very few were hurt, and most of them received very minor injuries.[39] At least fifty southeastern Nigerian women, from several ethnic groups, were shot to death or otherwise killed in the "riots."[40] How much the British understood of what the women told them would be judged by how they acted in return. By historical evidence, not a great deal was learned. Colonialism was too well entrenched to be rooted out by the women's grand egwu or even by their demonstrations of solidarity, although the last did give the British some pause. A few women were asked to take part in local politics, and the British became more interested in what women were thinking. The primary colonial solution, however, was not one that gives me a great deal of comfort: two "lady anthropologists" (only one of whom, Margaret Green, was really a scholar) were awarded Leverhulme Research Fellowships and dispatched to the scene of the "riots" to discover "more information about Ibo social organisation and particularly about women."[41]

Over sixty years later, Ohandum and their Ogu continue to perplex scholars, including women anthropologists, and to serve as one of the most intriguing cases of resistance in African and Africanist history. We still have not fully understood the proverbial messages embedded in the songs, dances, and verbal rhetoric of southeastern women in 1929, even as our investigations of the events continue. At most we may be applying what Trouillot calls "retrospective significances" to these events, trying to make them more relevant to our own understandings and categories (including gender) than to those unrecorded ones of Ohandum themselves. At worst we may be bending the meanings and values of Ohandum so far beyond what these courageous women could comprehend that they would no longer recognize them. This is not, however, to say that our interpretations and late-twentieth-century "significances" are without value— for us. It would also be very interesting to see what Ohandum would say about contemporary Igbo and other southeastern Nigerian women—women who are lawyers, bankers, farmers, traders, and professional politicians, as well as academics (including historians and anthropologists). During the Biafran civil war in the late 1960s, Igbo women demonstrated their continued commitment to defending their homeland, just as Ogoni women more recently showed great fortitude in demonstrating against the former federal military government and the multinational oil companies whose pipelines endanger their environment and their children's future. The importance of being a vulture of the marketplace has not been forgotten, even after women's place in those markets has been fatally disrupted.

Primary Documents

1. "Official List of Those Killed in the Ogu Umunwaanyi," Birrell Gray Commission, *Minutes of Evidence,* annexures 4 and 5. The following list of names and ethnic origins of Ohandum's dead has not, to my knowledge, previously been published. Although the Ogu Umunwaanyi has been often and justly cited in African history, it seems strange that we have never previously learned the (archivally recorded) identities of those who died during their resistance. I hope, by providing this information here, to begin further dialogue on these women and their real histories.

Table 11.1

Name	Gender	Town/Ethnic Origin	Where Killed
1. Alimi Aromashodu	M	Lagos	Opobo
2. Mary Nzekwe	F	Opobo	Opobo
3. Mary Okoronkwo Jaja	F	Opobo	Opobo
4. Rhoda Ronny Jaja	F	Opobo	Opobo
5. Regina Cookey	F	Opobo	Opobo
6. Leje Jaja	F	Opobo	Opobo
7. Nwa Nwa Waribo Uranta	F	Opobo	Opobo
8. Oruba	F	Opobo	Opobo
9. Eka	F	Opobo	Opobo
10. Omieseme	F	Nkoro	Opobo
11. Nwikpebu	F	Nkoro	Opobo
12. Barasua	F	Nkoro	Opobo
13. Tulu	F	Nkoro	Opobo
14. Abu	F	Nkoro	Opobo
15. Iweribara	F	Nkoro	Opobo
16. Adiaha Edem	F	Nkoro	Opobo
17. Adiaha Okonja	F	Anang	Opobo
18. Rebecca Thompson	F	Anang	Opobo
19. Ariwa Mie	F	Andoni	Opobo
20. Adiaha Ogbanaku	F	Andoni	Opobo
21. Wife of Sanitary Headman	F	Asaba	Opobo
22. Nwayi	F	Nkoro	Opobo
23. Nsukprumai	F	Nkoro	Opobo
24. Dubo	F	Ogoni	Opobo
25. Yako	F	Ogoni	Opobo
26. Yoti	F	Ogoni	Opobo
27. Oroni Jaja	F	Opobo	Opobo
28. Sui Dappa	F	Opobo	Opobo
29. Addah Igbi	F	Opobo	Opobo
30. Danuna	F	Ogoni	Opobo
31. Alale (Alali)	F	Ogoni	Opobo
32. Mary Tatare	F	Opobo	Opobo
33. Mary Udo Ekpo	F	Abak	Abak

34. Adiaha Umo	F	Abak	Abak
35. Unwa Udo Udom	F	Afaha Obong	Abak
36. Eyen Obot	F	Utu	Utu Etim Ekpo
37. Eyen Nwan	F	Ikot—Akpan—Awa	Utu Etim Ekpo
38. Enweke	F	Nsibung	Utu Etim Ekpo
39. Sekere Ama	F	Utu	Utu Etim Ekpo
40. Mary of Ubaku	F	Azumini	Utu Etim Ekpo
41. Adiaha Ukpong	F	Nung Ikot	Utu Etim Ekpo
42. Achonko	F	Udok Echiet	Utu Etim Ekpo
43. Mbeke	F	Utu	Utu Etim Ekpo
44. Ukwa Eyen Akpan	F	Ikot Isu	Utu Etim Ekpo
45. Etok Ama	F	Utu	Utu Etim Ekpo
46. Unwa Idiong	F	Ikot Nkum	Utu Etim Ekpo
47. Unwa Atai	F	Utu	Utu Etim Ekpo
48. Elizabeth (Eye Nnyang Umo)	F	Utu	Utu Etim Ekpo
49. Adiaha Ama	F	Utu	Utu Etim Ekpo
50. Okpo Ukot	F	Utu	Utu Etim Ekpo
51. Umo Udo Nta	F	Utu	Utu Etim Ekpo
52. Unidentified Ngwa (Owerri area) woman	F	unknown/Igbo	Utu Etim Ekpo

2. Aba Commission of Inquiry, *Notes of Evidence Taken by the Commission of Inquiry Appointed to Inquire into the Disturbances in the Calabar and Owerri Provinces, December, 1929* (London: Waterlow, 1930), pp. 114–15.

6th Witness, AHUDI (F[emale]. A[frican].), then came forward to give evidence, and was sworn.

> *The Chairman:* Where do you come from?
> *Witness:* Nsidimo.
> *The Chairman:* What do you want to say?
> *Witness:* I wish to say something about Chiefs. Women are very much annoyed. If I had a case with another in the Native Court, that case would not be heard until I kept borrowing money, about £10 in all. If I do not borrow money, the case would be kept waiting for six months. That is what Chiefs do. If I had a daughter and a Chief came to me to say he wanted to marry my daughter, he would pay only £5. He would not complete the proper dowry. If he fell out with his wife, for this £5 he paid, he would make another man pay £20. Caps are given to Chiefs by Government, but before they receive the caps they go to the poor men and say they must collect money for them because they are now capped Chiefs. Is it right that the poor should collect money for the Chiefs? I want to tell you that these disturbances will go on perhaps for fifteen years unless these Chiefs are decapped. All the Chiefs, when they appear before you, say all sorts of things to impress you that they are good men. All the Chiefs whom we ask to be deposed should be deposed, otherwise the trouble will go on. New

Chiefs whom the women say are good men, such are the people we want. If an action is brought against your husband, he will be punished. If an action is taken against your son, he will be punished. Chiefs take all the money. We are not armed with guns or matchets. We came in peace to ask you to make good Chiefs and to give us peace. We did not go to Umuahia to break shops. We ask you to bring peace in the land. You may take evidence for many days, but unless you come to a conclusion which will satisfy the women, we will follow you wherever you go. Formerly we never made demonstrations in this manner, but we do so now in order to show you that women are annoyed. If you come to a satisfactory conclusion which will satisfy all the women here, then peace will be restored. If not, then we will create trouble again. No doubt women like ourselves are in your own country. If need be we shall write to them to help us. We shall continue fighting until all the Chiefs have been got rid of, but until then the matter will not be settled. If a new man be appointed, then all the women should be present, and all the men should be present, and both should approve his appointment. And he shall be the man to judge our cases until the end of the world. These old Chiefs, whenever they return from Court, say that the District Officer says this and that, and fearing them, we do what the D. O. says. Fearing to refuse their instructions, we become poor, and we have not enough money to buy food. If you do not come to a satisfactory conclusion we will fight again. When we become annoyed we neglect our ordinary farm work. We should be engaged on ordinary duties, but we are here on this matter. When peace is restored we shall then see whether mothers and fathers of young girls will get their proper dowries. If a man gives his daughter in marriage he has to go and borrow money in order to pay his case, if he does not get the proper dowry. It does not matter who the Chief may be. Inasmuch as he is an old Chief, he should be deposed. Women are not claiming to be made Chiefs. New men should be appointed. If the old Chiefs are taken away, then we who have goats will find that the goats will have kids. If a man owns a portion of land the Chief takes it away from him and gives it to his women. When the Chiefs are all taken away then there will be peace, but if not, then there will be fighting again.

NOTES

I would like to acknowledge and thank all of those who have talked with me and shared their ideas, over the years, about the Ogu Umunwaanyi of 1929, particularly Doug Anthony, Mark Auslander, Ralph Austen, Jean Comaroff, Adeline Masquelier, Don Ohadike, Rosalind Shaw, Brad Weiss, and various members of the Naijanet, Nuafrica, and H-Africa e-mail lists, as well as the editors of this volume.

1.   Aba Commission of Inquiry, *Notes of Evidence Taken by the Commission of Inquiry Appointed to Inquire into the Disturbances in the Calabar and Owerri Provinces, December, 1929* (London: Waterlow, 1930), p. 278.

2.   A full description of the warrant chief system can be found in, among many others, A. E. Afigbo's *The Warrant Chiefs: Indirect Rule in Southeastern Nigeria, 1891–1929* (New York: Humanities Press, 1972), and Harry A. Gailey's *The Road to Aba: A Study of British Administrative Policy in Eastern Nigeria* (New York: New York University Press, 1970).

3.   The official casualty lists suggest that fifty-two women were killed outright and at least another fifty were wounded. These lists, however, are probably not accurate, since they enumerate only those women whose deaths were actually reported to the British or who ended up in hospital to be questioned and counted. For present purposes, however, they are the best sources we have for the death toll. See the first primary document reprinted in this chapter and annexures 4 and 5 of Birrell Gray Commission, *Minutes of Evidence Taken by a Commission of Inquiry Appointed to Inquire into Certain Incidents at Opobo, Abak, and Utu-Etim-Ekpo in December, 1929* (Public Record Office, file CO 583/176/7).

4.   Aba Commission, *Notes*, p. 179. Nina Emma Mba, *Nigerian Women Mobilized: Women's Political Activity in Southern Nigeria, 1900–1965* (Berkeley: University of California, Institute of International Studies, 1982), p. 92, notes that the more correct spelling would be *Oha nd'inyom*. I will use the colonial spelling throughout this chapter, because it does approximate the pronunciation of the phrase for English speakers and is the term used in the *Notes*, but Mba's orthography gives a better sense of the term's etymology in Igbo. The full term more literally means "the public/people/visitors who are part of *inyom* [womanhood, or the plurality of women]." This evokes the interstitial status of the women's movement: they are collected together to travel, on the basis of their status as exogamously married women now living in particular locations. They represent "the public" at large, but they themselves have a particular status in society, based on their gender. In non-Igbo-speaking areas of the southeast, the movement surely had other names. For example, Violetta Ekpo, in her article "Traditional Symbolism of the Women's War of 1929," in *The Women's Revolt of 1929: Proceedings of a National Symposium to Mark the Sixtieth Anniversary of the Women's Uprising in South-Eastern Nigeria*, ed. P. Chike Dike (Lagos: Nelag, 1995), p. 61, suggests that Ibibio women may have marched under the aegis of *Iban Isong*, one of several contemporary Ibibio women's associations.

5.   See, for example, the controversy surrounding who, exactly, looted "factories" in Mbawsi, Ayaba Native Court Area. In Aba Commission, *Notes*, p. 106, Chamberlain Jumbo, the African agent at G. D. Ollivant's trading station, swore, "No outside women [i.e., women from outside the trading station] really wanted to loot. They only wanted specially to burn down the native court, and having done that the station women went back to Aba and met the proper women trading. They brought them back to Mbawsi station saying that as the Umuahia women had looted the market and got a lot of stuff, they must therefore go to Mbawsi and loot the shops there. They therefore forced the other women into the shops, but they only took some stock fish. All the cases of theft of spirits were committed by station women."

6. Ibid., p. 804.

7. T. Obinkaram Echewa, *I Saw the Sky Catch Fire* (New York: Dutton, 1992).

8. Some of the most prominent of these works are Afigbo, *Warrant Chiefs;* Ekwere Otu Akpan and Violetta I. Ekpo, *The Women's War of 1929 (Preliminary Study): A Popular Uprising in South Eastern Nigeria* (Calabar, Nigeria: Government Printer, 1988); Dike, *Women's Revolt;* Gailey, *Road to Aba;* Judith Lynne Hanna, "Dance and the 'Women's War,'" *Dance Research Journal* 14, nos. 1–2 (1981–82): 25–27; Caroline Ifeka-Moller, "Female Militancy and Colonial Revolt: The Women's War of 1929, Eastern Nigeria," in *Perceiving Women,* ed. Shirley Ardener (London: Malaby, 1975), pp. 127–57; Elizabeth Isichei, *A History of the Igbo People* (New York: St. Martin's, 1976); Mba, *Nigerian Women Mobilized;* Susan Martin, "Gender and Innovation: Farming, Cooking, and Palm Processing in the Ngwa Region of South-Eastern Nigeria, 1900–1930," *Journal of African History* 25, no. 3 (1984): 411–27; Nkiru Nzegwu, "Recovering Igbo Traditions: A Case for Indigenous Women's Organizations in Development," in *Women, Culture, and Development: A Study of Human Capabilities,* ed. Martha C. Nussbaum and Jonathan Glover (Oxford: Clarendon, 1995), pp. 444–65; Margery Perham, *Native Administration in Nigeria* (London: Oxford University Press, 1937); Judith Van Allen, "'Aba Riots' or Igbo 'Women's War'? Ideology, Stratification, and the Invisibility of Women," in *Women in Africa: Studies in Social and Economic Change,* ed. Nancy J. Hafkin and Edna G. Bay (Stanford, Calif.: Stanford University Press, 1976), pp. 59–85, and "'Sitting on a Man': Colonialization and the Lost Political Institutions of Igbo Women," in *Women and Society: An Anthropological Reader,* ed. Sharon W. Tiffany (St. Albans, Vt.: Eden, 1979), pp. 163–87. I wrote my master's thesis on the Women's War in 1985 and have been working on a paper on the "prequel" to the Ogu Umunwaanyi, the *Nwaobiala* of 1925. See Misty L. Bastian, "Dancing Women and Colonial Men: The *Nwaobiala* of 1925," in *Wicked Women and the Reconfiguration of Gender in Africa,* ed. Dorothy L. Hodgson and Sheryl A. McCurdy (Portsmouth, N.H.: Heinemann, forthcoming). Without dwelling on Women's War materials, although the Nwaobiala certainly reached Nnobi, Ifi Amadiume, *Male Daughters, Female Husbands: Gender and Sex in an African Society* (London: Zed, 1987), also gives very valuable background information on Igbo women's political institutions in the nineteenth and early twentieth centuries. She also mentions the Ogu Umunwaanyi briefly in her most recent work, relating to ongoing Nnobi women's resistance actions during the colonial and post-colonial periods. See Ifi Amadiume, *Re-inventing Africa: Matriarchy, Religion, and Culture* (London: Zed, 1997), pp. 125–26.

9. Michel-Rolph Trouillot, *Silencing the Past: Power and the Production of History* (Boston: Beacon, 1995), p. 49.

10. Van Allen, Ifeka-Moller, and Mba have pointed toward the importance of this type of reading, but only Ifeka-Moller's academic orientation has been really conducive to the approach that I favor. Although Van Allen reveals a good deal about indigenous women's political organization to her readers, she does not give enough credence to that organization's poetics; and although Mba has written very movingly about southeastern Nigerian women's resistance to colonialism, she tends to ignore the religious dimension of Ohandum's practice in favor of a strictly economic explanation for the "war." Both of these

scholars come out of intellectual traditions that emphasize—and value—political and material realities over other forms of practice (e.g., cosmological or other, more aesthetic exegeses). Ifeka-Moller not only describes women's actions in late 1929 but attempts to contextualize those actions in a deeper fashion, moving from economics to religion in a way with which (in my opinion) many southeastern Nigerian women would be more comfortable.

11. Trouillot, *Silencing the Past,* p. 59.

12. Women protestors at Opobo, quoted in Perham, *Native Administration,* p. 209.

13. The Aba Commission was actually the second to investigate the events of late 1929. The Colonial Office first asked Major W. Birrell Gray and H. W. B. Blackall to interview witnesses in December 1929. (Their report can be found in the Public Record Office, CO 583/169/3, Sessional Paper No. 12.) Birrell Gray and Blackall's Commission of Inquiry evidently satisfied the local administration, who wished to dismiss the events of the Ogu Umunwaanyi as quickly as possible. See, for example, the comments of "S. J. F. J." in January 1931: "In the first place, it seems extremely unfortunate that two Commissions [which] were allowed to investigate the same set of circumstances connected with the actual disturbances should have arrived at different conclusions, thus placing the Nigerian Government in the predicament of having to choose between the two. It also seems very remarkable that Mr. Blackall, a Member of the first Commission was directed to appear as Counsel before the second" (Public Record Office, CO 583/176/9). The first commission mainly included male testimony in its published record, although Birrell Gray and Blackall also interviewed women.

14. It is interesting and evocative to learn that swearing on swords and other iron artifacts was a known practice in southwestern Nigeria, among Yoruba speakers, that was associated with the deity Ogun. See, for example, Adeboye Babalola, "A Portrait of Ogun as Reflected in Ijala Chants," p. 156, and J. D. Y. Peel, "A Comparative Analysis of Ogun in Precolonial Yorubaland," p. 279, both in *Africa's Ogun: Old World and New,* 2nd ed., ed. Sandra T. Barnes (Bloomington: Indiana University Press, 1997). Although Igbo and other southeastern peoples do not worship Ogun, they do have deities associated with iron and blacksmithing. Even today, some vestiges of the practice of swearing on blacksmithing tools or the products of smithing survive. In the early 1990s, I heard of a cabal of Igbo politicians swearing an oath for mutual gain on the engine of a Mercedes Benz.

15. Nwannedie of Ndume, for instance, desired to speak directly to the chairman of the commission on matters she had been delegated by Ndume women to bring to the administration's attention. See Aba Commission, *Notes,* p. 177. The chairman spoke to her outside of the hearing venue, but had her testimony entered into the commission's records.

16. For instance, the women massed on the road near Obor avoided a dangerous conflict with a military platoon by following their delegates' decision to sit down. The delegates, I should add, did not capitulate to military force without a demonstration of their resolve. The English officer in charge of the platoon gave them five minutes to sit, under the threat of fire or bayonet charge. In his words, "when I said 'half a minute to go,' suddenly the whole crowd sat down. I was flummoxed then to know what to do with them!" Ibid., p. 803.

17. "I asked them what their names were, and their answer was 'Ohandum.' I

asked them where they came from, and they answered 'Ohandum.' I asked them what they wanted and I received the same reply. I detained them, and said I was not going to listen to nonsense." Testimony of Capt. Royce, Aba Commission, *Notes*, p. 256.

18. Aba Commission, *Notes*, pp. 114–15.

19. See Mba, *Nigerian Women Mobilized*, p. 89.

20. See Misty L. Bastian, "Useful Women and the Good of the Land: The Igbo Women's War of 1929" (M.A. thesis, University of Chicago, 1985). There is a great similarity, for instance, in the lists of demands given by Ohandum and those sung by their sisters during the 1925 "Dancing Women's Movement." Several of these demands, notably those relating to women's fertility and authority over the land, are not "practical" in Western terms—for instance, that young girls should go naked and that all public areas are to be swept clean by women. Although I do not have the space to unpack these demands fully in this chapter, I have previously argued that both of these have to do with women's "transparency" and *mma* (beauty, wealth, well-being) in a changing moral, as well as political and social, environment. For a lengthy discussion of mma, transparency, and their role in Igbo gender construction, see Misty L Bastian, "The World as Marketplace: Historical, Cosmological, and Popular Constructions of the Onitsha Market System" (Ph.D. diss., University of Chicago, 1992), chapters 1 and 8.

21. Mba, *Nigerian Women Mobilized*, p. 72.

22. The Reverend E. N. Inyama quoted another Ogu song to the commissioners that included the metaphor of death's physical presence: "We are dying, our hearts are not good, for death is standing before us." Aba Commission, *Notes*, p. 168.

23. Nathaniel Cole, a forty-nine-year-old Sierra Leonean clerk for Nigeria Products, Ltd., described the women entering Utu Etim Ekpo to the Birrell Gray Commission: "At about a quarter to nine I saw a large crowd coming down the hill towards the factory, all women, singing and roaring. They were absolutely wild. I ran away to my house, thinking that they would not damage the factory. In my house I called my boy to give me a cup of tea; then I heard the noise of sticks beating the factory walls. My boy came and said 'Massa, the women are trying to break into the shop; Pack your things and run.'" Public Record Office, CO 583/169/3.

24. Testimony of Frank Ukoffia, Aba Commission, *Notes*, p. 324.

25. As per the testimony of Mark Emeruwa, Nwanyeruwa's first opponent in Oloko: "The District Officer asked me if I could write. I replied, 'Yes, Sir.' He drew me near to where he was sitting on a chair. He also examined one boy as to his capacity to write. Mr. Osuji was there as interpreter. He examined me and was satisfied that I could write. He gave me a note and instructed me to go to Mr. Anyanwu at Bende, who would give me a counting book. I did as I was ordered and Mr. Anyanwu gave me this book and showed me how records were to be entered." Ibid., p. 40. Later, the women of Oloko would relieve Emeruwa of his "counting book"—or, at least, the part of it not required by the district officer after the initial disturbances in the town. Other such books, as we can see, would follow.

26. Testimony of Opobo district officer Arthur Robert Whitman, Birrell Gray Commission, pp. 4–5.

27. Memo M. P. No. 18/1926, dated 9 March 1926, National Archives, Enugu, Nigeria. This is from a list of demands made by the Nwaobiala dancers.

28. See Aba Commission, *Notes,* pp. 539–40 for Dr. Hunter's testimony, and pp. 618–19 for the testimony of Nwannedie Mba, Nwanyioma's co-wife and "owner of her body."

29. Ibid., p. 740.

30. Ibid., p. 742.

31. Ibid., p. 201.

32. The testimony of Captain Alfred Thomas McCullagh shows how crowd control measures had already been tested in Ireland. He informed the Aba Commission that he had learned to use the Lewis gun against Irish civilians, "except at very close quarters." Mr. Blackall, acting in this instance as Crown Counsel, then noted that he had interviewed a Lieutenant Browning during the Birrell Gray Commission, who had suggested on the basis of his "eighteen months' experience in Ireland" that the Lewis gun was "more humane" because it "causes a smaller zone of fire and is more easily controlled and the moral effect is much greater than rifle fire." Ibid., p. 806.

33. Testimony of Nwoto of Okpuala, Ibid., p. 805.

34. Akulechula of Obowo sternly questioned the commissioners, after they asked her several times why she did not get permission from her husband to leave her home and join the Ogu: "Is not your mother a woman? Were you not born by a woman?" Ibid., p. 176. These questions are still part of Igbo women's rhetorical strategies when dealing with upstart men; I heard versions of them numerous times during the late 1980s in Onitsha. In those cases, as in the *Notes of Evidence,* the questions were generally treated by men as frustratingly unanswerable. During the Ogu itself, however, the female parentage of Europeans was questioned on at least one occasion. Lieutenant Richard Hill told the first commission of inquiry, "I moved up and down the fence [at Opobo] telling the women not to make a noise. They took no notice, some abused me in English and one took off her loin cloth and told me I was the son of a pig and not that of a woman." Birrell Gray Commission, *Minutes of Evidence,* p. 7.

35. Aba Commission, *Notes,* p. 191.

36. Lawrence Boadi, "The Language of the Proverb in Akan," in *African Folklore,* ed. Richard M. Dorson (Bloomington: Indiana University Press, 1972), p. 183.

37. Enyidia's speech is worth quoting at some length: "We said, 'What have we, women, done to warrant our being taxed? We women are like trees that bear fruit. You should tell us the reason why women who bear seeds should be counted.' Don't you agree that the world depends upon women—that it is the women who multiply the population of the world? We suffer at the hands of the Chiefs. They do many evil things and want to place the responsibility therefore upon women. We are not prepared to accept it." Later, upon being asked what the women's principal complaint was, Enyidia elaborated patiently, "Counting in order to tax women. Women come in contact with men, become pregnant and bring forth children. Such useful women are now asked to pay tax. That is our grievance." Aba Commission, *Notes,* p. 80.

38. Birrell Gray Commission, *Minutes of Evidence,* p. 43.

39. The one man who died was Alimi Aromashodu, a Lagosian goldsmith who accidentally stumbled into the line of fire at Opobo. As a measure of the deep, abiding patriarchal notions surrounding the inquiry at every level, his name is

the first one noted on the Casualty List appended to the Birrell Gray Commission's (1930) notes of evidence. I have deliberately preserved that order in the primary source that ends this chapter.

40.   These women have never been named in the literature. At the end of this chapter I reproduce the colonial administration's official casualty list. The list does not mention the deaths at Aba or any of the other deaths alleged at various towns, including Oloko, during the Ogu.

41.   M. M. Green, *Ibo Village Affairs* (1947; reprint, New York: Praeger, 1964), p. xiii. Green was particularly interested in Igbo linguistics, but she shows herself to be a very good ethnographer of the period in this volume. The other "lady anthropologist" was Sylvia Leith-Ross, the widow of a colonial administrator and eventually the first Lady Superintendent of Education in the Nigerian colony. For more on Leith-Ross, see Helen Callaway, *Gender, Culture, and Empire: European Women in Colonial Nigeria* (Urbana: University of Illinois Press, 1987), or read Leith-Ross's account of her 1934 experiences in the Nigerian southeast, *African Women: A Study of the Ibo of Nigeria* (1939; reprint, London: Farber and Farber, 1965).

12 "Emancipate Your Husbands!" Women and Nationalism in Guinea, 1953–1958

Elizabeth Schmidt

The Guinean branch of the *Rassemblement Démocratique Africain* (RDA), its detractors said, was a party of prostitutes, school drop-outs, and divorced women. It was aggressively opposed by the French colonial administration, by the so-called "traditional" chiefs who served as administrative spokesmen in the countryside, and by the esteemed notable families of Guinea. Yet this much disparaged party led Guinea to independence in 1958, advancing a wave of decolonization that ultimately spread across the African continent.

Founded in 1946, the RDA was an interterritorial alliance of political parties with branches in the colonies of French West and Equatorial Africa and in the United Nations trust territories of Togo and Cameroon. It promoted united action across colonial boundaries as a means of achieving its goals, which included greater political autonomy for the colonies and equality of political, economic, and social rights for colonial and metropolitan peoples.[1] RDA members suffered serious reprisals from the colonial administration; thus, many of their activities were clandestine. Although women did not participate in the founding of the alliance, they became increasingly involved in the RDA's popular mobilization against the colonial system.

In Guinea, one of eight colonies making up the federation of French West Africa, the turning point came during the seventy-day general strike of 1953, which included both labor and political demands. Women's crucial role in sustaining the strike, through material assistance and community mobilization, was recognized by male RDA leaders, who subsequently recruited them into the nationalist movement. Their involvement was critical to the anti-colonial struggle, from the 1954 legislative elections—rigged in favor of opponents of the RDA—through the September 1958 referendum, in which the population of Guinea overwhelmingly rejected the proposed constitution for the Fifth French Republic.[2] Guinea opted instead for immediate independence—and was the only French colony to do so.

Contextualized within current debates on nationalism and resistance to colonial domination, this chapter focuses on women's initiatives and the violation of gender norms as crucial, but under-studied, aspects of anti-colonial struggles. Unlike many of their male counterparts, female leaders of nationalist movements were seldom Western-educated Christian elites influenced by European Enlightenment ideas concerning individual rights and liberties. Nor were they generally aware of the nineteenth-century nationalist upheavals in Europe—popular resistance to empire that resulted in the establishment of numerous new nation-states. Rather, most had little, if any, formal schooling and virtually no direct contact with Westerners. In this way, female militants in Guinea strongly resembled their counterparts in Tanganyika and Kenya, as well as grassroots women activists in Nigeria.[3]

In Guinea, as in Tanganyika, female nationalists were predominantly Muslim and unschooled. In Kenya, women involved in anti-colonial activities were primarily peasants, rural laborers, and on the margins of urban society.[4] Western-educated Guinean women, whether Muslim or Christian, played little role in the anti-colonial struggle, choosing instead to preserve the few privileges they had acquired. As Kadiatou Meunier recalled, "The intellectual women were highly privileged. From this position of privilege, it was very difficult for them to see the need to fight colonialism. They were sheltered from the hardships of colonialism; they had the illusion that they had made it." Nonetheless, Meunier acknowledged, some elite women developed "consciousness and entered the struggle."[5] In contrast to Guinea, a vocal minority of Western-educated Christian women in South Africa, Nigeria, and Sierra Leone assumed significant leadership roles in their respective nationalist movements.[6]

If not Western notions of individual rights and national self-determination, what impelled Guinean market women, cloth-dyers, and seamstresses to violate gender norms, speaking out in public, traveling without escorts in the countryside, leaving their husbands and children—sometimes even resorting to divorce —to mobilize for a political party? How did these women leave their mark on the RDA, its methods, its program, and its goals? In what ways did preexisting "cultural systems" such as women's associations and regionally based ethnic organizations fundamentally shape the Guinean nationalist movement?[7]

This chapter argues that while other Guinean parties ignored women or opposed their political involvement, the RDA listened to women's demands and targeted issues of particular concern to them. Notably, the RDA promoted health, sanitation, and educational services that affected the well-being of women and their families. Acknowledging the power inherent in women's social relations and the relevance of their cultural associations, male leaders of the RDA supported women's use of these resources in mobilizing their families and communities. With the goal of bringing male laggards into line, the party leadership encouraged women to challenge their husbands, ignoring their marital responsibilities if necessary, all for the higher cause.

Yet there was an uneasy balance between leadership policy and grassroots male response. While the male-dominated RDA leadership publicly supported women's initiatives, male response at the household level did not always demonstrate such equanimity. The violation of the most entrenched gender norms, those pertaining to spousal relations and obligations, were rarely tolerated, resulting in tremendous domestic tension and upheaval. Thus women's emancipation in the domestic arena, while sometimes achieved, was neither widespread nor permanent.

African Women and Nationalism

During the late 1950s and 1960s, scholars of African nationalist struggles focused primarily on the Western-educated male elites who led the nationalist movements and assumed power after independence.[8] In the early 1970s, however, as social history gained prominence in the discipline, African peasants and workers, as agents of historical change, became important subjects of historical inquiry. Analyses sensitive to the centrality of women gradually superseded the presumption that men alone were the agents of African "modernization"—the backbone of emergent peasantries, capitalist farming sectors, and nascent African working classes.[9]

These revisions have been accompanied by a similar reevaluation of the "absence" of women from labor and nationalist struggles, as well as a redefinition of the terms of the debate.[10] The incorporation of women's vantage points into analyses of labor and nationalist movements has dramatically altered our understanding of the dynamics of these struggles, their premises, organization, and objectives.

In the case of Guinea, the importance of mass mobilization to the nationalist movement has received some attention, with Guinean historian Sidiki Kobélé Keita writing the most comprehensive account of the 1950s political movement, explicitly examining the popular roots of the struggle. Other authors, notably Morgenthau, Suret-Canale, and Rivière, have touched upon the movement's popular aspects.[11] However, even Keita's popular, and somewhat uncritical, account treats the "masses" as broad and undifferentiated and fails to describe the specific tactics of mass mobilization. While Keita mentions the crucial nature of women's role, he does not explore the dynamics of their involvement or the controversy surrounding it in depth. Meanwhile, the few other works remarking upon the central role of Guinean women offer no analysis of women's motivations, methods, and visions of a transformed society. Nor has there been any discussion of women's role in shaping the nationalist movement and defining the terms of the debate.[12] While these weaknesses have recently been addressed in scholarship pertaining to Tanganyika, a reexamination of nationalist movements more broadly has yet to occur.[13]

As Susan Geiger has demonstrated in the case of Tanganyika, women did not "learn nationalism" from the Western-educated male elites who dominated party politics. Instead, they brought to the party "an ethos of nationalism already present" in their trans-ethnic social and cultural organizations.[14] In Guinea, women's associations in the 1940s tended to be ethnically exclusive. However, within their own associations, women practiced mutual support and engaged in actions of solidarity that ultimately helped them to transcend ethnic boundaries. Associations such as *kabila* and *muso sere* (Malinke), *mamaya* (Susu), and *laba* (Peul) grouped women according to age or kinship and provided mutual aid in times of hardship or celebration. They also served social and community-building functions by organizing dances and ceremonies for marriages, baptisms, initiations, and funerals. Finally, these associations provided a separate space for women to dance and enjoy themselves without the hindrance of male authority.[15] Regionally based ethnic associations, with branches in various towns and neighborhoods, were equipped with women's auxiliaries that performed similar functions.[16]

Impressed by women's crucial role in the 1953 general strike, leading RDA men recognized the potential of women's organizations and made a conscious effort to capture their loyalty. Sékou Touré, a militant trade union leader and secretary general of the Guinean branch of the RDA, was particularly savvy in this regard. Women interviewed decades later frequently credited him personally with the party initiatives that benefited women. Although marriages, baptisms, and funerals continued to be organized under the auspices of various women's associations, from the early 1950s RDA women used such occasions to recruit new members.[17] According to the recollections of Néné Diallo, many of the mutual aid societies and women's auxiliaries of the ethnic associations were transformed into veritable organs of the RDA.[18]

The RDA Courts the Women

In the early 1950s, when women first became actively involved in the RDA, they were not intent upon violating gender roles and toppling male authority. They were proud to be the bearers of children, sustainers of the family, and guardians of the social order. Their involvement in political action was stimulated when their ability to fulfill these roles was threatened by colonial policies that impoverished their families. Relying on longstanding practices of female solidarity and collective action, they challenged the forces that prevented them from carrying out their duties. Temma Kaplan refers to this form of consciousness as "female." In contrast, women imbued with "feminist" consciousness challenge socially constructed gender roles, particularly those that perpetuate female inferiority and prevent women from exercising "full rights and powers" in the broader society.[19] For RDA women, as for so many women elsewhere on the continent, feminist consciousness evolved as their struggle unfolded.[20]

In order to attract women to its cause, the male leadership of the RDA consciously articulated demands that appealed specifically to women. Some were intended to lessen the burden of women's work. Others promoted the welfare of women and their families. For instance, as a result of the general strike of 1953, which was spearheaded by RDA-dominated trade unions, rations of white rice were added to workers' monthly wages. Women favored this type of rice because it was already hulled and thus did not have to be pounded with heavy mortars and pestles.[21]

Similarly, in 1954 the RDA advocated the construction of public water taps on the street corners of Conakry so that women would not have to walk long distances with buckets of water balanced on their heads. Nearby sources of water also freed young girls from onerous domestic chores and allowed them to attend school. According to former RDA militant Fatou Keita, "One day, Sékou Touré met the women and said the women's work should be alleviated. They shouldn't be carrying water on their heads, going long distances to look for firewood. . . . This was when the party introduced water taps in the compounds and on the street corners."[22] To lighten the burden of collecting firewood, the party encouraged women to make and use longer-burning charcoal. Moreover, at the party's initiative, Keita claimed, "The trains began to bring wood in their empty cars when they came to town; women no longer had to go long distances to find it. Later, they had tractors to help with their work in the fields." Whether or not these developments were, in fact, the result of party action, it is significant that Guinean women perceived them to be so.[23] The party also promoted the construction of markets and roads, increasing the prospects of commerce for women and for the rural population in general. It advocated the building of health clinics, hospitals, and maternity facilities, in both urban and rural areas, and demanded paid maternity leave and increased educational opportunities for girls as well as boys.[24] All of these proposals held a tremendous appeal for women.

Regional branches of the RDA also attempted to speak to women's concerns. However, they tended to view those concerns more narrowly than the national executive, focusing almost exclusively on pregnancy and birth-related matters. Invariably male-dominated, the branches echoed prevailing gender norms and values. In November 1954, for instance, the Mamou branch discussed the woeful inadequacy of a single eight-bed maternity facility, intended to serve a city of some ten thousand inhabitants. Because of insufficient space, pre- and postnatal consultations were performed in the open air, in good weather and bad. The hospital itself, which served the whole district, had only sixteen beds. The branch passed a resolution calling for the construction of new facilities in order to rectify the pitiful health conditions "which seriously jeopardize the lives of our women, our children, and our sick." In the same vein, the RDA branch in Dinguiraye petitioned the colonial administration to post a midwife to the local maternity facility. The male doctor was overburdened, and his "presence . . . during the birth process (rather than a midwife) constitutes an affront to the modesty of the women of the city," the male leadership wrote.[25]

While some female-oriented initiatives may have been conceived and presented to the women by male party leaders, others were clearly created by women themselves, particularly once they had been mobilized into party structures in the mid-1950s. In late 1954 or early 1955, for instance, a group of women from Kaporo, a suburb of Conakry, wrote to Guinea's director of public health. In their letter, reprinted in La liberté, the RDA's Guinean organ, they elaborated upon the difficulties they faced due to the lack of a medical clinic in Kaporo. Because few could afford the cost of transport, they wrote, women in need of medical attention were forced to walk fifteen to twenty kilometers to the nearest facility, in Dixinn. This included pregnant women who were required to make the trip weekly, wait all day on empty stomachs for their turn at the clinic, then make the return trip on foot. The authors petitioned the director of public health to build a clinic at Kaporo and to staff it with a qualified nurse and midwives so that the whole population, but especially pregnant women, "who produce children for the good of society," could be assured of adequate treatment.[26]

While early party initiatives largely bolstered established gender norms, women's commonly accepted roles also expanded. RDA women claim they were shown a certain respect in the party that they did not experience elsewhere. They were invited to speak at public meetings, to share their grievances, to mobilize not only their families and neighbors but total strangers in towns, villages, and hamlets across the country. According to Fatou Keita, before the transformations brought about by the party,

> Women were slaves. Wherever there were more than two men, women were not allowed to speak. It was Sékou Touré who brought about that change. The Socialists [*Démocratie socialiste de Guinée*] and the BAG [*Bloc africain de Guinée*] did not allow women to speak, but the RDA did. The other parties acted out of jealousy. They said that households would be split, that women would divorce their husbands if they were allowed to enter party politics. But women were clear that their involvement in politics was a good thing. And most went to the RDA. They thought that sending their daughters to school was a good thing, and many began sending their daughters to school.[27]

Néné Diallo echoed these sentiments: "We were all equal in the RDA, women and men. For women, when you worked you reaped the fruits for yourself, regardless of status and wealth. That is why we liked the RDA."[28]

The Mobilization of Women

Susan Geiger has aptly described the production of Tanganyikan nationalism as "women's work."[29] Among their various tasks, women "evoked, created and performed" nationalism through their songs and their dances.[30] Similarly, in Guinea, women sang and danced the message of independence. Oral transmission of information was crucial to the success of the RDA, which targeted the large mass of Guineans who had little or no formal education. According to Guinean scholar Idiatou Camara, women were considered the best sloganeers; as traditional story-tellers and singers, they were the practiced creators of ideas, images, and phrases that appealed to the non-elite population.[31]

Like the market women of coastal Nigeria, Guinean women used long-established networks to convey anti-government information.[32] The women's "bush telegraph" was highly effective. In the words of Idiatou Camara, "From the markets to the public water taps, from the train station to the taxi stands, information was transmitted along a chain." At their habitual meeting places, women popularized the slogans of the party, as well as new demands and grievances.[33] The public water taps and markets were especially important for this purpose. According to Fatou Keita, "The women congregated there and discussed where to go next. . . . News circulated fast in both places. If a woman went to get water, she stayed until the next person came and told her the news. The new arrival would wait and tell the next person, etc. This is how [RDA] news was spread."[34] While information circulated rapidly through informal channels, women also institutionalized the flow of information. According to former activist Mabalo Sakho, the market place was divided into sections, each one presided over by a female leader whose task it was to provide information to other section members. The leaders were the only ones authorized to disseminate news in the morning.[35]

Song was an essential educational and mobilizing tool for women, many of whom were not literate and therefore could not read the party tracts and newspapers. The songs dealt with recent political events, praised the RDA, and ridiculed the opposition. The lyrics were often sexually suggestive—or explicit. Their intention was to mock and shame rivals and laggards, as well as to mobilize RDA followers.[36] "Everything was with a song," recalled Néné Diallo. "There were countless songs. . . . Day after day, songs were made up. Everyone sang songs. We repeated the songs of others as they did ours. . . . There was not any one person singing the songs. There were many singers."[37] Fatou Keita concurred: "The women composed these songs. They did it spontaneously. There wasn't one author. When somebody found a song, they sang it. The next person heard it and sang it, and so on. It spread like that."[38] Fatou Diarra, another former militant, remembered,

> Women went to the markets every day. . . . If there was a new song, all the women learned it and sang it in the taxis, teaching one another. When there was an event, the leader went to the market with the song to teach it to the other women.
>
> After the 1954 elections, women sang at the markets that the colonial authorities had rigged the elections. "You women who go up, You women who go down. The other party has stolen our votes, Stolen the votes of *Syli*." All the women sang this song, so by the time they heard the election results, they already knew that they had been cheated, that the election had been rigged.[39]

The women who sang the songs at the market did so in teams. When the police came, they fled; political activities in the marketplace were prohibited.[40]

Some of the women's songs contained coarse language, ridiculing men who failed to join the RDA.[41] Embracing prevailing gender norms, women accused men of "behaving like women"—that is, of being cowardly and timid—and scorned those who were unwilling to stand up and fight. According to Kadiatou Meunier, contemptuous women claimed, "I don't want to be married to a woman like me, a man who is a coward."[42]

In other songs, women contrasted the ineffectual male population to the virility of Sékou Touré:

> Sékou Touré wears the pants.
> He is a handsome man.

> There is no other man who
> Dares stand in his way!
> Wear your pants, Handsome!

This song taunted reticent men, telling them that they were not big enough for Sékou Touré's pants; if they were equal to him, they would come out and support him. It also warned his opponents that their efforts were futile, and they might as well give up.[43] Some songs went further in their admonitions: if men were afraid of repression, they should give their trousers to the women, who would wear them in their place.[44] Women who sang these songs firmly believed that men should "wear the pants" in the family. Courage and initiative were not considered to be womanly traits; women assumed them only if men would not.[45]

Other songs were more graphic in insulting the manhood of those who failed to support the RDA or who joined rival parties. Between April and June 1955, police reports indicate that groups of RDA militants roamed the streets of Conakry singing the praises of Sékou Touré and casting aspersions on his chief rival, BAG leader Barry Diawadou. Diawadou had won the post of deputy to the French National Assembly in the rigged 1954 elections. Each day groups of women, organized by neighborhood, paraded before the home of Sékou Touré singing political songs. Then they marched in formation across the city, carrying banners and singing songs in which Barry Diawadou was characterized as a "dog" and as uncircumcised, the ultimate insult for an adult male.[46] According to police accounts, one of the songs went as follows:

> Barry Diawadou left Conakry
> To go to Upper Guinea,
> Because he found
> That *Syli* is always in the lead.
> Barry was slapped like a dog,
> The penis of Barry
> Is circumcised this time!

Even more serious than insulting a man's genitals was the denigration of his father's. In the following song, a double insult was intended. Barry Diawadou's father, Almamy Barry Aguibou, was the canton chief of Dabola, and thus a collaborator with the colonial regime.

> Barry Diawadou's father's penis,
> The saboteur's father's penis,
> Barry Diawadou left Conakry,
> He went to France.
> There he found his father's circumcision.
> Sékou Touré is always in the lead![47]

Among the other crucial tasks women performed were the sale and distribution of illicit party membership cards.[48] According to former activist Aissatou N'Diaye, the women had to work cautiously, concealing the cards from both government authorities and opposition party members:

The cards were hidden in their headscarves. The women would roll the cards into their scarves and put the scarves under their armpits. Over this, they wore big boubous. They went to compounds where they knew there could be Socialists and BAG members present, as well as RDA. The person selling the cards would lift her arms and boubou so that people would know she had something under her armpit. RDA people knew what that meant. Then they would ask her into the house and would buy their cards.[49]

On other occasions, the women strolled through hospital wards, visiting patients, nurses, and office workers. Operating according to code, they flashed hundred-franc notes, indicating that they had RDA cards to sell. If a customer wanted a card, the seller casually slipped it under papers scattered on the table, and the customer gave her a hundred-franc note in return. "We didn't know how to write, to compose a membership list. But the number of cards we sold indicated the number of members who joined each day," Mamayimbe Bangoura explained.[50]

Women also sold the party newspapers, such as *Le phare de Guinée, Coup de bambou*, and *La liberté*. They distributed party tracts, posted announcements of meetings, and popularized party slogans. During the early and mid-1950s, when the RDA was forced to work clandestinely, the women toiled at night, crisscrossing the town with pots of starch paste, posting tracts and announcements on baobab and mango trees in all the public places.[51]

RDA women also served as security guards. Market women, seated behind their platters of fruit, kept all-night vigils at the party headquarters and at the home of Sékou Touré, warning of attacks by members of rival organizations. They acted as sentinels during secret meetings, signaling the participants and dispersing the gathering as soon as they spied police vans.[52]

Finally, women gathered intelligence for the party. They had countless opportunities to observe activities in the neighborhood and informed party leaders of imminent actions against the RDA by the colonial government or by rival parties. According to Idiatou Camara, RDA women

> penetrated into the courtyards, pretending to take embers to the kitchen, and listened to the conversations. Or, in the seamstresses' workshops, at the popular hairdressers', during the ceremonies of marriage, baptism, circumcision, and funerals, they listened to everything and made note of all tendentious turns and unusual movements.

Posted in hospitals and at the marketplaces, taxi stands, and public water taps, women gathered information and reported to the RDA official responsible for their neighborhood or village. Mamayimbe Bangoura was so adept at slipping into enemy territory to ferret out information that she was called *Nyari*, or "Cat," out of respect for her stealth and agility.[53]

Similarly, when RDA men were imprisoned, their wives visited them, bringing not only food but information from the outside in the form of smuggled party newspapers and letters. On their return, they were able to inform party officials about prison conditions and whatever else their husbands had told them.[54] Even the police admitted that the inmates at the civil prison in Conakry were in permanent contact with the RDA through intermediaries, including visitors and wardens who transmitted correspondence.[55]

At first, RDA women used simple methods to penetrate prison security. During family visits, they slipped letters and journals to the prisoners or passed information orally. However, once these techniques were discovered by the authorities, they buried letters and newspaper clippings in the platters of rice they brought to feed the prisoners. When these means were uncovered, the women stuffed letters into aspirin bottles inserted into large pieces of cooked fish smothered in sauce. After the meal was finished, the return message was put into the bottle and hidden in the scraps the women carried home.[56]

Violation of Gender Norms

While these explicitly political roles for women were, for the most part, unprecedented, they were logical extensions of their preexisting caretaking functions. However, in 1954, in the aftermath of the general strike, gender norms were violated with a vengeance. That year, as a result of numerous brawls between rival political parties, RDA women organized "shock troops" in the large urban centers. In Conakry, the first group, led by Mafory Bangoura, a cloth-dyer and seamstress by profession, included Nabya Haidara, Khady Bangoura, Aissata Bangoura, Mahawa Touré, Néné Soumah, and N'Youla Doumbouya. At night, this women's brigade policed the neighborhood of Sandervalia, where Sékou Touré lived surrounded by members of opposing parties. Eventually, women's brigades were organized in all the principal neighborhoods of Conakry—Sandervalia, Boulbinet, Coronthie—and included the most active female members of the RDA.[57]

Unlike female security guards, the "shock troops" took punitive action against rival party members, men and women alike. Their primary opponents were members of the *Bloc africain de Guinée,* an ethnically based party founded in 1954 in order to more effectively counter RDA influence. In its defense of the status quo, the BAG was supported by the Peul aristocracy, the colonial administration, collaborating chiefs, and the most highly educated of the Western-educated elites, who coveted the crumbs of privilege thrown to them by the colonial regime.[58] Although women from these groups were active in the BAG, the party's traditionalism kept women from participating as actively as those in the RDA.[59]

RDA women fought with their hands and with clubs. Sometimes, mimicking male garb, they wore belts.[60] As a result of their violent activities, many members were arrested and imprisoned by the colonial authorities. Proudly, many assumed *noms de guerre.* N'Youla Doumbouya, for instance, noted for her daring and courage, was called "Montgomery, Eighth Army," after British general Bernard Law Montgomery, who led the successful North African campaign during World War II.[61]

Perhaps the most famous of the street fighters was Nabya Haidara, who was still legendary some four decades later. Haidara's female admirers referred to her as a "man in a wrapper" or a "man who had been given the wrong sex."[62] According to Idiatou Camara, Haidara dressed as a man and fought with a saber. When she was arrested, the police were said to have found some thirty sabers in her house, each engraved with her initials.[63] Whether tall tale or fact, Haidara's escapades are still eagerly retold. Aissatou N'Diaye claimed that on one occasion a member of a rival party, standing at his window, aimed his gun at a crowd of RDA supporters outside. Haidara "jumped into the air, grabbed the gun, and brought the man down." The man was wounded in the fray, and Haidara was sentenced to five months in prison.[64]

Although the shock brigades were not typical of women's work in the nationalist movement, they became a focal point for male anxiety over events they could no longer control. Many RDA men resisted women's emancipation, particularly in regions such as the Futa Jallon, which was dominated by the religiously conservative and socially hierarchical Peul. In Dinguiraye, an important religious center in the Futa, women lived in seclusion. According to Mira Baldé, "They stayed in their homes. They didn't even go to the market."[65] Léon Maka elaborated: "[Before the nationalist movement] in Dinguiraye, there was never a woman in the street. If by chance a man or a group of men were walking along a path and met a woman, the woman would hasten into the bush, covering her head with a cloth. She wouldn't get up until the men had passed."[66] Elsewhere in the Futa, Tourou Sylla remembered, "If men were gathered in a . . . compound and a woman wanted to cross the yard, she would have to bow down when passing."[67]

While the Futa Jallon was notorious for its religious and social conservatism, women's public roles were also circumscribed in other regions, albeit to a lesser degree. Generalizing about the country as a whole, Fatou Diarra noted, "Women did not speak in front of men. They did not stand up in the man's world to speak." This changed dramatically during the nationalist struggle, when women began to give public speeches to mixed gatherings.[68]

The transformation of gender roles did not occur smoothly, however. Fatou Keita explained, "Men liked the quiet of the colonial times, when their wives followed them. . . . There were no problems. After the party, it took a lot of readjusting. Men had to learn to do some things."[69] According to Bocar Biro Barry, a male activist in the RDA, Sékou Touré told the women that they should no longer accept their husbands' complete domination of their lives. "You must be able to go to the market yourselves. You must be able to accompany your children to school. Everything that men do, you must also be able to do."[70]

Although the RDA leadership encouraged the rank and file to accept, and even encourage, women's political activities, a discrepancy between theory and practice remained. While some husbands supported their wives' involvement in the nationalist struggle, many did not.[71] Wife-beating, marital breakdown, and the taking of additional, more subservient, wives were common responses. "For the husbands it was a shock," recounted Fatou Diarra. "They weren't used to seeing their wives outside the home. There were a lot of divorces, or the men married more wives."[72]

While refusing to relinquish their new-found roles, some women conceded the validity of their husbands' complaints. The marriage contract entailed certain mutually agreed upon responsibilities. If wives could no longer fulfill their designated roles, they were obliged to find surrogates who would. Because her political work entailed significant national and international travel, Fatou Keita was often unable to perform her wifely duties, which included cooking, childcare, and sexual relations with her husband. To win his consent for her political activities, Keita found her husband six additional wives to perform the requisite functions in her place.[73]

Some men were intensely jealous of their wives' loyalty to another man— Sékou Touré—and their willingness to follow his orders on a moment's notice. Others were concerned about their wives' attendance at late-night meetings that included men as well as women, a situation they associated with sexual promiscuity.[74] According to Bocar Biro Barry, "The men said, 'Fine! Since it is now Sékou Touré who is your husband, since it is his orders you are following and not mine, go then. Go marry him!' "[75]

Concern about women's rapid emancipation was not always confined to the rank and file. At times even the RDA leadership felt Sékou Touré was bordering on extremism. Barry recalled that male leaders in the party's political bureau said to Sékou Touré, "Truly, you are going too far. You are tearing households apart. . . . You are inciting women against their husbands." Unable to accept their wives' newfound roles, they exclaimed, "I am a member of the RDA—that is sufficient. My wife and my children need only to stay at home." However, Barry continued,

> It was there that [Sékou Touré] attacked them. He even attacked members of the
> political bureau, saying, "You are reactionaries. If you are of the RDA, you must be
> of the RDA entirely—that is, you, your wives, and your children."

Nonetheless, Barry concluded,

> There was something that wasn't public, but which was in each father, in each
> married man. He was suspicious when his wife abandoned the house with the children. . . . When [Sékou Touré] was to arrive at noon, by eight o'clock in the morning, all the women were in the streets. They didn't do any of their chores. They
> didn't mind the children. They didn't know whether they had gone to school or
> not. The women went into the streets and stayed there until noon, one o'clock, two
> o'clock in the afternoon, to wait for *that other man.* Upon returning home, the
> husband had nothing to eat . . . and there was a scene.[76]

Because of tensions within RDA households, the party quickly gained a reputation as a haven for prostitutes, loose women, and divorcées.[77] Rival political parties and the colonial administration eagerly capitalized on this image, railing against the evil of wifely disobedience. Fatou Diarra's husband, a civil servant, was a member of the *Démocratie socialiste de Guinée* (DSG), an elite party of highly educated intellectuals that disdained the nonliterate masses of the RDA base. Brought into the RDA by other women, she hid her RDA membership from her husband and stole away to meetings while he was at work. "Women were expected to follow their husbands," she recalled. "But I was RDA—like all the women."[78] According to a 1954 police report, Kémoko Kouyaté, a member of the RDA's board of directors and a childhood friend of Sékou Touré's, resigned from the RDA, publicly attacking the party's emancipatory policies. "Women who do not follow their husbands are condemned by religion," Kouyaté proclaimed. "A woman who engages in political activities other than her husband's is nothing more than a prostitute."[79] The same year, Fatoumata Traoré, sister of the president of the Siguiri RDA branch, was beaten bloody by the police because she refused to join her husband, who was active in the BAG.[80]

Members of rival parties peppered the police with allegations concerning the "dubious reputation" of women who were active in RDA associations. The police, for their part, were receptive to the notion that such groups constituted "a hotbed of prostitution."[81] When some forty women in Kankan joined the RDA, the governor of Guinea considered the event serious enough to write to the French West African high commissioner in Dakar, noting, "Among them are a number of notorious prostitutes, including: Kéritou Kaba, Kitiba Fanta Cissé repudiated by her husband, El Hadj N'Faly Kaba, Kiaka Kaba, Diaka Kaba, etc."[82]

Yet women continued to join the RDA. They did so, Néné Diallo explained, because they "had made up their minds."[83] According to Aissatou N'Diaye, "When we decided to join the struggle, we told our husbands that if, in the name of God and His Envoy, they would forgive us, we would appreciate it. But should they decide to divorce us for our politics, they could go ahead, because we intended to stick with the struggle of the RDA."[84] They chronicled their determination in song, asserting that, whether their husbands agreed or not, they were going to leave their homes to participate in the nationalist movement:

> Even when the rain pours,
> The women are out.
> Even when the sun shines,
> The women are out.
> Oh! How sweet the cause of *Syli*!
> Women of Guinea, the cause of *Syli* is sweet!
> Let's take the cause of *Syli* to heart.[85]

In the hope of avoiding complete marital breakdown, women called upon each other for assistance. As Fatou Keita recalled,

> The women in the movement organized to support the women who had problems at home. They told them to stick to their guns, that their husbands would follow them sooner or later. The women went to see the husbands and stressed that if

their wives turned out to be right and they had not supported them, they would be very ashamed in the future.[86]

As noted above, the public shaming of recalcitrant husbands was a common practice. Even women who violated female gender norms were quick to humiliate reluctant men with songs of ridicule that questioned their manhood.[87]

When shame did not suffice, sexual extortion was employed. In one particularly notorious speech, Sékou Touré threatened, "Each morning, each noon, each evening, the women must incite their husbands to join the RDA. If they don't comply, the women have only to refuse themselves to their husbands [at night]. The next day, they will be obliged to join the RDA."[88] In the same vein, a 1954 police report indicates that the RDA women's leader, Mafory Bangoura, took the floor during a party meeting in Conakry and invited "RDA women to refuse to have sexual relations with their husbands if they didn't join the party. They shouldn't worry; Sékou Touré would provide them with another husband —a real democrat." The audience sang in response,

> We will no longer share the bed
> Of any enemy of *Syli.*
> If not our legitimate husband,
> Sékou Touré will choose us
> A husband who is a democrat.[89]

A woman's refusal to engage in sexual relations with her husband constituted a serious violation of the marital contract—clear grounds for divorce. Some women left husbands who refused to join the party.[90] Others reportedly refused to marry men unless they could present an RDA membership card.[91] It was dramatic, exclaimed Bocar Biro Barry. "I tell you, the RDA infiltrated right into the homes!"[92]

In fact, the RDA had little interest in promoting marital discord or divorce. Rather, it hoped that women's membership would influence the men in their lives to join them in the nationalist struggle. According to Bocar Biro Barry, Sékou Touré encouraged the women in this endeavor, saying, "If you are with the RDA, it is up to you to emancipate your husbands."[93] Often, it worked. Mira Baldé noted that "there were lots of women who made their husbands wander into the movement. . . . The husbands weren't decided at first, but later they followed."[94] Even the tensions caused by women's independence sometimes had their payoff. Trailing their wives to late-night meetings, jealous husbands were often enticed into joining the party.[95]

Conclusion: Plus Ça Change . . .

Women continued to join the RDA, with or without their husbands' consent. As Tourou Sylla explained, people had to move with the times: "Once the sun rises, one cannot help but feel it."[96] The process of political mobilization raised women's consciousnesses, prompting women to take an interest in subjects previously off limits to them. They championed the nationalist cause in public, to audiences that included men as well as women.[97] They challenged a colonial authority that was composed primarily of men and, in the process, learned that they could also defy the authority of their own husbands.

Guinean women contested long-standing gender roles during the nationalist movement. However, in Guinea as elsewhere in Africa, gender roles were not permanently transformed. After independence, women frequently translated their new-found respectability into traditional terms. Nabiya Haidara, the famous woman street fighter who had gained the reputation of being a "man in a wrapper," was dramatically changed by her pilgrimage to Mecca. "You know the pilgrimage is very difficult," explained Aissatou N'Diaye. "One must be clean of some kinds of sins . . . to survive the experience."[98] The implication was that Haidara's activities as a street fighter had been improper, even sinful.

The circumstances working against women's post-independence emancipation were strongly rooted in the past. They were evident even during the nationalist period. For the most part, women themselves accepted the societally designated gender norms that undervalued women's capacities. Like their husbands, they generally believed that men should "wear the pants" in the family. They had donned the trappings of male authority only when their husbands would not. Unusual circumstances required abnormal tactics. When their husbands lacked courage and initiative, women followed the lead of another man, Sékou Touré. Even the most militant women rarely contested their husbands' right to multiple wives, the nature of their marital obligations, or the gendered division of labor in the domestic arena. Rather, they violated gender roles in order to create conditions in which they could once again fulfill them. In the end, during both the nationalist period and its aftermath, "female" consciousness held sway over "feminist."

Primary Document

Aissatou N'Diaye, interview by Elizabeth Schmidt, interpreted and translated from Susu by Siba N. Grovogui, Conakry, 8 April 1991. N'Diaye was an RDA member and grassroots leader of the nationalist movement during the 1950s.

The [general] strike was called in 1953. When it occurred, there was lots of suffering in the land. At that time Sékou [Touré] had begun his . . . activities. There was suffering, hunger, and people went naked. No one could afford to buy clothes. This was the result of the strike called by Sékou. The masses were having second thoughts about it. Men began giving their wives their pants. [Bakutui, or pantalons bouffants, are very loose, full pants which are worn by men in the hot climate of the Futa Jallon.] The women would take out the seams, tie the cloth into a scarf, and then take the cloth to a tailor to be sewn as a dress. That is what women resorted to, so as not to go about naked. The strike was very hard on people. . . .

So, men would take out their pants and give them to their wives so that they could make dresses. It was in this climate of hardship that the strike evolved. The strike was very tense and difficult. One day—listen to me! One day we went to see the young man, Sékou. At that time he was living here [pointing to a place in Sandervalia, by the sea]. It was Mafory's initiative. She said to me, "Aissatou, let's go see this young man. You know this is becoming worrisome." You know that there were three [political] parties. There were the Socialists, the BAG, and the RDA. She said, "Let's go see the young man." At that time they held a meeting at Cinema Rialto—at the movie theater near here. That is where they held the meeting. Workers were getting discouraged because there was no way out of the deadlock. . . .

Soon after [the strike ended] things heated up once again. That is when the RDA gained strength. The RDA really took off. And women had [Sékou Touré's] trust, because women had been supportive of him. The struggle really began in 1953, '54, '55.

[Sékou Touré] then met all the labor unions—here [pointing in a direction southeast of her house]. In this house, here, Ibrahima Touré's, we had our first headquarters. [Sékou Touré] met the labor unions, there. . . . That is where they spoke of what to do in the aftermath of the strike. Immediately afterward we really began [the political struggle].

As for me, Mafory came to tell me that [Sékou Touré] had asked us over. Upon our arrival, he told us that he had really called us to ask us to help him mobilize women on his behalf. He said he assumed that when one asks help from women, one has equally called upon their children. He said he meant it; he needed help from the women. He also said that he had nothing material, not money nor gold, to offer in return. If the women would help him, they would do it for the love of God, His Envoy [the Prophet Mohammed], and their cause.

He gave us this talk. "Why help the RDA?" he asked. He said, "Working for the RDA is working for oneself. In the RDA whatever you earn belongs to you." He said, "The RDA is for helping the disadvantaged." He said, "This is an example. . . . If you want to have a public gathering, for a wedding or anything else, you are required to seek an authorization, for which you must pay money. You go to the police to get the paper. Then when you get it, the police do not allow you to complete your ceremony. Before ten or eleven o'clock, the riot police will come to ask that you vacate the place. They will arrest some, including those organizing the ceremony, and send them to jail." That is what he told us. He said, "[The police] will send them to jail. You are not free, never free." He said that freedom and this kind of life are not comparable. One must be free even in poverty. He said there were many things he could relate to us, but he chose to stop there. He ended by telling us that in the name of God and his Prophet, Mohammed, "I, Ahmed Sékou Touré, ask that you stand up for something. There are three parties at present, represented by Barry Diawadou, Barry III, and myself, Sékou. Barry Diawadou is BAG; Barry III, Socialist; me, I am RDA." Well, as I have told you, we simply said, "Okay, we will see what we can do."

It was then that he sent us the membership cards—in 1954. He sent us cards.

The cards for the women were given to Mafory because she was the national president. . . . That day I was among those who collected the cards. We began mobilizing the women. . . .

You must know that women brought about independence. It was really the women. Women launched membership drives. . . . We had our first meeting in [Lengebunji], a neighborhood in Boulbinet. Membership cards were distributed there. . . .

Well, I took my cards. I was given two assistants. Every other day I would go out with one of them. Their role was to take down the names of new members. The cards were twenty francs. We mobilized lots of women. From then on, whenever there were meetings you could not see anybody but RDA people. There was no other party in town but RDA. Wherever we went there was trouble, because there were many battles. We had to fight our way—sometimes with some Peuls. Supporters of Barry III and Barry Diawadou got scared [she laughs].

NOTES

1. Pierre Kipré, *Le congrès de Bamako ou La naissance du RDA en 1946, Afrique contemporaine,* vol. 3 (Paris: Éditions Chaka, 1989), pp. 135, 137–38, 162.
2. For a discussion of official interference in the 1954 legislative elections, see Ruth Schachter Morgenthau, *Political Parties in French-Speaking West Africa* (Oxford: Clarendon, 1964), pp. 106, 240.
3. See Susan Geiger, *TANU Women: Gender and Culture in the Making of Tanganyikan Nationalism, 1955–1965* (Portsmouth, N.H.: Heinemann, 1997), pp. 14, 31, 42–44; Cora Ann Presley, *Kikuyu Women, the Mau Mau Rebellion, and Social Change in Kenya* (Boulder, Colo.: Westview, 1992), pp. 158–59; Nina Emma Mba, *Nigerian Women Mobilized: Women's Political Activity in Southern Nigeria, 1900–1965* (Berkeley: Institute of International Studies, University of California, 1982), pp. 193, 197; Cheryl Johnson, "Madam Alimotu Pelewura and the Lagos Market Women," *Tarikh* 7, no. 1 (1981): 1–10; Cheryl Johnson, "Grassroots Organizing: Women in Anti-Colonial Activity in Southwestern Nigeria," *African Studies Review* 25, no. 2 (1982): 138–39.
4. See Geiger, *TANU Women*, pp. 42–44; Presley, *Kikuyu Women*, pp. 124–73.
5. Kadiatou Meunier (pseudonym), interview, 18 January 1991. Unless otherwise noted, all interviews were done in Conakry and translated from French by Elizabeth Schmidt, assisted by Siba N. Grovogui.
6. See Cherryl Walker, *Women and Resistance in South Africa* (London: Onyx, 1982), pp. 135–36, 156, 160–62; Mba, *Nigerian Women Mobilized,* pp. 142–45, 151, 193; Johnson, "Grassroots Organizing," pp. 148–49; Cheryl Johnson-Odim and Nina Emma Mba, *For Women and the Nation: Funmilayo Ransome-Kuti of Nigeria* (Urbana: University of Illinois Press, 1997), pp. 64–68; LaRay Denzer, "Constance A. Cummings-John of Sierra Leone: Her Early Political Career," *Tarikh* 7, no. 1 (1981): 20–32; LaRay Denzer, "Women in Freetown Politics, 1914–61: A Preliminary Study," *Africa* 57, no. 4 (1987): 443–45.
7. I am grateful to Susan Geiger for referring me to Benedict Anderson's argu-

ment that nationalism "has to be understood by aligning it, not with self-consciously held political ideologies, but with the large cultural systems that preceded it, out of which—as well as against which—it came into being." Benedict Anderson, *Imagined Communities: Reflections on the Origin and Spread of Nationalism*, 2nd ed. (New York: Verso, 1991), p. 12.

8.   See, for instance, Thomas Hodgkin, *Nationalism in Colonial Africa* (New York: New York University Press, 1957); James S. Coleman, *Nigeria: Background to Nationalism* (Berkeley: University of California Press, 1958); David Apter, *Ghana in Transition* (Princeton: Princeton University Press, 1963).

9.   See, for instance, Janet M. Bujra, "Women 'Entrepreneurs' of Early Nairobi," *Canadian Journal of African Studies* 9, no. 2 (1975): 213–34; George Chauncey, Jr., "The Locus of Reproduction: Women's Labour in the Zambian Copperbelt, 1927–1953," *Journal of Southern African Studies* 7, no. 2 (1981): 135–64; Marcia Wright, "Technology, Marriage, and Women's Work in the History of Maize-Growers in Mazabuka, Zambia: A Reconnaissance," *Journal of Southern African Studies* 10, no. 1 (1983): 71–85; Luise White, "A Colonial State and an African Petty Bourgeoisie: Prostitution, Property, and Class Struggle in Nairobi, 1936–1940," in *Struggle for the City: Migrant Labor, Capital, and the State in Urban Africa*, ed. Frederick Cooper (Beverly Hills: Sage, 1983), pp. 167–94.

10.   See, for instance, LaRay Denzer, "Towards a Study of the History of West African Women's Participation in Nationalist Politics: The Early Phase, 1935–1950," *Africana Research Bulletin* 6, no. 4 (1976): 65–85; Denzer, "Women in Freetown Politics," pp. 439–56; Margarita Dobert, "Civic and Political Participation of Women in French-Speaking West Africa" (Ph.D. diss., George Washington University, 1970); Susan Geiger, "Anti-colonial Protest in Africa: A Female Strategy Reconsidered," *Heresies* 9, no. 3 (1980): 22–25; Susan Geiger, "Women in Nationalist Struggle: TANU Activists in Dar es Salaam," *International Journal of African Historical Studies* 20, no. 1 (1987): 1–26; Susan Geiger, "Tanganyikan Nationalism as 'Women's Work': Life Histories, Collective Biography, and Changing Historiography," *Journal of African History* 37, no. 3 (1996): 465–78; Geiger, *TANU Women;* Caroline Ifeka-Moller, "Female Militancy and Colonial Revolt: The Women's War of 1929, Eastern Nigeria," in *Perceiving Women*, ed. Shirley Ardener (London: Malaby, 1975), pp. 127–57; Johnson, "Grassroots Organizing," pp. 137–57; Johnson-Odim and Mba, *Women and the Nation;* Mba, *Nigerian Women Mobilized;* Presley, *Kikuyu Women;* Timothy Scarnecchia, "Poor Women and Nationalist Politics: Alliances and Fissures in the Formation of a Nationalist Political Movement in Salisbury, Rhodesia, 1950–6," *Journal of African History,* 37, no. 2 (1996): 283–310; Judith Van Allen, "'Aba Riots' or Igbo 'Women's War'? Ideology, Stratification, and the Invisibility of Women," in *Women in Africa: Studies in Social and Economic Change*, ed. Nancy J. Hafkin and Edna G. Bay (Stanford, Calif.: Stanford University Press, 1976), pp. 59–85; Walker, *Women and Resistance.*

11.   Sidiki Kobélé Keita, *Le P.D.G.: Artisan de l'indépendance nationale en Guinée (1947–1958)* (Conakry: I.N.R.D.G./Bibliothèque Nationale, 1978); Morgenthau, *Political Parties;* Jean Suret-Canale, *La république de Guinée* (Paris: Éditions sociales, 1970); Claude Rivière, *Guinea: The Mobilization of a People,* trans. Virginia Thompson and Richard Adloff (Ithaca: Cornell University

Press, 1977). Unfortunately, Keita's path-breaking book has not been widely circulated outside of Guinea.

12. See especially Dobert, "Civic and Political Participation of Women." A notable exception to this generalization is Idiatou Camara's unpublished undergraduate thesis: Idiatou Camara, "La contribution de la femme de Guinée à la lutte de libération nationale (1945–1958)," Mémoire de fin d'études supérieures, Conakry, IPGAN, 1979 (Archives nationales de Guinée, AM-1339). Unfortunately, this unique work, preserved in the National Archives of Guinea, is available only in that country.

13. The transformative nature of women's involvement in the nationalist move-ment is central to Geiger's pioneering work on Tanganyika. Scholars of other countries have yet to follow her lead. See Geiger, *TANU Women;* Geiger, "Tanganyikan Nationalism."

14. Geiger, "Tanganyikan Nationalism," pp. 468–69.

15. Archival materials from the French West African collection are housed in the National Archives of Senegal in Dakar. Mamady Kaba, interview, 15 January 1991; Fatou Diarra, interview, 17 March 1991; Fatou Keita, interview (inter-preted and translated from Susu by Siba N. Grovogui), 7 April 1991; Siba N. Grovogui, personal communication, 6 March 1998; Camara, "Contribution de la femme," pp. 38–39, 62; 17G613, Guinée française, Services de police, Conakry, "Renseignements a/s réunion des comités R.D.A. de Conakry, le mercredi 8 mai dernier à 20 heures," 10 May 1957, no. 1065/423, C/PS.2.

16. Léon Maka, interview, 20 February 1991; Fatou Keita, interview, 7 April 1991; Néné Diallo, interview (interpreted and translated from Susu by Siba N. Grovogui), 11 April 1991; Camara, "Contribution de la femme," p. 14.

17. Camara, "Contribution de la femme," pp. 55, 57, 67; Fatou Diarra, interview, 17 March 1991; Fatou Keita, interviews, 7 April and 24 May 1991; Sidiki Kobélé Keita, interview, 9 April 1991. For a similar discussion pertaining to Tanganyika, see Geiger, "Tanganyikan Nationalism," pp. 470, 472; Geiger, *TANU Women,* p. 58.

18. Néné Diallo, interview, 11 April 1991. Also see Léon Maka, interview, 20 Feb-ruary 1991.

19. For an in-depth discussion of "female" versus "feminist" consciousness, see Temma Kaplan, "Female Consciousness and Collective Action: The Case of Barcelona, 1910–1918," *Signs: Journal of Women in Culture and Society* 7, no. 3 (1982): 545–66. For African women's collective action in response to threats to family well-being and economic survival, see Mba, *Nigerian Women Mobi-lized,* pp. 297, 299; Johnson, "Grassroots Organizing," pp. 140–41, 143, 148; Julia C. Wells, "Why Women Rebel: A Comparative Study of South African Women's Resistance in Bloemfontein (1913) and Johannesburg (1958)," *Jour-nal of Southern African Studies* 10, no. 1 (1983): 55–70.

20. For women's collective action in response to violations of their rights or threats to their interests, see Shirley Ardener, "Sexual Insult and Female Mili-tancy," in *Perceiving Women,* ed. Ardener, pp. 29–53; Ifeka-Moller, "Female Militancy," pp. 127–57; Johnson, "Grassroots Organizing," pp. 137–57; Mba, *Nigerian Women Mobilized;* Van Allen, "'Aba Riots,'" pp. 59–85; Walker, *Women and Resistance,* pp. 158, 163; Denzer, "Women in Freetown Politics," pp. 447–48.

21. While the addition of rice to the ration packet had been demanded by male

trade unionists since 1947, it is likely that women initiated the demand for hulled (white) rice. See Fatou Keita, interviews, 7 April and 24 May 1991; Fatou Diarra, interview, 17 March 1991.

22. Fatou Keita, interview, 24 May 1991. Also see Keita, *P.D.G.,* 338.

23. Fatou Keita, interview, 24 May 1991. Also see Fatou Diarra, interview, 17 March 1991; Camara, "Contribution de la femme," p. 40.

24. Fatou Keita, interview, 28 April 1991; "La population féminine de canton de Kaporo écrit à M. le médecin-colonel-directeur de la santé publique de la Guinée française à Conakry," *La liberté,* no. 43 (18 January 1955): 3; "Résolution" [R.D.A. sous-section de Mamou], *La liberté,* no. 45 (1 February 1955): 2; "Motion rélative à l'affectation d'une sage-femme à Dinguiraye" [R.D.A. sous-section de Dinguiraye], *La liberté* (25 September 1956): 4; 17G573, Guinée française, Services de police, Kankan, "Renseignements a/s réunion du R.D.A. section Kankan le 5 octobre 1947," 6 Oct. 1947, no. 1082/105 C; Camara, "Contribution de la femme," pp. 40, 66–67.

25. "Résolution," p. 2; "Motion," p. 4. Also see Keita, *P.D.G.,* p. 338.

26. "Population féminine," p. 3; also see Camara, "Contribution de la femme," p. 66.

27. Fatou Keita, interview, 28 April 1991; also see Fatou Diarra, interview, 17 March 1991.

28. Néné Diallo, interview, 11 April 1991; also see 2G55/152, Guinée française, gouverneur, "Rapport politique pour l'année 1955," no. 281/APA, p. 81.

29. Geiger, "Tanganyikan Nationalism," pp. 465–78; Geiger, *TANU Women,* p. 162.

30. Geiger, "Tanganyikan Nationalism," pp. 467, 469, 471–72; Geiger, *TANU Women,* p. 162.

31. Camara, "Contribution de la femme," p. 65.

32. For comparison, see Mba, *Nigerian Women Mobilized,* p. 194; Ifeka-Moller, "Female Militancy," p. 132; Van Allen, "'Aba Riots,'" pp. 68–69, 72; and Bastian's chapter in this volume.

33. Camara, "Contribution de la femme," p. 65.

34. Fatou Keita, interview, 24 May 1991; also see Camara, "Contribution de la femme," p. 67.

35. Mabalo Sakho, interview (interpreted and translated from Susu by Siba N. Grovogui), 19 June 1991. For a similar description of the structure and use of Lagos markets, see Mba, *Nigerian Women Mobilized,* p. 194.

36. Léon Maka, interview, 20 February 1991. For examples of such use of song elsewhere in Africa, see Mba, *Nigerian Women Mobilized,* p. 150; Ardener, "Sexual Insult," pp. 19–30, 36–37; Ifeka-Moller, "Female Militancy," pp. 132–33; Van Allen, "'Aba Riots,'" pp. 61–62; Geiger, "Tanganyikan Nationalism," p. 473.

37. Néné Diallo, interview, 11 April 1991.

38. Fatou Keita, interview, 24 May 1991; also see Léon Maka, interview, 20 February 1991.

39. Fatou Diarra, interview, 17 March 1991. *Syli* is the Susu word for "elephant." It was the symbol of the RDA, and by extension, for Sékou Touré personally.

40. Aissatou N'Diaye, interview (interpreted and translated from Susu by Siba N. Grovogui), 8 April 1991.

41. Léon Maka and Mira Baldé (Mme. Maka), interview, 25 February 1991.

42. Kadiatou Meunier (pseudonym), interview, 18 January 1991.
43. Fatou Keita, interview, 7 April 1991.
44. 17G586, Guinée française, Services de police, "Renseignements *Objet:* Réunion publique R.D.A. à Conakry et ses suites," 8 September 1954, no. 2606/942, C/PS.2.
45. Ibid.; Fatou Diarra, interview, 17 March 1991.
46. 17G586, Guinée française, Services de police, "Renseignements a/s R.D.A. Conakry," 19 April 1955, no. 811/332, C/PS.2; 17G586, Guinée française, Services de police, "Renseignements *Objet:* RDA à Conakry," 27 April 1955, no. 867/353, C/PS.2; 17G586, Guinée française, Services de police, "Renseignements *Objet:* Incidents en Guinée," 3 June 1955, no. 1095/463, C/PS.2; 17G586, Guinée française, Services de police, "Renseignements *Objet:* R.D.A. à Conakry," 6 June 1955, no. 1106/469, C/PS.2. Also see 17G573, Guinée française, Services de police, "Renseignements a/s attroupement R.D.A. devant le commissariat de police de Mamou, le 15 Mai 1956," 19 May 1956, no. 929/324, C/PS.2; Archives nationales de Guinée,: 1E41, Guinée française, Services de police, "Renseignements a/s conference publique tenue le lundi 14 janvier 1957 à Conakry, salle du Cinema 'Vox,' par le P.D.G.-R.D.A.," 15 January 1957, no. 89/50/C/PS.2.
47. 17G586, Guinée française, Services de police, "Renseignements *Objet:* R.D.A. Conakry," 14 June 1955, no. 1158/490, C/PS.2; Morgenthau, *Political Parties,* p. 222, 240. These Susu songs were transcribed and translated into French by the police. The English translations are my own.
48. The discussion that follows relies heavily on the work of Idiatou Camara. (See "Contribution de la femme," pp. 52–65.) Camara conducted extensive interviews with female activists in the mid-1970s, the results of which appear in her undergraduate thesis. Geiger describes strikingly similar activities undertaken by female activists in Tanganyika. See Geiger, "Tanganyikan Nationalism," pp. 472, 473; Geiger, *TANU Women,* pp. 59, 160.
49. Aissatou N'Diaye, interview, 8 April 1991.
50. Mamayimbe Bangoura, quoted in Camara, "Contribution de la femme," p. 58.
51. Camara, "Contribution de la femme," pp. 52, 61–65. According to the Institut fondamental de l'Afrique noire (Dakar, Senegal), the Guinean branch of the RDA published three successive periodicals during the period under consideration: *Le phare de Guinée* (1947–49); *Coup de bambou* (1950); *La liberté* (1951–60).
52. Camara, "Contribution de la femme," pp. 61–65; Keita, *P.D.G.,* p. 326.
53. Camara, "Contribution de la femme," pp. 61–63, 65.
54. Fatou Keita, interview, 7 April 1991; Camara, "Contribution de la femme," pp. 63–64.
55. 17G586, Guinée française, Services de police, "Renseignements *Objet:* Militants RDA arrétès à la suite d'incidents," 18 March 1955, no. 605/250, C/PS.2.
56. Camara, "Contribution de la femme," pp. 63–64.
57. Camara, "Contribution de la femme," pp. 82–84, 128; Keita, *P.D.G.,* pp. 341, 345.
58. Morganthau, *Political Parties,* pp. 232–33, 240–42, 247, 251–52.
59. Fatou Keita, interview, 28 April 1991.
60. Camara, "Contribution de la femme," p. 83; Mamady Kaba, interview, 15 January 1991; Namankoumba Kouyaté, interview, 31 January 1991.

61. Camara, "Contribution de la femme," pp. 63, 83–85.
62. Aissatou N'Diaye, interview, 8 April 1991; Mamady Kaba, interview, 15 January 1991; Léon Maka, interview, 25 February 1991.
63. Camara, "Contribution de la femme," pp. 84–85.
64. Aissatou N'Diaye, interview, 8 April 1991; 17G586, Guinée française, Services de police, "Renseignements à propos de decisions judiciaires rendues à Conakry," 26 Mai 1955, no. 1057/440, C/PS.2.
65. Mira Baldé, interview, 19 May 1991.
66. Léon Maka, interview, 20 February 1991.
67. Tourou Sylla, interview (interpreted and translated from Maninka by Siba N. Grovogui), Mamou, 30 May 1991.
68. Fatou Diarra, interview, 17 March 1991; also see Bocar Biro Barry, interview, 29 January 1991; Mamadou Béla Doumbouya, interview, 26 January 1991; Fatou Keita, interview, 28 April 1991; Mira Baldé, interview, 25 February 1991.
69. Fatou Keita, interview, 7 April 1991.
70. Bocar Biro Barry, interview, 29 January 1991.
71. See Nima Bah, interview, 31 January 1991; Fatou Keita, interview, 7 April 1991; Aissatou N'Diaye, interview, 8 April 1991.
72. Fatou Diarra, interview, 17 March 1991; also see Aissatou N'Diaye, interview, 8 April 1991; Néné Diallo, interview, 11 April 1991; Bocar Biro Barry, interview, 29 January 1991; Namankoumba Kouyaté, interview, 31 January 1991; Léon Maka, interview, 20 February 1991; Mabalo Sakho, interview, 19 June 1991; 2G55/152, Guinée française, gouverneur, "Rapport politique pour l'année 1955," no. 281/APA, 81; Camara, "Contribution de la femme," p. 57.
73. Fatou Keita, interview, 7 April 1991.
74. Note the romantic nature of the songs women sang about Sékou Touré and *Syli*. Bocar Biro Barry, interview, 29 January 1991; Fatou Keita, interview, 7 April 1991; Camara, "Contribution de la femme," p. 59.
75. Bocar Biro Barry, interview, 29 January 1991.
76. Bocar Biro Barry, interview, 29 January 1991; also see Mamadou Béla Doumbouya, interview, 26 January 1991.
77. Independent and mobile female nationalists in Tanganyika and Kenya risked similar condemnation. See Geiger, *TANU Women,* pp. 45, 59–60; Presley, *Kikuyu Women,* pp. 158–59.
78. Fatou Diarra, interview, 17 March 1991; Morgenthau, *Political Parties,* p. 233.
79. 17G586, Guinée française, Services de police, "Renseignements a/s KOUYATE Kémoko," 27 September 1954, no. 2715/1000, C/PS.2.
80. Camara, "Contribution de la femme," p. 57.
81. Archives nationales de Guinée, 1E41, Guinée française, Services de police, "Renseignements a/s creation d'une association féminine," 20 November 1951, no. 2219/C/PS.2.
82. 17G565, Guinée française, gouverneur, Conakry, au haut commissaire, Dakar, 3 June 1950, no. 188, PS.
83. Néné Diallo, interview, 11 April 1991.
84. Aissatou N'Diaye, interview, 8 April 1991.
85. Aissatou N'Diaye, interview, 8 April 1991; Léon Maka, interview, 20 February 1991; Namankoumba Kouyaté, interview, 31 January 1991.
86. Fatou Keita, interviews, 7 April and 24 May 1991.

87. Fatou Keita, interview, 7 April 1991; 17G586, Guinée française, Services de police, "Renseignements," 8 September 1954.

88. Quoted in Claude Rivière, "La promotion de la femme guinéenne," *Cahiers d'études africaines* 8, no. 31 (1968): 408; also see Camara, "Contribution de la femme," pp. 56–57; Bocar Biro Barry, interview, 29 January 1991.

89. 17G586, Guinée française, Services de police, "Renseignements," 8 September 1954; also see Camara, "Contribution de la femme," pp. 56–57.

90. Bocar Biro Barry, interview, 29 January 1991; Kadiatou Meunier (pseudonym), interview, 18 January 1991.

91. Camara, "Contribution de la femme," p. 56.

92. Bocar Biro Barry, interview, 29 January 1991.

93. Bocar Biro Barry, interview, 29 January 1991; also see Camara, "Contribution de la femme," pp. 56–57.

94. Mira Baldé, interviews, 20 and 25 February 1991.

95. Camara, "Contribution de la femme," p. 59.

96. Tourou Sylla, interview, 30 May 1991. Also see Néné Diallo, interview, 11 April 1991.

97. Léon Maka, interview, 20 February 1991.

98. Aissatou N'Diaye, interview, 8 April 1991.

13 Guerrilla Girls and Women in the Zimbabwean National Liberation Struggle

Tanya Lyons

> They were swift and deadly and strong. They ran all night chanting the songs of freedom, fifty miles a night to kill in the morning, and when they ran they breathed together, so perfectly in step that the velvet black air of the veldt drummed with their running. Even the men of the freedom army were afraid of them and they knew it and it made them feel powerful.[1]

Sara Maitland's fictional narrative of women freedom fighters running to battle captures a heroic image of women fighting for national liberation in Africa. The roles and experiences of women in the Zimbabwean national liberation struggle, however, are not captured by this fictional representation. In this chapter, I explore the ways in which women's roles have been glorified in the discourse of war—a process which has silenced women's voices and experiences in the history of anti-colonial struggle in Zimbabwe.

In April 1980, Zimbabwe won its long struggle for independence against the oppression and exploitation of colonialism and the Rhodesian white settler regime.[2] The actions of women in Zimbabwe's anti-colonial liberation struggle were crucial for the success of the guerrilla war. Women in rural villages provided food, clothing, and shelter to the guerrillas, often risking their lives to do so.[3] Young women and men became *chimbwido*s and *mujiba*s (messengers and carriers), providing information on the whereabouts of Rhodesian soldiers to the guerrillas. By 1972, when the armed struggle against white minority rule was in full swing, women were being trained to fight; this was one of the most significant developments of the guerrilla war.

During the 1970s, Zimbabwean women guerrilla fighters were hailed internationally as women who rose above traditionally subordinate gender positions in order to fight equally with men in the struggle for national independence.[4] This era coincided with the United Nations Decade for Women (1976–85), which culminated in the mid-term World Conference on Women in Copenhagen in 1980. Spearheading research on the role of women in southern African liberation struggles, Richard Lapchick and Stephanie Urdang[5] drew attention at that time to the connections socialists were making between national liberation and women's emancipation.[6] For example, Guinea-Bissau's revolutionary leader, Amilcar Cabral, argued that a revolution would not be complete without a transformation in the social roles of both men and women, and that women had to fight for and earn equality with men.[7] Samora Machel, the late president of Mozambique, argued that "[t]he liberation of women is a fundamental necessity for the revolution, the guarantee of its continuity and the precondition for its victory."[8] Influenced by the socialist revolutionary successes in Mozambique and Guinea-Bissau, Robert Mugabe, the president of the Zimbabwe African National Union (ZANU), explained that his organization had "learned through the liberation struggle that success and power are possible when men and women are united as equals."[9]

Internationally, socialist feminists expected that women in southern Africa would be liberated as their nations gained independence. Because Zimbabwean women were more actively engaged in guerrilla fighting than their counterparts in Mozambique, Namibia, or Guinea-Bissau, their liberation seemed even more assured. But their active involvement did not ensure their automatic equality or access to the fruits of independence.[10] As a result, many scholars have focused their attention on understanding why equality was not gained after national independence,[11] rather than on what women experienced during the liberation war as guerrilla fighters.[12] I argue that that very experience of engagement in the struggle for liberation can provide important answers as to why African women did not automatically achieve equality with men after national independence.

The First *Chimurenga*

Throughout the colonial period, Zimbabwean women were actively involved in anti-colonial resistance. One woman in particular played a major role during the First *Chimurenga* (anti-colonial struggle) in 1896–97, when both the Matabele and Shona communities fought against colonization and white settlement initiated by the British South Africa Company.[13] Charwe, the female medium possessed by the spirit Nehanda, is celebrated in Zimbabwe today as the leader of the uprisings. Some claim she took up arms herself and was a military adviser to the people.[14] She was arrested for the killing of Native Commissioner Pollard[15] and was sentenced to be hanged. On the scaffolding she refused to submit and stated that her bones would rise again in the fight against colonialism. Eighty years later, during the Second Chimurenga, spirit mediums claiming to be possessed by Nehanda advised and inspired guerrilla fighters,[16] and Charwe's name was invoked by the nationalist parties to encourage young women to join the armed struggle.

The Second Chimurenga

Black consciousness and African nationalism in Zimbabwe began to develop in the 1930s, and were solidified in the late 1940s and 1950s with the Southern Rhodesian African National Congress and the City Youth League.[17] During this political stage of the struggle Zimbabwean women set the scene for their active involvement in anti-colonial agitation.[18] The nationalist movement was clearly male-dominated, and women's roles were seen as mainly supportive. Yet the National Democratic Party (NDP) was banned soon after it was formed in 1960, after thousands of women protested in Salisbury (now Harare), the capital, and over two thousand were arrested. Women in the NDP organized a demonstration against the approval of a new constitution which cemented white domination by allocating only fifteen out of sixty-five parliamentary seats to Africans. Sally Mugabe remembered,

> We didn't tell our husbands about our plans. Early one morning, we left our homes, and by 7 a.m. we were all assembled in the foyer of the Prime Minister's office in the city centre to protest in a peaceful manner, by means of placards, against the new Constitution. The placards read: "Women Do Not Accept This Backward Constitution," "Give Us Our Land and Country," and "One Man One Vote." Soon our numbers had increased to the extent of over 1,500 women. The police were in their hundreds with dogs.[19]

Thousands of women were arrested, beaten, and jailed. Sally Mugabe's husband, Robert Mugabe, then a leading nationalist and currently the president of Zimbabwe, argued that the women organized the large protests because the men "had failed to respond to the nationalist call for several strike actions." Indeed, some men actually hindered the women's actions:

> Men—husbands, I mean—came to prison and threatened their wives with divorce unless they agreed to the payment of fines, which the husbands had readily brought. They told them that unless that were the case they could find other wives in their place by the time they returned. Women had shown greater courage and resolve, indeed, far greater commitment, than the cowardly men.[20]

The *Zimbabwe Review*, the official organ of the Zimbabwe African People's Union (ZAPU), later cited these demonstrations as proof that women were determined "to play their role in freeing Zimbabwe."[21] Women in Salisbury organized follow-up protests as the arrested women faced charges in the courts. At midnight on 8 December 1961, Prime Minister Edgar Whitehead banned the NDP and all gatherings. David Martin and Phyllis Johnson have argued that he did so because the NDP refused to accept the new constitution.[22] But as Bhebe has pointed out, since the ban coincided with the women's protests, their actions were the catalyst which shifted the struggle to a more militant level. Yet the women's actions in 1961 have not been accorded much importance in narratives of Zimbabwean political history. Robert Mugabe simply praised the women as civic cheerleaders for the male-led nationalist movement:

> Public rallies were always a successful feature when our women attended them in large numbers, chanting slogans and nationalist songs, ululating and dancing. This gave the meetings the necessary and rousing effect which boosted morale and gave the impetus to go on with the struggle until final victory.[23]

The banning of the NDP did not, as white Rhodesians hoped, produce a moderate nationalist movement; rather, African nationalism grew more militant.[24] The Zimbabwe African People's Union (ZAPU) formed from the remains of the NDP, and in 1963 the Zimbabwe African National Union (ZANU) split off from ZAPU. In 1965, after Ian Smith's Rhodesian Front announced the Unilateral Declaration of Independence from Britain, these two major nationalist movements resorted to armed struggle, spearheading the Second Chimurenga from 1965 to 1980. ZAPU led the initial stage of armed struggle in the 1960s, building up its armed forces, the Zimbabwe People's Revolutionary Army (ZIPRA), in Zambia. From 1972, however, ZANU's armed wing, the Zimbabwe African National Liberation Army (ZANLA), dominated the struggle, although in 1975 ZIPRA and ZANLA united briefly to form the Zimbabwe People's Army, as attempts were made to change the course of the revolution.[25] ZANLA resurfaced as the dominant military wing in 1976, and remained so until the end of the war in 1980.

Many young Zimbabweans volunteered for or were recruited into ZIPRA and ZANLA and trained for guerrilla warfare outside Rhodesia, mainly in Zambia and Mozambique. Many young men and women were sent back across the border to Rhodesia to fight and to educate and politicize the rural peasants on the need for revolution and armed struggle. These "freedom fighters" aimed to liberate Zimbabweans from the shackles of colonization.

When the armed struggle began, young women were provided with new opportunities to negotiate their traditional gender roles,[26] while young male guerrillas began to realize the need for women's support and challenged the authority of elders by giving women new and different opportunities. David Maxwell has argued that "some young girls seized the opportunity of the war to escape the drudgery of domestic chores and replace them with the attentions of 'heroic' young men with guns."[27] But how did women perceive these new opportunities? Did they see them as a means of escaping traditional gender roles?

Many of the women ex-combatants I interviewed for this research in Zimbabwe, sixteen years after liberation was won, were reluctant to talk about their experiences during the war.[28] Some had not previously discussed their experiences, even with their husbands or children. As one woman said, "I have never talked to anybody about this. [It] is very difficult for me to relate because [the war] was very difficult."[29] When they returned to Zimbabwe after fighting the war, many were called prostitutes or murderers by their communities, families, and in-laws. Remaining silent about their actions was easier than confronting such labels and countering the abuse. For many, the experiences of war were just too terrible and they wanted simply to forget. Nonetheless, some of the women ex-combatants agreed to speak about their experiences as part of their broader efforts to win public recognition of their roles in the war, in order to gain access to rehabilitation schemes and funding; that is, to gain the fruits of independence that even now they have not seen.[30]

Although recruits were being trained as early as 1963 for guerrilla warfare, and some women were being sent from Rhodesia to be educated in other countries, it was not until 1972 that the first women were recruited into the liberation armies as part of an essentially guerrilla strategy. Women's access to ZIPRA and ZANLA varied, and their reasons for joining differed. Women who volunteered to join the armed struggle did not stop to think about the gendered implications of doing so, but joined as Zimbabweans in order to free the country from oppression. Sekai became a security officer within ZANLA. She recalled, "I decided to join the struggle because I wanted to liberate Zimbabwe."[31] Rudo began her involvement in the armed struggle as a chimbwido in the rural areas of Rhodesia. She remembered,

> I used to bring information from very far distances [to the comrades]. Later on . . . I went to training. [When] I was finished my training I was pregnant. . . . Military training is not only jumping and the like. You have some lessons . . . it makes you stronger. Sometimes you happen to discover yourself. You discover what you are, and what you are really made of.[32]

(Pregnancies like Rudo's were not uncommon and caused problems for the military command, as I will discuss below.) After completing three years of school, sixteen-year-old Nhamo joined the nationalist forces in 1974. One of her girlfriends from the Mount Darwin area had heard that some people were being educated by the nationalist forces in their camps overseas and across the borders in Zambia and Mozambique. She suggested to Nhamo that they should both go to join the nationalist freedom fighters to receive this education. At first they went to Botswana, where they were recruited to go to Zambia, and later they stayed in ZAPU's Nampundu Camp.[33]

At first, women who joined up were mainly used to carry supplies and weapons to the front. For example, Maria remembered that

> [o]ne of the important roles that was played by female combatants was in the transportation of ammunition between Mozambique and Zimbabwe. Because in our culture here, women carry loads on the head, on the shoulders, even on the back. Whereas the men here culturally would only use their hands to carry.[34]

Carrying ammunition was dangerous but necessary, and women often faced ambushes and attacks from Rhodesian soldiers. In 1973, more women began to demand training in order to protect themselves. Nhamo, for example, recalled that

> [o]ur job was mainly to carry weapons to the border. . . . In 1975–76 I became a teacher, and in early 1976 I was sent to Mozambique . . . to . . . [a] camp near the border. There were less than fifty women there and only a few men, mainly com-

manders. It was dangerous to be so close to the border, as there was always the threat of attack.

In 1976, Nhamo was given three months' training in guerrilla tactics at Tembwe Camp in Mozambique.[35]

While some young women joined the armed struggle voluntarily, other girls and boys were press-ganged or abducted from their schools and forced to join the fighters. In January 1977, ZIPRA guerrillas took children at gunpoint from Manama Mission School in Matabeleland South, near Botswana's border. Taurai remembered how the Rhodesians had sent the children's parents to Botswana to collect them, but

> only a few Form One students turned back. . . . The rest of the school, which was more than five hundred students, had been convinced that by joining the liberation struggle, you'd be freeing yourself of a lot of conflict and a lot of colonialism within the country. . . . After our parents had gone back to Rhodesia, we then went to Zambia.[36]

After finishing two years of school in 1973, Teurai Ropa (Joyce Nhongo)[37] joined the freedom fighters, first in Zambia and later in Mozambique. After she had joined she was rapidly promoted:

> I was just lucky to be one of the few who were chosen as leaders at that time. I was one of the few women who got trained to either do the commissariat work, the political training, or the military training. . . . When selections for women representatives to the Central Committee or Politburo were being carried out, I was the only one to be chosen to be the Politburo member. And when Mrs. [Sally] Mugabe came to join us, she then became the second one.[38]

During and after the war Teurai Ropa was portrayed as a heroine of the liberation war, particularly in ZANU's propaganda. She was the symbol of the heroic African woman warrior, with baby in one hand and gun in the other. Teurai Ropa's training camp was attacked while she was heavily pregnant. She gave birth soon after and her child was sent to Zambia for protection while she stayed in Mozambique to continue the struggle.[39] The war was not confined inside Rhodesia's borders.

When the Rhodesian forces attacked ZANU's Nyadzonia Camp in Mozambique in 1976, there were heavy casualties. Monica's experience highlights the special brutality of war for refugees and untrained recruits:

> I had not seen a gun; I had not seen anything. All I had come to was to join the struggle. . . . As we were sitting on the ground . . . cars came, and everybody else who was there were going to the cars, especially those who had been there for a longer time than us, because to them cars signified training . . . and I sat there with my other three colleagues, because, we thought, we have just arrived and our chances of going to get training had maybe not come. . . . I asked, "How did the Rhodesians get through to the camp in the cars?" I don't know how . . . and the next thing we are sitting there, and well *pah pah pah!* [gestures to indicate guns going off][40]

The Rhodesian soldiers used Mozambican uniforms, cars, and weapons to infiltrate the camps, and some white soldiers had painted their faces black: "[A]fter gathering together part of the camp population and shouting slogans they opened fire indiscriminately with light weapons but also anti-tank and anti-aircraft guns."[41] Monica explained that thousands of refugees, mainly women and children, were killed during the attack:

> I went running because I had not been trained, then I had no tactics I knew, I [had] no practice with a gun shooting. And the shock of it and everything. . . . As you are running you would actually feel the bullets "whoosh," and you'd see the other guy in front of you falling, you'd see the whole head coming off, and actually when that was happening. I'll tell you these people were refugees, people who didn't know anything about the war. You know, some of them would even stop the bullets with their hands, because they just thought "what is this?" You hear this zoom!

Monica was eventually trained for guerrilla warfare, but was not sent to the front inside Rhodesia. "I was appointed," she recalled, "to [guard a camp], as much as I wanted to go to the front, since I had come to fight the enemy, they always wanted people who would look after the camps. We were given our rifles, to go and guard the women in this camp, Osibisa. All our camps had guards."[42]

Women who had joined the war to liberate Zimbabwe, the same women who were being attacked in their training camps across the border, were described by the nationalist movement as both liberated and fighting for equality with men. In 1978 Teurai Ropa, then heading ZANU's Department of Women's Affairs, asserted, "Gone are the days when all women did was to sew, knit, cook, commiserate with and mourn for their fallen soldiers. Now they too participate in the fighting, they too face the music."[43] In 1979 she repeated these sentiments: "Today's women are not only mere bedroom women to produce children as the concept used to be, they are in the vanguard liberation struggle in Zimbabwe. This oppressive and exploitative system has affected women to the same degree as it has affected men."[44]

In 1978 ZANU suggested that women in ZANLA were being deployed to the front, especially as "the political commissars, medics, logistics, security, intelligence, teaching etc. It was at this time that women detachments were put in the Manica Province and Tete [in Mozambique] for actual combat duties led by their women commanders and proved to be successful in their operations."[45] For example, Teurai Ropa said at the time that "women were going into combat at the front in large numbers. The climax was the shelling of Umtali under women commanders in 1978."[46] Here she said that women military leaders were among the 450 ZANLA guerrillas who crossed the border of Mozambique and attacked Umtali (Mutare). However, she later claimed that it was not women but men who attacked Umtali in 1978, saying that there were only a few women actually at the front; they were mainly found in the liberated zones inside Zimbabwe. She explained that it was expedient to promote the image of women fighting at the front to solidarity groups in the West, rather than try to explain the importance of women's roles in supporting men's actions.[47] In 1996 the Zimbabwe National Liberation War Veterans Association (ZNLWVA) asserted that women were mainly used to carry weapons and supplies to the front; women's units were not deployed specifically to front-line attacks.[48] Despite the experiences of Teurai Ropa and the claims she made during the war, the ZNLWVA argued that most women filled traditionally defined gender roles within the guerrilla training camps.

Yet clearly some women did fight in combat. For example, Freedom Nyamubaya remained in Rhodesia after crossing the border from Mozambique.[49] There she commanded operations and carried out various ambushes and surprise attacks between 1977 and 1979. Another woman combatant, Rudo Hondo, was promoted to ZANLA's general staff in 1977 and was given the command of female guerrillas in Manica Province. Hondo was "one of the very first women officers in the battlefield. But being a female commander did not confine her duties to those of her gender—many battles were fought with men including under her command and victories achieved."[50] In February 1978, Hondo and the thirty fighters she commanded in the Jiri area were attacked by helicopters, paratroopers, and infantry. The Rhodesians had heard of her "unique military prowess,"[51] and after a fierce battle they managed to capture her. Refusing to tell them anything and misleading them about her identity, Hondo eventually managed to escape just before the 1980 elections and independence. Apart from these examples, however, most of the women I have interviewed were not in front-line combat, and those who were were not willing to talk about it. These ex-combatants did not want to be remembered as either "murderers or victims,"[52] nor did they want to admit that their actions may not have been quite so "heroic" as they were portrayed.[53]

Differences

Within the discourse of Zimbabwe's liberation war, "the stories of most of [the women] . . . have blended together over time, to constitute a group of anonymous ones."[54] Not only are women's experiences blurred, so too is the fact that they were involved in two separate parties, ZAPU and ZANU. Because the history of women's involvement in the liberation war has been mainly based on ZANU women's experiences, ZAPU women's experiences, which differed significantly from ZANU women's, have been obscured.

ZAPU insisted on placing women and men in separate training camps. At Victory and Mkushi Camps in Zambia, women were trained in military tactics and taught skills to prepare them for the new Zimbabwe. Ruth stated that ZIPRA treated its women differently than ZANLA, by sending fewer across the border into Rhodesia to fight or to be subjected to attacks on the front lines:

> In Zambia . . . it was very very rare for women to come in and operate. . . .
> [Women] were mainly used for spreading [political ideology] . . . as commissariats as well as instructors for military training. They were very good. [The

commanders] mainly did not want to send women combatants to the front to come and fight. They usually sent men. That is why in Zambia the females were more protected. They were more advantaged than the females in Mozambique.[55]

However, when Mkushi Camp was attacked by Rhodesian forces in 1978 because it was training women guerrilla fighters, the myth of protection was shattered and the nationalists received a severe blow. ZAPU claimed that the women killed in Mkushi had been unarmed refugees, but some who survived the attack stated that they were trained in military tactics. ZIPRA, specifically, was training at least one thousand women for active urban guerrilla warfare, but the war ended before they were deployed.[56] Tsitsi spoke of her experience in Mkushi Camp in Zambia as dominated by military training:

> In Mkushi life was not all that different [for men and women], because we were
> the first group of women to train there. So we had more advantages than men. In
> our camp there were a few men. These were instructors and old men who used to
> cook food for us. We trained heavily . . . we were very much anxious to do so.[57]

While ZAPU ex-combatants discussed how well they were trained for urban guerrilla warfare, Jane Ngwenya, ZAPU's National Secretary for Women's Affairs, had argued in 1979 that women were fighting differently than men in ZAPU:

> So we are fighting side by side with our men; we are not left behind. While
> our men are holding guns and deployed outside to fight, women are fighting in
> another wing of the struggle, because they try to help themselves through self-help
> schemes. They have trained themselves, they are prepared for a new Zimbabwe.

During the late 1970s, Ngwenya encouraged women to participate in more traditional female roles, especially looking after the children: "We have got a lot of programs for them—knitting, sewing and some of them are political commissars who continue to educate themselves about the political situation at home. Those women are doing fantastic work."[58] Ngwenya's emphasis on the domestic capabilities of women, rather than on their combat abilities, situates ZAPU women within the traditional female roles of women in war—as cheerleaders and maids of all work, rather than revolutionaries or active nationalists. Compared to ZAPU in Ngwenya's account, ZANU was not averse to promoting the idea that its women were actively involved in military actions. Yet Teurai Ropa's recent claims that women were not as involved in combat as previously portrayed suggests that ZANU women also did not fight like men, and that it is no longer expedient to argue that they did.

Equality

The question of equality between women and men in the training camps becomes problematic when we consider the differences between women's treatment and deployment in ZAPU and ZANU. Sally Mugabe argued that women's roles in the liberation war were "not that of a weak feminine force of cooks, nurses, mothers, and entertainers; they had been equals with the men in every role and phase of the liberation war."[59] ZANU's propaganda, which promoted women's participation in the struggle, trumpeted claims of equal treatment in the training camps. Robert Mugabe, for example, stated that women fighters

> have demonstrated beyond all doubt that they are as capable as men and deserve equal treatment, both in regard to training and appointments. It is because of their proven performance that we have agreed to constitute a Women's Detachment with its own commander who should become a member of the High Command. It is also necessary . . . that . . . we should promote more women to the High Command. . . . Although in the High Command there is only one woman. . . . In the General Staff, there are scores of women officers, while in the Army generally several thousands of women cadres gallantly serve in one role or another.[60]

ZANU ex-combatant Maria said, "I think we were just like men!"[61] and Sekai stated that, while women carried more than men to the front, they all suffered equally in the camps. When there was not enough food to go around, it was divided equally among the recruits.[62] Yet there was not always equality between the sexes in the training camps. One woman ex-combatant remembered that there was equal treatment in some areas, but not in others:

> Women were given equal treatment even when . . . going through military training we were just being mixed up with the men and if we show that military commander we can command and everybody will be saluting you and everything. . . . But [what] was disappointing was that they would try to fall in love with [you] or to make you love the guys [that is, try to have sex with you] and . . . when you're in the hardships promising you that you can have soap you can have . . . luxury . . . even sugar . . . where you could go for four days without food . . . so they started kind of buying out women.[63]

These references to exchanges of sex for soap reveal that the extent of equality between the sexes varied from person to person and from camp to camp. Some women clearly experienced more equality than others.[64]

The Problem with Women

While the veneer of women's equality was being polished to make ZANU's international image shine, many young people began to enjoy their freedoms from older cultural strictures or constraints. By 1976, thousands[65] of young women had joined up with ZAPU and ZANU. The traditionally male-led nationalist movement now had to incorporate increasing numbers of women who had military training, and many more women who wanted training in order to fight the Rhodesians. However, the inclusion of women in the training camps resulted in disruptions of traditional gender roles, and a "woman problem" emerged, especially within ZANU. In the late 1970s, relations between men and women became a moral, political, and military problem for the ZANU

High Command in Mozambique. In July 1978, at Pfutskeke Base in Mozambique, the ZANU Defence Secretariat held a rally at which its members discussed the "problems of women." According to Teurai Ropa, the main problem was that young women were misbehaving, which was "bad for the revolution." She asked,

> What kind of families were you brought up in? Were you ever taught discipline? . . .
> I don't indulge in other people's love affairs. That is out with me. . . . At this stage
> the revolution demands our transformation.[66]

Teurai Ropa was frustrated by the lack of discipline shown by women in training. Clearly, sexual relationships were developing which were affecting military and guerrilla training and deployment, as well as complicating the maintenance of customary marriage practices already threatened by the prospect of socialist revolution.

Marriage

Women who were having sexual relationships with men, especially those using contraceptives, were labeled prostitutes. In July 1979 the ZANU Commissariat Department produced a report, "On Marriage," which argued that marriage was essential to prevent prostitution and the use of contraceptives:

On Marriage
It is consistent with our customs and it is a natural process that a man or woman who has become of age should marry, if he or she so wishes. To refuse suitable partners from marrying can have disastrous consequences, inter alia,:-
a) The rate of prostitution will escalate. Men will spoil women with the knowledge and understanding that they will not have any responsibility to bear down on them.
b) women will practice birth control to avoid having "fatherless" children. When they have done this, they will engage themselves, freely, into prostituting.
c) The cultural value of marriage will disappear, etc.
Viewed from this angle, marrying is a convenient and unavoidable process. The question of marriage becomes a complicated issue in the course of our struggle. More often the meaning and essence of marriage is abused and the responsibilities accruing the marriage come into conflict with the commitment each individual has, to our revolutionary struggle. Some of the reasons why marriages are a failure in our struggle are,:-

1) By coming to the revolution, a majority of our youths feel freed from parental restrictions and see the revolution as something that justifies their ego for youthful mischief.
2) The presence or grouping of many girls induces infatuation which is oftenly misinterpreted as love. This brings about 'short term' love affairs and results in the changing of boyfriends or girlfriends regularly.
3) Lack of strong action to end prostitution.

4) Youths engage into prostitution whilst they are still very young and fail to be rebuked strongly by adult comrades or their responsible authorities.

REMEDY:-
Probably a remedy lies in the four headings stated below:-
a) Outline procedure to be followed before getting into marriage.
b) Draft regulation governing marriages.
c) Impose penalties for breach of these regulations.
d) Intensify orientation on our culture with emphasis on marriage and "internal discipline."

Pamberi Na President Mugabe!
Pamberi Ne Z.A.N.U.
signed _____
MEYA URIMBO (Chief Political Commissar)[67]

The party's emphasis on marriage reveals certain contradictions in the role and position of women in ZANU's camps. The Department of Women's Affairs was formed to deal with the increasing problems with women in the camps, and since women were blamed for men's bad behavior, the policies made regarding marriage were largely ineffective.

Lobola

Lobola (bridewealth) was central to questions of marriage, and challenges to both lobola and marriage have heralded transformations in many southern African societies. Some leaders of ZANU's High Command and of the Department of Women's Affairs espoused the abolition of lobola in order to promote the liberation of women. Naomi Nhiwatiwa explained at a conference in Los Angeles in 1979 how ZANU had

> eliminated one of the major sources of women's oppression in our tradition, the concept of dowry [lobola], which actually entitled a man to own his wife. . . . [I]n the liberated areas [ZANU] arranges the marrying of people, so people get married in the party. People are getting married, and they are not getting married with the dowry system.[68]

The rhetoric, however, did not reflect much commitment. ZANU kept records of marriages so that lobola could be claimed by parents after the war.[69] Julia Zvobgo explained that ZANU did not challenge African customs, because they could not afford to lose the support of the traditional chiefs and of parents in the countryside, who were crucial to the success of the guerrilla war.[70] For example, Teurai Ropa, who, because she was appointed to the High Command, was often described as one of the most liberated women in ZANU, had lobola paid for her. She said,

> When I met my husband he was already a commander in ZANLA. . . . We were married in the party. Yes, he paid full lobola when we came back to Zimbabwe,

and we had two daughters already. Then we had a Chapter 37 [Constitutional] marriage.[71]

Despite Nhiwatiwa's confident declaration, the persistence of lobola during and after the liberation war reflected the nationalist movement's unwillingness to radically change the social and economic position of women.[72]

Contraceptives

The use of contraceptives reveals much about contests over change for women in the liberation armies. Leading ZANU women, such as Sally Mugabe and Naomi Nhiwatiwa, agreed that contraception was not promoted as an option for women within the party.[73] It was assumed that women using the contraceptive pill (the form of contraception focused on) would become prostitutes. Instead, women were encouraged to be the mothers of the next generation of soldiers.[74] Yet even such motherhood presented a problem. Women's access to contraception varied, and many women, like Rudo, became pregnant while they were in training.[75] Within ZANU, pregnant women were sent to the women and children's camp, Osibisa, in Mozambique. Many women did not want to be sent there because once arrived they would no longer train as guerrilla fighters or be sent back to Zimbabwe to fight. Teurai Ropa confirmed that many women became frustrated, and she "tried to organise some projects such as knitting, sewing, cookery, animal husbandry and gardening."[76] However, the war and the movements of people made this difficult. The party thus saw women's sexual behavior as a problem because it reduced the number of able fighters. At a party meeting Comrade Catherine argued that

> [w]e have plenty of officers, two months pregnant who were removed from their departments to this base Ossibissa to wait for the day of their delivery. I think that as these comrades are still fit to carry on with their duties . . . they should be sent back for a month or two before they deliver . . . plus some women at Ossibissa have very big children ranging to two years, can't the mothers be returned to their departments to take up duties so that we abandon a lot of corruption in the way of gossipping?[77]

Men's sexuality, however, was never seen as problematic; nor were men implicated in ZANU's "problem with women," although Comrade Rumbidzai pointed out to a ZANU meeting that "male comrades [also need] to have similar lessons [on discipline] because they are mainly responsible for the corruption."[78] In 1996, it was further argued that many of the women ex-combatants labeled prostitutes had actually been raped by senior male combatants.[79] The problems associated with women's alleged behavior and the questions of marriage, lobola, and contraception, however, had no place in a narrative foregrounding women's equal roles in the liberation war. Women fighters were glorified in nationalist rhetoric, while the fundamental problems associated with the inclusion of women in a guerrilla or military force remained obscured.

How Many Women?

The most obvious glorification of women's roles is revealed when we question the numbers of women involved as guerrilla fighters and the actions they performed. In 1985, the Ministry of Community Development and Women's Affairs estimated that 250,000 women had been "actively involved in the liberation struggle."[80] However, Norma Kriger has identified "a misleading picture of the extent to which women participated as fighters in the guerrilla army." She suggests that at various times during the war, ZANU spokespeople like Sally Mugabe and Naomi Nhiwatiwa created this picture, apparently "by conflating women who were full-time fighters with those who did some military training in the camps, but were primarily engaged in agricultural work, education, or other tasks."[81]

In 1979, Naomi Nhiwatiwa stated that ZANLA's forces were one-third women.[82] Sally Mugabe also suggested that about twenty thousand women inside the country and two thousand outside it were fighting.[83] However, others have "put the number of trained female fighters in Zimbabwe at between 1,500 to 2000."[84] This significant drop in numbers occurs when we distinguish between women combatants and those performing supportive tasks in the training camps. Unfortunately, as Teurai Ropa acknowledged, no records were salvaged from the war:

> During that time there were many raids. Even though records were kept but time and time again they kept on being stolen by the regime, or burnt out. So, to tell you the truth we are just going by statistics [we are guessing]. . . . As early as 1974–1975 the numbers were small. Say one thousand, I wouldn't dispute. Towards 1978–1979, the numbers were tremendous, 20,000–36,000. The camps were crowded with children and [adults]. This was not all women. It was inclusive. There were actually more men than women. And towards the end we had more school pupils, although they were not more than [adults] who were to be assigned for fighting in the front.[85]

Serious difficulties arise when we use these problematic statistics to calculate the extent of women's participation, particularly in relation to claims for compensation by women ex-combatants. For example, the ZNLWVA considers that women make up only 20 percent of war veterans.[86] This figure excludes many women involved in the struggle as teachers, nurses, mothers, and chimbwidos, and those women who, nonliterate or isolated in rural communities, are unable to register as war veterans. Because there are no statistics on how many women combatants were demobilized after 1980, it is virtually impossible to get an accurate count of women ex-combatants.[87]

Beginning with the First Chimurenga, in 1896–97, Zimbabwean women were involved in anti-colonial action until political independence in 1980. As African nationalism increased, women's roles were seen as supportive of a male-dominated movement. However, in 1961, the National Democratic Party needed women to protest against a proposed new Rhodesian constitution. Although women's actions and desires for change were thwarted by their husbands, who bailed them out of jail, their actions led to significant shifts in the structure of the nationalist parties and eventually spearheaded armed revolutionary struggle.

When the armed struggle began in 1965, young male guerrillas realized that women's support was necessary for their survival in the rural areas, and young women saw an opportunity to escape their customary gender roles. Although it took nearly a decade of guerrilla training and warfare, male nationalists eventually realized the importance of incorporating women into the armed struggle. Most women were initially recruited to carry weapons and material to the front, but were eventually trained as guerrilla fighters when it became obvious they were vulnerable to attacks while in their training camps and while crossing the borders.

A focus on ZANU in the discourse of Zimbabwe's liberation has masked the differences between women in the different parties. Claims of equal treatment between the sexes in the training camps are contradicted by some women ex-combatants. Stories of rape and of "sex for soap" have been effectively obscured in Zimbabwe's narrative of national liberation. Promises of equality rang hollow in the face of failed attempts to challenge traditional practices and attitudes to marriage, lobola, and contraception, and simultaneously demonstrated a lack of real commitment to women's liberation and the difficulties inherent in projects of social transformation.

In order to promote and encourage women's roles in the struggle, leading ZANU women inflated the number of women involved in the war as actual guerrilla fighters, and in so doing further glorified "women in the struggle." This glorification, in turn, has obscured a more fundamental "problem with women" in the liberation struggle. What ZANU saw as a "problem with women" in its guerrilla training camps was the difficulties posed by "women's problems," such as pregnancy and prostitution. I have argued that, by associating the problems with women, the nationalist party ignored men's roles in them.[88] This chapter began with a heroic image of fighting women and argued that women in Zimbabwe's liberation struggle are still glorified as African women warriors. Yet this glorified image does not reflect the pain and suffering women endured while fighting in anti-colonial struggles. Sara Maitland's story encapsulates women's experiences of war:

Neme had been with the Women's Corps when they had run all night to the small village where the Children's Camp was and there she had seen three hundred and eighty-two babies of the revolution being shelled to death, there she had seen seven and eight-year-old children arm themselves with kitchen knives against the coming assault. . . . the enemy poured over the river and burned and stabbed and raped and looted. . . . Nonetheless victory finally came. . . . Through villages of song and isolated farmsteads of flowers the Women's Corps had run, cheering and laughing. Neither pregnancy or syphilis had deterred Neme from running with them.[89]

Guerrilla girls and women were integrated into the Zimbabwean national liberation struggle and their roles were important to its outcome. However, women did not fight equally with men, as was often claimed in nationalist propaganda. Women fought differently than men, in ways that were no less important, and their efforts need to be recognized. As Rudo asked,

> How could I have been called a "terrorist" [during the war] and today I can't be called a hero with my fellow comrades? If ever one crossed the border, going to join the struggle, and that person managed to fight during the war, or died during the war, or they survived, that person is a hero, because it's "mission accomplished"! The pride we have is hidden. You know, the way we are living, you can't be proud. You don't want to be identified, because we are living in poverty.[90]

NOTES

1. Sara Maitland, "Justice and Mercy," in *Women Fly When Men Aren't Watching: Short Stories* (London: Virago, 1993), p. 143.
2. When Zimbabwe was colonized in 1893 it was named Rhodesia after Cecil Rhodes, who had discovered it with the British South Africa Company. In 1898, after the First *Chimurenga* (anti-colonial struggle), it was divided into Southern and Northern Rhodesia. In 1964 political independence was granted to Northern Rhodesia, which became Zambia. Southern Rhodesia then became known as Rhodesia. After the Second Chimurenga, in 1979, an internal political agreement settled on the name Zimbabwe/Rhodesia, but in 1980 the name Rhodesia was dropped after national independence. Zimbabwe literally means "House of Stone."
3. Sita Ranchod-Nilsson, "This Too Is a Way of Fighting: Rural Women's Participation in Zimbabwe's Liberation War," in *Women and Revolution in Africa, Asia, and the New World,* ed. Mary Ann Tétreault (Columbia: University of South Carolina Press, 1994), pp. 62–88.
4. See, for example, Miranda Davies, ed., *Third World, Second Sex: Women's Struggles and National Liberation: Third World Women Speak Out* (London: Zed, 1983); Alexis DeVeaux, "Zimbabwe Woman Fire!" *Essence,* July 1981, p. 111; Jan Jindy Pettman, *Worlding Women: A Feminist International Politics* (Sydney: Allen and Unwin, 1996).
5. Richard E. Lapchick and Stephanie Urdang, *Oppression and Resistance: The Struggle of Women in Southern Africa,* based on materials prepared for the World Conference of the United Nations Decade for Women, Copenhagen, 1980 (Westport, Conn.: Greenwood, 1982).
6. However, in 1995, fifteen years after independence, Ngwabi Bhebe and Terence Ranger argued that there had been no "satisfactory gendered accounts of the war and its aftermath." Ngwabi Bhebe and Terence Ranger,

eds., *Soldiers in Zimbabwe's Liberation War,* 2 vols. (Harare: University of Zimbabwe Publications, 1995), vol. 1, p. 5.

7.   Stephanie Urdang, *Fighting Two Colonialisms: Women in Guinea-Bissau* (New York and London: Monthly Review, 1979), p. 17. In Guinea-Bissau Amilcar Cabral promoted women's equality with men in the struggle for national liberation from Portuguese colonization, yet he believed that it was not necessary to train women specifically for guerrilla warfare because there were enough men. Women's involvement was therefore to be based on traditional gender roles, supporting men as nurses, teachers, and cooks. Amilcar Cabral, *Revolution in Guinea: Selected Texts,* trans. and ed. Richard Handyside (New York: Monthly Review, 1970); Amilcar Cabral, *Return to the Source: Selected Speeches,* ed. Africa Information Service (New York: Monthly Review, 1974).

8.   Samora Machel, *Mozambique: Sowing the Seeds of Revolution* (Harare: Zimbabwe Publishing House, 1981), p. 20; Stephanie Urdang, *And Still They Dance: Women, War, and the Struggle for Change in Mozambique* (London: Earthscan, 1989).

9.   Robert Mugabe, "Message to the World Conference of the United Nations Decade for Women," delivered by Sally Mugabe, Copenhagen, July 1980, cited in Lapchick and Urdang, *Oppression and Resistance,* p. 108.

10.   Lapchick and Urdang, *Oppression and Resistance,* have argued that Zimbabwean women's actions were "responsible for the increased acceptance of women as equals in all areas by Zimbabwean men." However, they assumed that any gains made for women in the early independence excitement would persist, and this was not the case. For example, while a Ministry of Women's Affairs was established in 1980, it had been subsumed into various other ministries and portfolios by the early 1990s.

11.   Kathy Bond-Stewart, *Independence Is Not Only for One Sex* (Harare: Zimbabwe Publishing House, 1987); Elinor Batezat et al., "Women and Independence: The Heritage and the Struggle," in *Zimbabwe's Prospects: Issues of Race, Class, State, and Capital in Southern Africa,* ed. Colin Stoneman (London: Macmillan, 1988), pp. 153–73.

12.   Both Stephanie Urdang's study of Mozambique and Cleaver and Wallace's study of women in Namibia focus on the effects of war on women in general, and on how women cope during crisis. Both studies admit that relatively few women became active guerrilla fighters, hence their research has focused not on women guerrilla fighters but on women in general. See Urdang, *And Still They Dance;* Tessa Cleaver and Marion Wallace, *Namibia Women in War* (London: Zed, 1990).

13.   For the roles and experiences of women during this period, see Elizabeth Schmidt, *Peasants, Traders, and Wives: Shona Women in the History of Zimbabwe, 1870–1939* (Harare: Baobab; London: James Currey, 1992), pp. 36–42.

14.   Lapchick and Urdang, *Oppression and Resistance,* p. 103: Christine Sylvester, "African and Western Feminisms: World-Traveling the Tendencies and Possibilities," *Signs: Journal of Women in Culture and Society* 20, no. 4 (1995), p. 943.

15.   Terence Ranger, *Revolt in Southern Rhodesia, 1896–7* (London: Heinemann, 1967), p. 209.

16.   See David Lan, *Guns and Rain: Guerrillas and Spirit Mediums in Zimbabwe* (London: James Currey, 1985).

17.   See Brian Raftopoulos and Ian Phimister, eds., *Keep On Knocking: A History of the Labour Movement in Zimbabwe, 1900–1997*, Zimbabwe Congress of Trade Unions (Harare: Baobab, 1997).

18.   Lapchick and Urdang provide a brief overview of women's involvement during the 1940s and 1950s in *Oppression and Resistance*. They cite women's support of the 1948 general strike as the key to its success, and argue that women's commitment to the struggle was demonstrated when some women were arrested alongside men in 1959 when the Southern Rhodesian African National Congress was banned. Substantial research on women's involvement in the early nationalist stage has yet to be done, hence I can only generalize here. For an overview of women's involvement in Zimbabwean history, see Ruth Weiss, *The Women of Zimbabwe* (Harare: Nehanda, 1986), and Raftopoulos and Phimister, *Keep On Knocking.*

19.   Sally Mugabe, quoted in Sarah Kachingwe et al., eds., *Sally Mugabe: A Woman with a Mission* (Harare: Department of Information and Publicity, ZANU PF, 1994), p. 17.

20.   Robert Gabriel Mugabe, "First Zimbabwe Women's Seminar," in *Our War of Liberation: Speeches, Articles, Interviews, 1976–1979* (Gweru: Mambo, 1983), pp. 75–76.

21.   *The Zimbabwe Review*, 20 October 1973, p. 6.

22.   David Martin and Phyllis Johnson, *The Struggle for Zimbabwe: The Chimurenga War* (London: Faber and Faber, 1981), p. 68.

23.   Mugabe, "First Zimbabwe Women's Seminar," p. 75.

24.   Ngwabi Bhebe, "The Nationalist Struggle, 1957–1962," in *Turmoil and Tenacity: Zimbabwe, 1896–1990*, ed. Canaan S. Banana (Harare: College Press, 1989), p. 102.

25.   David Moore, "The Zimbabwe People's Army: Strategic Innovation or More of the Same?" in *Soldiers in Zimbabwe's Liberation War*, ed. Bhebe and Ranger, vol. 1, pp. 73–86.

26.   Terence Ranger, *Peasant Consciousness and Guerrilla War in Zimbabwe: A Comparative Study* (London: James Currey, 1985), pp. 206–207.

27.   David Maxwell, "Local Politics and the War of Liberation in North-East Zimbabwe," *Journal of Southern African Studies* 19, no. 3 (1993): 375; Mike Kesby, "Arenas for Control, Terrains of Gender Contestation: Guerrilla Struggle and Counter-insurgency Warfare in Zimbabwe, 1972–1980," *Journal of Southern African Studies* 22, no. 4 (1996): 561–84.

28.   In 1996, I interviewed women ex-combatants through the Zimbabwe National Liberation War Veterans Association. The interviews were conducted in English. Most of the women preferred to remain anonymous, fearing that their compensation payments might be stopped if they criticized the ruling party or the history of the war. I have therefore given them pseudonyms in this chapter. I asked them why they joined the struggle and what their experiences were as women. They did not feel comfortable talking about wartime political situations and hence shed very little light on the wider significance of women's involvement.

29.   Monica, interview, Harare, August 1996.

30.   In 1998 over fifty thousand ex-combatants in Zimbabwe were awarded

Z$50,000 plus Z$2000 a month as war veterans' compensation. It is unknown exactly how many women benefited from this scheme.

31. Sekai, interview, Harare, September 1996.

32. Rudo, interview, Harare, September 1996.

33. Nhamo, interview, Harare, September 1996.

34. Maria, interview, Harare, September 1996.

35. Nhamo, interview, Harare, September, 1996.

36. Taurai, interview, Harare, September 1996.

37. During the struggle recruits were asked to take new names so that their families would not be persecuted by the Rhodesians if they were caught. Teurai Ropa, meaning "spill blood," was the name taken by Joyce Mujuru, who became the most publicized woman guerrilla fighter when she was promoted to head the ZANU Department of Women's Affairs in Mozambique in 1978. She married a ZANLA commander, Rex Nhongo, during the war. After independence she became the youngest and first female minister in the first democratically elected government of Zimbabwe. When I interviewed her in 1996, she was the Minister for Information, Posts, and Telecommunications. In 1998 she became the Minister for Water Development and Rural Resources. In the text I refer to her as Teurai Ropa to avoid confusion.

38. Teurai Ropa (Joyce Mujuru), interview, Harare, October 1996. Some people have suggested, however, that she was promoted only because she was Rex Nhongo's girlfriend and not because she was the best person for the job. Dzino (a male ex-combatant), interview, Harare, August 1996.

39. When I interviewed her she said that she never fought in combat inside Zimbabwe, since her role was to coordinate ZANU's Department of Women's Affairs in Mozambique.

40. Monica, interview, Harare, August 1996.

41. Martin and Johnson, *The Struggle for Zimbabwe*, p. 241.

42. Monica, interview, Harare, August 1996. Osibisa Camp was specifically for ZANU and ZANLA women who were pregnant or with children. The politics of this camp are discussed below in more detail.

43. "Comrade Teurai Ropa: Women Have Total Involvement in Struggle," *Zimbabwe News* 10, no. 2 (May–June 1978): 30.

44. "The Role of the Zimbabwe Women in the Liberation Struggle," *Zimbabwe People's Voice*—ZANU PF United Kingdom Edition (1979), p. 11.

45. ZANU Archives, "Women's Affairs" folder: Tsatsayi Constantino, ZANU archivist, "The Role of Women in the Liberation Struggle," unpublished notes, Harare, 1996. Access to the ZANU Archives in Harare was restricted. Some documents specifically relating to women's issues had been filed in a folder titled "Women's Affairs." Other relevant documents were scattered throughout the archives, but were difficult to access for security reasons.

46. ZANU Archives, "Women's Affairs" folder: Teurai Ropa, "ZANU Women's Affairs (League)," undated but between March 1978 and May 1979.

47. Teurai Ropa (Joyce Mujuru), interview, Harare, 5 March 1997.

48. John Gwitira (Executive Director, Zimbabwe National Liberation War Veterans Association), interview, Harare, 19 August 1996. The Zimbabwean film *Flame* was controversial for its depiction of women fighting with guns. The ZNLWVA attempted to ban it for misrepresenting the role of women in the war. I have discussed this saga in more detail in "Guns and Guerrilla

Girls: Women in the Zimbabwean National Liberation Struggle" (Ph.D. diss., Department of Politics, University of Adelaide, 1998).

49. Freedom Nyamubaya, interview, Marondera, October 1996. Nyamubaya is a published author of short stories and poems and now works for a nongovernmental organization in Zimbabwe. She is an outspoken woman ex-combatant.

50. "Rudo Hondo: Heroine of the Liberation Struggle," *The People's Voice*, 13–19 March 1994, p. 13.

51. Ibid.

52. "They Are Teaching Our Women How to Murder," *The African Times*, 15 February 1978, pp. 8–9.

53. Norma Kriger, "The Politics of Creating National Heroes: The Search for Political Legitimacy and National Identity," in *Soldiers in Zimbabwe's Liberation War*, ed. Bhebe and Ranger, pp. 139–62.

54. Christine Sylvester, "Simultaneous Revolutions and Exits: A Semi-skeptical Comment," in *Women and Revolution*, ed. Tétreault, p. 418.

55. Ruth, interview, Harare, September 1996.

56. Taurai, interview, Harare, September 1996.

57. Tsitsi, interview, Harare, October 1996.

58. Jane Ngwenya, "Women and Liberation in Zimbabwe," in *Third World, Second Sex*, ed. Davies, pp. 82–83.

59. Sally Mugabe, "'Women's Struggle for Liberation': Roland Buck Interviews Sally Mugabe, Wife of the Prime Minister of Zimbabwe," *West Africa* 3336 (1981): 1531–32.

60. Mugabe, "First Zimbabwe Women's Seminar," p. 78.

61. Maria, interview, Harare, September 1996.

62. Sekai, interview, Harare, September 1996.

63. Anonymous female ex-combatant, interview by David Moore, Canada, 26 April 1994.

64. Weiss, *Women of Zimbabwe*, p. 95.

65. It is difficult to estimate exactly how many women joined up and how many were trained, as most records were destroyed during the war.

66. ZANU Archives, "Women's Affairs" folder: Teurai Ropa at ZANU Defence Secretariat, Rally held at operational farm base on 20th July 1978, Pfutskeke Base (Present: Teurai Ropa Nhongo plus 36 women cadres, and 6 General Staff and Field Commander E. Mhuru [all men]).

67. ZANU Archives, "Women's Affairs" folder: "On Marriage," ZANU Commissariat Department HQ, 6 July 1979.

68. Naomi Nhiwatiwa, interview by Carol B. Thompson, in *Women's Studies International Forum* 5, no. 3–4 (1982): 249.

69. Angeline Shenje-Peyton, "Balancing Gender, Equality, and Cultural Identity: Marriage Payments in Post-colonial Zimbabwe," *Harvard Human Rights Journal* 9 (1996): 115–16.

70. Norma Kriger, *Zimbabwe's Guerrilla War: Peasant Voices* (Harare: Baobab, 1995), p. 193.

71. Teurai Ropa (Joyce Mujuru), interview, Harare, October 1996.

72. The nationalists' concern with lobola was the precursor to post-independence debates on marriage and bridewealth which reveal divisions between urban and rural women, and between literate and illiterate ones. In 1995 most women in the rural areas agreed that lobola benefited them personally and

wished it to be upheld. It was mostly urban educated women who argued that it had to be eliminated for the oppression of women to end. See W. N. Tichagwa, "Lobola and Women's Status and Role in Society," in *Culture Survey* (Harare: Zimbabwe Women's Resource Centre and Network, 1995).

73.   Mugabe, "Women's Struggle for Liberation," and Naomi Nhiwatiwa as quoted in Weiss, *Women of Zimbabwe*.

74.   This designation of women as mothers of soldiers is different from the title "Mothers of the Revolution," as the unsung heroines of the liberation struggle have been called for their acts in support of the guerrillas as women and mothers in the rural areas. See Irene Staunton, ed., *Mothers of the Revolution* (Harare: Baobab, 1990).

75.   Amy Kaler, "Fertility, Gender, and War: The 'Culture of Contraception' in Rhodesia" (Ph.D. diss., University of Minnesota, 1998).

76.   ZANU Archives, "Women's Affairs" folder: Teurai Ropa, ZANU, Department of Women's Affairs, "Report for the Year Ending 31st December 1978," pp. 1–2.

77.   ZANU Archives, "Women's Affairs" folder: Comrade Catherine, ZANU Defence Secretariat HQ, 29 July 1978, Department of Women's Affairs—REF DSWS/01, Minutes of Central Committee, High Command General Staff Meeting (Female Comrades), 27 July 1978, p. 5.

78.   ZANU Archives, "Women's Affairs" folder: Teurai Ropa at ZANU Defence Secretariat, Rally held at operational farm base on 20th July 1978, Pfutskeke Base (Present: Teurai Ropa Nhongo plus 36 women cadres, and 6 General Staff and Field Commander E. Mhuru [all men]).

79.   "Female Combatants Raped or Consented," letter to the editor, *The Financial Gazette*, 15 May 1997, p. 7, and *The Financial Gazette*, 1 May 1997; "Brace Up for Stunning Revelations from War Victims Compensation Scam," *Zimbabwe Standard*, 4–10 May 1997, p. 11. See "Focus on Sexual Violence and War: When Will We Tell Our Own Story? A Woman Called Sarah," *Social Change and Development* 40 (1996): 25–26; *The Daily Gazette*, 15 August 1994. Women ex-combatants whom I interviewed at the Zimbabwe National Liberation War Veterans Association, Harare, August 1996, also confirmed the occurrence of rape. However, they agreed that many women fell in love and had consensual sex as well. The debate is discussed in my Ph.D. dissertation, "Guns and Guerrilla Girls."

80.   Ministry of Community Development and Women's Affairs, *Women in Construction and Reconstruction in Post-independence Zimbabwe* (Harare: UNICEF, 1985), p. 12, cited in Batezat et al., "Women and Independence," p. 156.

81.   Kriger, *Zimbabwe's Guerrilla War*, pp. 191, 192.

82.   Naomi Nhiwatiwa, in *Women's Liberation in the Zimbabwean Revolution: Materials from the ZANU Women's Seminar, Maputo, Mozambique, May 1979* (San Francisco: John Brown Book Club, Prairie Fire Organizing Committee, 1979), p. 24.

83.   Kriger, *Zimbabwe's Guerrilla War*, p. 191; Sally Mugabe, quoted in Lapchick and Urdang, *Oppression and Resistance*, p. 101.

84.   Julia Zvobgo, quoted in Weiss, *Women of Zimbabwe*, p. 106.

85.   Teurai Ropa (Joyce Mujuru), interview, Harare, October 1996.

86.   John Gwitira, interview, Harare, 19 August 1996. Also see *Re-integration*

Programme for War Veterans in Zimbabwe: A Participatory Development Plan (Harare: ZNLWVA, 1996).

87. Petronella Maramba, "Tracer Study on Women Ex-Combatants in Zimbabwe," incomplete and unpublished manuscript (Geneva: International Labour Organisation, December 1995). This report is missing crucial tables and graphs enumerating women. If 20 percent of the 50,000 ex-combatants who received compensation payments in January 1998 were women, the estimated 250,000 women involved in the war are seriously underrepresented, and obviously many men are too.

88. The socialist feminist literature on Zimbabwean women in the struggle has given this problem little attention. "Conflicts between men and women have often been glossed over, but they did exist." Batezat et al., "Women and Independence," p. 157.

89. Maitland, "Justice and Mercy," p. 63.

90. Rudo, interview, Harare, September 1996.

Contributors

Jean Allman teaches African history at the University of Illinois. She is the author of *The Quills of the Porcupine: Asante Nationalism in an Emergent Ghana* (1993) and, with Victoria Tashjian, *"I Will Not Eat Stone": A Women's History of Colonial Asante* (2000). Her research on gender, colonialism, and social change has appeared in the *Journal of African History, Africa, Gender and History,* and *History Workshop Journal.*

Teresa Barnes is the author of *"We Women Worked So Hard": Gender, Urbanization, and Social Reproduction in Colonial Harare, Zimbabwe, 1930–1956* (1999) and, with Everjoyce Win, *To Live A Better Life: An Oral History of Women in the City of Harare, 1930–70* (1992). Her work on gender and Zimbabwean history has appeared in *Signs,* the *Journal of Southern African Studies,* and *African Studies Review.* She is a lecturer in the Department of History at the University of the Western Cape in South Africa.

Misty L. Bastian is Assistant Professor of Anthropology at Franklin & Marshall College in Lancaster, Pennsylvania. With Jane Parpart, she co-edited *Great Ideas for Teaching about Africa* (1999), and she has published articles in numerous venues on gender, popular culture, media, and religious practice in Nigeria.

Susan Geiger was Professor Emeritus of Women's Studies at the University of Minnesota. She was the author of *TANU Women: Gender and Culture in the Making of Tanganyikan Nationalism, 1955–1965* (1997) and over a dozen articles on African women's history and the uses of life history in historical research. She co-edited two previous anthologies, and served on the editorial board of *Signs* for four years.

Heidi Gengenbach is Assistant Professor of History at the State University of New York at Buffalo. Her doctoral dissertation, "Where Women Make History: Pots, Stories, Tattoos, and Other Gendered Accounts of Community and Change in Magude District, Mozambique, c. 1800 to the Present," received one of the Gutenberg-e Electronic Book Prizes for 1999 from the American Historical Association, and will be published as an e-book by Columbia University Press in the coming year. Her research on gender, women's communities, and feminine forms of history-telling in rural southern Mozambique has been published in the *International Journal of African Historical Studies* and the *Journal of Southern African Studies.*

Holly Hanson is Assistant Professor of History and African and African-American Studies at Mount Holyoke College. Her book *Landed Obligation: The Practice of Power in Buganda* is forthcoming in the Heinemann Social History of Africa Series, and she is currently working on a study of social change in colonial Uganda titled "Bad Heirs: The Dilemma of Private Property for an African Colonial Elite."

Sean Hawkins is Assistant Professor in the Department of History at the University of Toronto. His *Writing and Colonialism in Northern Ghana: The Encounter between the LoDagaa and "the World on Paper," 1892–1991* (forthcoming) analyzes representations of identity, political authority, beliefs, knowledge, women, marriage, and kinship by both colonial and postcolonial observers. His previous work on the history of the LoDagaa has appeared in *Africa,* the *Journal of Religion in Africa,* and the *Canadian Journal of African Studies.* He is presently writing a history of kinship in twentieth-century Africa.

Lynette A. Jackson teaches African history at Barnard College, Columbia University. She has written numerous articles and chapters for anthologies on questions of social power and health in Africa. Her particular emphasis has been the intersections of gender, space, and the medical subject. She is currently writing a book which explores the domestication of colonial conquest in Zimbabwe through the history of the Ingutsheni Mental Hospital and the narratives of its patients.

Tanya Lyons teaches in the Globalisation Program at Flinders University in Adelaide, Australia, focusing on African history and politics. Her Ph.D. thesis, "Guns and Guerrilla Girls: Women in the Zimbabwean National Liberation Struggle," will be published in 2001. She has published an article on the dilemmas of Western feminist fieldwork in Africa, and is currently writing about the roles of white Rhodesian women in the Zimbabwean liberation struggle. She has conducted training workshops in gender analysis in Indonesia and is currently researching community attitudes to globalization from a gendered perspective. She is also Secretary of the African Studies Association of Australasia and the Pacific.

Gertrude Mianda is Associate Professor of Women's Studies and Sociology at York University/Glendon College. She is the author of *Femmes africaines et pouvoir: Les maraicheres de Kinshasa* (1996). Her ongoing research is on gender, education, and colonialism in the Belgian Congo. She has worked in the fields of women and development and postcolonialism and feminism, with a focus on francophone African immigrant women in Canada.

Nakanyike Musisi is currently Director of Makerere Institute of Social Research at Makerere University, Kampala, Uganda. She has published a number of chapters and articles on Baganda women in journals and edited collections. Her research interests are diverse, covering such areas as state formation, customary law, education, and environment.

Elizabeth Schmidt is Professor of African History at Loyola College in Maryland. She is the author of *Decoding Corporate Camouflage: U.S. Business Support for Apartheid* (1980) and *Peasants, Traders, and Wives: Shona Women in the History of Zimbabwe, 1870–1939* (1992). Her next book, *Mobilizing the Masses: Gender, Ethnicity, and Class in the Nationalist Movement in Guinea, 1939–1958*, will be published by Heinemann. Her work on women in African colonial history has also appeared in *Signs*, the *Journal of Southern African Studies*, *African Economic History*, and several edited collections.

Victoria B. Tashjian teaches African history at St. Norbert College in De Pere, Wisconsin. Her research interests and publications are concerned with gender, marriage, work, and "customary law" in west Africa. She is the co-author, with Jean Allman, of *"I Will Not Eat Stone": A Women's History of Colonial Asante* (2000).

Jane Turrittin is a social anthropologist with fieldwork experience in Mali and with West Indian and African women in Toronto. She is involved in research on equity issues in nursing in association with the Faculty of Nursing at the University of Toronto, and has published several articles based on this research.

Wendy Urban-Mead is a Ph.D. candidate in history at Columbia University in New York. The material for her chapter in this book grew out of her master's thesis at the University at Albany. She is currently writing a dissertation on faith and gender in colonial Matabeleland, Zimbabwe.

Index

Italicized page numbers refer to illustrations.

Childbirth: medicalization of, 41n7, 106; and local knowledge systems, 73; and post-menopausal women, 73; and maternal mortality, 77; importance of, 78; French techniques in, 81; and social control, 105. *See also* Maternal and infant health; Midwives; Traditional birth attendants

Chimbwidos (messengers). *See* Nationalism, Zimbabwe

Chimurenga, 306–308, 318, 320n2. *See also* Nationalism, Zimbabwe

Christianity: conversion to, 23–26, 49, 229; and Western biomedicine, 24–27; and literacy, 52; rejection of polygyny by, 52; illness and, 103; conceptions of the family in, 153, *155*

Church Missionary Society (CMS), 71, 95, 97, 104, 225, 267

City Youth League (Zimbabwe), 307. *See also* Nationalism, Zimbabwe

Civilization: colonial notions of, 6; material objects associated with, 6, 52; Christianity and, 39; healing and, 39; mission stations and, 51; dress and, 56; literacy and, 56; *mission civilisatrice*, 71; writing and, 97; women's emancipation and, 99; scientific discourse and, 100; illness and, 103; decline of Baganda and, 104–105; *évolués'* belief in, 145, 154–155; évolué concepts of, 148; French language as sign of, 149, 157; and children's education, 151; and the home, *152*. *See also* Christianity; Dress and fashion; *Évolués*

Colonial binaries: challenging of, 1, 28–29, 61, 83; collaboration v. resistance, 2, 20, 40n6; medical, 103; and gendered mobility, 182

Colonial chronologies, 1–2, 28

Colonial economies: and monetization, 9, 217, 231, 237, 249–50, 253, 264, 269

Colonial education: and gender, 8; Gayaza Girls School, 22; and the Portuguese in Mozambique, 28, 32; Bessie Price and African girls' education, 51; women's struggles with, 73; for girls in Buganda, 99; and moral crisis, 105; sexual segregation in, 144, 146; in Belgian Congo, 146–48; and domesticity, 146–48; French literacy training, 147; morality and, 152; women's salaried work and, 157; and nursing, 147, 157, 171; and gender chaos, 253. *See also* Midwives

Colonial encounters: as strategic engagement, 20–22, 27–29, 38–39, 47n60, 50; ethnography of, 107

Comaroff, Jean and John, 49

Concubinage: Sechele and, 55, 60; defining marriage and, 240; vs. marriage, 250. *See also* Marriage; Marriage payments

Consciousness, female v. feminist, 285, 296, 300n19

Cook, Dr. Albert (Buganda), 95, 101–102, 105, 108–19

Cooper, Barbara, 123, 239

Cooper, Frederick, 169, 209

Coquery-Vidrovitch, Catherine, 3

Coup de bambou, 290

Customs and traditions: Kéita's questioning of, 73; midwives and the struggle against, 75; infant care, 79; and gender discrimination, 80; and girls' education, 81; the role of *magnamagans,* 81; of family ideals, 93; in Buganda, 98; colonial codification of, 98; Dr. Albert Cook's ideas on, 100; and customary law, 133. *See also* Adultery; Divorce; Initiation; Marriage; Native Courts; Spirit mediums

Dakar Medical Training Center, 85n3, 86n8

Danquah, J. B., 244

das Neves, Diocleciano Fernandes (Mozambique), 22

Démocratique socialist de Guinée, 294

Depopulation, colonial fears of, 100, 105

Diagne, Blaise, 71

Diallo, Néné, on Guinean nationalism, 285, 287, 288, 294

Diarra, Fatou, on Guinean nationalism, 288, 292–94

Diawadou, Barry (Guinea), 289, 297

Dioune, Sokona, on midwives in French West Africa, 81–83

Divorce: and native law, 126–27; meanings of, 128–29; double standard and, 133; in pre-colonial Asante, 243, 252; and sexual relations, 295

Domesticity, 3, 59, 144, *152,* 155, 166. *See also* Christianity; Civilization; *Évolués*

Doumbouya, N'Youla, on Guinean nationalism, 291

Dress and fashion, 29, 37, 52, 55, 81, 224. *See also* Civilization

Echewa, T. O., 261

L'École des sage-femmes, 72

L'École Jules Carde, 72

L'École le Dantec, 72

Economic autonomy, 83, 120, 125, 132, 248–49, 252. *See also* Women's work

Ethnicity: Tsonga, 43n36; midwives and, 79, 82; and hierachy, 97–100

Évolués: and education, 8; and Western bio-medicine, 71; self-representations, 73; on gender relations, 144–63 passim; ideas of civilization, 145; on bridewealth, 149; and Christian training, 149; on polygyny, 149, 153; on prostitution, 149; on motherhood, 151; on women working, 151; and marital authorization for work, 151; on patrilineal succession, 153, 155

Farming. *See* Women's work
Female circumcision, 91n77
Feminism: and recognition of power differ-ences, 64n15; Western socialist feminists, 306; socialist feminist literature on Zim-babwe, 326n88
Ferguson, Fergus, on *Ogu Umunwaanyi,* 269
Fleming, Dr. Andrew, on venereal disease in Buganda, 197, 200
Fortes, Meyer, 241, 248
Fosuwa, Yaa, on marriage in Asante, 252
Freedom fighters. *See* Nationalism, Zimbabwe
Frelimo, 39n2
French colonial health service, 72, 75–77, 88n40. *See also* Midwives
French West Africa, 71–91 passim, 282–304 passim

Gaza Nguni, 21
Geiger, Susan, 284–85, 287
Ghana (Gold Coast), Northern Territories of, 116–43 passim
Gosa, Furiana, on compulsory venereal disease exams in Zimbabwe, 204–205
Green, Margaret, on *Ogu Umunwanyi,* 272, 281n41
Grewal, Inderpal, 170
Grier, Beverly, 248
Guinea, 9, 282–304 passim
Guyer, Jane, 119

Haidara, Nabya, on Guinean nationalism, 291–92
Harries, Patrick, 168
Hawkins, Sean, 249
Hay, Jean, 2, 3
Healers: old women (*masungukati*) as, 25; and borrowing, 27. *See also* Indigenous knowl-edge systems; Midwives; Postmenopausal women; Traditional birth attendants
Health Union (French West Africa), 80, 83
Historiography: of African women, 2; nature

of, 2–4; of gender, 3; early collections in women's history, 10n4; early monographs in women's history, 11n5; on agricultural and rural transformation, 11n7; on women's organizations and resistance, 12n8; on women in cities, 12–13n9; on domesticity and sexual politics, 13n10; on mission en-counter, 49–50, 62n4, 63nn6,11; on conver-sion and literacy, 65–66n27; on Western bio-medicine in French West Africa, 86n8; on colonial attempts to control women, 118; on colonial courts and customary law, 118–19, 211n3; on colonial education, 144; on labor migration, 164, 166–68; women's pre-colonial political power and authority, 220–221; on women's political power, 233nn12; on economic change and its impact on women's daily lives, 238, 255n6; of *Ogu Umunwaanyi,* 277nn8,10; on nationalism, 283, 284, 298nn3,6, 299n10; on national lib-eration and women's emancipation, 306, 321nn7,10
Hondo, Rudo, on armed struggle in Zim-babwe, 312

Igbo Women's War. *See Ogu Umunwaanyi*
Imam, Ayesha, 3
Indigenous knowledge systems: local medi-cines, 23, 109; reproduction and birth, 88n29; Dr. Albert Cook's views on, 101; medicine, 109. *See also* Healers; Midwives; Traditional birth attendants
Indirect rule: in Buganda, 98; in Asante, 237. *See also* Ashanti Confederacy Council; Chiefs; *Lukiiko*
Influenza epidemic, 197
Initiation: *bojale,* 53, 57, 60, 66–67n37, 67n41; Sechele's children and, 69n69
Interracial relationships, 29–31, 34, 37, 56, 68n57

Jochelson, Karen, 165–66
Johnson, Phyllis, 307
Johnston, Sir Harry, 97–98

*Kabaka*s (kings of Buganda): Ndawula, 223; Suuna, 223; Junju, 223, 230–32; Mutesa, 224–25, 226–27; Mwanga, 225, 227, 235n53; Mwanga and execution of Christians and Moslems, 225
Kaplan, Temma, 285
Kéita, Aoua: and childbirth in West Africa, 71–91 passim; *Femme d'Afrique,* 72; career and career posts of, 72–85, 90n57; versus tradi-

women, 80; and class, 81–83; versus TBAs, 81; training of, 88n37. *See also* Colonial education; Western biomedicine

Missions: missionaries, 23, 128, 224–25; and literacy, 58; records of, 24, 26, 50, 60; mission doctors, 25, 109; on initiation, 53; on polygyny, 53; on rainmaking, 53; and colonial education, 144; education and Igbo women's responses to, 265, 269. *See also* Christianity; Civilization; Moffat, Mary; Moffat, Robert; Western biomedicine

Mitchell, Dr. J. P. (Mulago Hospital), 100–102

Moeketsi, Mary (South Africa), 174–75, 178

Moffat, Mary, 52, 54

Moffat, Robert, 48–49, 50, 53, 59. *See also* Sechele

Monica (on armed struggle in Zimbabwe), 310–11

Moral crisis, colonial fears of, 105, 107, 125

Moral Purity Campaign (Buganda), 106

Morgenthau, Ruth, 284

Mozambique, 7, 19–47 passim

Muchineripi, Loice (on travel and mobility in southern Africa), 179–80

Mugabe, Robert, 306–307, 308, 314

Mugabe, Sally, 307, 313–314, 317–318

Mujibas (carriers). *See* Nationalism, Zimbabwe

Mulago Hospital, 105

Musisi, Nakanyike, 230

Namasole. *See* Queen mothers

National Democratic Party (Zimbabwe), 307, 319. *See also* Nationalism, Zimbabwe

National liberation. *See* Nationalism, Zimbabwe

Nationalism, Guinea: women and, 9–10, 282–304 passim; and market women, 283; and seamstresses, 283; women's sale of membership cards, 289–290; women's sale of newspapers, 290; and violation of gender norms, 291–295; women's brigades, 291; shock troops, 291

Nationalism, Zimbabwe: history of, 10, 305–26 passim; *chimbwidos*, 305; *mujibas*, 305; formation of ZANU and ZAPU, 308; launch of armed struggle, 308; impact of armed struggle on gender roles, 308; pregnancy and freedom fighters, 309; training for armed struggle, 311; differences between ZAPU and ZANU, 312–13; problem of uncontrollable women, 314–15, 319; sexual relationships and, 315; marriages and armed struggle, 315–316; contracep-

tives and armed struggle, 317–18; rape of women freedom fighters, 317, 319, 325n79; numbers of women fighters, 318; 1948 general strike, 322n18

Native Authority courts, *See* Native courts

Native courts: imposition of, 6; records of, 8; in Northern Territories (Gold Coast), 116–43 passim; on adultery, 128–33; and marriage, 249–51; and colonial rule, 253; as target of *Ohandum*, 261. *See also* Chiefs; Customs and traditions; Sources, discussions of

Native Domestic Labor Committee (Zimbabwe), 196

N'Diaye, Aissatou (on Guinean nationalism), 292, 294, 296–98

Ngano, Martha (Zimbabwe), 175

Ngwenya, Jane, on armed struggle in Zimbabwe, 313

Nhamo, on armed struggle in Zimbabwe, 309

Nhiwatiwa, Naomi, on armed struggle in Zimbabwe, 316–18

Nigeria, 9

Notes of Evidence (Aba Commission of Inquiry), 261–63, 268, 274–75

Nursing. *See* Women's work

Nwanyeruwa (on *Ogu Umunwaanyi*), 262

Nwaobiala ("Dancing Women's Movement," Nigeria), 264, 266, 270, 279

Nwoto (on *Ogu Umunwaanyi*), 268

Nyamubaya, Freedom, in armed struggle in Zimbabwe, 312

Nyrenda, Mary, on travel and mobility in southern Africa, 174–175, 178, 179

Ogu Umunwaanyi: history of, 9, 260–81 passim; and taxation, 264; and bridewealth, 264; first deaths, 266; list of those killed, 273–74, 276n3. *See also Ohandum*; Chiefs

Ohandum (Women of All Towns, Igbo), 261–68; first deaths of, 266; and marketplace, 266–67; testimony of, 268–72; as vultures, 269–71. *See also Ogu Umunwaanyi*

Okali, Christine, 251

Okpopo, Emena (on *Ogu Umunwaanyi*), 271–72

Ope (Sechele's daughter), 48–49, 52–61

Opperman-Mfazi, Edith, 174

Passes and influx control, 167, 168, 192–193, 201–203. *See also Chibeura*; Labor migration; Reproduction; Women's work

Patriarchy: indigenous and colonial, 3, 194; reconfigurations of, 9, 217; Aoua Kéita's struggles against, 73; and colonial project, 93, 118; illusions of, 120–21; colonial, 133–34; and education in the Belgian Congo, 147; controls in rural areas, 169; women's escape from, 177; fears of unruly women, 198; and *chibeura*, 209

Paul, Graham, and *Ogu Umunwaanyi*, 269

Pawnage, 120, 240–41, 244, 247–49, 256n14

Phare de Guinée, Le, 290

Politics: gendered forms of power and authority, 7, 9, 217, 219–21, 231. *See also* Chiefs; Indirect rule; Queen mothers

Polygyny: and Kwena royal women, 57; Aoua Kéita's opposition to, 82; eradication of, 84; *évolués'* position on, 148, 153–54; and Christian morality, 153, 155

Postmenopausal women, 43n35, 73, 84

Price, Bessie (Elizabeth): letters of, 48–50; childhood, 51; and rapport with Bantsang, 57; on Christian message, 59; marriage to Roger Price, 65n19

Price, Roger, 51

Primary documents (appended to chapters): missionary journals, 61–62; autobiography, 84–85; colonial medical records, 110–111; native court cases, 134–35; written/transcribed histories, 231–32; colonial government archives, 182–83, 209–11, 273–75; life stories, 231–37, 254–54, 296–96. *See also* Sources, discussions of

Prostitution: accusations of, 37; *évolués'* fears of, 152; colonial fears of, 175–76; and urban strategies, 178; and male migrants, 198; and *Ogu Umunwaanyi*, 263; and perceptions of women nationalists, 293–294; and perceptions of women freedom fighters, 308–309, 319. See also *Chibeura*

Proverbs, 270–72

Queen mothers: importance of, 1; in Buganda, 9, 219–36 passim; Queen Mother Muganzirwaza, 221, 224; as king-makers, 222; in Ganda oral tradition, 223; Queen Mother Nanteza, 223–24; end of power in Buganda, 226–31

Racism, 1, 80, 102–103

Ranger, Terrence, 178–79

Rassemblement démocratique africain: and Aoua Kéita, 72, 82; in Guinea, 282–304 passim. *See also* Nationalism, Guinea

Rattray, R. S., 237, 239, 240, 242, 247–49

Renamo, 19, 39n1

Reproduction: of labor force, 1, 2, 198, 209; as woman's role, 108, 126; and the reserves, 191–92; women's reproductive labor, 217; struggles to control, 252–53. *See also* Labor migration; Women's work

Rhodesia Industrial and Commmercial Workers Union, 208

Rhodesian Front, 308. *See also* Nationalism, Zimbabwe

Rhodesian Landowners' and Farmers' Association, 200

Rivière, Claude, 284

Roberts, Penelope, 244

Romance, 37–38

Ropa, Teurai, on armed struggle in Zimbabwe, 310, 311–12, 315, 316–17, 318

Roscoe, John (Christian Missionary Society), 98

Royal women: importance of, 7; in Gaza, 23; and conversion, 60; in Buganda, 217, 230; in Dahomey, 220; in Asante, 220; in Lagos, 220. *See also* Queen mothers

Rudo, on armed struggle in Zimbabwe, 309

Rumbidzai, on armed struggle in Zimbabwe, 317

Ruth, on armed struggle in Zimbabwe, 312

Sakho, Mabalo, on Guinean nationalism, 288

Sand River Convention, 50. *See also* Sechele

Schmidt, Elizabeth, 238

Scientific knowledge, 100–105

Scott, Johanna, on compulsory venereal disease exams in Zimbabwe, 206–207

Sechele (Kwena king), 48–49, 50, 53–54, 66n29

Seduction, 121, 130–31

Sekai, on armed struggle in Zimbabwe, 309

Sewing. *See* Women's work

Sexually transmitted diseases: colonial perceptions of, 100, 105–106, 112n1; Dr. Albert Cook's work on, 107; examinations for, 191–93, 197, 203–206; compulsory examinations for, 191–217 passim; and male migrant workers, 193, 197; treatment of, 200. *See also* Chibeura; Western biomedicine

Shope, Gertrude, on travel and mobility in southern Africa, 171, 174, 180

Slavery, 120, 244, 138n14, 258n47

Smith, Ian, 308. *See also* Nationalism, Zimbabwe

Song: and the *Ogu Umunwaanyi*, 261, 264–65; and nationalist struggle in Guinea, 287–89, 295

Sources, discussions of: life histories, 1, 20, 28, 30, 45; life stories, 1, 7, 29–31; court cases,

176, 179, 200; cash-crop farming, 238–39, 242–46, 248, 249–53. *See also* Midwives; Traditional birth attendants
World Conference on Women, 305–306

Yellow Peril, 196. *See also* Black Peril

ZANU. *See* Nationalism, Zimbabwe
ZAPU. *See* Nationalism, Zimbabwe
Zeleza, Paul, 4
Zimbabwe (Southern Rhodesia), 191–215 passim; census results in, 176

Zimbabwe African National Liberation Army (ZANLA). *See* Nationalism, Zimbabwe
Zimbabwe African National Union (ZANU). *See* Nationalism, Zimbabwe
Zimbabwe African People's Union (ZAPU). *See* Nationalism, Zimbabwe
Zimbabwe National Liberation War Veterans Association (ZNLWVA), 312, 318
Zimbabwe People's Revolutionary Army (ZIPRA). *See* Nationalism, Zimbabwe
Zimbabwe Review, 307
Zvobgo, Julia, on armed struggle in Zimbabwe, 316